Whoever Hears You Hears Me

Whoever Hears You Hears Me

Prophets, Performance, and Tradition in Q

Richard A. Horsley
Professor of Religion
University of Massachusetts Boston

with Jonathan A. Draper
Professor of New Testament
University of Natal, South Africa

TRINITY PRESS INTERNATIONAL
Harrisburg, Pennsylvania

Parts of chapter 2 were previously published as "Weber, Theissen, and 'Wandering Charis-matics' in the *Didache*" in the *Journal of Early Christian Studies* 6, no. 4 (1998): 541–76, copyright © 1998 Johns Hopkins University Press, and are used here with permission.

Trinity Press International, P.O. Box 1321, Harrisburg, PA 17105
Trinity Press International is a division of the Morehouse Group.

Library of Congress Cataloging-in-Publication Data
Horsley, Richard A.
    Whoever hears you hears me : prophets, performance, and tradition
in Q / Richard A. Horsley with Jonathan A. Draper.
        p.   cm.
    Includes bibliographical references and index.
    ISBN 1-56338-272-5 (pbk. : alk. paper)
    1. Q hypothesis (Synoptics criticism)   I. Draper, Jonathan A.
    II. Title
    BS2555.2.H67   1999
    226'.066 – dc21   99-44775

Printed in the United States of America

99   00   01   02   03   04   10   9   8   7   6   5   4   3   2   1

Contents

Abbreviations x

Acknowledgments ix

Introduction 1
    Richard A. Horsley

    Questioning Inappropriate Assumptions and Concepts
        for a Clearer View of Q / 2
    Toward an Understanding of Oral Communication and of Q as
        Oral-Derived Literature / 5
    The Sequence of Chapters on Q Discourses / 11
    A Note on the Presentation of Q Discourses / 12

1. The Teachings of Jesus and Liberal Individualism 15
    Richard A. Horsley

    Aphorism and Individualism / 15
    The Reductionist Hermeneutics of Modern Liberalism / 18
    Harnack's Different Reading of Q / 22

2. Wandering Charismatics and Scholarly Circularities 29
    Jonathan A. Draper

    The Theory of Religious Role Adoption and Its Implications / 30
    Weber's Charisma and Theissen's Wandering Charismatics / 34
    Apostles and Prophets in the *Didache* / 40
    Weber and the *Didache* vs. Theissen's Wandering Charismatics / 44

3. The Historical Context of Q 46
    Richard A. Horsley

    A Brief History of Galilee / 48
    Social Forms and Power Relations in Galilee and Roman Palestine / 52

4. The Contours of Q 61
    Richard A. Horsley

    The Quest for Control of Q: Of Theology and Stratigraphy / 61
    Q as a Sequence of Discourses / 83

5. ISRAELITE TRADITIONS IN Q   94
   Richard A. Horsley

   Survey of Q Discourses and Israelite Traditions / 95
   Great / Official vs. Little / Popular Tradition / 98
   Contested Israelite Traditions in Q / 104

6. THE ORAL COMMUNICATION ENVIRONMENT OF Q   123
   Richard A. Horsley

   Limited Literacy in Western Antiquity / 125
   Uses of Writing in Relation to Oral Communication / 128
   Manuscripts and Oral Communication in Judea and Galilee / 135
   Implications for Q / 144

7. RECENT STUDIES OF ORAL-DERIVED LITERATURE AND Q   150
   Richard A. Horsley

   Recognition of Orality in the Synoptic Tradition, Q, and Mark / 151
   Immanent Art and Ethnopoetics / 160
   The Theory of Verbal Art and Q / 166

8. RECOVERING ORAL PERFORMANCE FROM WRITTEN TEXT IN Q   175
   Jonathan A. Draper

   Toward a Model of Oral Communication / 175
   Oral Communication Surviving in the Written Medium / 183
   Toward Hearing Q Discourses in Measured Verse / 186
   Application of the Model: Q 12:49–59 in Measured Verse / 189

9. THE COVENANT RENEWAL DISCOURSE: Q 6:20–49   195
   Richard A. Horsley

   The Coherence and Covenantal Character of the Discourse / 195
   The Continuing Importance of Covenantal Patterns and Teaching / 201
   The "Text" of Q 6:20–49 / 209
   Q 6:20–49 as a Covenant Renewal Discourse / 216
   Covenant Renewal in the Popular Tradition vs. Sapiential
       Covenantal Teaching / 225

10. PROPHETIC ENVOYS FOR THE RENEWAL OF ISRAEL: Q 9:57–10:16   228
    Richard A. Horsley

    Toward Contextual Interpretation / 228
    The Text of the Mission Discourse in Oral Performance / 234
    Metonymic Referencing and Resonance in the Mission Discourse / 237
    Function of the Mission Discourse in the Communities of
        the Q Movement / 248

11. THE ANNOUNCEMENT AND TESTING OF THE PROPHET 250
    Jonathan A. Draper

The Announcement of the Prophet: Q 3:7–9, 16–17, 21–22 / 251
The Testing of the Prophet: Q 4:1–13 / 254
The Sequence of Discourses / 258

12. THE KINGDOM OF GOD AS THE RENEWAL OF ISRAEL 260
    Richard A. Horsley

Other Q Discourses Addressed to the Life of the Renewal
    Movement / 261
Q Discourses Addressed to Communities of a Movement
    under Attack / 270
Q Discourses That Sanction Discipline and Solidarity in
    the Communities / 275

13. THE RENEWAL OF ISRAEL OVER AGAINST ITS RULERS 277
    Richard A. Horsley

Against the Jerusalem Rulers: Q 13:29–28, 34–35 + 14:16–24 / 279
The Prophetic Woes against the Pharisees and Scribes: Q 11:39–52 / 285

14. THE RENEWAL MOVEMENT AND THE PROPHET PERFORMERS OF Q 292
    Richard A. Horsley

Shift in Assumption (Oral vs. Written) Requires Shift in Approach / 292
The Renewal Movement Evident in Q Discourses / 295
Prophetic Performers of the Q Discourses / 300

INDEX OF REFERENCES 311

GENERAL INDEX 322

Acknowledgments

We are deeply indebted to and greatly appreciate the earlier work of Werner Kelber, who pioneered study of orality with regard to the Synoptic Gospel tradition, that of Joanna Dewey and Pieter Botha, who pioneered application of oral studies to the Gospel of Mark, and that of Susan Niditch, who pioneered study of orality and literacy in the Hebrew Bible. We would like to express special gratitude to Ellen Aitken for patient tutoring in oral studies and for a critical reading of an earlier draft of many of the chapters below. Larry Wills, Joanna Dewey, Pieter Botha, Eugene Boring, and Melanie Johnson-DeBaufre also read a draft of several chapters and offered many helpful criticisms. Ann DiSessa and Judi Roberts, multicompetent staff at the University of Massachusetts Boston, facilitated the project in many ways. Special thanks also to Laura Whitney and her staff at the Andover-Harvard Library and to the staff at the Episcopal Divinity School–Weston College Library for their patient assistance in locating books and journals. Appreciation finally to research assistants Marcus Aurin, Heather Kaplow, Karen Brownell, and Leila Kohler for their valiant efforts in search and discover missions.

ABBREVIATIONS

AGJU	Arbeiten zur Geschichte des antiken Judentums und des Urchristentums
BETL	Bibliotheca ephemeridum theologicarum lovaniensium
CBQ	*Catholic Biblical Quarterly*
HTR	*Harvard Theological Review*
JBL	*Journal of Biblical Literature*
JR	*Journal of Religion*
JSNT	*Journal for the Study of the New Testament*
JSNTSup	Journal for the Study of the New Testament — Supplement Series
NovT	*Novum Testamentum*
NTAbh	Neutestamentliche Abhandlungen
NTS	*New Testament Studies*
SNTSMS	Society for New Testament Studies Monograph Series
TDNT	*Theological Dictionary of the New Testament*
TU	Texte und Untersuchungen zur Geschichte der altchristlichen Literatur
WdF	Wege der Forschung
WMANT	Wissenschaftliche Monographien zum Alten und Neuen Testament
WUNT	Wissenschaftliche Untersuchungen zum Neuen Testament
ZKG	*Zeitschrift für Kirchengeschichte*
ZTK	*Zeitschrift für Theologie und Kirche*

INTRODUCTION

Richard A. Horsley _____

Modern people are intrigued by the teachings of Jesus. Indeed, the teachings of Jesus are about all that is left for those who no longer believe he was the Son of God and was resurrected from the dead or who find it difficult to deal with Jesus as a healer and exorcist. Luckily for modern Western children of the Enlightenment, the nineteenth-century scholars who pioneered the development of "New Testament science," particularly in Germany, could not help but notice that the Gospels of Matthew and Luke shared a great quantity of Jesus' teaching, often in verbatim parallel passages, that did not appear in the Gospel of Mark. Concluding that Matthew and Luke must have been following a common literary source for these sayings, in the same way as they were following Mark in most of their narratives, scholars hypothesized a "source" of Jesus' sayings or speeches behind Matthew and Luke. We thus came to have "Q," short for *Quelle*, the German word for "source." The delineation of Q was exciting to liberals at the end of the nineteenth century and the beginning of the twentieth because it enabled them to bypass all of the miraculous stories in the Gospels and move directly to the teaching of the great prophet that was far more palatable to the modern scientifically oriented mind. And once it was recognized that the Gospel of Mark, presumably the first account of Jesus, had its own particular theological point of view and could not be used as a historical source out of which to reconstruct the life of Jesus, Q seemed like a godsend of a whole collection of seemingly reliable sayings readily available as source materials in the quest for the historical Jesus.

During the heyday of close study of individual sayings and stories of Jesus through much of the twentieth century, interest in Q as a collection of Jesus' sayings declined. Partly in connection with the discovery of the *Gospel of Thomas*, another collection of Jesus' sayings, interest in Q revived after midcentury. A number of factors motivate the revival of interest in and study of Q. It offers a view of Jesus very different from that found in Mark or Paul or in other believers in or followers of Jesus. Understood as a collection of individual sayings of Jesus, it is attractive to those who have learned, from Bible study in church or academic training in biblical studies, to focus on one verse or saying at a time. And, with the parallels in the *Gospel of Thomas* and other sources in the Gospel tradition, it offers some of the key sources for renewed interest in the historical Jesus. Further, to the scholarly as well as popular imagination, it is intriguing to get behind the written Gospels to an earlier, more "original" source through which Jesus

1

might be understood. It is surely significant that, well over a hundred years after Q had been delineated by nineteenth-century scholars, a semipopular book was published, in a shrewd marketing ploy, with the title *The Lost Gospel*. Now we can again be privy to what those earliest followers of Jesus knew before it all became lost — into two of the long-since-familiar canonical Gospels!

Questioning Inappropriate Assumptions and Concepts for a Clearer View of Q

Intensive study of Q has been carried on in the United States and Canada during the past two decades, particularly in the Q Seminar of the Society of Biblical Literature. In the reading of papers amid scholarly give and take, an unusual sophistication has been developed in the analysis of the sayings of Jesus in Q. A collective adoption of a certain scholarly paradigm of the stratification of Q along the lines of different types of sayings has become the basis of an impressive production of scholarly articles and books on Q, now called "the Sayings Gospel" — which presumably lends it added authority. The extraordinary sophistication and incisive precision of this stimulating scholarship also have a flip side in its relative isolation from other biblical and historical scholarship. European scholarship of Q works with very different hypotheses. Many New Testament interpreters do not believe in the existence of Q and quietly chuckle at the erudite discussions of the stratigraphy of a document that is hypothetical in the first place. And much of the analysis of Q materials, like much interpretation of Gospel literature generally, is done in the relative vacuum of historical knowledge about the historical situation in which the literature originated.

Significant breakthroughs in recent interpretation of Q have resulted from abandoning previous assumptions about it that turned out to be unwarranted. Some of these assumptions were rooted in the Christian theology from which much of the conceptual apparatus of New Testament studies is derived, and some of them were about the historical situation which Q presupposed and addressed. One way of viewing the evolution of recent scholarship on Q is as a process of recognition that one Christian theological concept after another does not apply to Q, that one feature after another of what was assumed to be early Christianity does not appear in Q. It was long assumed that Q had or presupposed a christology, like other early Christian literature. But while Paul is so familiar with Jesus as Christ that the latter almost sounds like his second name, the title *Christ* (Greek for "Messiah") does not appear in Q. Paul presents Jesus' principal title as *Kyrios* ("Lord"). But in Q *kyrios* is little more than a form of addressing Jesus as "sir" or "master" or an authoritative teacher (Q 6:46; 7:6; 9:59).[1] "Son of God the Father" appears more promising as a title for Jesus (as in 4:3, 9; 10:22), but John

---

1. So also James M. Robinson, "The Son of Man in the Sayings Gospel Q," in *Tradition und Translation: Zum Problem der interkulturellen Übersetzbarkeit religiöser Phänomene: Festschrift für Carsten Colpe zum 65. Geburtstag*, ed. Christoph Elsas et al. (Berlin: Walter de Gruyter, 1994), 317–18.

and the Q people generally are also children of God elsewhere in Q (as in 6:35; 7:35; 11:2–4). Nor does Q have a "Wisdom christology," for in Q Jesus is not identified with or substituted for Wisdom but is represented as one of Wisdom's children or one of the prophets Wisdom sent (Q 7:35; 11:49–51).

It was the thesis that Q had a distinctive (apocalyptic) Son of Man christology of its own that led many to recognize that Q was a unique document from a discrete group that had a particular viewpoint, different from other early Christian literature. But that also has recently been recognized as questionable. In most of its occurrences in Q the phrase "son of man," as an idiomatic expression, "refers indefinitely to a human and by implication to Jesus himself. . . . The ability to use the term to refer to Jesus during his public ministry would seem . . . to be due to the term's use as an unimpressive Aramaic idiom with an implied reference to the speaker."[2] And once the old composite scholarly picture of the supposed Jewish apocalyptic "Son of Man" is recognized to be without ancient basis in Judean texts prior to the time of Jesus and Q, then it can be discerned more clearly that the Q sayings referring to the "son of man" in the future judgment do not portray a figure coming as the judge on the day of judgment. The latter is Matthew's portrayal of Jesus and the Son of Man at his parousia (Matthew 24–25). In Q 12:8–9, the "son of man" is a defender or accuser at the divine court of judgment, but other figures in Q, such as the Queen of the South and the Ninevites, fulfill a similar role (Q 11:31–32). In Q 17:24, 26, 30, "the day(s) of the son of man" are declared analogous to "the days of Noah" (and "the days of Lot"). In those sayings, as in that of 12:39–40, "the son of man" would appear to be a reference to Jesus as an accuser or defender at the future judgment, as in 12:8–9, or perhaps as a symbol for the future restoration of the people of Israel, as in the influential passage in Dan. 7:13–14, 27. Not only is Q uninterested in the crucifixion and resurrection preaching that drives Paul and appears prominently in Mark, but Q utterly lacks Paul's exalted Lord and Matthew's Son of Man coming in judgment.[3]

This book attempts to explore how Q may appear to us if we continue stripping away Christian theological concepts and assumptions and certain assumptions about and pictures of the historical context that do not apply to these speeches of Jesus. The major assumption that must be challenged and relinquished is that Q can and should be dealt with as if it were a written text, as opposed to oral tradition. The majority of the book, chapters 6 through 14, will be devoted to exploring the alternative — that in the predominantly oral communication environment of antiquity, Q was an oral-derived text that calls for interpretation as it was performed orally before groups of people. That requires major rethinking of the appropriate questions to be asked and conceptual apparatus to be used in attempting to understand the Q material in its function as oral performance in a particular historical context. Before even raising the issue of Q as an oral-derived text, however, a number of other theological assumptions and historical concepts

---

2. Ibid., 325.
3. John S. Kloppenborg, " 'Easter Faith' and the Sayings Gospel Q," *Semeia* 49 (1990): 71–99.

that determine current interpretation of Q can be challenged more or less on the basis of present knowledge in the fields of New Testament studies and Jewish and ancient Mediterranean history, and a number of alternatives can be delineated.

Certain theological assumptions and positions prominent in recent studies of Q should be challenged on the basis of fuller awareness of the history and sociology of modern Western theological knowledge. Chapter 1 of this book argues that a certain line of interpretation of selected Q sayings resembles the statements of liberal theology of a century ago, which suggests that this interpretation has more to do with the continuing attraction of liberal individualistic theology than with Q materials themselves. One senses that the extreme individualism of renewed liberal theological interpretation of Q is inappropriate to and incommensurate with this ancient "text" of Jesus' speech. That the hypothesis of the "wandering charismatics" continues to be adapted in studies of Q and the early Jesus movement, particularly in America, despite serious criticism of the hypothesis's lack of historical basis and weakness in sociological theory, suggests that the hypothesis may mesh with certain concerns of the interpreters rather than with the material interpreted. In chapter 2, Jonathan Draper presents yet another telling criticism of the wandering charismatics thesis, in particular of its limited textual basis in Harnack's now-questionable interpretation of the *Didache* and its selective theoretical basis in Weber's concept of charisma, which in turn is based on the same, now-questionable, use of the *Didache*.

Other theological assumptions and historical concepts must be challenged on the basis of a more precise knowledge of the ancient historical context in which Q originated and which it addressed. It is evident in much of recent Q interpretation that older Christian theological schemes persist in New Testament scholarship after historical knowledge has become more cognizant of the diversity and complexity of the historical situation of Roman Palestine in which Jesus worked and the Q materials originated. Thus recent treatments of Q assume, on the one hand, a monolithic Jewish society which certain sections condemn as a whole and a monolithic Jewish culture to which certain sayings in Q are counter, and, on the other hand, a quasi-cosmopolitan Hellenistic cultural atmosphere in the same geographical area that can account for the resemblance of many Q sayings to the sharp cultural criticism of the ancient Cynic philosophers. As the necessary historical context that should rather be presupposed in the rest of the inquiry, therefore, chapter 3 presents a more complex and precise picture of Hellenistic Judea and Galilee under Roman rule. In contrast to an older picture that took Jerusalem and the Pharisees as representative of Judaism, we can now recognize a society recently subjected to Roman rule, with the Herodians and Jerusalem high-priestly families at the top as the wealthy and powerful client rulers for the Romans, their Pharisaic and other scribal representatives as mediators with the people, and the vast majority of Judeans and Galileans living in agrarian villages that conduct their own community affairs according to Israelite traditions. The fundamental class division between rulers and ruled is further compounded by the historical regional differences between the Galileans, who had only recently come under and then been removed from Jerusalem rule, and the Jerusalemites, who focused on the political-economic-religious institution of the temple, still undergoing the massive rebuilding in grand Hellenistic style begun by Herod the Great.

The examination in chapter 4 of the grand paradigm of Q's stratigraphy adopted by many participants in the Q Seminar concludes that, for all its sophistication and generation of scholarly energy, this hypothesis appears to be based primarily on modern theologically rooted scholarly assumptions and concepts. The criteria by which the two principal strata are sorted out — that is, the classification of sayings into sapiential and apocalyptic, the supposed prophetic condemnation of "all Israel," and the apocalyptic motifs that distinguish the secondary layer — are difficult to find in the Q material itself and would appear to be derived from modern scholarly concepts in the field of New Testament studies. The principal studies out of which the grand hypothesis of Q stratigraphy was developed, however, contain the seeds of an alternative view of Q. The implications of John S. Kloppenborg's groundbreaking "composition criticism"[4] are that Q was a coherent series of discourses rather than a collection of sayings.

Recent interpretation of Q, particularly in America, tends to downplay the importance of its grounding in Israelite culture and to emphasize its similarities with Hellenistic Greek culture. This is due partly to the training of most New Testament scholars primarily in Hellenistic Greek literature and culture rather than Hebrew and Aramaic, partly to the needs of the modern Western Christian claim of universalism over against supposed Jewish particularism, and partly to the individualism of modern Western culture generally. Yet the presence of Israelite tradition in Q materials is pervasive, if only we look for it, as explored in chapter 5. Once we recognize the complex political-economic-religious structural division in ancient Roman Palestine, however, we must also recognize that Israelite tradition was far from unitary. As in other historical agrarian societies, Israelite tradition was contested, between the great tradition of the rulers and their scribal retainers, on the one hand, and the little tradition(s) of the great peasant majority, on the other. Thus, to complicate matters, it appears that Q discourses were grounded in the Israelite popular tradition over against the "official" tradition based in Jerusalem.

Toward an Understanding of Oral Communication and of Q as Oral-Derived Literature

Since not only the Israelite popular tradition(s) generally but also the great tradition in its cultivation even by scribal teachers was oral, we are led to a major recognition that biblical studies, devoted as it is to the interpretation of sacred

---

4. John S. Kloppenborg, *The Formation of Q: Trajectories in Ancient Wisdom Collections* (Philadelphia: Fortress, 1987).

texts, has been resisting for some time: that the communication environment of Palestine in particular and Hellenistic Roman antiquity in general was oral. Much of the discussion of orality and literacy during the last few decades has drawn a stark contrast between them, treating them as two very different mentalities with distinctive and even opposing characteristics. This opposition between oral societies / culture and literate societies / culture appears to have contributed to the reluctance of some to recognize that until the dramatic increase in literacy and public education in the modern era, the vast majority of people in any historical society were illiterate, and literacy was confined to a tiny fraction, usually the elite or those who served the ruling elite. Thus communication in nearly every area of life was predominantly oral. In these traditional societies, however, there was a certain degree of interaction between writing and oral communication. Writing, particularly official or sacred writing, had a considerable influence on the vast majority of illiterate people, directly and indirectly. Chapter 6 attempts to present a summary of the more nuanced scholarly investigation and treatment of literacy and orality and their interaction in the ancient world, with a focus on ancient Israel, Greece, and the Roman Empire, the key societies and cultures that would have influenced the circumstances and the movement from which Q in particular and New Testament literature in general emerged. The composite sketch that emerges from these recent studies is that oral communication was predominant in ancient societies generally, more so in the villages and towns than in the cities, and more so among ordinary people than among the elite. Writing and even the writing down of literature were in effect ancillary to oral communication and oral performance. The implications are clear: written texts, such as we believe Q to have been, were oral-derived texts, copies or transcripts of communication that took place concretely in oral performance before a group. It thus seems inappropriate to deal with Q as if it were a printed text and according to the interpretive habits ingrained in moderns socialized into print culture. "The fixation on authorial intent, on language as self-legitimating discourse, on the reduction of tradition to processes of textual transmission and stratification, and on the perception of ancient chirographs as visualizable, disengaged objects opens a vast conceptual gap that separates our own typographic rationalities from ancient media sensibilities."[5]

But how can biblical interpreters, trained to study and interpret sacred texts by intensive immersion in the assumptions and habits of print culture, become more sensitive to ancient media sensibilities? How can we retrain our minds to appreciate the different hermeneutics of oral-derived texts that were originally alive in oral performance? How can we rescue from an exclusive procedure in terms of texts — and from the previous dichotomy between textuality and orality — an oral-derived "text" such as Q that, "while surviving only in writing, still depends fundamentally on a pre-textual oral-traditional dynamic and on an oral-

---

5. Werner Kelber, "Jesus and Tradition," *Semeia* 65 (1994): 162.

traditional idiom that to an extent persists in the textual arena"?[6] Fortunately, interpreters of other oral-derived texts in other academic fields have already begun to deal with similar problems. By attending to explorations by pioneers in related fields we can gain both some perspective on our own subject matter and some sense of how other fields deal with oral-derived texts. We can at least temporarily move away from exclusive reliance on the microscopic analysis of sayings pursued by Q scholars and other biblical scholars and explore a more macroscopic inter-disciplinary approach, looking to others who deal with oral performance and/or oral-derived texts for ideas and procedures we can adapt to fit our peculiar oral-derived texts. It so happens that ethnographers of speech, classics scholars, and others experienced in the oral-traditional analysis pioneered by Milman Parry and Albert Lord are beginning to communicate with one another and are adapting sociolinguistics to their needs. The literature is already vast, and we pretend only to have scratched the surface. What we survey, summarize, and adapt in chapters 7 and 8, however, seems very fitting and potentially illuminating for an attempt at hearing the discourses of Q. It must be appropriately adapted, however, in adjustment to the particular political-economic-religious structure and dynamics of first-century Roman Palestine.

It may be useful to anticipate, in a simplifying summary, the difference that the approach we are exploring to oral-derived texts makes vis-à-vis standard studies of Q and other materials of or about Jesus. In contrast with focusing on and attempting to establish (1) the transmission (2) of an individual saying (3) to another individual (4) who cognitively grasped the meaning of its words, this evolving approach to an oral-derived text focuses on and attempts to appreciate (1) the public performance (2) of a whole discourse or set of discourses focused on issues of common concern (3) to a community gathered for common purposes (4) who in the performance experience certain events verbally enacted and/or are affected by the performance. The transmission, individual sayings, individuals, and cognitive meaning would all have been included in the broader process of public performance of discourses addressed to communities who experienced events in verbal enactments, as can be seen in some brief elaboration.

1. The public performances were probably regularly repeated and in more than one community. The problem of mere transmission of Jesus' sayings is no longer a problem, for it happens as a corollary, as a side effect, as it were, in regular public interactional performance in which the message must resonate with the hearers or it will no longer be performed.

2. The message or "text(s)" performed were short speeches focused on con-cerns of the community listening. What modern New Testament scholars take as individual sayings were components of larger units of communication. A lit-erary genre such as that of *logoi sophōn* was not needed as an occasion and form to generate the collection of sayings. Sayings were already repeatedly embed-

---

6. As it is put by John Miles Foley, addressing the concerns of biblical interpreters, in "Words in Tradition, Words in Text: A Response," *Semeia* 65 (1994): 172.

ded in speeches, which were at some point written down, transcribed into the manuscript(s) presumably used by Matthew and Luke. The Q speeches as oral performances would have been developing and changing; but without the control of variant versions in writing, it would be difficult to delineate compositional layers. "Composition" would be difficult to differentiate from performance. And the modern literary concept of authorship may simply be inappropriate. Such oral-derived texts "were viewed as constituents of a collective cultural enterprise or of a communal memory."[7]

3. Performance of Q discourses before a community involved in a conflictual life situation meant that the text always had an immediate historical social context. Only to modern scholars do Q discourses appear as individual sayings abstracted from a social situation. As discourses devoted to a subject of concern to a movement, they were embodied and alive in and through regular performance in a recurrent and often problematic situation. Q discourses were also always interactive insofar as some members of the movement recited the speeches to others, which was the point of the discourses. Composition and text had something to do with the circumstances and needs of the hearers with whom they resonated, or else they would have been discontinued in performance.

4. To establish the mere meaning of the words and sayings in the discourses would not take us very far in understanding what was happening in the performances of the discourses. We must seek further for the function or effect and significance of the communication in the historical social context. Insofar as some of the discourses would have been performatory, that is, verbal enactment, then certain events were happening in the performance of those discourses. Renewing a covenant, commissioning envoys to expand the movement, praying for the kingdom as a way of helping make it a social reality, or pronouncing woes against the Pharisees and thus calling down divine judgment upon them — all enact events through performative utterances and accomplish far more than transmitting sayings to preserve their memory! Performing a covenant renewal, teaching people to pray for the kingdom, and reassuring those anxious about the necessities of life also consolidate communities of people and enable them to maintain their solidarity and purpose through difficult life situations, in all of which the meaning of the words is only part of what is happening.

But how do things happen? How does performance work? How does performance have its effects in and among the hearers? Recently developed theories of oral performance in studies of oral-derived literature suggest that performance in a particular context must resonate with the cultural tradition shared by performer and listeners. "Performance is the enabling event, tradition the enabling referent."[8] This will be difficult for the field of New Testament studies, particularly studies of Jesus and Jesus' sayings and actions — again, because the field is so

---

7. Kelber, "Jesus and Tradition," 155.
8. A proverb coined as a key thesis for John Miles Foley, *The Singer of Tales in Performance,* Voices in Performance and Text (Bloomington: Indiana University Press, 1995).

strongly determined by Christian theological concerns. Christian interpretation tends to downplay the influence of the supposedly particularistic Jewish culture from which Jesus and the disciples came and to favor the supposedly more universalistic Hellenistic culture in which the Christian church grew and was decisively shaped. Virtually by definition, Jesus is the source, the originator, of new teaching and action. Although it has undergone some severe overdue criticism recently, the criterion of "double dissimilarity" (from preceding Jewish materials and from succeeding Christian ecclesial materials) for establishing authentic sayings of Jesus illustrates an orientation that had not disappeared with the rejection of this criterion. Jesus and the movement(s) he inspired are somehow new departures over against Judaism and Israel. The bias in the field is clearly to look for similarities of Jesus' teachings with Hellenistic Greek culture and for differences with the Jewish culture from which he came, despite the insistence that Jesus was Jewish.

One solution in some recent studies of Q is to find that Galilee was less Jewish and more cosmopolitan Hellenistic than previously allowed. As indicated in chapter 3, however, recent historical and archaeological studies of Galilee suggest that it is highly unlikely that the cities just being developed in Galilee by its first resident ruler, Herod Antipas, would have brought much by way of cosmopolitan Hellenistic culture to the towns and villages. The cultural tradition presupposed by Jesus and the earliest Jesus movements in Galilee would have been Israelite. And the examination of Israelite tradition in Q in chapter 5 confirms that it is far more pervasive in Q than is often acknowledged. If Jesus is to be approached in his own historical context, then he must have been working out of the Israelite popular tradition. Galileans, Judeans, and their Israelite tradition were undergoing the impact of foreign conquest and to a degree the impact of an alien culture as well, so there was tension and conflict aplenty in which that tradition was implicated. But however creatively and effectively Jesus must have been drawing on Israelite tradition as he addressed his people in the midst of their crisis situation, our task as we attempt to hear and appreciate Jesus' speeches as performed by some of his followers before others of his followers is to become as aware as possible of how the Israelite tradition was being drawn upon and used creatively in addressing the crisis of the first century in Galilee and Judea.

Scholars of oral-derived literature lay great stress on the cultural tradition for the effectiveness of oral performance and the importance, therefore, for the modern interpreter to have as thorough an acquaintance as possible with the tradition with which an oral-derived text resonates. To cite only two scholars who recently addressed the concerns of biblical studies:

> Each work of verbal art is nourished by an ever-impinging set of unspoken but implicitly articulated assumptions shared among the discourse community. To remove the event from the biosphere of tradition is therefore to sap its cognitive lifeblood, to deprive it of very obvious potential for conveying meaning, to silence the echoes that reverberate through it.... What will be required ... is an informed audience alive to their illocutionary force, ... auditors who can invest the entexted utterance with its due heritage of performative meaning. Without that experience and

ability no reader or auditor can construe the map of textual signals in traditional context.... Once such an audience has been "written out of existence" by decades of exclusively textual discourse, ... it is left to scholars to reestablish analytically — and artificially — what we can of the lost context of oral tradition.[9]

We must learn to think of a large part of tradition as an extratextual phenomenon [shared experiences, etc.].... Tradition in this encompassing sense is a circum- ambient contextuality or biosphere in which speaker and hearers live. It includes texts and experiences transmitted through or derived from texts. But it is anything but reducible to intertextuality. Tradition in this broadest sense is largely an invisible nexus of references and identities from which people draw sustenance, in which they live, and in relation to which they make sense of their lives. This invisible biosphere is at once the most elusive and the foundational feature of tradition.[10]

For exploration of Q as an oral-derived text those extratextual aspects of the tradition out of which it must be understood are of special importance, given Q's apparent origins in and resonance with, not the Israelite great tradition as cultivated in scribal circles, but the Israelite popular tradition. However, although the latter was oral, its existence and contents must be projected on the basis of parallels in the written great tradition, as indicated in chapter 5. Because the ways in which a performed text references the tradition with which it resonates in the hearers provide the principal indicators of the performance context and the register of the text, an exploration of the Israelite tradition will figure prominently in the chapters devoted to particular Q discourses.

One hesitates to bring the term and concept "tradition" into the discussion in yet another prominent and elastically vague sense when it is already overworked in other, related meanings that are also vague. It will be potentially confusing to use the term with multiple meanings, which will require close attention to context. But for most of the meanings in which "tradition" will be used, no satis- factory alternative term has emerged. There may be one exception. For "tradition" in the sense of the handing down or on of a particular cultural memory or say- ing or custom or ritual, a prominent usage in biblical studies, we can substitute "transmission" in most instances. In most cases it will be clear from context where "tradition" is being used for one of those particular memories of sayings or cus- toms. Similarly, with an adjective attached it will be clear when "tradition" is being used for a broader line of tradition, such as "the prophetic tradition," or used to describe a particular kind or style of tradition carried in certain social circles, such as "scribal/sapiential tradition." Most important for this attempt at exploration of Q as an oral-derived text is the broadest sense of tradition, as indicated in the quotations above: the comprehensive cultural heritage of Is- rael. And it is important to keep in mind that even though we are dependent largely on textual artifacts of this tradition for our knowledge of it, it was largely extratextual at the time in a predominantly oral culture, carried in memory and

---

9. Foley, "Words in Tradition," 171.
10. Kelber, "Jesus and Tradition," 159.

oral communication. Finally, to add an important qualification and subdivision that may not be pertinent in other cases such as archaic (Homeric) Greece, it is clear, given the political-economic-religious structure and dynamics of Galilee and Judea in late second-temple times under Roman rule, that Israelite tradition was contested, primarily between, on the one hand, the Israelite great tradition based in Jerusalem and cultivated in scribal and ruling circles and, on the other hand, the Israelite little tradition(s) that were cultivated orally and almost certainly with certain regional variation among the villagers who comprised the vast majority of the people.

The Sequence of Chapters on Q Discourses

We begin with Q 6:20–49 and 9:57–10:16 (chapters 9 and 10) for several reasons. They are the longest and most schematic discourses with clear internal indications of their purpose and performance context. Q 6:20–49 also can easily be seen to reference a very rich vein of Israelite tradition and offers an opportunity to deal with a broader form, that of covenant renewal, central to Israelite tradition. We begin with these discourses also, however, because so much recent Q interpretation has focused on sayings taken out of these discourses, insisting that they are by definition sapiential in form and sapiential in significance. We want to problematize that term/concept right at the outset and to insist that the meaning contexts of those sayings, however sapiential they may be, are those of covenant renewal and mission in a popular movement, a far cry from the circles of scribes and sages who cultivated sapiential teaching and left some of it in sapiential literature. In chapter 11 we then move back to the first two discourses of Q, the speech of John announcing the coming of one who is apparently a prophet of fulfillment and judgment and the story of the testing of the prophet in the wilderness by the devil, both of which heavily reference the wilderness roots of Israel's origins and Israel's founder's and renewers' testing and preparation. That leads to confirmation of the suggestion at the end of chapter 4 that the first several Q discourses, while each devoted to a particular concern of a movement, have an intelligible sequence as well.

Chapters 12 and 13 are then devoted to less extensive treatment of many of the other discourses in Q, some insofar as they address concerns internal to the communities of the movement and others insofar as they pronounce prophetic condemnation on the Jerusalem rulers and their representatives. All of the discourses dealt with thus appear to be addressed to concerns of a movement (which apparently originated in Galilee) for the renewal of Israel, based in village communities and standing over against the ostensible rulers of Israel and their Pharisaic representatives based in Jerusalem. While covering most of the Q discourses at some point, we do not pretend to be offering a comprehensive survey of Q materials.

The last chapter attempts to pull together conclusions about the Q movement generated by the previous chapters, examining particular discourses and also exploring how we might understand the performers of the Q discourses in relation to Jesus, for whom they speak, and to the communities, to whom they speak.

A Note on the Presentation of Q Discourses

In an experimental attempt to present the speeches of Jesus in Q in such a way that their oral patterning can be appreciated by us moderns who usually work through the medium of print, we have attempted to block out the texts in such a way that a modern hearer who does not know ancient Greek can still glean some sense of the parallelism of lines, the repetition of sounds, the positioning of key terms within lines, verses, and stanzas. We have also provided translations so that the sense of the speech is approximated, and even some of the patterning of language, if not sounds, may come through in the blocking of the translation. The rationale and particular scheme we are using are explained further in chapter 8. We hope that by reading the transliterated discourses aloud several times until the parallelism of lines and repetition of sounds are familiar to the ear, even readers without knowledge of Greek can obtain a feel for the oral performance. Those familiar with music and/or poetry will appreciate the importance of the hearing of sounds in what was originally the oral performance of these speeches in Q. Jesus himself presumably spoke Aramaic, but we have these speeches in Greek. After prolonged debate, scholars have in the main concluded that we cannot move behind the Greek of our texts into a reconstructed Aramaic. All that may remain in some cases are some parallelism of lines and certain other patterns in the Greek that may derive from Aramaic speech patterns. We have made no attempt to analyze such possible connections and influences and work with the Greek text available through the Gospels of Matthew and Luke. Throughout our blocking of the Q text in transliteration and translation, we have depended heavily and appreciatively on, although not always followed, the Q text produced by the International Q Project. We are grateful to the staff of James M. Robinson at the Institute for Antiquity and Christianity in Claremont, California, for making a working draft of the reconstructed text of Q available to us. We hope that the presentation of the Q text blocked out in measured verse not only will help make credible that Q discourses were performed orally but will also enable modern hearers to appreciate some of the sound and sense of the speech in these discourses.

The reading, reflection, and considerable rethinking behind this exploration of Q discourses as oral-derived literature developed during a half-year in which Jonathan Draper and I together attempted to come to grips with the oral communication environment of antiquity, how to understand the interaction of writing and orality in traditional societies, and how to approach oral-derived texts whose oral hermeneutics carry over into their textualization. We feel that we have only begun what will be a long process of rethinking in the field of biblical studies as we attempt to move from the assumptions and habits of the print culture in which we have been socialized into greater appreciation of the oral performance in which the teachings and actions of Jesus were communicated in the early communities of his followers. Draper and his colleagues at the School of Theology at the University of Natal in Pietermaritzburg, South Africa, have long since realized that they must listen to their students, many of whom come from and still live among Zulu and other peoples whose communication is still predominantly oral. They are courageously attempting to adjust their scholarly biblical study in the direction of the people for whom ultimately they are training an educated clergy with university degrees. There are signs elsewhere as well that university-based biblical scholars are recognizing that established academic biblical study is not the only mode in which the biblical tradition can be appropriated.

For whatever illustrative value it may have in connection with issues of oral performance and a situation in which we are attempting to appreciate an oral performance in a language and culture we do not know (or know well), let me tell of my experience of a three-hour Easter service of a Zulu Anglican congregation. The whole service was conducted in Zulu by several officiants, including Jonathan Draper, who was serving as the temporary priest of the parish. Although I could not cognitively understand the words of the liturgy in Zulu, even I, a country Methodist boy, was familiar enough with the actions and gestures of the liturgical drama to have a rough sense of what was happening up front. Meanwhile, whenever the liturgists up front left off for a while, the hundreds of Zulu people jammed into the benches in the church building would burst into traditional Zulu songs — until the liturgists quieted them down for some more formal prayers, hymns, and lessons. When it came time for the sermon, Draper, who felt confident enough of his grasp of the language to say the liturgy in Zulu, thought it best to preach in English, with periodic breaks so that his Zulu assistant could repreach that section of the sermon in Zulu. It was evident to me that many of the Zulus present who did not know much English were "hearing the word" pretty well in Draper's English even before they heard it again in their native Zulu, when their antiphonal response became even more active. And I, having heard a section of Draper's sermon in English, could then gain at least some sense of the sounds that my Zulu fellow listeners were hearing in Zulu as the preaching progressed. It was vividly evident that more was happening in oral performance than the mere cognitive meaning of the words and sentences and that much of the communication depended on the communication context, the familiarity of what was being performed, and the continuing community before and in interaction with whom the performance was happening.

Chapter 1

THE TEACHINGS OF JESUS
AND LIBERAL INDIVIDUALISM

Richard A. Horsley _____

Aphorism and Individualism

Recent studies of Q have taken modern scholarly treatment of the Synoptic Gospel tradition to its logical extreme. Under the pressures of Enlightenment reason, scientific interpreters of the Gospels had to jettison virtually all narrative material in the Gospels as potential sources for reconstruction and understanding of Jesus. The superhuman beings and miraculous elements in most narratives could not be accommodated. All that remained were Jesus' teachings, separated from the longer narratives that placed them in a broader context of dramatic political-religious conflict. By around 1920, form critics such as Rudolf Bultmann worked out a method for tracing the development of Jesus' sayings among his followers so that they could determine what seemed earliest and most "authentic."[1] It became and still is a standard assumption that in the beginning were individual sayings that only later became combined in various ways and for various reasons. The discovery of the *Gospel of Thomas* earlier in the twentieth century provided a powerful confirmation of this assumption insofar as it consists of 114 separate *logia*, most of which are separate or paired individual sayings. Although earlier interpreters of Q sometimes described it as a collection of speeches, it became standard to label it the "Synoptic Sayings Source" and, more recently, the "Sayings Gospel." Even those who have more recently recognized that the component sayings are configured in larger "clusters" or "discourses" assumed that the individual sayings were originally independent and proceeded by categorizing, characterizing, and analyzing individual sayings.[2]

Categorization of individual sayings by form enabled recent interpreters to construct a homogenous, supposedly original layer or "document" comprised of relatively simple sapiential sayings unencumbered with more troubling prophetic pronouncements and apocalyptic motifs. The sayings that thus remain in the original "collection" are relatively simple and suggestive aphorisms and admonitions.

---

1. Rudolf Bultmann, *The History of the Synoptic Tradition* (Oxford: Blackwell, 1963 [1921]).

2. For example, John S. Kloppenborg, *The Formation of Q: Trajectories in Ancient Wisdom Collections* (Philadelphia: Fortress, 1987).

"These sayings put us in touch with the earliest stage of the Jesus movement when aphoristic discourse was the norm."[3] Having thus been isolated as individual aphorisms and admonitions and stripped of any literary and historical context on the basis of which their meaning can be discerned, these sayings provide attractive subject matter for modern European and American interpreters whose orientation to reality is dominated by two interrelated characteristics peculiar to modern Western culture: an unquestioning individualism and the closely related separation of a personal religious-cultural dimension from the political-economic dimensions of life.

The individualism of the modern interpreters, which neatly matches their isolation of the individual sayings from literary and historical context, is the determining factor in recent scholarly analysis and interpretation of Q. This comes vividly to the fore in a recent interpretation of the supposedly earliest layer of Q written for a more general, less scholarly market.[4] What is assumed by most interpreters is stated explicitly and repeatedly: the aphorisms and imperatives "were addressed to individuals."[5]

The most telling — and, in comparison with previous studies of Jesus and the Gospels, astounding — indicator of just how pervasively individualistic such interpretation of Q can be is the understanding of the "kingdom / rule of God." Because they cannot find the precise phrase "kingdom of God" in Judean prophetic and apocalyptic literature, recent Q interpreters resort to supposed parallels from Hellenistic and Hellenistic Jewish philosophical texts, where the precise phrase is equally as difficult to find. In the elite intellectual circles of Hellenistic philosophy, "kingdom" was "a metaphor for the 'sovereignty' manifest in the 'independent bearing,' 'freedom,' 'confidence,' and self-control of the superior person, the person of ethical integrity who thus could 'rule' his 'world' imperiously."[6] That is, "the concept of the rule of God [was] an alternative realm or way of life everywhere available to daring individuals," the metaphors of which are largely taken from the realm of nature.[7] The principal feature of the Q sayings that is not derived from Hellenistic philosophy is their representation of God as Father. Q interpreters then find in this a universalism that corresponds to the individualism of Jesus' teachings.[8]

This individualistic interpretation of "the kingdom of God" in Q is all the more striking because it does not appear to be derived from a consideration of the kingdom of God sayings in Q read with close attention to their contents and literary contexts. Nearly all of the kingdom sayings often assigned to the original layer of Q (6:20; 10:9, 11; 11:2–4; 12:31), like those often assigned to

3. Burton L. Mack, *The Lost Gospel: The Book of Q and Christian Origins* (San Francisco: HarperSanFrancisco, 1993), 110.

4. Ibid.

5. Ibid., 120, 127, 128.

6. Ibid., 126.

7. Ibid., 127.

8. Ibid., 27–28.

a secondary redactional layer (7:28; 11:20; 13:28–29; 16:16; 22:28–30), seem to refer to some dramatic change in the historical situation, not to some sort of individual self-confidence. Moreover, the political metaphor of the kingdom of God is embellished (explicitly or implicitly in the context) with other social-political metaphors in most of those sayings (6:20; 7:28; 9:60; 10:9, 11; 11:2–4, 20; 12:31; 13:28–29; 16:16; 22:28–30) and with agricultural and domestic metaphors in others (9:62; 13:18–19, 20–21). While metaphors from nature are found in Q, they do not happen to crop up in kingdom sayings. The individual kingdom is not found in but read into the kingdom of God sayings in Q.

As can be seen in the Q interpreters' reduction of the kingdom of God to a matter of individual self-confidence, their individualistic interpretation also abstracts and generalizes away from the particular circumstances of historical life. The aphorisms and admonitions of the earliest layer of Q, it is claimed, pertain to individual character (*ethos*) and attitude. "Life in general is under review and conventional values are under critique," but only with regard to a change in individual attitude and behavior.[9] Taking the sayings as isolated aphorisms abstracted from context leads to vague, generalized readings. Since they are assumed to be isolated sayings, separate from any particular context, it is not surprising that "none of them specifies the circumstances" and that they seem only to "solicit a heightened awareness" in a general way that cannot be further specified. The sapiential sayings of the supposedly earliest layer of Q thus isolated do resemble the somewhat detached generalizations about life found in Jewish wisdom books and the gnomologia collected by Hellenistic philosophers: "Life is more than food." Far from directly attacking the wealthy, as did the Hebrew prophetic sayings, Q sayings merely offer a suggestive critique of those who claim superior status based on wealth in ways similar to Cynic philosophers in Hellenistic cities.[10] The pithy aphorisms of the original Q do not protest the structures of power but merely call the "readers" to "see through the emptiness" of power. Some of the sayings even "invite introspection" in a way that resembles the hermeneutics explicit and implicit in the *Gospel of Thomas* (see esp. 1–2): the aphorisms provoke reflection and are to be carefully pondered. "Overall the message is that customary pretensions are hollow.... There must be a better way to live."[11]

The earliest layer of Q sayings correspondingly calls not for social reform but for a change of individual lifestyle. "There is no suggestion of a program to change the system that supports questionable values."[12] "The way society worked in general was taken for granted."[13] The better lifestyle that the Q aphorisms and admo-

---

9. Ibid., 111, 124.

10. In this regard recent Q interpreters are inconsistent. While claiming that the earliest Q sayings have virtually no trace of the particulars of Israelite culture, including characterization of God, they then find Q sayings to be somehow countercultural, and that in ways that resemble Hellenistic philosophical culture, particularly the Cynic! See Mack, *Lost Gospel*, 114–19; and Leif Vaage, *Galilean Upstarts: Jesus' First Followers according to Q* (Valley Forge, Pa.: Trinity Press International, 1994).

11. Mack, *Lost Gospel*, 111.

12. Ibid.

13. Ibid., 120.

nitions recommend, while vague in the extreme, is discernibly countercultural, a relatively unobtrusive rejection of traditional values and codes tempered by a certain "etiquette" in begging and troublesome public encounters. "One should discard unnecessary trappings and live the simple, unencumbered life."[14] The earliest Q people, apparently comfortable in their life circumstances, are admonished by Q's critique of riches (e.g., Q 6:20) toward voluntary poverty (e.g., Q 12:22–31) and renunciation of family (Q 9:59–62; 14:26; both literalistically understood).[15] Even in the midst of the (vaguely) "rough and ready circumstances of Galilee," therefore, the earliest Q people, their personal ethos or character thus informed by Jesus' aphorisms and admonitions, could thus lead a countercultural way of life with carefree equanimity (Q 12:4–7, 22–31).

The Reductionist Hermeneutics of Modern Liberalism

To anyone acquainted with the history of modern theology and biblical studies this recent interpretation of the supposedly earliest layer of Q seems familiar. Roughly a hundred years ago liberal theologians were articulating the same interpretation of the sayings of Jesus in general. The sentences and phrases of Adolf von Harnack in particular continue to echo in the books and articles of recent interpreters of Q, as comes to mind from a review of Harnack's 1899–1900 public lectures on "the essence of Christianity," published in English under the title *What Is Christianity?* in 1900.[16] Because Gospel studies have become ever more complex in the course of the last century, recent interpreters of Q have retreated to a far more limited "data base," but their basic interpretation of the so-called earliest layer of Q strongly resembles Harnack's interpretation of Jesus' teachings in general.

Harnack and other liberal theologians had already retreated from any scientifically indefensible materials in the Gospels and focused only on "the leading features of Jesus' message." Reluctant, as university intellectuals, to claim knowledge of what Jesus actually said, they focused on "the reflection and the effects which he produced in those whose leader and master be became,"[17] just as it is intellectually more comfortable today to focus on the earliest layer of Q as the effects Jesus produced in his followers. And in that connection the dominant agenda is immediately clear: "Individual religious life was what he wanted to kindle and what he did kindle."[18] Or, as Ernst Troeltsch put it: the Gospel's "first outstanding characteristic is an unlimited, unqualified individualism."[19] As with recent Q interpreters, so with Harnack the most telling indicator of how modern

---

14. Ibid., 113.
15. Ibid., 113–14.
16. Adolf von Harnack, *What Is Christianity?* with introduction by Rudolf Bultmann (New York: Harper & Row, 1957 [1900]).
17. Ibid., 10.
18. Ibid., 111.
19. Ernst Troeltsch, *The Social Teaching of the Christian Churches* (New York: Harper & Brothers, 1960 [original German ed. 1911]), 55.

Western individualism dominates the reading of Jesus' teachings emerges in connection with the kingdom of God. "The kingdom of God comes by coming to the individual, by entering into his soul and laying hold of it."[20] Harnack delivered his lectures just before the "apocalyptic" understanding of Jesus' teachings became prominent, thanks to Johannes Weiss and Albert Schweitzer, while recent Q interpreters have been at pains to free Jesus' teaching from the embarrassment of apocalypticism by sorting out an early layer of apocalyptic-free sapiential sayings.

Along with their focus on the individual, the teachings of Jesus are "above all questions of mundane development"; they are not "concerned with material things" but with individuals' souls, their attitudes, and their behavior.[21] "Such an individualism is only possible at all upon this religious basis, . . . and it is only in common relationship with God, in a realm of supernatural values, that natural differences disappear."[22] In the realm of religion, Jesus' gospel "contains no statutory or particularistic elements" but is "religion itself."[23] Eager to find in Jesus' teachings the universalism they saw in classical culture, the liberal theologians showed the way in simply ignoring any undesirable Israelite/Jewish particularism that might contaminate the gospel. Harnack, moreover, could even claim that Jesus' teaching "never uses any ecstatic language, and the tone of stirring prophecy is rare."[24] To free Jesus' teachings from such troubling prophetic elements a century later, it was necessary to differentiate an early nonprophetic layer from a secondary prophetic-apocalyptic layer in Q itself. The most influential part of Harnack's interpretation of the kingdom of God as what "comes to the individual" was perhaps his emphasis on God as Father. Harnack's reduction of Jesus' message to individualism and individual religiosity was summarized in a now-famous phrase: "the idea of God the Father and the infinite value of the human soul."[25]

With Jesus' focus on "individual religious life" and its transcendence of mundane matters, it is clear that he "laid down no social programme for the suppression of poverty and distress" and "did not interfere with economical conditions and contemporary circumstances."[26] Rather, Jesus' teachings focus on freeing the individual from the accepted ways of the world. Although Harnack did not use the recent buzzword "countercultural," he found Jesus criticizing conventional values and behavior as he offers what is in effect an alternative lifestyle. "He of-

---

20. Harnack, *What Is Christianity?* 56.
21. Ibid., 116.
22. Troeltsch, *Social Teaching,* 55.
23. Harnack, *What Is Christianity?* 63.
24. Ibid., 35.
25. Ibid., 63; Troeltsch, *Social Teaching,* 52, 55.
26. Harnack, *What Is Christianity?* 97; Harnack also writes: "With this [the Lord's] prayer we ought also to confront all those who disparage the Gospel by representing it as an ascetic or ecstatic or sociological pronouncement" (65). Cf. Troeltsch, *Social Teaching,* 59–62, on Jesus' attitude toward the state and economics. "In the teaching of Jesus there is no trace of a struggle against oppression. . . . The message of Jesus was not a programme of social reform" (60–61).

fers men an inexorable alternative."[27] Like recent Q interpreters, Harnack found in Jesus' teachings a particular concern with liberating individuals from possessions and cares. "Jesus regarded the possession of worldly goods as a grave danger for the soul, as hardening the heart, entangling us in earthly cares."[28] "A man is not really free, strong, and invincible, until he has put aside all his cares and cast them upon God."[29] "Upon those who were anxious to devote their whole lives to the preaching of the Gospel . . . he enjoined the renunciation of all that they had."[30] The teachings of Jesus, such as the parables, thus exhibit and inculcate in his followers "an inner freedom and a cheerfulness of soul in the midst of the greatest strain."[31]

The principal difference between Harnack's interpretation of Jesus' teachings in their effects on his disciples and recent interpretations of an ostensibly early layer in Q pertains to the social implications. Somehow, left unexplained by Q interpreters, the sapiential teachings of Jesus in the original collection of Q led to "social formation" of house-based gatherings of people and a resentment by Jesus' followers at their rejection by the rest of Israel, that is, a kind of sectarianism that withdrew from society as a whole. Harnack and other liberals, however, saw more of a social-ethical aspect to Jesus' teaching in general. "The Gospel is a social message, . . . the proclamation of solidarity and brotherliness, in favour of the poor."[32] A communal dimension remains, along with a sense of individuals' responsibility in the larger society and an ethical idealism about the future. "Our riches do not belong to us alone. . . . [W]e are administrators in the service of our neighbor." "Jesus' disciple ought to be able to renounce the pursuit of his rights, and ought to co-operate in forming a nation of brothers, in which justice is done, no longer by the aid of force, but by free obedience to the good, and which is united not by legal regulations but by the ministry of love."[33] "The fire of judgment and the forces of love were what [Jesus] wanted to summon up so as to create a new humanity. . . . [H]e saw on his horizon not only the judgment, but also a kingdom of justice, of love, and of peace, which though it came from heaven, was nevertheless for this earth."[34] Although they find an eventual formation of small communities in the Jesus movement, recent Q interpreters project a far more individualistic reading of their earliest layer of Q sayings than Harnack's

---

27. Harnack, *What Is Christianity?* 37.

28. Ibid., 93; cf. 84.

29. Ibid., 86. Except for the last phrase about God, this interpretation rather remarkably parallels Mack's comparison of Jesus' kingdom as individual self-confidence and self-sufficiency with ancient Cynic teaching. Troeltsch had compared Jesus' religiously based moral freedom with that articulated in Stoic philosophy (*Social Teaching,* 64–69).

30. Harnack, *What Is Christianity?* 95. Again, except insofar as Harnack claims that Jesus' followers were not to beg for a living, his interpretation in 1900 resembles that of Q interpreters who draw the Cynic analogy nearly a century later.

31. Ibid., 36.

32. Ibid., 101.

33. Ibid., 112.

34. Ibid., 122.

interpretation of Jesus' teachings in general, which was still fired by a hopeful ethical idealism.

The residue of ethical idealism in Harnack's individualistic interpretation, however, only serves to highlight the remarkable similarity of recent Q scholars' individualistic interpretation to that of liberal theology a century earlier. How do we explain this remarkable similarity, even in certain key phrases, this striking revival (or is it continuity?) of liberal theology in interpretation of Jesus' teachings? Several interrelated factors may play a role, as we glance over the development of theologically based biblical interpretation in relation to the dominant Western liberal-intellectual culture.

One prominent factor is the continuing dominance of liberal individualism in Western society, particularly in American intellectual culture. Intellectual discussion and academic analysis proceed on the assumption that people are and should be separate individuals, which downplays or ignores the reality and importance of social groups and social relationships. Correspondingly, it is assumed in the still-prevailing Western intellectual culture that various dimensions of societal life are separate spheres, embodied in separate political, economic, religious, and familial institutions. Relations among these spheres take place primarily through individuals, who play various roles. Almost by definition, religion becomes a matter of individual faith, embodied in some mix of feelings, attitudes, beliefs, and dispositions. The Gospels, historically literature of Christianity, therefore, are viewed almost by definition as strictly religious documents; Jesus is seen as primarily a religious teacher; and his sayings are understood as addressed to individuals and their character, attitudes, and behavior. This common cultural assumption is shared by Q interpreters, who articulate it pointedly with regard to Jesus' aphorisms and admonitions.

Another factor is the formative and continuing influence of liberal theology, such as Harnack's treatise on Jesus' teaching and Troeltsch's tour de force on ethical teachings. Originally published in English and German in 1900, Harnack's *What Is Christianity?* had gone through fourteen printings and had been translated into fourteen languages by 1927. It was reissued in a paperback edition in the United States in 1957. As Bultmann, himself a powerful voice in perpetuating liberal individualism in theology, wrote in the introduction to the new edition, the work "exerted an extraordinary influence . . . on the educated classes generally."[35] Troeltsch's *The Social Teaching of the Christian Churches*, originally published in 1911, was reissued in paperback in 1960. Through such readily available paperback editions the influence of liberal theology continued after midcentury, particularly in educated circles. In the United States in particular, liberal theology fired with ethical idealism was a factor in the social gospel movement, with its agenda of building the kingdom of God on earth. The devastating experience of World War I, of course, decisively undermined such idealism in Europe. Half a century later the failures of movements to change social reality led theologians and other intellectuals, both in North America and Western Europe, to

---

35. Bultmann, introduction to *What Is Christianity?* vii.

withdraw into a relatively disengaged culture criticism. Late twentieth-century Gospel interpreters thus cannot summon the idealism of their predecessors in liberal theology. Yet if anything, individualism became more pronounced in the course of the twentieth century, particularly in North America, which has far less of a tradition of corporate social solidarity and responsibility than European countries. As Bultmann wrote prophetically in 1957, "this 'liberal' understanding, at the very least, contains active impulses which though now obscured nonetheless preserve their legitimacy and will recover their validity."[36]

Yet another factor, surely, is the similarity of recent Q scholars' position in the dominant culture to that of leading liberal theologians a century ago. Liberal theologians such as Harnack and Troeltsch were members of an intellectual elite based in German universities. They were trying to find a way of making theology and religion respectable in wider academic circles which, particularly in Germany, placed a high value on classical antiquity, with emphasis on its humanism and universalism. In Christian theological circles, this led to a devaluation of the Jewish origins of Christianity as parochial and political and to an emphasis on how Christianity built on the supposedly more universalistic Hellenistic heritage in becoming the true religion, universal as well as purely spiritual. Achieving intellectual respectability also meant accepting the value of modern science and its criteria of truth and meaning. That reinforced the reduction of religion to a sphere separate from politics and economics and focused on the individual and the individual's feelings, attitudes, and moral behavior. Not only do the theologically trained recent interpreters of Q stand in the same theological tradition. But in their role as an intellectual elite attempting to make theology and religion respectable in academic circles, they also share many of the concerns of their liberal theological forebears a century earlier.[37]

Harnack's Different Reading of Q

Harnack also produced the first book-length study of Q, but not until several years after his highly influential lectures on "the essence of Christianity." At a few points in the study he made statements reminiscent of his earlier interpretation

---

36. Ibid., viii.

37. Many of the observations here about recent "American" Q studies also pertain to recent "American" studies of the "historical Jesus," particularly those associated with the "Jesus Seminar." In a recent essay, Werner Kelber places the latter, along with more "conservative" reaction to them, in the broader perspective of the history of Christian thought ("The Quest for the Historical Jesus: From the Perspectives of Medieval, Modern, and Post-Enlightenment Readings, and in View of Ancient, Oral Aesthetics," in *The Jesus Controversy*, ed. Werner Kelber [Harrisburg, Pa.: Trinity Press International, 1999]). A supplement to Kelber's analysis might be the observation of how individualistic both Crossan's and Johnson's constructions of Jesus are. Crossan's Jesus, particularly striking in the more popular *Jesus: A Revolutionary Biography* (San Francisco: HarperCollins, 1993), is virtually a monk (e.g., as an itinerant teacher who enjoys open commensality), which may not be surprising for a scholar rooted in Catholic tradition. Johnson's Jesus in *The Real Jesus* (San Francisco: Harper-Collins, 1996) resonates with an individualistic pietism, which resonates in both American Catholic and Protestant traditions.

of Jesus' teachings in general. In Q, for example, he found a solid basis for his view of "the purely religious and ethical elements" of Jesus' message, including "the renunciation of earthly rights, earthly goods, and earthly cares."[38] Harnack's study of Q, however, is most striking for his discussion of aspects of Q that have disappeared from, been deemphasized by, or been denied in the revival of Q studies during the last few decades.

First, and perhaps most remarkable and important, in his investigation and reconstruction of the text of Q, Harnack understood and described it as "essentially a collection of discourses."[39] In more recent discussion of Q, it is usually understood as a collection of sayings. Even the very recent compositional analysis that finds Q to consist of a set of "clusters" or "speeches" understands the latter to be constructed out of originally separate individual sayings. Harnack, however, took the contents of Q as he investigated it just under the surface of the Gospels of Matthew and Luke to consist of seven narratives, thirteen groups of sayings that included some parables, and twenty-nine single sayings, with a few more separate parables. He further saw that the narratives are mostly dialogues or speeches set up by a question, thus further enlarging the size and number of discourses or "groups of sayings." Moreover, many of "the twenty-nine shorter or longer sayings . . . may be regarded with more or less probability as parts of discourses." He thus discerned the basic contours of the Q "sermon" and "mission" discourse, as well as the fuller scope of other discourses.[40] He reconstructed all of this in an investigation that followed the Matthean order, which he concluded was closer to the original. If he had worked on the same principle of more or less contiguous sayings material but followed the Lukan order instead, he would undoubtedly have found even greater coherence in the Q text — for example, Luke 6:20–49 has in continuous sequence what appears in Matthew as separate "groups" of "beatitudes" ("love your enemies . . ."; "do not judge . . .") and the double house parable, and Luke 9:57–10:16 has in continuous sequence what appears in Matthew as somewhat more scattered "single sayings."

Besides discerning a compilation of discourses and not simply a collection of sayings, Harnack sensed an order and coherence in those discourses that have not been noticed in more recent Q studies. He noticed that the discourses themselves cohere around a given "subject matter."[41] Besides that, he observed that the discourses have a "definite arrangement of subject matter" into "an order which is natural and intelligible," almost seeming "chronological":[42] the preaching of the Baptist; the story of the temptation; the Sermon; the charge to the disciples concerning their mission; the discourse concerning the Baptist; the woes against

38. Adolf von Harnack, *The Sayings of Jesus* (New York: Putnam's Sons, 1908 [1907]), 250–51, 231.

39. Ibid., 181; note how the title of the English translation skews Harnack's conclusion (the German title is *Sprüche und Reden Jesu*).

40. Ibid., 164–67.

41. Ibid., 165.

42. Ibid., 178–79, 181.

the cities; thanksgiving to the Father; the section about Beelzebul and the sign
of Jonah; the woes against the Pharisees; the warning against false Christs and
the discourse concerning the parousia; the coming of the Son of Man as thief
in the night and the faithful and unfaithful steward; and the disciples governing
the twelve tribes of Israel.[43] He even noted that this sequence of discourses has
coherence as a document. "Q appears to be more homogeneous than any of the
three" Synoptic Gospels. For example, "the geographical horizon of Q is bounded
[largely] by Galilee."[44] Moreover, strikingly absent are "the Passion and the narratives leading up to the Passion.... Herein lies the fundamental difference between
the gospels and Q. The latter, in fact, was not a gospel at all in the sense that the
Synoptics are."[45] "Indeed," Harnack even commented, "if one keeps in mind the
contemporary Jewish fashion, the composition of such a work [i.e., a compilation
of discourses] is a priori probable," suggesting that he had in mind some sort of
literary genre of teachings that Q is following.[46]

Second, and somewhat surprising, given the German cultural atmosphere and
theological agenda at the time and his own previous emphasis on the universalism evident in Jesus' teachings, Harnack recognized both the Semitic linguistic
background and the Jewish societal horizon of the Q discourses. Behind the vocabulary, syntax, and style of the Q discourses he found Semitic expressions.[47]
Moreover, Q stands prior to any crystalization of "Christian" identity separate
from Jewish society:

> The controversy of Christianity with Judaism as between two distinct religious
> principles... [is] wanting [in Q]; only in reference to divorce does Jesus go be-
> yond the Law. Elsewhere it is said that the Law abides so long as heaven and earth
> remain. The Jewish horizon and Jewish sentiment are also shown in the fact that
> the bliss of the Kingdom of God is pictured as a sitting at meat with Abraham, Isaac,
> and Jacob, and in the promise to the apostles that they should rule the twelve tribes
> of Israel.[48]

Q is neither "national" nor "antinational" in its stance.[49] That is a remarkably
blunt recognition, although Harnack proceeded immediately to read the words
against "this generation" and the woes against the Pharisees as a rejection of
the Jews generally, who are to be replaced by the Gentiles in the kingdom with
Abraham, much as do more recent studies of Q.[50]

Third, although he still projected certain Christian theological and biblically
derived concepts onto Q (e.g, the parousia, because he is giving priority to Matthew's version), Harnack noticed that terms prominent in other New Testament

---

43. In other lists Harnack includes other discourses, such as "Do not be anxious, etc.," and "Not
peace but a sword, etc." (ibid., 165).
44. Ibid., 167–68.
45. Ibid., 170.
46. Ibid., 181.
47. Ibid., 147–63.
48. Ibid., 229–30.
49. Ibid., 171.
50. Ibid., 230.

literature, such as "Christ" and "Lord," were not applied to Jesus in Q, that Q was not particularly interested in particular disciples or "the disciples" in general, and that Q lacked interest in and any reference to the passion or crucifixion of Jesus. Since he took "the Son of Man" as Jesus' self-reference in Q, he also made little of an exalted, heavenly Jesus-figure. Compared with more recent studies of Q, Harnack's study was relatively less encumbered by Christian theological categories developed separately from and/or later than Q.

Fourth, because he was attempting to deal with Q as a work of literature and not a mere collection of sayings, Harnack carried out an analysis of the vocabulary, grammar, and style of the document as a whole. He noted, for example, the dominance of simple verbs, most of which were those in common use, over compound verbs,[51] which were also relatively common — a relatively small ratio of compound verbs by comparison with more sophisticated literature such as Luke-Acts or the Epistle to the Ephesians. Unusual words and phrases are very rare. A large number of adjectives are used as substantives. Prepositions used in more sophisticated Greek writing are rare.[52] In grammar, Q's discourses are very simple, and in style they feature frequent interrogatives, parataxis, and parallelism, along with frequent unclassical constructions.[53] Harnack took many of these as indicators of a Semitic idiom behind Q's Greek. They may also be indicators of an oral-derived text, as we shall explore in chapters 7 to 14.

Harnack's analysis and treatment of Q thus stand in contrast to his earlier interpretation of Jesus' teachings in general. In contrast to the earlier selection and interpretation of separate sayings, he understood and treated Q as a collection of discourses, whole "groups of sayings," arranged by topics but having an overall coherence. In contrast to the earlier denial of any particularism in the sayings of Jesus, he found Q to be embedded in Jewish society and anticipating the fulfillment of Israelite promises. And, in comparison with German theology at the time and Q studies since, he projected relatively less of a Christian theological conceptual apparatus onto Q.

By contrast, the revival of Q studies in the last several decades has resorted to the liberal theology Harnack articulated a century ago, while ignoring or departing from his work on Q. Once form criticism focused attention on the individual sayings of and stories about Jesus, little attention was paid to Q as a document. The revival of Q studies after midcentury presupposed and arose partly out of form criticism and viewed Q as a collection of individual sayings. Not until the very recent composition criticism of Q was the existence of clusters of sayings even acknowledged, and even then the discourses were understood to have been gradually built up out of separate sayings. And classification of individual sayings by form, for example, "sapiential" vs. "prophetic and apocalyptic," still determines

51. In 475 places, 166 simple verbs compared with over 82 compound verbs in 168 places.
52. Harnack, *Sayings of Jesus,* 147–58, on "vocabulary."
53. Ibid., 159–63, on "grammar and style": the usual connective is *kai; de* is not used much; clauses with "for" (*gar*), "in order that" (*hina*), and "so that" (*hopōs*) are infrequent; final clauses occur often with the infinitive.

the results of such composition criticism, in the direction of stratification of Q into layers determined by those same classifications. Similarly, the need to free Jesus of Jewish particularism evident in liberal theology a century ago still seems to drive recent Q studies' construction of an early layer of Jesus' sayings free of particularism, including references to Israelite tradition. Correspondingly, these recent studies of Q emphasize far more than Harnack the "secondary" prophetic sayings in Q that condemn "all Israel." Recent Q studies, moreover, still project Christian theological concepts onto Q, although some important recognitions of Q's distinctive "theology" have emerged.

This contrast between the ways in which Harnack and more recent scholars understand Q, juxtaposed with the recent Q interpreters' perpetuation of the older liberal theological understanding of Jesus' sayings, points toward some critical reexamination of assumptions and approaches in the study of Q.

First, establishing the teachings of Jesus as universalistic and individualistic appears to be a distinctive project of liberal theology, perhaps without wider authorization and applicability. By the time of Harnack, liberal theologians had been forced to retreat from most Gospel narratives to what seemed defensible teachings of Jesus in general. Liberal individualist Q scholars have now retreated even further, to a far smaller set of aphorisms and admonitions in a supposedly early sapiential layer of Q, on the basis of which they find teaching that closely resembles what Harnack found in a wider range of Jesus' sayings. A persistently vital liberal theology appears to be informing investigation into Q. As has often been pointed out, however, even in theological and biblical studies, liberal individualism is peculiar to modern Western culture. Harnack and other liberals insisted that Jesus did not found communities or even suggest that his disciples organize a "church." Recent Q studies do assert that somehow, in a way that remains unexplained, "social formation" of communities in a Jesus movement emerged.[54] But it is virtually impossible to discern how new community formation could have emerged from the individualistically focused and directed sapiential sayings they assign to the earliest layer of Q. Investigation of Q must be refocused in broader, more complex ways that will accommodate historical social forms and (political-economic-religious) power relations into the analysis from the beginning.

Second, Harnack's reconstruction of Q as consisting primarily of discourses, not a collection of individual sayings, combined with the conclusion of recent compositional analysis that Q was eventually composed in discourses, suggests that the intervening understanding of Q as a collection of sayings was dependent on the historical development of Gospel studies. As noted above, form criticism focused attention on isolated sayings, and the discovery of the *Gospel of Thomas* reinforced this focus, which continues unabated in investigations of the historical Jesus. Not surprisingly, Q studies proceeded with the same focus. Yet to be faced in studies of Synoptic Gospel materials and the historical Jesus, however,

---

54. Mack, *Lost Gospel*, 128–30.

are the severe problems of focusing on isolated sayings for purposes of historical reconstruction. The historical meaning of Jesus' sayings depends upon a historical meaning context. The latter depends upon a historical literary context, in and through which the historical context can be discerned. Once the Gospels were seen not only to contain "mythical" and "miraculous" elements but to be composed from a confessional point of view, form criticism and subsequent studies of Jesus' sayings purposely isolated the sayings for analysis of form and, ironically, of meaning. But that indicates that the meaning context for the isolated sayings is supplied by the modern scholarly interpreter, now without consideration of the original literary context which would provide the best and perhaps the only guide to the historical meaning context.[55] The approach that Harnack offered nearly a century ago, before Gospel scholarship narrowed its focus to isolated individual sayings, suggests an alternative focus for study of Q. Harnack recognized that the sayings of Q were grouped in discourses focused on issues or topics and discerned some coherence in the whole sequence of discourses as well. Focusing on the discourses rather than on the individual sayings would attend to the literary contexts that constitute meaning. Attending to the whole sequence of discourses would attend to an even wider, more complex literary context that could provide some clues to historical context as well. The analysis of recent Q studies in chapter 4 will result in further reasons for focusing on Q as a sequence of discourses.

Third, very recent recognitions of how distinctive Q was in comparison with early "Christian" literature are reinforced by the fact that Harnack applied relatively less of the standard Christian theological apparatus to Q than did the Q studies that revived after the middle of the twentieth century. It is significant that many breakthroughs have been made in recent Q studies simply by recognizing that a given Christian theological concept does not apply. In recent studies it was finally recognized, as Harnack had said long ago, that Q not only does not refer to the crucifixion or passion of Jesus, but does not appear to presuppose some sort of Markan or pre-Markan passion. Harnack also noted that Q is prior to any separation of some proto-Christian identity over against the wider Jewish heritage, something re-recognized only in the last decade of Q studies (see now Jacobson). Following the same line of critical investigation, it may now be possible to realize that the parousia is a Matthean overlay (Matthew 24), even that Q speaks not so much of a "future" or "apocalyptic Son of Man" as of the "day(s) of the son of man," referring apparently to a future time of judgment (see esp. Q/Luke 17:23–37). Instead of applying such Christian theological concepts and questions to Q, it should be possible to examine the Q discourses on their own terms to discern what were their concerns and functions in the community that cultivated them. After taking some first, tentative steps in this direction in the second half of chapter 4, we attempt to explore new possibilities in most of the remaining chapters.

---

55. Exemplified in the highly sophisticated works of Mack, *Lost Gospel*, and John Dominic Crossan, *The Historical Jesus: The Life of a Mediterranean Jewish Peasant* (San Francisco: HarperCollins, 1991).

Fourth — a particular example of the previous general differentiation between Christian theological concepts and Q realities — Harnack acknowledged that Q not only was situated within Israelite tradition but also proclaimed the fulfillment of Israelite history. That is a significant break with the standard Christian view of a universalist and spiritual Christian religion and even of Jesus as making a decisive break with an overly particularist and political Judaism. Recent Q studies picture Q as in but not of Jewish society. That is, the supposedly earliest layer of Jesus' teachings in Q lacks particularism, while the supposedly secondary layer of Jesus' sayings condemns "all Israel" for its rejection of Jesus' (Q people's) teaching. Now that Jewish historians and Gospel scholars alike have recognized the considerable diversity within late second-temple Jewish society, however, including the class differences between villagers and Herodian or high-priestly rulers and their scribal and Pharisaic representatives, Q studies should be ready to explore more precisely how Q and the movement that produced it positioned themselves within Galilean and/or Judean society. Chapter 5 will explore the extent and ways in which Q discourses are embedded in and arise out of Israelite tradition, which will then inform the investigation in the subsequent chapters. In connection with the movement that produced and cultivated the Q discourses, however, it is necessary to reexamine critically a highly influential modern scholarly concept that has determined how the Q people are constructed in recent Q studies, the subject of chapter 2.

Chapter 2

WANDERING CHARISMATICS
AND SCHOLARLY CIRCULARITIES

Jonathan A. Draper _____

The picture of early Palestinian Christianity originating in a movement of "wandering charismatics" has decisively influenced recent interpretation of Q. Most influential has been the suggestive sociological construction of Gerd Theissen, who pictures early Christianity as a movement of wandering charismatics called into being by Jesus as the Son of Man and the "bearer of revelation," who depended for sustenance on local communities of sympathizers.[1] Despite severe criticism of Theissen's uncritical treatment of texts and conservative structural-functional sociological method,[2] interpretations of Q and historical constructions of the history of the "Q people" and other Jesus movements continue to follow the picture he presented.[3] The recent presentations of Jesus and/or the Q people as analogous to vagabond Cynic philosophers build on the foundation laid by Theissen, despite minor disagreements with him on particulars.[4] The continuing scholarly popularity of Theissen's seriously flawed theory and thesis of the wandering charismatics invites further critical examination of its problematic theoretical

---

1. Gerd Theissen, *Sociology of Early Palestinian Christianity* (Philadelphia: Fortress, 1978).

2. Wolfgang Stegemann, "Vagabond Radicalism in Early Christianity? A Historical and Theological Discussion of a Thesis Proposed by Gerd Theissen," in *God of the Lowly: Socio-Historical Interpretations of the Bible,* ed. Willy Schottroff and Wolfgang Stegemann (Maryknoll, N.Y.: Orbis Books, 1984), 148–68; John H. Elliott, "Social Scientific Criticism of the New Testament and Its Social World," *Semeia* 35 (1986): 1–33; Richard A. Horsley, *Sociology and the Jesus Movement* (New York: Crossroad, 1989). The principal proof texts cited by Theissen, mainly from mission discourses (Mark 6:6–56; Matt. 10:1–11:1; Luke 9:1–11; 10:1–24), seem instead to provide evidence of a purposeful strategy, a mission of sending and returning, rather than of radical itinerancy; see Jonathan A. Draper, "Wandering Radicalism or Purposeful Activity? Jesus and the Sending of Messengers in Mark 6:6–56," *Neotestamentica* 29, no. 2 (1995): 187–207.

3. John Dominic Crossan, "Itinerants and Householders in the Earliest Jesus Movement," in *Whose Historical Jesus?* ed. W. E. Arnal and M. Desjardins (Waterloo, Ont.: Wilfrid Laurier Press, 1997), 7–24.

4. Burton L. Mack, *The Lost Gospel: The Book of Q and Christian Origins* (San Francisco: HarperSanFrancisco, 1993); L. E. Vaage, *Galilean Upstarts: Jesus' First Followers according to Q* (Valley Forge, Pa.: Trinity Press International, 1994); see the critique by H. D. Betz, "Jesus and the Cynics: Survey and Analysis of a Hypothesis," *JR* 74 (1994): 453–76; and Richard A. Horsley, "Jesus, Itinerant Cynic or Israelite Prophet?" in *Images of Jesus Today,* ed. J. H. Charlesworth (Valley Forge, Pa.: Trinity Press International, 1994), 68–97, esp. 74.

roots. It appears that Theissen grounded his study on two social-scientific models, one acknowledged and one unacknowledged, neither of them discussed at all. The one is Hjalmar Sunden's theory of religious role adoption, acknowledged in a note; the other is Max Weber's theory of charismatic leadership as an explanation of new religious movements, which goes unmentioned. Theissen's adoption of both theories, however, is selective, inappropriate, and problematic.

The Theory of Religious Role Adoption and Its Implications

Theissen's use of the concept of roles, fundamental to his construction of the origins of Christianity, has gone unchallenged. According to the role theory of Sunden,[5] whom Theissen is adapting, the individual forms her or his consciousness by observing, experimenting with, and internalizing roles from the ongoing social interactions around her or him. Sunden combines this with his understanding of the psychology of perception (the relation between outward stimuli and inner receptiveness), arguing that sense data are not immediately apprehended by the human subject but are mediated by a network of experientially and culturally derived expectations that function as an interpretive filter and condition the person's response.

In terms of religious tradition, actual historical events (raw empirical data as they are experienced and interpreted by a community) are understood from a religious point of view as the activity of a god or gods in relation to a people or persons, that is, as salvation history. This salvation history is passed on in religious tradition. It encodes within the tradition the culturally determined pattern of relationships between the god or gods and mythical human beings or heroes (using myth in the technical sense as archetypal, whether the human beings concerned are historical beings or not). In other words, religious tradition encodes both the role of the god or gods and the role of particular human beings in relationship with the god or gods. In a time of disaster, crisis, or uncertainty, a person may adopt from the religious tradition a particular role that seems to match the situation. In internalizing this role (e.g., wisdom teacher, prophet, warrior, priest, mystic, bride), the person also internalizes the role of god in relation to the adopted human role (e.g., Law-Giver, Savior, King, Judge, Lover). God is thus experienced interactively as an objective presence within and over against her or him. Along with the role, the person adopts the expectation that god will act in relation to her or him as god did toward the adopted role model. A pattern of appropriate behavior is also adopted along with the role. This adoption of a particular role

---

5. Hjalmar Sunden's book, which was originally published in Swedish and translated into German as *Die Religion und die Rollen: Eine psychologische Untersuchung der Frömmigkeit* (1966), has never been translated into English. Its influence was, it seems, limited to pastoral theology in Germany and Scandinavia. Sunden's theory seems to be influenced primarily by the work of anthropologists (such as Ralph Linton, H. J. Mead, R. H. Turner, K. Kerenyi, and C. Kluckholm) who documented the influence of culture on the formation of character (as opposed to what they considered "innate"), rather than psychologists.

is then confirmed or disconfirmed by two things: the recognition of her or his adopted role by others (i.e., conferral of status; this is central)[6] and the particular configuration and experience of actual events in the environment (though these cannot easily disconfirm the role once adopted, since actual events are interpreted through the cultural framework and experienced as the will of god). One further aspect of Sunden's theory is that he particularizes it in terms of actual persons or heroes from a particular culture, rather than leaving things at a general level (e.g., a person adopts the role of Moses in relation to Yahweh or Paul in relation to the God of Jesus Christ).

When a person adopts a particular role, especially when she or he does so over a long period of time, her or his experience is filtered through the configuration of expectations and experiences implicit in the role. The person becomes the re-ligious role and experiences the encoded role of god as a living, acting Other in relation to herself or himself. The person can act for god, speak for god, and know what god has done or will do, in conformity with the role which has been adopted, because, Sunden argues, gods and spirits are best viewed psychologically as roles which are real for the group in which a person lives.[7] When this stage is reached, everything which happens serves as a confirmation of the self-understanding of the person in a particular role, since everything is filtered through the interpretive framework. The pattern structures and gives meaning to the perceptual content. In this way, the social or personal crisis which gave rise to the adoption of the religious role is resolved or accepted for the individual. Where the crisis or un-certainty is a widespread phenomenon in the society at large, the claims of the person to embody a particular religious role in the culture may be enthusiastically accepted by a group of followers who see in her or him a resolution of their own crisis or uncertainty facing them collectively. Their acceptance of the person's claims then acts as status confirmation for that person. For this immediate circle of followers, their acceptance by the leader would in turn act as status confirma-tion of their role as followers, together with a wider public acceptance of that person's claims. They will themselves then be adopting particular religio-cultural roles from the religious tradition: for example, the followers of the prophet, the army of god, and so on.

Sunden's psychological theory is immensely problematic, and the whole field of the construction of the mind and consciousness is hotly debated. Theologians and historians need to tread warily. Sunden's role theory has been overtaken by further developments in the field of psychological theory, and there is no need to enter further into the psychological debate. Our interest is to test the foundations of Theissen's hypothesis in terms of its own presuppositions. However, we might retain from Sunden's formulation an understanding that religious experience will be socially conditioned and that the kinds of religious roles that people play will be part of the ongoing conversation of the culture from which they emerge. More

---

6. Sunden, *Die Religion*, 18.
7. Ibid., 10–11, 29.

specifically, these roles should be clearly formulated in terms of a specific religio-cultural tradition and should include an understanding of how the role of the religious figure or hero in that culture relates dyadically to the role of god.

Theissen's real interest lies in the wandering charismatics and local communities, with whom he begins his account without further ado. A consideration of the role of bearer of revelation is only then considered. Sunden's theory, however, would demand first a detailed investigation of the particular role or hero in the religious tradition of Israel which Jesus has internalized or is understood by his followers or "status confirmers" to have adopted, as well as the particular role of God in relation to that role, before anything could be said about his followers. They would be adopting a role in relation to [a role in relation to God] in relation to God. Theissen offers no explanation as to why the followers of Jesus should have become wandering charismatics after his death. One is left to assume that Theissen envisages them adopting the role of Jesus, who is assumed to have been a wandering charismatic himself, and so they continued the behavior appropriate to the role of Jesus, namely, wandering charismatic asceticism. However, there are obvious problems with the use of this model. If we were following Sunden's theory, then we would first have to ask what particular role from the religio-cultural tradition of Israel Jesus' followers had internalized in relation to the role he had adopted, together with the particular role of God in relation to Jesus in relation to them. Sunden provides models of just such behavior in religious movements he has analyzed, for example, that of James Naylor in the period of the English Civil War of the seventeenth century.[8] Naylor is understood to have adopted a number of roles from the Bible successively but always specifically (i.e., from Abraham to Christ).

For Sunden a religious role is provided by a religious tradition, its interpretation of history as salvation history. A role is encoded in the tradition dyadically: the role of god and the particular human role. Such roles are not invented but stand in continuity with a religio-cultural tradition, even if that continuity is a dynamic and developing one. New religious movements arise in response to a crisis or an uncertainty in a time of social upheaval and change, but they derive their inspiration from their own specific religious traditions. In applying the model of Sunden to such a situation of crisis, we would need to explore first of all the role or roles from the religio-cultural tradition adopted by the leader of the movement. It is simply inappropriate and misleading to begin by applying the model to the followers of the leader. We need to begin by asking what role Jesus adopted from the possible roles available to him from or latent within the cultural tradition of Israel, which was the basis of his particular religious experience of the role of God and the behavior he considered appropriate to the role he had adopted.

"Bearer of revelation" does not seem to be immediately recognizable as a role within Israelite culture of the first century C.E., or at least it is misleading. It is too vague. Theissen himself suggests that this is a role expressed "in various

---

8. Ibid., 14–20.

christological titles."[9] This is a problematic formulation because the various christological titles express different roles. Theissen argues that the most important title used by the Jesus movement was "Son of Man," but that is the most difficult of all to see in terms of roles. If "Son of Man" means "human being," it is hard to envisage this as a role at all! Even if it did have a titular significance, this would have implied the role of the heavenly judge, which is really a role of God. In Daniel, the role is delegated to a heavenly being in Daniel and in the case of the Christian community, it could only be applied to a postresurrection Jesus returning as a heavenly judge. It is thus not a human role, strictly speaking, since there is no implication that the earthly Jesus acted out the role of (heavenly) judge; indeed, his earthly role is specifically contrasted with the future role of judge in those texts which apply it to him. It is difficult to see how one could get from a supposed use of the "role of the Son of Man" by Jesus to the adoption of the "role of wandering charismatics" by his followers.

What appears to lie behind the pseudo-scientific title "bearer of revelation" is the role of prophet. If so, then Sunden would go on to ask, "What sort of prophet?" and "In what relationship to God?" But nothing we know about the prophets of Israel suggests that they were wandering figures. Itinerant mendicants were no part of the religio-cultural tradition of Israel, even if there might be specific occasions when a prophet or his or her followers were in transit, on an embassy, in flight, or in hiding.

The role of sympathizers in local communities envisaged by Theissen is also problematic when considering the religio-cultural tradition of Israel. It is far from clear that "sympathizer" is a role in Sunden's sense at all. In any case, it assumes a situation of private religion, where people in towns and villages could withdraw from public life into the sphere of religion. However, in the tradition of Israel, the whole people is the covenantal people, and religion is a public and obligatory aspect of a holistic understanding of life. Of course, an individual could receive someone or not receive someone who asked for accommodation or refuge. But life was a public affair, and villages in Israel made decisions corporately. The ability to form separate communities in opposition to each other is more a feature of cities than of villages.

This very brief survey shows that the psychological theory of roles does not really provide any helpful support for the threefold construction of roles suggested by Theissen, since there are no clear religio-cultural precedents for them. There are prophets and the possibility that the prophets had followers and supporters. It is also likely that once the gospel left rural Palestine, it was accepted by sympathetic groups of supporters within the cities. However, our examination of Sunden's role theory shows that nothing in that theory explains the extraordinary use of the problematic title "wandering charismatics" to refer to persons supported by local communities. The term and its popularity must come from somewhere

---

9. Theissen, *Sociology*, 24.

other than role theory. It must come from the second and unacknowledged sociological model, that of Weber's charismatic legitimation.

Weber's Charisma and Theissen's Wandering Charismatics

Part of the reason for the tenaciousness of Theissen's model is that its roots reach deeply into the history-of-religions theory of emerging Christianity developed by Adolf von Harnack on the basis of the *Didache*, which has become an unrecognized consensus in New Testament scholarship.[10] From the beginning Harnack saw the potential of this text to provide the missing link in the development or rather degeneration from a "charismatic" early Christianity with its "ministry of the Word" into the "early Catholic Church" based on priests, rituals, and hierarchy.[11] This concept of *Frühkatholizismus* was and to some extent remains central to German Protestant thinking. In 1902 Harnack formulated this theory in his work of pivotal importance in Western scholarship, *The Mission and Expansion of Christianity in the First Three Centuries*.[12] Harnack saw in the *Didache* a threefold order of itinerant charismatics — apostles, prophets, and teachers — as the earliest form of Christian ministry; he proposed that this order, operative in the "period of Christianity," was gradually replaced in the "period of the Church" by local hierarchical bishops, priests, and deacons as the earlier order became corrupt.[13] The assumption that word comes first and that structure comes as a secondary feature of decline derives, of course, from Lutheran theology. It is quite possible to read the evidence the other way around in the *Didache* and argue that prophets are an intrusion into a settled and structured community.[14]

Harnack's thesis was developed prior to the theory of charisma propounded by Max Weber in his *Wirtschaft und Gesellschaft*, published posthumously.[15] It seems that Weber both read and utilized Harnack's celebrated work as he worked on his magnum opus between 1916 and his death in 1920.[16] Weber's thesis of the routinization of charisma is in some respects a sophisticated restatement of the concept of *Frühkatholizismus*. Theissen's application of Weber to the wandering charismatics of the *Didache* may thus be a species of circular reasoning. Weber's

---

.10. Adolf von Harnack, *Die Lehre der zwolf Apostel*, TU 2, 1–2 (Leipzig: Hinrichse, 1884). The text discovered and published first by Bryennios in 1883 caused a sensation, but it was in the version and commentary of Harnack that most Western scholars read it.

11. Harnack, *Die Lehre*, 94–95, 157.

12. Adolf von Harnack, *The Mission and Expansion of Christianity in the First Three Centuries* (London: Williams & Norgate, 1908 [1902]).

13. Ibid., 319–68.

14. As I have attempted to do in "Torah and Troublesome Apostles in the *Didache* Community," in *The Didache in Modern Research*, ed. J. A. Draper, AGJU 37 (Leiden: E. J. Brill, 1996), 340–63.

15. English translation, Max Weber, *Economy and Society I–II*, trans. and ed. G. Roth and C. Wittich (Berkeley: University of California Press, 1968).

16. Weber (ibid., 472, 511) cites Harnack both as an authority for the delineation of Christianity as an urban religion and in a reference to the *Didache* in the context of charismatic teachers. The absence of footnotes in the original work, which was in any case only a first draft, makes the identification of the work(s) of Harnack that Weber is using difficult.

theory is developed on the basis of Harnack's interpretation of the *Didache* and is then applied by Theissen to the same work to obtain his "analysis of roles." The fit is perfect, needless to say, which may be why Theissen's analysis of roles has its apparently "self-evident" character for many modern scholars schooled in both Harnack and Weber as independent traditions in theology and sociology.[17]

The ascetic-charismatic interpretation of the *Didache* rests on the combination of 6:2–3 with 11:3–12. *Didache* 6:2–3 was understood as referring to ascetics who kept the "whole yoke" of the Lord and became "perfect," while ordinary Christians did the best they could.[18] The passage is interpreted on the basis of Matthew's redaction of the story of the rich man in 19:21: "If you would be perfect, go, sell what you possess and give to the poor, and you will have treasure in heaven; and come, follow me."[19] This is then combined with speculation about homeless radicalism and possible spiritual marriage of the charismatics in 11:3–12. The scene is set for a continuing interest in asceticism and itinerant radicalism, on the one side by Protestant scholars interested in describing a romanticized spirit-filled church before its decline into hierarchy, and on the other side by Catholic scholars interested in discerning a continuity of religious asceticism from the first disciples of Jesus on into the development of monasticism and religious orders.

Harnack's work on the *Didache* was developed further toward what emerged as the wandering charismatics construct by scholars such as G. Kretschmar, who found evidence in *Didache* 11–13 for itinerant apostles, prophets, and teachers, whom he viewed as self-evidently ascetics and whom he subsumed under the designation "prophets."[20] In the period of the *Didache*, he argued, these itinerant charismatics were supported by "settled" Christians in villages, for whom they constituted the pastors and community officials. They came from outside, although provision was made for them to settle if they wished. This was very different from the Pauline communities, where the charismatics were local and settled. It was only at the end of this developmental process of the text that the communities became self-sufficient and appointed their own officials as bishops and deacons, who gradually replaced the declining order of charismatics.[21] At the beginning of

---

17. For an overview of the history of research into the *Didache*, see my introduction to *The Didache in Modern Research*, 1–42. Part of my earlier text is taken up and modified here.

18. Harnack, *Die Lehre*, 19–22; and R. Knopf, *Die zwei Clemensbriefe*, Handbuch zum Neuen Testament (Tübingen: J. C. B. Mohr, 1920), 1:20–21.

19. Such a procedure would be problematic if, as is likely, the *Didache* is independent of Matthew. See Jonathan A. Draper, "The Jesus Tradition in the Didache," in *The Didache in Modern Research*, 72–91; for a contrary opinion, see C. M. Tuckett, "Synoptic Tradition in the *Didache*," in *The Didache in Modern Research*, 92–128.

20. G. Kretschmar, "Ein Beitrag zur Frage nach dem Ursprung frühchristlicher Askese," *ZTK* 61 (1964): 27–64; now also in K. S Frank, ed., *Askese und Mönchtum in der alten Kirche*, WdF 409 (Darmstadt: Wissenschaftliche Buchgesellschaft, 1975), 129–79; cf. Kretschmar, "Das christliche Leben und die Mission in der frühen Kirche," in *Kirchengeschichte als Missionsgeschichte I: Die Alte Kirche*, ed. H. Frohnes and U. W. Knorr (Munich: Kaiser, 1974), 94–123. See also E. Peterson, *Frühkirche, Judentum und Gnosis: Studien und Untersuchungen* (Rome: Herder, 1959), 146–82, 209–20; A. Vööbus, "Celibacy a Requirement for Admission to Baptism in the Early Syrian Church," *Estonian Theological Society in Exile* 1 (1951); and A. Adam, "Erwagungen zur Herkunft der Didache," *ZKG* 68 (1957): 1–47.

21. Kretschmar, "Beitrag," 36–39.

the whole process, of course, were the first circle of disciples, for whom personal union with Jesus meant following him in a life of wandering. The "disciples" of Matthew then lived on in the itinerant apostles, prophets, and teachers of the *Didache,* but the settled members of the communities were no longer called to this life of discipleship in the narrow sense.

These studies all argue that the origin of Syrian asceticism lay in a continuation of primitive Christian itinerant discipleship among the charismatic prophets and teachers who worked as missionaries in the Palestine-Syrian Jewish communities under the new apocalyptic conditions inaugurated by the Messiah. After the separation of church and synagogue, Syrian Christianity sought to reshape the call of Jesus to discipleship into a rule of life, which in the end produced an unresolved tension between radical asceticism as a requirement for all Christians and the compromise of a two-tier ethic. The studies of the *Didache* since Harnack — that is, those by Kretschmar and others — had an obvious influence on Theissen. He describes his original presentation of *Wanderradikalismus* as a "further development" of Kretschmar's ideas.[22] And citations from the *Didache* figure prominently in his reconstruction.[23]

Weber's sociology has been attacked or modified by many sociologists and anthropologists but continues to be influential. Theissen relies extensively on the theories of Weber, though he uses them eclectically and rarely with proper acknowledgment. In particular he uses Weber's theory of "charisma." It is clear that Weber's concept of charismatic legitimation lies behind Theissen's theory that Jesus founded a movement of wandering charismatics who "handed on what was later to take form as Christianity,"[24] although again it is never specifically stated. When Theissen's thesis is compared with Weber's model, however, obvious problems emerge. Theissen treats Weber's typology in a static fashion, whereas Weber conceives of it dynamically as part of an evolutionary process.[25] And Theissen uses

---

22. Gerd Theissen, "Wanderradikalismus: Literatursoziologische Aspekte der Überlieferung von Worten Jesu im Urchristentum," in *Studien zur Soziologie der Urchristentums,* WUNT 19 (Tübingen: J. C. B. Mohr [Paul Siebeck], 1989), 79–195, esp. 86 n. 90; Eng. trans.: "The Wandering Radicals," in *Social Reality and the Early Christians* (Minneapolis: Fortress, 1992), 33–59, esp. 40 n. 20.

23. For example, Theissen, *Sociology,* 9, 10, 11, 13, 19, 20, 21, 28, 33, 39, 44. Building on Theissen's thesis of "wandering charismatics," Klaus Niederwimmer ("Zur Entwicklungsgeschichte des Wanderradikalismus im Traditionsbereich der Didache," *Wiener Studien* 11 [1977]: 145–67; Eng. trans.: "An Examination of the Development of Itinerant Radicalism in the Environment and Tradition of the Didache," in Draper, *The Didache in Modern Research,* 321–40) constructs a process of integration and stabilization between the itinerant charismatics and the local officials of the supporting local communities, which is none other than the process of early catholicization. The thesis of Harnack is reconfirmed. See also W. Rordorf and A. Tuilier, *La doctrine des douze apôtres (Didache),* Sources chrétiennes 248 (Paris: Cerf, 1978), 49–64. Yet another restatement of this thesis is Steven J. Patterson, "Didache 11–13: The Legacy of Radical Itinerancy in Early Christianity," in *The Didache in Context,* ed. C. Jefford (Leiden: E. J. Brill, 1995), 313–29. Patterson takes up the thesis elaborated earlier in C. N. Jefford and S. J. Patterson, "A Note on Didache 12.2a (Coptic)," *Second Century* 7 (1989–90): 65–75. However, his textual reconstruction based on the Coptic manuscript has been challenged by F. S. Jones and P. A. Mirecki, "Considerations on the Coptic Papyrus of the Didache (British Library Oriental Manuscript 9271)," in Jefford, *The Didache in Context,* 47–87.

24. Theissen, *Sociology,* 8; cf. idem, "Wanderradikalismus," 79–104.

25. Cf. J. H. Schutz, "Charisma and Social Reality in Primitive Christianity," *JR* 54 (1974): 51–70;

only certain aspects of Weber's concept of charisma outside of his conception as a whole.

At the risk of oversimplification, the following summary of Weber's concept of charisma can be used to compare with Theissen and with his principal source, the *Didache*.

Charismatic Legitimation. Weber's discussion of charisma comes in his thesis concerning the three different kinds of "legitimate domination" he sees at work in society.[26] The first two are traditional and legal-rational, which characterize most normal societies. However, in times of upheaval and stress, a third kind of legitimation emerges, charismatic. A leader arises from outside the normal channels of authority in a given society, "considered extraordinary and treated as endowed with supernatural, superhuman, or at least specifically exceptional powers or qualities" which are not available to ordinary people.[27] Moreover, "in order to live up to their mission the master as well as his disciples and immediate following must be free of the ordinary worldly attachments and duties of occupational and family life."[28] The charismatic is often a force for revolutionary change in society in a time of crisis. The social structure corresponding to charismatic authority consists of the leader; her or his personal staff constituting a "charismatic aristocracy," united by discipleship and loyalty; and a wider loosely defined circle of supporters.

The Routinization of Charisma. A crucial feature of Weber's theory of charismatic legitimation is that it is fundamentally transformed by the death or removal of the leader. Charismatic domination is extraordinary and so is effective only in *statu nascendi,* and when the tide wanes, it either dies or turns into an "institution": "It cannot remain stable, but becomes either traditionalized or rationalized, or a combination of both."[29] This is caused by the desire to transform it from the unique and transitory into a permanent possession of everyday life. The crisis

---

idem, *Paul and the Anatomy of Apostolic Authority,* SNTMS 26 (London and New York: Cambridge University Press, 1975); B. Holmberg, *Paul and Power: The Structure of Authority in the Primitive Church as Reflected in the Pauline Epistles* (Philadelphia: Fortress, 1980); and M. Y. MacDonald, *The Pauline Churches: A Socio-Historical Study of Institutionalization in the Pauline and Deutero-Pauline Writings* (Cambridge: Cambridge University Press, 1988). These scholars have attempted to follow through the sociological suggestions of Theissen concerning authority in Paul in a more consistent fashion. Holmberg and MacDonald combine Weber's developmental theory of charisma with the concept of institutionalization drawn from the sociology of knowledge.

26. For criticism of Weber's concept of charisma see Peter Worsley, *The Trumpet Shall Sound* (New York: Schocken, 1957), who points to the reciprocal role played by the followers in conferring or withdrawing charismatic authority; A. Weights, "Weber and 'Legitimate Domination': A Theoretical Critique of Weber's Conceptualisation of 'Relations of Domination,'" *Economy and Society* 7 (1978): 56–73, pointed out Weber's individualism, idealism, and evolutionism. Nevertheless, Weber's category of charismatic leadership is a valuable theoretical model. Kenelm Burridge, *New Heaven, New Earth: A Study of Millenarian Activities* (New York: Schocken, 1969), has offered a revision based on his understanding of millenarian movements as an attempt to formulate the "New Human Being" in the face of social disintegration.

27. Weber, *Economy and Society,* 241.

28. Ibid., 1113.

29. Ibid., 246.

for charismatic authority becomes acute with the disappearance of the charismatic leader. This precipitates a problem of succession,[30] which the community may solve in various ways, including acquisition of legitimacy by a designated successor nominated by the charismatic leader before she or he dies.[31]

Weber's model envisages the inevitable routinization of the administrative staff of the charismatic movement immediately after the death of the leader.[32] The followers and disciples of the leader settle down and transform the movement originated by the charismatic leader into an institution. This may take various forms, including ritualized begging in the case where "the administrative staff [of the charismatic leader] may seek and achieve the creation and appropriation of individual positions and the corresponding economic advantages for its members."[33]

The model of the bearer of revelation, the wandering charismatics, and the local communities presented by Theissen and others obviously develops this possibility in Weber's description of the succession crisis. However, the difference is that they do not really envisage ritualized begging as a right of successors of the charismatic leader. Instead, they envisage the local communities in control of the process of providing strictly controlled rations for a strictly defined period. In other words, these hypothetical wandering charismatics are bound by rules and regulations. The question this raises is what to do with the only accounts we have of the behavior of the post-Easter followers of Jesus in Paul and Acts, namely, that they settled in Jerusalem and busied themselves with financial organization, as Weber's model would lead us to expect. Theissen, who is inordinately uncritical of the historical value of the evidence of Luke-Acts elsewhere,[34] at this point rules the evidence of Acts out of court, on the grounds that it reflects Hellenistic influence.[35]

Religious Virtuosi. A greatly neglected aspect of Weber's theory of the routinization of charisma is his typology of the religious virtuoso,[36] which he provides in his discussion of methodologies of religious salvation, where "the gap between the unusual and routine religious experiences tends to be eliminated by evolution towards the systematization and rationalization of the methods for attaining religious sanctification."[37] The systematization of charisma can take the form of "world-rejecting asceticism" or of "inner-worldly asceticism." The latter seeks to transform the world by ascetic activity in fulfillment of the perceived will of God.

---

30. Ibid., 246–49.

31. The community may "manipulate the tradition" to place such a designation on the lips of the leader before he dies, as in Matt. 16:18 and John 20:22.

32. This point is obviously overlooked also by R. P. Martin, "Patterns of Worship in New Testament Churches," *JSNT* 37 (1989): 59–85, using Weber at second hand.

33. Weber, *Economy and Society,* 250.

34. As shown by Horsley, *Sociology,* 45–46.

35. Theissen, *Sociology,* 8.

36. Cf. I. M. Zeitlin, *Jesus and the Judaism of His Time* (Cambridge: Cambridge University Press, 1988), 47–48.

37. Weber, *Economy and Society,* 541–44.

The former renounces the world, flees from it, and seeks to "find rest in god and in him alone."[38] Unfortunately there is a lack of clarity in Weber about the exact location of the religious virtuoso in the unfolding process of routinization and how it relates to the model of the charismatic leader. It appears to be located primarily in the advanced stage of routinization, since it is rule-bound.

Theissen builds on the model of the ascetic virtuoso when describing the later history of *Wanderradikalismus* in the church.[39] Such virtuosi, he argues, have their value in times of "social fluidity" when there is the "urgency of social change." Again, the influence of Weber is unacknowledged. But what is the relationship between such later wandering charismatics and the earlier wandering charismatics Theissen describes? The goal of the religious virtuoso in Weber is rule-oriented preservation of charisma "to provide a secure and continuous possession of the distinctive religious acquirement."[40] Theissen's wandering charismatics, whom he describes as "ethically motivated heroes of renunciation" (*ethisch motivierte Verzichtleistler*),[41] really seem to fit the description Weber provides for religious virtuosi. A standing feature of the wandering charismatics, as Theissen has defined them, is extreme ascetic behavior governed by rules. But charisma in its *statu nascendi*, which is how the Jesus movement should be characterized during Jesus' lifetime as the bearer of revelation, is by its nature opposed to rules. Hence, following Weber's model, Jesus himself could not have started a movement of wandering charismatic power revealed in the charismatic leader in a time of crisis among his followers.

Weber's ascetic virtuosi withdraw from the "world," from social and psychological ties with the family, from the possession of worldly goods, and from political, economic, artistic, and erotic activities.[42] Nevertheless, they maintain a dialectic with the world, since it is the area of the exercise of their vocation.[43] Such virtuosi inevitably become a closed group, with special religious status and privileges, an exclusive class.[44] The ascetic virtuoso has an ambivalent attitude toward money: she or he is forbidden to earn, ask for, or accumulate it, yet when it comes to her or him, it is a sign of God's blessing.[45] A further mark of the world-rejecting ascetic is a lack of concern with theological issues or questions of ultimate meaning. Ultimate meaning is not her or his responsibility but is God's.[46] She or he is an agent of the will of God, which is unsearchable in its ultimate significance.[47] She or he is God's "tool," and the success of her or his action is the success of God's self.[48]

---

38. Ibid., 544–51.
39. Theissen, *Sociology*, 119.
40. Weber, *Economy and Society*, 538.
41. Theissen, *Sociology*, 117.
42. Weber, *Economy and Society*, 542.
43. Ibid., 543.
44. Ibid., 542.
45. Ibid., 543.
46. Ibid., 548.
47. Ibid.
48. Ibid., 548–49.

Between Priest and Prophet. This model of religious virtuosi also connects with Weber's description of the competitive relation between priest and prophet. The virtuosi are by nature prophetic and charismatic, although in the process of routinizing charisma. Weber confuses the issue somewhat by failing to distinguish between the prophet as a revolutionary charismatic leader, such as set out in his forms of domination, and the prophet as part of a prophetic renewal movement. He does nevertheless envisage such a prophetic movement as a constant phenomenon in early Christianity.[49] This raises the inevitable question of the place of such a prophetic movement in the process of routinization. Weber argues that "primarily, a religious community that arises in connection with a prophetic movement may be a renewal movement as a result of routinization."[50] Yet he allows also that a prophetic movement may be a renewal movement in an established community.[51] Since the Christian prophet is not the "founder" of the Christian community, it is legitimate to suppose that she or he must be rather a "renewer" in Weber's terms.

The emergent prophet, for Weber, represents a threat to the existence and livelihood of the settled traditional leaders of the community, whom Weber calls "priests" in contrast to "prophets." The competition between prophet and priest ensures the formation of a corpus of teaching, oral or written, since the priest's material survival depends on it.[52] In terms of the development of early Christian tradition, one would expect that the emergence of prophetic virtuosi in the community would be accompanied by the collection and codification of the tradition, whether the preprophetic tradition or the prophetic tradition itself or a combination of both.

Apostles and Prophets in the *Didache*

The *Didache* is a community rule, providing guidance and regulation for the life of a community, not a romantic reconstruction of a bygone era or merely "advice on a wide variety of practical subjects."[53] As one might expect of a community rule, the *Didache* has been edited and updated to meet the changing needs of the community it serves.[54] Such "updating" can be seen particularly in the sections dealing with apostles and prophets. The component sections of the *Didache* devoted to particular topics begin consistently with a standard formula: "And concerning X, do as follows," as in 6:3; 7:1, 4; 9:1; 10:1.[55] In striking contrast, the introduction to what seems to have been instructions only on "apostles" in 11:3–6 appears

---

49. Ibid., 440.
50. Ibid., 452.
51. Ibid., 439.
52. Ibid., 457.
53. David E. Aune, *Prophecy in Early Christianity and the Ancient Mediterranean World* (Grand Rapids, Mich.: Eerdmans, 1983), 208.
54. J.-P. Audet, *La Didache: Instructions des apôtres* (Paris: Gabalda, 1958).
55. The debate concerning the function of the *peri de* formula, especially in the letters of Paul, has been well summarized by Margaret M. Mitchell, "Concerning PERI DE in 1 Corinthians," *NovT* 31

to have been edited, with the addition of "and prophets, according to the ordinance of the gospel." Moreover, a section on "prophets" in 12:7–12 would then appear to have been inserted in between the instructions pertaining specifically to apostles in 11:3–6 and those pertaining to hospitality to other travelers belonging to the movement in 12:1–5, which have the same literary form and style.[56] The introduction of "the ordinance of the gospel" here and in 15:4, furthermore, in effect undermines the authority of the *Didache* itself, which already offers instruction on matters such as prayers, alms, tithing, and accommodating apostles and other visitors. It is highly significant that the instruction regarding treatment of prophets is a secondary addition to those concerning apostles, which apparently represent a prior historical stage.

The chief function of the apostles that can be gleaned from the sparse information is that they have a representative function, since they are to be received "as the Lord,"[57] unlike ordinary Christian travelers who come "in the name of the Lord" (12:1) and are simply received and tested. There is no indication that the apostles are limited to a particular number, twelve. They are to stay the minimum amount of time in the community. They are usually unknown personally to the community in which they arrive seeking accommodation, so that strict rules are needed.[58]

Most significantly, there is no suggestion that the apostles are wandering to and fro,[59] nor that they have any charismatic or ecstatic function beyond that of representation. No mention of special endowment with the Spirit is made. The instructions would serve those on a specific embassy with letters of recommendation from the community which sent them.[60]

(1989): 229–56. It had a background in Semitic usage as well, as in the way in which the Damascus Document introduces a new halakhah (CD 9:8; 10:10, 14; 16:10, 13).

56. Niederwimmer, "Itinerant Radicalism."

57. Cf. ibid., 330.

58. Ibid., 322. It is not clear why Niederwimmer considers these instructions to be apologetic for the creeping decay of the institution (ibid., 333). Hospitality with coreligionists or conationals was a crucial question for any traveler in the Greco-Roman world. See R. MacMullen, *Roman Social Relations 50 B.C. to A.D. 284* (New Haven: Yale University Press, 1974), 83–85. Cf. 3 John 5–8.

59. Although this has been widely taken for granted since Harnack (*Die Lehre*, 104) described them as "von Ort zu Ort wanderten." See Gerd Theissen, " 'Wir haben alles verlasser' (Mc. X, 28), Nachfolge unde soziale Entwurzelung in der judisch-palastinenischen Gesellschaft des 1. Jahrhunderts n. Chr.," *Studien zur Soziologie*, 106–41; Kretschmar, "Beitrag," 27–67; Niederwimmer, "Itinerant Radicalism," 328, 329–30, 333, gives no evidence for his confident assertion: "What is envisaged is obviously not an isolated event, but a repeated and regular one."

60. The important feature of the Jewish *shalichim* is that they were appointed for a specific task, and only for the duration of that task did they have their plenary function. They were not missionaries (in our modern sense of religious evangelism) nor necessarily even teachers, though rabbis seem usually to have been chosen for religious delegations. Hospitality toward such *talmid chachamim* was enjoined as especially meritorious (*b. Ber.* 10b; *b. San.* 92a). They were not regular officers of the community, yet they must have been a common feature of life in the Jewish diaspora, keeping communities in touch with one another and with the center of Jewish religious life in Palestine. See C. K. Barrett, "Shaliach and Apostle," in *Donum Gentilicium: New Testament Studies in Honour of David Daube*, ed. E. Bammel, C. K. Barrett, and W. D. Davies (Oxford: Clarendon, 1978), 88–101, esp. 96. The debate has a long pedigree; see J. B. Lightfoot, "The Name and Office of an Apostle," in *St. Paul's Epistle to the Galatians* (London, 1865), 93–94; A. von Harnack, *The Mission and Expansion of Christianity*

Early Christian apostles, like their Jewish counterparts, would have need of hospitality from coreligionists in their journey to their destination. Their purpose would also vary: it could be administrative, disciplinary, instructive, or financial. It is sheer speculation to suggest that their task was an "eschatological proclamation, call to repentance, exorcism."[61] Of course, at their final destination, their letters of introduction would also guarantee their right to stay until their business had been completed. In the communities through which they passed on their journey, however, they could command only one night's accommodation and provision for the next day's journey. The necessity to which the instructions refer, which would make two days' stay imperative, is probably the Sabbath (or later perhaps Sunday), when travel is prohibited. A longer stay than that would show that the apostle was not in earnest in his journey.[62] Ordinary Christian travelers, who come in the Lord's name, are given slightly more leeway, since the occasion and circumstances of their travel could be diverse. Moreover, the possibility that they might wish to settle is accepted, although with stringent controls to prevent them becoming parasitic on the community. Since, however, the community is not obliged to provide them with hospitality, it can afford to be flexible.

If the instructions concerning prophets represent a redaction of the instructions concerning apostles, then it also follows that the redaction deliberately associates prophets with the apostles (perhaps Matthew does the same in attaching 10:40–42 to the account of the commissioning of the Twelve by Jesus). The present form of the text uses the archaic authority of the apostles to legitimate the emergent prophetic class.[63] confusion occasioned by the title of the section is more or less intentional.

The instructions of the *Didache* allow the following characteristics of the

---

(London: Williams & Norgate, 1908), 1:327–34; K. H. Rengstorf, s.v. "Apostolos," *TDNT*, 1:407–47; cf. E. Käsemann, "Die Legitimität des Apostels," *Zeitschrift für die neutestamentliche Wissenschaft* 41 (1942): 33–71; contra A. Ehrhardt, *The Apostolic Succession in the First Two Centuries of the Church* (London: Lutterworth, 1953), 17; W. Schmithals, *The Office of Apostle in the Early Church*, trans. J. E. Steely (London: SPCK, 1971), 98–110.

61. Niederwimmer, "Itinerant Radicalism," 330. Barsabbas and Silas in Acts 15:22–35 represent such apostles (they are *apestalkamen*, v. 27), delegates who carry a letter of authorization from those who send them. In this case, the letter itself authorizes these delegates to add further instruction by word of mouth (v. 27). Such a letter might also instruct the community to collect their tithes to send back with the delegates. Since the delegates have a specific task in the community to which the letter is addressed, they are authorized to spend whatever time is necessary to complete the task (v. 33). However, the letter would not authorize them to spend long periods in other communities on their journey to and from Antioch! From Christians along the road from Jerusalem to Antioch they could expect overnight hospitality. My analysis here does not imply that I consider this letter to be historically authentic, simply that it provides an unambiguous example of what such apostolic activity involved.

62. There seems to be no justification for Aune's assertion that these instructions "reflect the suspicious attitudes of rural peasants toward outsiders, even if those outsiders are Christians" (*Prophecy*, 225). Similar strict rules are laid down by the rabbis for the traveling poor (*m. Peah* 8:7; *t. Peah* 4:8; *j. Peah* 21a). These rules would clearly be needed, regardless of whether the community involved were rural or urban.

63. Contra the assertion of David Hill, *New Testament Prophecy* (Atlanta: John Knox, 1979), 186, and others that the *Didache* is typical of the decline of prophecy.

prophets to be determined. To begin, their authority is no longer representative, as was that of the apostles. It is directly inspired by the Spirit (*lalounta en pneumati*), so that the prophet may not be tested or judged. This would be a sin against the Holy Spirit (11:7).[64] The prophet's authority is directly charismatic. The only test of the prophetic vocation which is permitted is that the prophet must possess the "lifestyle of the Lord" (*tous tropous tou kyriou*, 11:8), which Theissen, without more ado, identifies with Christ's renunciation of home, family, and regular income.[65] The prophet is prohibited from demanding food or money or indeed anything else from the community (11:9, 12). It is not stated that he would also be subject to the limited stay allowed to visitors to the community, nor that he would be entitled only to the provision specified in the hospitality rules of 11:4–6; 12:1–5. According to chapter 13, at least, the prophet is entitled to the firstfruits if he chooses to settle in the community. Complete consistency between lifestyle and teaching is required of the prophet (11:10). This demand for conformity to rules involves "certification" — that is, the prophet must be "tested" (*dedokimasmenos*) and found to be "genuine" (*alethinos*, 11:11), presumably on the basis of the "lifestyle of the Lord" (11:8), before he is allowed to practice.[66]

Bizarre and extreme forms of behavior, which are not permitted to the average member of the local community, are permitted to and even expected from the prophet. The prophet is not permitted to extend such behavior to ordinary members (11:11). This extreme kind of charismatic behavior is defined as "performing a mystery of the church" (*poiōn eis mystērion ekklēsias*), which is not subject to the judgment of the community but only to the judgment of God.[67] It is compared to the behavior of the prophets of the Old Testament. The prophets in the community of the *Didache* are thus beyond the authority of the established leaders of the community. Even in the matter of the cult, the thanksgiving meal of the community, the prophets are permitted to celebrate as they wish (*hosa thelousin*, 10:7), thus supplanting the carefully codified eucharistic prayers of the community (9–10).

Finally, the prophets are severely restricted in terms of financial matters. They may order food for others but not eat of it themselves (11:9). They may not directly ask for financial support for themselves, though they may ask it on behalf of others in need (11:12). In this matter they may not be judged. The interesting thing is the ambiguity which is introduced into their economic situation by *Didache* 13.

---

64. Cf. 1 Thess. 5:19–20. Mark 3:28–29 could find its original *Sitz im Leben* in the kind of setting envisaged by the *Didache*. See M. Eugene Boring, *Sayings of the Risen Jesus: Christian Prophecy in the Synoptic Tradition* (Cambridge: Cambridge University Press, 1982), 162; contra Aune, *Prophecy*, 240–42.

65. Theissen, "Forschungsgeschichtliche Einordnung," 91; cf. Niederwimmer, "Itinerant Radicalism," 331–32. In "Social Ambiguity and the Production of Text," in *The Didache in Context*, ed. C. N. Jefford (Leiden: Brill, 1995) 306–7, I have argued that *tous tropous kyriou* refers more to the possession of the Jesus tradition by the prophets.

66. Aune, *Prophecy*, 226.

67. There is no evidence for the idea of spiritual marriage which is widely seen behind this text; e.g., Niederwimmer, "Itinerant Radicalism," 331–32; G. Bornkamm, s.v. "Mysterion," *TDNT*, 4:824–25.

It seems that at a certain point prophets began a transition from the status of outsiders to a settled status within the community. This at least is the implication of *Didache* 13, where they are given not only the right to settle but also the right to be supported by the community. They are to receive the firstfruits of the community, which were probably already collected in the Jewish fashion. That they could do this indicates that a major social upheaval had occurred in the wider movement. If the apostles of 11:4–6 had ceased to visit the community, to collect money, and to give instructions from Jerusalem, then this would have provided the social conditions for such a transition from the status of the prophets as outsiders to that of settled community leaders. It still does not confirm that such prophets were itinerants prior to settling, only that they came from outside the community. It also does not settle the question as to whether prophets might also are emerging from within the community. However, since this possibility is not mentioned, it seems that the burning issue relates to prophets coming from outside.

This would not have been without consequences, in terms of a struggle with the settled leaders of the community, as 13:2 shows. Bishops and deacons, the original local leaders, are in danger of being despised and their authority overlooked: "For they exercise the ministry of the prophets and teachers, even they [*kai autoi*]. Do not despise them, for they too [*autoi*] are your honorable ones, with the prophets and teachers" (15:2). It is more usual to see this text as evidence of emergent settled leadership in the local communities, but it should in my opinion be read the other way around. Certainly Phil. 1:1 and *1 Clement* 42 show that bishops and deacons were mentioned together as the local leadership at a very early time.

Weber and the *Didache* vs. Theissen's Wandering Charismatics

Theissen's and others' failure to discern different layers in the text of the *Didache* has led to the confusion of apostles and prophets. Their notion of wandering charismatics is a synthesis of the characteristics of these two different types of figures, one that fits their selective use of Weber's concept of charisma. If we are to use Weber's model appropriately, however, the apostles are not wandering vagabonds but representatives of the successors of the charismatic leader who settled in Jerusalem and who claimed authority on the basis of their representation of Jesus' delegated charisma. Paul stands out as a glaring contradiction to this, but then he himself acknowledges his own unique position, even that others denied that he was an apostle (1 Cor. 9:2). His commission from the Lord is an exception to the rule (Galatians 1). It is Paul who redefined the meaning of apostle in claiming authority for himself (2 Corinthians 10–13).

While there is no evidence in the *Didache* that the apostles were charismatic figures, the prophets clearly were. As portrayed in the *Didache*, they fit Weber's concept of virtuosi. They show a secure and continuous possession of charisma and live a radically different lifestyle of renunciation. Their position is characterized by economic ambivalence in that while they are forbidden to ask for money, the provision of the community's firstfruits to them ensures they get it as a blessing from God. Their religious charisma is required to be proved by rational ethical conduct within the world. They form a closed status group in the community. Finally, there is little evidence of an interest in theological definition and development, judging by the danger areas regulated by the instructions. These seem more interested in practical problems and material abuse. It seems that there is a widespread agreement between Weber's scheme of the religious virtuosi and the prophets of the *Didache,* which may help us grasp the social dynamic of the community. They are figures of the advanced process of routinization rather than direct successors of the charismatic leader.

Thus the prophets represent a new phase in the history of the *Didache* communities, at the time of crisis in authority when the apostles are no longer visiting them. In their place come the prophets, who claim to represent a continuity with the origins of the Jesus movement. They constitute a challenge to the settled order of the communities, one based on uncompromising insistence on its original norms, which is also a threat to the bishops and deacons.

Once the ostensible textual basis and methodological presuppositions for the picture of the origins of Christianity as a movement of wandering charismatics are examined critically, that picture turns into a chimera. Modern scholars such as Theissen have unwittingly brought a seventy-year scholarly argument full circle. Successive generations of scholars did not question the sources and concepts of their predecessors. The greatest irony is that Theissen and others not only oversimplified the concept of charisma they borrowed from Weber but also failed to note that Weber was dependent on Harnack's questionable earlier construction of the development of early Christianity on the basis of the then newly discovered *Didache.* In a further irony, it turns out that Weber's theory of charismatic legitimation, flawed as it may be, is at least somewhat useful in understanding the sequence of authority figures discerned through a critically examined sequence of the *Didache,* whereas New Testament scholars' static and oversimplified adaptation of Weber has been used to manipulate texts and to distort history.

The results of this critical examination of the wandering charismatics thesis for study of Q are not far to seek. It is a modern scholarly construct, not an identifiable historical type of behavior. The prophets discussed in the *Didache* seem more clearly identifiable as historical charismatic figures active in Syria roughly in the second generation of early Christianity. Whether they were generally itinerant is not at all clear. It seems difficult, moreover, to discern any pattern or consistency in their roles in local communities. Hence it is difficult to discern without considerable further consideration whether they would have been appropriate carriers of Q materials.

Chapter 3

THE HISTORICAL CONTEXT OF Q

Richard A. Horsley _____

Exploration of Q depends upon the historical context in which it is understood —
unless interpretation of Q is to remain in the service of modern theology or a
resurgent liberal construction of Jesus and his movement. A consensus of sorts has
emerged among recent interpreters of Q that it originated in or near Galilee, because the only place-names in Q are of the Galilean towns Capernaum, Chorazin,
and Bethsaida (Q/Luke 10:13–15). But how Galilee should be understood is by
no means clear. Wildly divergent assumptions and/or claims are made about
Galilee in Jesus and Gospel studies generally. Indeed, society in Roman Palestine
in general and in Galilee in particular has not been investigated with very precise
attention to social structure and dynamics. For Galilee itself, historical sources
other than the Gospel materials about Jesus and the histories of the historian
Josephus are scarce. And archaeological explorations of Galilee have only begun
during the last twenty years and have produced little evidence for the time of Jesus
and his movement(s). Interpretation of the limited evidence available, moreover,
is disputed in this undertheorized area of historical study. Partly because of the
recently revived interest in investigation of the historical Jesus, however, more
precise and critical studies of history and society in Galilee are emerging. As
we move toward a critical examination of Q and its recent scholarly treatment,
several factors indicate the importance of first establishing more precisely the
historical context in which it originated and functioned.

First, the usual construction of the "historical background" of "early Christian" texts is still heavily determined by Christian theological concepts. According
to the older standard Christian theological-historical scheme, the parochial and
overly political religion of "Judaism" was replaced by the universalistic and purely
spiritual "Christianity." Stated in such bald terms, this scheme now seems utterly simplistic. Yet it is remarkably resilient in New Testament scholarship, and
vestiges of it still determine interpretation of Q. In a widely read standard interpretation of "Judaism and Hellenism" (published as recently as 1973), when
faced with a "Hellenism" in which a cultural "universalism" had developed, "Judaism" (in the Maccabean War) turned away from a universalizing "reform" in
which it might have become a "world religion." It was left for "Christianity" to
break away from the resulting parochialism and political particularism and finally

establish a universalistic religion.[1] In the revival of Q studies after the middle of the twentieth century, as we shall note, Q or some Q material was seen to pronounce condemnation of "Judaism" or "all Israel" because of its rejection of Jesus and his message, even though no Q sayings state this is so many words. The most extreme form of this modern scholarly scheme claims that in contrast to Jewish resistance to Hellenistic forms of culture and governance, Greco-Roman Galilean society was already an ethnic mix of peoples who had acquired universalistic and individualistic Hellenistic culture.[2] It was thus a ready-made matrix for the "individual freedom" and "natural and simple lifestyle" that emerged in the Q sayings. Not only does this approach ignore how diverse Palestinian society and culture were in the late second-temple period. It also fails to recognize that religion was embedded with political-economic aspects of life. One might say that in Palestine there was no such historical entity as Judaism yet. We are dealing rather with a complex society or societies the political-economic-religious structure and dynamics of which must be historically investigated. The respective situations in Galilee, Samaria, and Judea may have more to do more with their different regional histories under a succession of empires and with the political-economic-religious relations between rulers and ruled than with ethnic relations and reified abstractions of culture.

Second, recent American Q studies in particular present a decisive set of Q sayings as calling for "unconventional" or "countercultural" attitudes and behavior without attention to precisely what would have been "conventional" and what "culture" they were countering.[3] Again, such characterizations of Q materials beg rather than address questions of social-cultural diversity and ruler-ruled relations in "Jewish" Palestine in general and Galilee in particular. Statements about attitudes and behavior in Q may have to do with social location and power relations as well as with differing regional histories.

Third, even the sociology-of-literature approach that finds wandering charismatics or itinerant radicalism behind Q and other Jesus sayings that it reads as calling for behavior counter to social conventions focuses on individuals in abstraction from fundamental social forms and relations.[4] As noted in chapter 1,

---

1. Martin Hengel, *Judaism and Hellenism* (Philadelphia: Fortress, 1974), in two "summary" sections, 303–14.

2. Burton L. Mack, *The Lost Gospel: The Book of Q and Christian Origins* (San Francisco: Harper-SanFrancisco, 1993), 51–68. Mack cites no sources for his remarkable sketch of Galilee as ethnically mixed and culturally Hellenistic. It is difficult to imagine that the principal archaeologists and historians of late second-temple / early Roman Galilee would claim responsibility for "the picture now being painted by archaeological and sociological analyses of first-century life and times in Galilee" (48). The lack of historical nuancing can be seen in the statement that "even the Semitic component of the Galilean population needs to be carefully nuanced lest the fact of Jewish presence in Galilee allow the myth of a common Jewish culture to continue" (60–61).

3. For example, Mack, *Lost Gospel*, who presents a puzzling scenario of Q people as countercultural vis-à-vis an ethnically mixed Hellenized Galilean culture that has already broken with its traditional ethnic cultures; and John S. Kloppenborg, "Literary Convention, Self-Evidence, and the Social History of the Q People," *Semeia* 55 (1991): 77–102, who apparently assumes that Galilean and nearby culture and conventions are Jewish.

4. Particularly important in this connection, because so many studies of Q have simply adopted

such an orientation to the individual is peculiar to the modern West. In ancient Palestine, as in most historically known societies, persons apparently were understood to be embedded in certain fundamental social forms and social relations, particularly the family and the local village community.

Many of the most crucial steps in understanding the distinctive viewpoint of Q have been taken simply by ceasing to view the text in terms of a given Christian theological concept. Significant further steps can be taken by ceasing to view the historical context of Q in terms of modern Christian constructions of Judaism and modern Western assumptions of social individualism. A brief review of the history of Galilee, from the viewpoint of the Galileans rather than from that of its rulers, will provide perspective for a brief analysis of the social forms and political-economic-religious structure and dynamics of historical power relations in Galilee.[5]

A Brief History of Galilee

According to biblical traditions, the Israelite tribes were able to establish themselves in hill-country villages in Palestine during the twelfth and eleventh centuries B.C.E.[6] Here they formed an independent peasant society based in scattered villages and held together apparently by "covenant(s)" to maintain cooperative and mutually supportive relations among their constituent households and to come to each others' aid when threatened by predatory would-be rulers from without.[7] The tribes located in Galilee come prominently to the fore in the Israelite victory song in Judges 5 named after the heroine Deborah, one of the oldest pieces of Hebrew poetry in the Bible. In one of the fierce struggles to maintain their freedom as a people against the Canaanite city-states, whose kings fielded professional armies of horses and chariots,

---

his thesis, is Gerd Theissen, "Wanderradikalismus: Literatursoziologische Aspekte der Überlieferung von Worten Jesu im Urchristentum," *ZTK* 70 (1973): 245–71; and idem, *Sociology of Early Palestinian Christianity* (Philadelphia: Fortress, 1978).

5. The following sketches of the history of Galilee and of political-economic-religious forms and power relations in ancient Palestine are based on Richard A. Horsley, *Galilee: History, Politics, People* (Valley Forge, Pa.: Trinity Press International, 1995); idem, *Archaeology, History, and Society in Galilee* (Valley Forge, Pa.: Trinity Press International, 1996); and idem, *Sociology and the Jesus Movement* (New York: Crossroad, 1989). For textual, archaeological, and scholarly references, see the text and notes in those works. Cf. the first recent comprehensive scholarly treatment of ancient Galilee in Sean Freyne, *Galilee from Alexander the Great to Hadrian: A Study of Second Temple Judaism* (Wilmington, Del.: Michael Glazier, 1980).

6. See the stories in Joshua 8–11 and the summary in Judg. 1:16–33 (in which the Hebrew often translated "inhabitants of" the land/city should be translated rather "rulers of" the land/city); contrast the picture in the schematic passages in 10:40–43; 11:16–23. Biblical references for the following historical sketch are offered, partly because they provide key textual sources for the history and partly because it is important to have a sense of how the history was remembered in late second-temple times (around the time of Jesus) for understanding Q, as will be further explained in subsequent chapters.

7. For example, see the covenantal ceremonies and law code in Exodus 20–24.

> The people of the LORD marched down...against the mighty....
> The chiefs of Issachar came with Deborah....
> Zebulun is a people that scorned death;
> Naphtali too, on the heights of the field.
> The kings came, they fought,
> at Taanach, by the waters of Megiddo.
> The torrent Kishon swept them away....
> March on, my soul with might!

This early victory song represents the Galilean tribes coming down out of the hill country to fight against chariot forces from the fortified city of Megiddo in the great plain just to the south of Galilee. The Hebrew term *ha-galil* was apparently a secondary shortening for *galil ha-goyim*, "circle of the peoples," probably a reference to the peoples or city-states that surrounded the hilly and mountainous country just to the north of the great plain between the Mediterranean and the Sea of Galilee and that periodically competed for political-economic domination of the area.

The Galilean tribes along with those in the central hill country of Palestine managed to maintain their independence as a free peasantry for several generations.[8] When it proved impossible to hold their own militarily against the professional armies of the Philistine city-states on the coastal plain, Israel generated popularly "anointed" (messiah) kings or chieftains to lead them into battle (1 Samuel 8–12; 2 Sam. 2:1–3; 5:1–3). The popularly anointed David, however, used his own mercenary troops to conquer the Jebusite (non-Israelite) city of Jerusalem as a capital, where he consolidated his power over Israel (2 Samuel 5–7). The twelve tribes' attempts at rebellion proved ineffective against David's professional military forces (2 Samuel 15–20). David's son Solomon (961–922) then established an imperial monarchy over Israel and the conquered Canaanite city-states and constructed the temple in Jerusalem, as well as luxurious palaces and fortresses, by means of forced labor (1 Kings 5–9). To help pay off the heavy indebtedness incurred by these massive development projects, Solomon even ceded twenty villages in Galilee, along with the Galilean peasants who worked the land, to King Hiram of Tyre (1 Kings 9:10–11).

Not happy with their subjection to the Davidic monarchy and particularly to forced labor, ten of the twelve tribes rebelled after the death of Solomon (1 Kings 12). Only Judah, along with the tiny tribe of Benjamin, remained under the Davidic monarchy and its temple in Jerusalem. The continuing independent spirit of the northern Israelites succeeded in preventing their popularly acclaimed kings from establishing a dynasty until Ahab and Jezebel succeeded in consolidating power in the newly constructed city of Samaria. Once again, under the leadership of Elijah and Elisha and the enclaves of "prophets" (*bene-nabi'im*), the Israelite villagers managed to resist the exploitative rule of their monarchs, and eventually

---

8. Technically speaking, this is a contradiction in terms, since peasants are, by the usual definition, agrarian people subject to lords or rulers who forcibly appropriate their surplus produce, that is, what they do not need for subsistence.

the army overthrew Ahab's dynasty (1 Kings 17–22; 2 Kings 1–10). Thereafter, however, popular resistance movements disappear from the biblical narratives. Instead, resistance took the form of oracles of indictment and judgment against the rulers' exploitation and injustice delivered by individual prophets such as Amos and Hosea in the north, and Micah, Isaiah, and Jeremiah in Judah.

The Assyrian Empire conquered the northern monarchy in Samaria in 722 B.C.E. and replaced the deported Israelite ruling class in the capital city of Samaria with an aristocracy imported from elsewhere in the empire. A critical examination of pertinent biblical narratives and Assyrian inscriptions, however, suggests that the Assyrian regime followed the usual Near Eastern imperial practice of leaving the peasantry on the land in their semi-independent and largely self-sufficient village communities.[9] Thereafter, for the next six centuries, Galilee and the central hill country around Samaria were subject to a series of ancient Near Eastern and Hellenistic empires in separate administrative districts. Thus, for more than eight hundred years following the death of Solomon, when they rebelled against Davidic rule and the Solomonic temple built by forced labor, the Israelite villagers in Galilee lived separately and independent of Jerusalem rule.

The kingdom of Judah was also conquered and the ruling class in Jerusalem deported by the Babylonian Empire in 587 B.C.E. The Persian imperial regime, however, restored the Judean ruling class later in the sixth century B.C.E. and sponsored the building of the second temple, as well as the consolidation of the indigenous Judean laws and traditions that eventually became parts of the Torah. After four centuries under the same succession of empires that Galilee had been under, the Judean villagers and ordinary priestly families resorted to guerrilla warfare in an eventually successful struggle against attempts by their own high-priestly rulers and the Seleucid imperial regime in Syria to "reform," that is, Hellenize, the ruling institutions of city and temple in Jerusalem (see 1 and 2 Maccabees). The brothers and successors of the charismatic military leader Judas the Hammer (Maccabee), however, consolidated their own power by obtaining appointment as high priest by the Seleucid emperor and established the Hasmonean dynasty in the Jerusalem temple-state. Expanding their power in the vacuum of weakening Seleucid imperial power, the Hasmonean priest-kings first conquered Samaria to the north, destroying its temple, and Idumea to the south, forcing the inhabitants to be circumcised and to obey the "laws of the Judeans." In 104 B.C.E., they also took control of Galilee and forced the inhabitants to be circumcised and to live according to the "laws of the Judeans." More than eight hundred years after they had rebelled against Davidic rule and the Solomonic temple, the Galileans were again under Jerusalem rule.

The hundred years that Galilee was again under Jerusalem rule — the hundred years just before Jesus was born — included first a time of intense turmoil, followed by a long period of tyranny, at the end of which popular rebellion broke out

---

9. Evidence and argument for this conclusion in Horsley, *Galilee*, 26–27.

in both Galilee and Judea.[10] Hasmonean conquests and arrogance evoked the resistance, apparently by Pharisees and/or other scribal circles. Turmoil within the Hasmonean regime coincided with the Romans' finally moving to take control of the eastern Mediterranean. In 63, the Romans conquered the area and laid greater Judea (including Idumea, Samaria, Perea, and Galilee, as well as Judea proper) under tribute, while leaving the Hasmonean regime in the Jerusalem-based temple-state. For more than twenty-five years Galilee and other areas of Palestine were simply decimated by Roman military actions and then civil wars raging in Palestine parallel to those in the Roman Empire at large. The last three years of this chronic warfare found the Judean people and particularly the Galilean people resisting conquest by the Idumean strongman Herod, whom the Roman Senate had appointed as their client-king of the Judeans.

When Herod had finally conquered the people over whom he had been designated king, he ruled with an iron fist while exploiting the productive peasantry to the limit, yet without destroying his economic base.[11] He established his own Hellenistic-style administration. Yet, like the Romans, he also left the high-priestly aristocracy and temple intact, except that he replaced the Hasmoneans with a succession of hand-picked high-priestly families, including one from Egypt and one from Babylon. There thus emerged two layers of rulers, two aristocracies in Jerusalem, the high-priestly and the Herodian. Herod established security forces and fortresses around his realm, built many impressive cities and monuments in honor of Caesar, and rebuilt the Jerusalem temple in grand Hellenistic style — all at tremendous cost, underwritten by his subjects' produce. Galilee he ruled, like the Hasmoneans before him, from fortified towns, the most important of which was clearly Sepphoris, in which he built a royal fortress-palace to which goods collected from nearby villages such as Nazareth, Cana, and Japha were taken and stored. When the tyrant finally died, popular rebellions broke out in every major district of his realm, led by men acclaimed by their followers as kings. In the area of Galilee around the fortress town of Sepphoris, the popular messianic movement that emerged — right around the time Jesus of Nazareth was supposedly born — was headed by Judas son of the brigand chief Hezekiah, whom Herod had killed a generation earlier as the military governor of Galilee.

The Roman reconquest was devastating, at least in the areas of the insurrection. In Galilee they burned (the area around?) Sepphoris and enslaved the people, a collective trauma that would have reverberated among the villages in the area such as Nazareth. Once the reconquest was completed, the Romans appointed Herod's eighteen-year-old son, Antipas, as ruler of Galilee and Perea, across the Jordan River. Previously the rulers of Galilee had always ruled from a

---

10. Horsley, *Galilee*, chap. 2, is an attempt critically to reconstruct the history of Galilee under Jerusalem rule in this period, for which few sources exist. The many important references to Josephus's accounts are given there.

11. For the reign of Herod in general, see now Peter Richardson, *Herod: King of the Jews and Friend of the Romans* (Columbia: University of South Carolina Press, 1996); for Herod's rule of Galilee in particular, see Horsley, *Galilee*, 56–61.

distant imperial or Judean capital, an advantage for a peasantry trying to avoid expropriation of its produce by the royal tax collectors. Antipas, however, established his capital directly in Galilee, first rebuilding the city of Sepphoris and then founding the new capital city of Tiberias along the Sea of Galilee, both apparently according to Hellenistic-Roman political forms and political-cultural styles.[12] Thus within about twenty years he engaged in two massive building projects, all the more remarkable considering the limited territory (Galilee and Perea) and thus the limited tax base from which he was drawing his resources. These two capitals, which between them overlooked nearly every village in lower Galilee, placed his tax collectors in command of the desired resources.

Social Forms and Power Relations in Galilee and Roman Palestine

This sketch of the history of Galilee in relation to that of Judea should make possible recognition of several important factors that affect the reading of Q, assuming that Q materials at least originated and developed in a Jesus movement in Galilee.

The fundamental social forms of a traditional agrarian society such as that in Galilee were households and villages, which were interrelated sets of households. Households or families were the basic units of production and consumption, more or less self-sufficient in producing nearly all the food consumed and clothing and other necessities used, while also producing whatever surplus was demanded by their rulers. Villages were semi-independent, self-governing, and virtually self-sufficient communities.[13] Individual people in Galilee or any similar ancient agrarian society were thus embedded in and integral to both families and village communities.[14] In such a society there were also no broader social forms or organizations that cut across and/or united villages except for the occasional, and quickly suppressed, popular social movements, such as the rebellions led by popularly acclaimed kings after the death of Herod.

The form of both self-governance and communal political and religious life was what is called a synagogue in the Gospels. This becomes more obvious once we both acknowledge that the Greek term *synagoge* means "assembly" and recognize that archaeologists have not found evidence of synagogue buildings with any

---

12. On Antipas's transformation of Galilee, see Horsley, *Galilee,* 64–66 and chap. 7; and idem, *Archaeology,* chap. 2.

13. For more extensive discussion of households and villages in Galilee, including a gathering and discussion of literary and archaeological evidence, see Horsley, *Galilee,* chaps. 8–9; and idem, *Archaeology,* chaps. 4–5.

14. It is understandably difficult for people from highly complex modern society, in which multiple options are available for individual actors in most of their multiple social roles, to imagine that there were extremely few options outside of one's ascribed position embedded in the fundamental and traditional social forms of family and village. But it is utterly unhistorical and inappropriate to project an abstract modern Western individualism onto Galileans (or Samaritans or Judeans, etc.) at the time of Jesus.

frequency in Galilean villages until late antiquity (suggesting the conclusion that they were not built — as community centers — until then). From earlier Judean texts, from somewhat later rabbinic evidence for such traditional Galilean villages, and from inscriptional evidence in nearby areas, it appears that the local village assembly had a handful of officers who presided at meetings, took care of collecting and distributing goods for the destitute, administered beatings ordered by local courts established on an ad hoc basis by the assemblies, and attended, for example, to construction projects of the local assembly (water works, etc.).[15]

Elevated far above the villages were various types of rulers who commanded and expropriated the surplus products of the villagers in various forms. "To rule in aristocratic empires is, above all, to tax."[16] Monarchs such as Solomon dominated the Israelites with professional armies and expropriated from them both the produce of labor in taxation and forced labor itself for building projects such as the temple (1 Kings 4 and 5 describe how these political-economic arrangements were institutionalized). Temple-states such as that in Jerusalem claimed produce from the villagers as tithes and offerings for God (as laid out in Neh. 10:32–39 and Sir. 7:31; 50:1–21). Empires such as the Seleucid and Roman took tribute from the villagers, often expecting the local rulers such as the high priests of the Jerusalem temple-state to collect the taxes for them. Herod and his son Antipas in Galilee expropriated the resources they demanded in direct taxation. When the Romans left the high priesthood in place and then installed Herod as well, the result was a multiple layer of rulers and multiple demands on the produce of the peasantry. The position of Roman client rulers such as the high priests in Jerusalem and Antipas in Galilee depended upon the pleasure and potential military support of the Romans. All levels of the rulers' tributary relationship with the producer-peasants were maintained by the threat of punitive military action, by which the relationship had been established in the first place — as the Galileans living in Nazareth and nearby villages well knew from the devastating losses they suffered in the Roman retaliatory reconquest in 4 B.C.E. Except for its extraction of tithes, taxes, and tribute, sanctioned by religious rites or military forces, however, the Roman imperial regime, the local Herodian regime, and the Jerusalem temple-state did not directly govern the people, having nothing like

---

15. Evidence and discussion are laid out in Horsley, *Galilee*, chap. 10. Kloppenborg, "Literary Convention, Self-Evidence, and the Social History of the Q People," *Semeia* 55 (1991): 85–86, apparently assumed that these village officers in Galilee and surrounding areas were scribes at the lower levels of a sort of administrative bureaucracy. Yet there is nothing in the rabbinic evidence to suggest that such local officers of village assemblies were somehow also scribes, that is, literate, and nothing in the inscriptional evidence from the Hauran, other than the minimal literacy of the inscriptions themselves, to suggest that those behind the Greek terms for the corresponding local officers were also scribes. "Village scribes" (*komogrammateis*) appear only in sources from Egypt, which was unique in antiquity for having been bureaucratized by the Ptolemies. But even the "village scribes" turn out to be only semiliterate, according to the analysis of the evidence by Herbert C. Youtie, "*Bradeos graphon*: Between Literacy and Illiteracy," *Greek, Roman and Byzantine Studies* 12 (1971): 239–61.

16. John H. Kautsky, *Politics of Aristocratic Empires* (Chapel Hill: University of North Carolina Press, 1982), 73, 150.

the modern state's apparatus of disciplinary control, mass media, and surveillance apparatus.[17] Rulers generally did not intervene in local community affairs as long as their tax revenues were forthcoming.

The high-priestly rulers (and Herod the Great) in Jerusalem and Herod Antipas in Galilee, however, did employ what sociologists would call retainers in certain administrative capacities. Among the functions of the scribes and the Pharisees, who apparently were a political interest group among the scribal retainers, were the cultivation and interpretation of the Torah, the laws of Moses. In one account of their activities under the Hasmoneans, Josephus reports that they also promulgated certain additional "rulings" (nomima) for the people that were not contained in the books of Moses, rulings that were part of the official law of the state or not, depending on the disposition of the ruler. (John Hyrcanus rescinded them; Alexandra Salome restored them [Ant. 13.295–98, 408–9].) According to a scholarly view prominent in the last few decades, the Pharisees had withdrawn from political affairs under Herod the Great. That view seems doubtful, however, since Josephus portrays them as actively involved in political-religious affairs, even in high places, in mid–first century C.E.[18] The importance of the Pharisees has been blown out of proportion because they appear as the principal opponents of Jesus in the Gospels and because they have been understood as the precursors of rabbinic Judaism. Virtually the only sources that portray the Pharisees as active in Galilee, except for an occasional reference of individual sages living in Galilee in rabbinic sources (e.g., Johanan ben Zakkai), are the Gospels. The picture of the scribes and Pharisees as having Jesus virtually under surveillance in the beginning of the Gospel of Mark, moreover, is hardly credible historically. No more credible historically are Matthew's programmatic harangues against them (Matthew 23) and Luke's portrayal of Jesus as dining with them (Luke 14:1). Nevertheless, it seems highly likely that the scribes and Pharisees would have extended their activities into Galilee once the Hasmoneans brought the area under the temple-state. These actions would have been the same ones they carried out in Judea itself, that is, cultivation and application of the Torah and other laws of the Judeans. The Herodians who appear both in Josephus's narratives and in the Gospels apparently served in somewhat similar capacities, officially and unofficially, as representatives and administrators for Herod the Great, with a basis in Jerusalem, and then for the regime of Herod Antipas and his successors, the Agrippas, based in Sepphoris and / or Tiberias.[19]

In the political-economic-religious relations between Galileans and Jerusalem, the class differences between rulers and ruled were compounded by differences

---

17. Anthony Giddens, *The Nation State and Violence* (Berkeley: University of California Press, 1986).

18. See Steve Mason, *Flavius Josephus on the Pharisees: A Composition-Critical Study* (Leiden: E. J. Brill, 1991); and Horsley, *Sociology*, 73–75.

19. See the sketch of Antipas's and successor administrations in Sepphoris and Tiberias in Horsley, *Galilee*, chap. 7. Antipas's administration would also have employed scribes; but it is not clear that "lesser managers" and "supervisors of public works" would have also been scribes, as suggested by Kloppenborg, "Literary Convention," 86.

in historical experiences. It should first be emphasized, against any insinuation that Galilee was somehow predominantly Gentile, that the Galileans were almost certainly predominantly of Israelite heritage. That first-century C.E. Galilee was not Judea proper and not predominantly Judean in population does not mean that its people were not of Israelite heritage. Despite the relative decline in population following the Assyrian conquest in 722, evident from archaeological surface surveys (which are not particularly reliable indicators anyhow), the most compelling reading of the fragmentary evidence, including Assyrian inscriptions and standard ancient Near Eastern imperial treatment of conquered villages, suggests that the Israelite people were left on the land in Galilee and in the hill country around Samaria. Social-economic life in self-governing, semi-independent village communities, moreover, is generally run according to time-honored tradition and custom, which would have been Israelite in the case of Galilean villages populated by the tribes of Issachar, Zebulun, and Naphtali. Presumably, therefore, Galilean village communities would have been living according to the same Mosaic covenantal tradition to which Elijah and Amos and Hosea had appealed in the people's struggles and protests against the monarchy in Samaria. And that would have been more or less the same Mosaic covenantal tradition that continued in the villages of Judah, to which prophets such as Micah and Isaiah and Jeremiah appealed in their prophecies against the Davidic kings and their officers in Jerusalem. That the Galileans appear to have observed the Sabbath and practiced circumcision and reacted to violations of the prohibition against images does not mean that they were Judeans but that they were of Israelite heritage and shared these Israelite traditions with the Judeans.[20] That the Galileans were Israelite in heritage means also that they shared a long tradition of opposition to and prophetic protest against exploitative and unjust rulers, domestic as well as foreign. For the descendants of northern Israelites, of course, the Israelite tradition included resentment of and rebellion against Jerusalem rule.

That Galileans were still Israelite in heritage and were viewed as Israelite by the ruling circles in Jerusalem seems to be reflected in the differing accounts given by the Judean historian Josephus of the Hasmonean expansion into Idumea and Galilee.[21] Whereas the Hasmoneans reportedly conquered the Idumeans, in Galilee they merely took control of the people by driving out the Itureans, who had taken control of that area when Seleucid imperial power declined (Josephus, *Ant.* 13.257–58, 318–19). That in both cases, according to Josephus, the Hasmoneans required the people to "be circumcised" and to live according to the laws of the Judeans should not be read as a report of a (forced) religious conversion, on the standard old paradigm that the relations between the Hasmoneans and these newly subjected peoples were merely matters of religion. Terms such as

---

20. This is illustrated by several incidents in first-century C.E. Galilean history, as discussed in Horsley, *Galilee*, 147–55.

21. On the following, see the attempt to restate the issues in more appropriate historical terms in ibid., chap. 2.

"laws of the Judeans" indicate political as well as religious relations. Being circumcised was probably understood as a rite of incorporation into the "body-politic" (in traditional terms as the children of Abraham), and living according to the laws of the Judeans probably pertained primarily to the relations between village communities and the temple-state, since ancient states did not govern within the local communities they controlled and taxed.

Such village communities would have remained self-governing according to local tradition and customs, as noted above. Considering the intense turmoil within Judea, even within the Hasmonean regime in Jerusalem, during the generations after the takeover of Galilee, it seems highly unlikely that representatives of the temple-state such as scribes and Pharisees would have been forcing local villages to conform their local community affairs and self-governance to the laws of the Judeans. Nevertheless, in the same way as such scribal representatives of the Jerusalem temple-state "interpreted" and applied the Torah and / or "the laws of the Judeans" for Judean villagers and promulgated additional new "rulings" for the people that were not already in the books of Moses (Josephus, *Ant.* 13.257–58), they must have done so also for Galilean villagers as well during the century of Jerusalem rule in Galilee. Thus Galileans would have been familiar with the scribes' and Pharisees' political-economic-religious role as legal interpreters and teachers and representatives of the Jerusalem temple-state's interests in general. The continuing Galilean cultivation of Israelite tradition in comparison with the Israelite tradition cultivated (partly in written form) in Jerusalem by Pharisees and other scribal circles would correspond with what anthropologists and others refer to as the interrelation between the great tradition of the elite and the little tradition of ordinary people, which we will apply to Q materials in chapter 5.

As indicated by their different historical experiences, a significant difference between Galilean villagers and their popular Israelite tradition and the Judean villagers and their popular tradition may have existed with regard to the temple and the high-priestly rulers in Jerusalem. The Judean villagers in the immediate environs of Jerusalem lived out of a long tradition of political-economic-religious affairs focused on the temple and administered by the high priesthood along with the ordinary priests and Levites. They had presumably paid tithes to the priests and Levites and made offerings in the temple for centuries. The coherence of Judean life, focused on the temple, had been powerfully reinforced in mid–second century B.C.E. by the struggle against the Hellenizing reform and a prolonged and successful guerrilla war against the Seleucid armies. The "courses" of ordinary priests, many of whom lived in Judean villages but served in the temple during the three major pilgrimage festivals and the weeks assigned to their particular course, must have provided further connections between the Judean villagers and the temple apparatus. The outlying villages that came under Jerusalem's control only after the Maccabean revolt would have been correspondingly less assimilated to the temple-state.

The villagers of Galilee, however, who came under Jerusalem rule only a hundred years before Herod's death and Jesus' birth and then were removed from the temple-state's jurisdiction during the lifetime of Jesus, would presumably have had a somewhat ambivalent relationship with the temple and high priesthood.[22] Conceivably Jerusalem rulers who were fellow Israelites would have been more acceptable than completely foreign Hellenistic or Roman imperial rulers. Coming under the Hasmonean priest-kings who, in taking over Galilee as well as Samaria, had reunited all formerly Israelite territories under Jerusalem rule for the first time since Solomon may well have also stimulated among the Galilean villagers an awareness of belonging to Israel as a whole. Although only a limited number of Galileans would have made the long journey to a pilgrimage festival at some point in their life, such journeys would have further enhanced a sense of connection to the rest of Israel and the temple itself. On the other hand, several factors would have worked against the development of an attachment to the temple and high priesthood. The Hasmoneans, after all, had imposed their polity, the laws of the Judeans, including their rule and taxation, on the Galileans. To enforce internal compliance and to defend their expanded frontiers vis-à-vis Tyre and other principalities to north, the Hasmoneans had installed garrisoned fortresses in Galilee, with Sepphoris as the principal military-administrative town. They thus maintained a Jerusalemite military-administrative presence in Galilee that evidently evoked the resentment of Galilean peasants, who drowned such "gentry" in the Sea of Galilee during the turmoil of Herod's conquest of the area, according to Josephus's account (*Ant.* 14.450; cf. *B.J.* 1.326). Herod as well ruled through these military-administrative fortresses. And again at the first opportunity, the tyrant's death, the Galileans attacked the royal fortress and arsenal in Sepphoris (*Ant.* 17.271; *B.J.* 2.56). The hostility to the scribes and Pharisees expressed in the Synoptic Gospel traditions in Q and Mark certainly suggests that Galileans also resented the activities and rulings of these representatives of the Jerusalem temple-state (e.g., Mark 7:1–13; Q/Luke 11:39–52). Generally, Galileans were reluctant and slow to render up their dues to the temple and priests.[23]

The Galileans were not alone in their opposition to the temple, the incumbent high priests, and/or their scribal and Pharisaic representatives. Dissident Judean scribal and/or priestly circles produced sharp criticism in literature such as the Epistle of Enoch (*1 Enoch* 94–105) and the literature of the separatist community at Qumran. A virtual civil war erupted in the opposition to Alexander Janneus early in the first century B.C.E. Herod's appointment of his own creatures to the high priesthood created a vastly enlarged priestly aristocracy of declining legitimacy. Their ostentatious wealth and residences and increasingly predatory behavior toward the people during the course of the first century C.E. deepened the already wide chasm that existed between rulers and ruled. Not surprisingly,

---

22. On the whole subject, see ibid., chap. 6.

23. Freyne, *Galilee*, 277, 280, 282, 285, 293–94, lays out the evidence, yet comes to the conclusion that Galileans were nevertheless deeply attached to Jerusalem and the temple. He repeats these conclusions that appear to run counter to the evidence in "Galilee-Jerusalem Relations according to Josephus," *NTS* 33 (1987): 600–609.

some of the popular protests in Jerusalem itself focused against the high priests,[24] and some of the popular movements in the countryside were implicitly anti-temple and/or anti-Jerusalem.[25]

Therefore, although it is difficult to pin down with any precision, an ambivalent relationship between Galileans and the temple-state must have become established during the hundred years that Galilee was directly under Jerusalem rule. After the death of Herod, of course, Augustus set Galilee under Antipas. Following his reign, Galilee was ruled either by one of the Agrippas or by Roman governors. Nevertheless, at the outbreak of the great revolt in the summer of 66 c.e., the provisional high-priestly government in Jerusalem immediately attempted to reassert Jerusalem's control in Galilee by sending the team of "generals" that included Josephus (Josephus, B.J. 2.562–68). The priestly aristocracy in Jerusalem thus still apparently viewed itself as the rightful rulers of the area. And the Gospels portray Jesus of Nazareth as focused on Jerusalem rather than Sepphoris or Tiberias and moving into a direct face-off with the temple and high priesthood rather than Antipas in the climax of their narratives. If the overall plot of the Gospels and the prophetic materials in the Synoptic Gospel tradition have any historical credibility, then at least one Galilean prophet and his movement saw Jerusalem as having significance, even if it was an extremely ambiguous one. Finally, at least a few Galileans, led by John of Gischala, fled to Jerusalem after the Romans reconquered Galilee in 67 (Josephus, B.J. 4.106–16), suggesting that some Galileans chose to continue the resistance to Roman rule in solidarity basically with Israelite peasants from various districts of Judea.

The impact of Antipas's direct rule in Galilee, both political-economic and cultural, must have been intense, particularly during the generation of Jesus and his followers. Herod the Great had exploited his tax base to the fullest, while presumably the villagers simultaneously yielded up their tithes and offerings to the priesthood and temple. Antipas's construction of two cities within twenty years, combined with the immediate presence of the capitals and tax collectors with easy access to the surrounding villages, must have intensified the economic pressure on the Galilean peasantry. Nor did Antipas show much sensitivity to the cultural traditions of his subjects. According to Josephus's account, he had Tiberias built on the site of a cemetery and uprooted several villages and/or numbers of villagers in order to populate his new capital (Ant. 18.36–38). Antipas's cities, moreover, were apparently designed as centers of Roman-Hellenistic culture, as exemplified in the Roman-style theater built at some point during the first century in Sepphoris and by the very title "Tiberias" (after the emperor Tiberius) and the significant number of "Greeks" in that city.[26] It would be a projection of

---

24. See Richard A. Horsley, *Jesus and the Spiral of Violence: Popular Jewish Resistance in Roman Palestine* (San Francisco: Harper & Row, 1987), chap. 4.

25. The popular prophetic and messianic movements, discussed in Richard A. Horsley, "Popular Messianic Movements around the Time of Jesus," *CBQ* 46 (1984): 471–95; and idem, "'Like One of the Prophets of Old': Two Types of Prophets at the Time of Jesus," *CBQ* 47 (1985): 435–63.

26. See further Horsley, *Galilee*, chap. 7.

early modern times to imagine that the Galilean peasants received any mutual benefits from these cities suddenly imposed on the landscape or even that they interacted in any active way with Sepphoris and Tiberias — other than rendering up their produce in taxes, of course.[27] It cannot be coincidental, given the paucity of evidence from this period for popular figures or movements ("during the reign of Tiberius all was quiet"), that the prophet John the Baptist condemned Antipas (*Ant.* 18.116–19) and that Jesus and his movement emerged in Galilee under Antipas. The pressures that intensified during the reign of Antipas continued to reverberate among the Galilean people. The massive peasant strike against the plan of the emperor Gaius to place his bust in the temple was a protest against this blatant violation of the command against images, but like other such protests it had deeper roots in political-economic discontents. And after effective Roman control of the area by the threat of force broke down at the outbreak of revolt in 66, it became evident just how intense was the Galilean villagers' hostility to their rulers based in Sepphoris and Tiberias. According to the Jerusalem-sent general on the scene, the Galileans were eager to attack Sepphoris, which remained steadfastly loyal to Rome, and they cooperated actively with the popular party in Tiberias against the Herodian elite who administered that area for Agrippa II. The hostility of the Galilean villagers to their urban rulers appears to have been more intense than usual for traditional agrarian societies.

From this survey of more precise recent reconstruction of history, social forms, and political-economic-religious relations in ancient Galilee, it is evident that the assumptions about Galilee in previous Q studies are historically unwarranted. Galilean culture was neither an overly parochial Jewish religion that the Q people transcended nor a Hellenized Gentile culture already on its way toward universalism. The vast majority of Galileans were villagers apparently living according to their Israelite heritage. Their lives, moreover, were embedded in the traditional social forms of family and village community. After the Hasmonean takeover the "laws of the Judeans" and perhaps a renewed awareness of that Israelite heritage became more of a factor in Galilee, perhaps partly through a periodic presence of scribal-Pharisaic representatives of Jerusalem in the area. The Roman client ruler Antipas imposed Roman-Hellenistic political culture on the Galilean landscape in the building of Sepphoris and Tiberias. But far from having a Hellenizing effect on the populace, the immediate presence of foreign rulers and ruling institutions within view of their ancestral villages evoked the Galileans' hostility. If anything, the increased economic pressures of Antipas's rule and his imposition of Roman-Hellenistic political culture would have driven the Galileans into deeper attachment to their traditional Israelite heritage. Those who would interpret Q sayings as vaguely countercultural must explain which culture is being countered, the traditional Israelite heritage in which Jesus and his followers were rooted, or the Jerusalem-based scribal culture represented by scribes and Pharisees, or the

---

27. In addition to the treatment in ibid., see the evidence and arguments in Horsley, *Archaeology,* chaps. 2 and 3.

newly imposed Roman-Hellenistic imperial culture. Those who would interpret Q sayings as calling for voluntary poverty and abandonment of home and family must explain the absurdity of addressing such a call primarily to people who were already marginal and under increasing economic pressure — that is, already mired in poverty and struggling to keep their households and village communities from disintegrating any further. It is difficult, finally, to discern how the abstract individualism of the itinerant radicalism thesis fits in any way the circumstances of first-century C.E. Galilee. Q must rather be read against the more precisely sketched background of social forms, regional and class differences, and political-economic-religious relations in Roman Palestine emerging in recent historical and archaeological studies of Galilee. This will become all the more urgent once we examine the extent to which Q is grounded in Israelite tradition and recognize that, as an oral-derived text, it would have functioned in communal contexts.

Chapter 4

THE CONTOURS OF Q

Richard A. Horsley _____

The Quest for Control of Q: Of Theology and Stratigraphy

How we read a document depends a great deal on the assumptions we bring to the reading and the interests we have in the reading. The assumptions that determine our reading include those about what sort of literature the document is and the kind of communication and messages we can expect from such literature. For much of the twentieth century, during the prominence of form criticism in the study of Synoptic Gospel materials, Q was used mainly as a source of individual Jesus sayings. Little attention was paid to Q itself as a document. It was viewed mainly as the Synoptic Sayings Source. So long as New Testament studies still assumed a monolithic early Christianity, interest focused on the early Christian kerygma of Christ's crucifixion and resurrection, as articulated in Paul's letters, early Christian preaching, and the Gospel of Mark. Insofar as Q was viewed as a document at all, it occupied a subordinate role as catechetical material for instruction of early Christians supplemental to the preaching of the gospel.[1] In the last generation, however, Q came to be understood as a distinctive message of and about Jesus different from that in the Gospel of Mark, even as it continued to be analyzed as a collection of sayings.[2] Debates about the distinctive message of Q, however, are finally leading to the recognition that Q is not a collection of sayings but a series of speeches or discourses.[3]

Much of the scholarly energy devoted to the form and message of Q during the last generation has focused on a hypothesis about a hypothesis. The very existence of Q is a hypothesis, that the Gospels of Matthew and Luke must have depended on a common source for their common materials that they did not derive from Mark. In recent decades specialists on Q have proposed various versions of a hypothesis that Q was produced in two or more layers of sayings that

---

1. See the convenient summary and documentation in John S. Kloppenborg, "The Sayings Gospel Q," in *Q-Thomas Reader*, ed. John S. Kloppenborg et al. (Sonoma, Calif.: Polebridge, 1990), 17–18.

2. Summaries in James M. Robinson, "The Q Trajectory: Between John and Matthew via Jesus," in *The Future of Early Christianity: Essays in Honor of Helmut Koester*, ed. Birger Pearson et al. (Minneapolis: Fortress, 1991), 173–94; and Kloppenborg, "Sayings Gospel Q."

3. The thrust of Richard A. Horsley, "*Logoi Prophētōn* Reflections on the Genre of Q," in Pearson et al., *The Future of Early Christianity*, 195–209.

have distinctive characteristics and emphases, even different representations of Jesus. After sorting out the materials in Q into different layers largely on criteria of literary form and theological content, these specialists then use those layers to reconstruct different stages in the history of a Jesus movement and its theology. Although this scholarly delineation of strata as a secure basis for historical reconstruction has dominated American and, to a degree, German studies devoted to Q, it is rather narrowly based in the field of New Testament studies generally. "The revival of Q studies over the past generation took place in large part within the strand of the Bultmannian movement led by Günther Bornkamm . . . [and] documented in the work of [three of] his pupils."[4] Building on this German scholarship, Helmut Koester and James M. Robinson then laid the fundamental groundwork for delineating the different strata in Q in the 1960s.[5] They and a group of their students and others influenced by their work have focused on refining the hypothetical strata within Q (for example in the Q Seminar of the Society of Biblical Literature). It has recently been claimed that there is now a virtual consensus around the fuller elaboration and refinement of the hypothesis by John S. Kloppenborg that the formative stratum of Q was a series of sapiential clusters of sayings, which was then redacted in a secondary layer of judgmental prophetic and apocalyptic sayings, followed finally by a tertiary layer that added such materials as the temptation story.[6]

Critical Examination of Recent Stratigraphy of Q

Kloppenborg articulates clearly the assumptions that determine his and others' analysis of Q. Although the completed Q consisted of many coherent clusters of sayings, the compositional process that led to Q began with "originally independent sayings and groups of sayings. Naturally this presupposes and builds upon the results from form-critical analysis."[7] Form-critical analysis is the type practiced in the dominant Bultmannian scholarly tradition; in Rudolf Bultmann's words, it "proceed[s] from the analysis of the particular elements of the tradition." In the case of Q this means the "originally independent sayings," almost to

---

4. Robinson, "The Q Trajectory," 182.

5. The programmatic, foundational studies are James M. Robinson, "LOGOI SOPHON: On the Gattung of Q," 71–113; Helmut Koester, "GNOMAI DIAPHOROI: The Origin and Nature of Diversification in the History of Early Christianity," 114–57; and idem, "One Jesus and Four Primitive Gospels," all in *Trajectories through Early Christianity* (Philadelphia: Fortress, 1971), 158–204.

6. John S. Kloppenborg, *The Formation of Q: Trajectories in Ancient Wisdom Collections* (Philadelphia: Fortress, 1987).

7. Kloppenborg, *Formation of Q*, 98, as he notes, adopted the assumptions and method of Dieter Lührmann, *Die Redaktion des Logienquelle*, WMANT 33 (Neukirchen-Vluyn: Neukirchener Verlag, 1969); Dieter Zeller, "Redaktionsprozesse und weckselnder 'Sitz im Leben' beim Q-Material," in *Logia: Les paroles de Jesus — the Sayings of Jesus: Memorial Joseph Coppens*, ed. Joel Delobel, BETL 59 (Leuven: Leuven University Press, 1982), 395–409; and Arland D. Jacobson, "Wisdom Christology in Q" (Ph.D. diss., Claremont Graduate School, 1978). In *The First Gospel: An Introduction to Q* (Sonoma, Calif.: Polebridge, 1992), Jacobson describes the assumptions and method of Lührmann as "the form-critical decomposition of sayings compositions" (48).

the exclusion of Bultmann's original recognition that "the life of the community must be used to render the forms [of the literary tradition] themselves intelligible."[8] Besides assuming that the sayings in Q were "originally independent" and therefore must be the starting point of analysis, Kloppenborg and others begin with the assumption that there must have been different strata in Q. Since "of course one cannot assume that the compositional themes governing one section of Q were those of the final redactor," one must apparently assume the opposite. "Hence it is necessary . . . to reconstruct one or more redactional stages."[9] Finally, like most recent scholarly investigators of Q, Kloppenborg, Koester, and Robinson assume and employ the standard conceptual apparatus of theologically grounded New Testament studies, particularly that stemming from the German scholarly tradition. The following review of Kloppenborg's elaborated hypothesis of different strata in Q and its roots in Robinson's and Koester's work on the genre of Q proceeds on the basis of their own assumptions and conceptual apparatus before raising questions about them.[10] The review will prepare the ground for an alternative approach, perspective, and hypothesis.

Kloppenborg assigns five complexes of Q sayings — Q/Luke 3:7–9, 16–17; 7:1–10, 18–35; 11:14–26, 29–32, 39–52; 12:39–59; and 17:23–35 — to the same secondary redactional stratum on the basis of three "common features" indicated by his analysis of the compositional and redactional history of the sayings and units that comprise these complexes.[11] First, the *projected audience* "consists of the impenitent and the opponents of the community preaching. . . . The target group of the final form of the Q woes and the five speeches as a whole . . . includes all of Israel."[12] Second, the *form* typical of this stratum of Q is that of *chriae* that criticize the response of "this generation" to the preaching of the kingdom and that encapsulate the *prophetic judgment sayings and apocalyptic words* "typical of this stratum."[13] Third, correspondingly preponderant in this stratum are *motifs* related to the theme of judgment, such as imminence of judgment and the parousia, with

---

8. Rudolf Bultmann, *The History of the Synoptic Tradition* (Oxford: Blackwell, 1963), 5.

9. Kloppenborg, *Formation of Q*, 98.

10. The following review builds upon my previous examinations in Richard A. Horsley, "Questions about Redactional Strata and the Social Relations Reflected in Q," 186–203, and John S. Kloppenborg's response, "The Formation of Q Revisited: A Response to Richard Horsley," 204–15, in *Society of Biblical Literature 1989 Seminar Papers*, ed. David J. Lull (Atlanta: Scholars Press, 1989); Richard A. Horsley, "*Logoi Prophētōn?* Reflections on the Genre of Q," in *The Future of Early Christianity: Essays in Honor of Helmut Koester*, ed. Birger Pearson et al. (Minneapolis: Fortress, 1991), 195–209; and idem, "Wisdom Justified by All Her Children: Examining Allegedly Disparate Traditions in Q," in *Society of Biblical Literature 1994 Seminar Papers*, ed. Eugene H. Lovering (Atlanta: Scholars Press, 1994), 733–51. Cf. parallel criticisms of the stratigraphy of Q in Christopher M. Tuckett, "On the Stratification of Q," *Semeia* 55 (1991): 213–22; idem, *Q and the History of Early Christianity: Studies on Q* (Peabody, Mass.: Hendrickson, 1996), 52–75, esp. 71–72; and John J. Collins, "Wisdom, Apocalypticism, and Generic Compatibility," in *In Search of Wisdom: Essays in Memory of John H. Gammie*, ed. Leo G. Perdue et al. (Louisville: Westminster/John Knox, 1993), 165–87.

11. Kloppenborg, *Formation of Q*, 166–70.

12. Ibid., 167.

13. Ibid., 169.

Israel obstinately rejecting John, Jesus, and the Q preachers while the Gentiles respond positively, thus highlighting Israel's unfaithfulness.[14]

These same three common features function prominently throughout Kloppenborg's analysis of particular sayings as the criteria according to which this secondary redactional stratum of Q is determined. Thus Q appears to have a "polemic against Israel's lack of recognition," and "Israel is guilty of rejecting God's envoys" (etc.),[15] while certain texts "speak of actual Gentile belief," and "the theme of Gentile response and faith occurs in Q" with frequency, such that Q can be seen to have an "interpretation of Gentile faith as an *Unheilszeichen* for Israel."[16] Certain sayings are found to be "apocalyptic predictions" or "apocalyptic judgment" or "eschatological" events.[17] Similarly, in this stratum of Q one supposedly finds apocalyptic *topoi* such as "war" and the "division of families" and apocalyptic motifs such as "nearness of the end," the parousia, and "impending catastrophe."[18]

When one closely examines the complexes of sayings assigned to this redactional stratum of Q, however, it is difficult to find the "common features" used as the criteria for distinguishing it from the supposedly primary layer. With regard to *projected audience*, little of the material in these five complexes in fact appears to be "directed at the 'outgroup'" of the impenitent and the opponents. Indeed, only one of the five clusters as a whole, Q/Luke 11:14–26, 29–32, 39–52, appears to be clearly directed at the outgroup of this generation as the ostensive or implied audience. The majority of the material in these clusters consists of rationalizations, exhortations, and particularly sanctions directed at the in-group of Jesus' followers (the Q people) themselves (7:18–23, 24–28; 12:39–46, 51–53, 57–59; 17:23–35) or is not particularly threatening in the first place (11:14–26). The only sayings that could possibly be understood as rationalizations of the rejection and persecution encountered by Q preachers are 11:29–32 and 49–51, and perhaps 3:7–9 and 7:31–35. But there is no reason internal to these Q passages to think that "this generation" refers to Israel as opposed to Gentiles. The only occurrence of "Israel" is in 7:9. Here, in this one saying, one Gentile responds positively to Jesus. Yet the point of the story in Q 7:2, 6–9 is not to exemplify a mission to Gentiles,[19] but to challenge or embarrass Israel into fuller response. Except for this reading of Q 7:2, 6–9, there is no indication in Q of "actual Gentile belief." Q 11:31–32 cites the traditions of the Queen of the South's response to Solomon's wisdom and the Ninevites' response to Jonah's preaching as historical prototypes for or contrasts to the response of "this generation" to "something greater," but not as Gentile response to Jesus or preaching of the

---

14. Ibid.

15. Ibid., 120, 147; see also 119, 125, 127, 236–37, 238.

16. Ibid., 236, 119–20; see also 193, 196, 226.

17. Ibid., 103, 108, 128, etc.

18. Ibid., *topoi*, 151; nearness of the end, 152, 155, 166; parousia, 102, 150, 152, 163, 165; catastrophe, 152–53, 164.

19. As Kloppenborg admits in *Formation of Q*, 119.

kingdom. Q 10:13–15 does not "predict Gentile faith" but offers a hypothetical contrast to the lack of repentance in two particular towns (and not "Israel"). Q 13:28–29 speaks of the eschatological gathering of a dispersed Israel (as can be seen by comparison with Judean texts such as Ps. 107:3; Isa. 27:12–13; 43:5–6; Hos. 11:11; Zech. 8:7–8; 10:10; Bar. 4:4; 5:5; *1 Enoch* 57:1; *Pss. Sol.* 11:2–3), not "an actual Gentile mission."[20] There is simply no basis in Q for "Gentile faith" as a significant theme, let alone its interpretation as an *Unheilszeichen* for Israel.

As for the "common feature" of *form*,[21] only one of the *chriae* listed (11:29 + 31–32) actually criticizes the response of "this generation" to the preaching of the kingdom. Moreover, of the sayings that these *chriae* "encapsulate," while many are "prophetic sayings," only one of them (17:23–24) appears to be classifiable as what Bultmannian form criticism would label "apocalyptic words," and only three of the nine sayings that supposedly articulate a threat seem actually to do so (i.e., possibly 12:39, 54–55; and 17:37b; but not 11:20, 23, 24–26, 33, 34, 36; and 12:57–58). Although Kloppenborg views Q as ultimately composed of clusters of sayings or speeches, his characterization and categorization generally proceed by individual sayings, as if they were the basic intelligible unit of communication and meaning.

The third supposedly common feature of apocalyptic *motifs* is even less in evidence in the sayings clusters designated as a secondary stratum in Q. The notion that the parousia occurs in Q comes from Matthew's reshaping of Q sayings in his eschatological discourse (Matthew 24–25). But "(the day of) the son of man" in Q/Luke 12:40; 17:24, 26, 30 is a symbol for the judgment and not a reference to an individual figure of redemption/judgment or his "coming." Moreover, judgment is not particularly "imminent" in Q, except perhaps in the tone of the Baptist's preaching (3:7–9, 16–17). Q/Luke 12:54–56 does not point to "signs of the end" or "the impending catastrophe" but refers to a present crisis, and the division of families in 12:51–53, which also refers to a present crisis, is a prophetic, not an apocalyptic, motif (see Mic. 7:6).[22] Finally, only in 11:29–32 and 49–51 (and not in 7:31–35; 11:19–20, 24–26, 33–36; 12:57–59) does lack of response to John, Jesus, or Q preachers constitute grounds for condemnation. As with the projected audience, so with the motifs, there is little or no basis for the claim that Q has a polemic against Israel in contrast to the positive response of the Gentiles.

Strictly speaking, only two short passages in Q, 11:29–32 and 11:49–51, actually attest the three common features used as criteria for the secondary, judgmental layer, and then not quite in the distinctive way Kloppenborg has characterized them: that is, they are prophetic sayings (not apocalyptic sayings) in form; they contain the motif of rejection of Jesus' preaching as a basis for condemnation (but no apocalyptic traits); and they also focus on "this generation"

---

20. Cf. ibid., 119–20, 236, building on the study by Joachim Jeremias, *Jesus' Promise to the Nations* (Philadelphia: Fortress, 1982), 55–63, that became a commonplace in New Testament studies.

21. Kloppenborg, *Formation of Q*, 168–69.

22. See ibid., 151–52.

(but not "Israel") as the projected audience. It hardly seems justified, however, to assign five large complexes of sayings to a particular "redactional stratum" on the basis of only two sayings, both in the same complex, that actually manifest the "common features" used as criteria.

Most of the rest of Q (6:20–49; 9:57–62 + 10:2–16, 21–24; 11:2–4, 9–13; 12:2–12; 12:22–34; and 13:24–30) is assigned to a formative "sapiential" stratum, according to Kloppenborg's grand hypothesis, again on the criteria of the same "common features" of *audience, form,* and *motifs*.[23] The supposedly distinguishing common features, however, do not run consistently across the constituent clusters of the "formative" stratum and/or do not distinguish them from the clusters of the "redactional" stratum.

First, the clusters of the sapiential stratum cannot be differentiated from those of the judgmental stratum on the basis of *implied audience* for two principal reasons. As noted above, most of the supposedly secondary clusters are addressed to the in-group of the Q community, just like the sapiential clusters. Moreover, at least two clusters of the formative layer include material ostensibly addressed to outsiders, which must then be explained as redactional insertions (e.g., Q/Luke 10:13–15; 13:28–30, 34–35; 14:16–24). Yet that same conclusion could be drawn about certain materials in the supposedly secondary clusters (e.g., that Q/Luke 7:31–35, ostensibly directed to outsiders, is a redactional addition to 7:18–28, which is addressed to the community).

Second, the argument from characteristic *forms,* which again proceeds by characterization and categorization of individual sayings, is especially weak. In order to purify the sapiential layer, it must be purged of prophetic sayings, which are explained as later insertions. Even the material that remains, however, is not particularly sapiential "with respect to traditional forms of conventional wisdom" and appears "sapiential" only by comparison with materials in the "apocalyptic" secondary layer.[24] Since the supposedly secondary layer is not particularly apocalyptic in form, this ostensible distinction between the strata would appear to collapse. Since the supposedly formative layer contains "some rather specialized instructions which go beyond what is usually understood as sapiential admonitions," such as sayings pertaining to mission, discipleship, and the Holy Spirit,[25] there appears to be no basis for its characterization as distinctively and consistently sapiential. Even if, recognizing the inapplicability of the modern concept "apocalyptic" to Q materials, we used "prophetic" as the contrasting concept, the problem would remain. As Kloppenborg himself points out, there is fundamental unclarity in the definitions of the terms "wisdom" and "prophecy," and the Q material itself is ambiguous with regard to just such a distinction. It is pertinent to remember that form criticism originally understood *form* to include function and

---

23. The following observations respond to the summary titled "Sapiential Speeches in Q" in ibid., 238–43.

24. Burton L. Mack, "The Kingdom That Didn't Come: A History of the Q Tradents," in *Society of Biblical Literature 1988 Seminar Papers,* ed. David J. Lull (Atlanta: Scholars Press, 1988), 613.

25. Kloppenborg, *Formation of Q,* 239–40.

that in any case individual sayings must always be understood in literary context (and meaning context) and cannot be understood by purely "formal" categories.[26]

Third, the *motifs* claimed as characteristic for the supposedly formative layer, like the forms, do not run consistently across the component clusters, and it is questionable whether the texts cited actually illustrate the motifs listed. Finally, it is at least curious that while the term *sophia* (= "wisdom") does not occur in the sapiential clusters, it plays a prominent role at key points in the apocalyptic / judgmental clusters and is projected into an additional redactional judgmental saying (Q 7:35; 11:31, 49; 13:34).

Kloppenborg's elaborated hypothesis of Q strata, furthermore, does not explain the structure and the coherence of either the formative stratum or the redacted document, other than as a series of sayings clusters. The references adduced as evidence for characteristic structural features throughout the formative layer are not convincing, in some cases (12:13–14; 12:33a) not even clearly part of Q. Kloppenborg offers no principle or reason that the various "sapiential clusters" would have belonged together as a coherent formative document rather than simply functioned as separate clusters.[27] The hypothesis as developed has the judgmental materials, even clusters of them, already in circulation, apparently in the Q community, prior to their combination in the secondary layer, which was supposedly superimposed on the formative layer already in existence as a document. The developed hypothesis, however, does not adequately explain away an obvious alternative possibility: that the various clusters that supposedly constituted the formative layer were first brought together in the same redaction that joined them with the judgmental clusters, which were also brought together at that point.[28]

Arguments from the most developed hypothesis of different strata in Q thus do not stand up to critical scrutiny. The common features that supposedly characterize the sayings clusters assigned to the different strata either fail to appear in the clusters or do not appear consistently across the various clusters. The hypothesized layers cannot in fact be differentiated according to the stated criteria of these features. Not only do the clusters assigned to the apocalyptic / prophetic stratum not pronounce judgment against all Israel, but also most of them are addressed directly to the Q community itself, not outsiders, in the same way that most of the supposedly sapiential clusters are directed to the Q people. Not only does the material in the supposedly apocalyptic / judgmental clusters not take the form of apocalyptic sayings, and not only is much of the material in the sapiential stratum not particularly sapiential; in fact, much of the material in both strata would be described as prophetic according to traditional form-critical criteria of form and function.

---

26. Ibid., 37; when Kloppenborg nevertheless claims (239) that "it is the sapiential, not the prophetic, element which comes to the fore" in the hypothetical earlier stratum, he lists numerous sayings that other scholars have labeled as "prophetic."

27. Similarly, Tuckett, *Q and the History of Early Christianity*, 72–73.

28. Similarly, ibid., 72–74.

Problematic Concepts and Categories

The above examination indicates that the common features used as criteria for assigning Q materials to separate sapiential and apocalyptic/judgmental layers are not found in (or are not distinctive to) the sayings clusters that supposedly comprise those layers. This suggests that the concepts being applied are inappropriate to Q and Q materials.[29] It is precisely because of ever more sophisticated analyses of texts, such as Kloppenborg's careful investigation of the composition of Q, that we are realizing just how diverse were the communities of Jesus' followers and their understandings of Jesus. Yet we have not adjusted the conceptual apparatus of New Testament studies to accord with that diversity. It seems that we are still applying to Q materials concepts that were derived from a simpler, more synthetic earlier scholarly understanding of early Christianity that is not being expressed in Q. We may be particularly suspicious of key concepts heavily influenced by the Christian theology and christology out of which New Testament studies developed, such as the break of Christianity from Judaism, the parousia of Christ, and christological titles such as "the Son of Man." The following critique focuses on the work of Kloppenborg, Koester, and Robinson both because their work is most fundamental in the quest to discern and control different strata in Q and even more because their work also leads to other possibilities, once we question certain standard scholarly concepts in the field.

Most obviously determined by traditional Christian theology is the claim that the judgmental layer is aimed against "all Israel." In arguments to this effect, readings of Q texts are rooted in traditional constructs of Christianity as the true, universal, and spiritual religion that broke away from Judaism, which was an overly parochial and political religion — as the gospel of Christ, which the Jews rejected but the Gentiles eagerly received, overcame and displaced Judaism's overemphasis on the Law.[30] Many interpreters seem simply to assume that "this generation" (Q/Luke 7:31; 11:29–32, 50–51) refers to "(all) Israel" and that "Jerusalem" whose house is desolate (13:34–35) must be a symbol for "(all) Israel" and that the many people "coming from east and west" (13:28–29) must be Gentiles who are displacing the Israelites in the kingdom of God.[31]

There is growing awareness, however, not only that Q comes from one community or movement among a diverse range of Jesus' followers, but also that it comes from a period (50–70 C.E.) prior to the separation of self-consciously Christian groups from their origins in Israelite traditions. Q is increasingly being located

---

29. That is, the criteria used in sorting out the strata in Q are derived from modern New Testament scholarship more than from the text of Q, as suggested in Horsley, "Logoi Prophētōn?" 196. Similarly, Werner Kelber, "Jesus and Tradition: Words in Time, Words in Space," Semeia 65 (1994): 154: "Are we not operating on modern standards of literary and theological consistency if we use wisdom and apocalyptic as defining criteria for separating strata in the tradition?"

30. It is interesting that Q has recently been included in the category of "gospel."

31. Some American studies of Q during the 1980s and 1990s carry over this stereotype, deeply rooted in theologically determined New Testament scholarship, from redactional studies of Q done in the 1960s and 1970s in Germany, such as that by Lührmann (Die Redaktion der Logienquelle, 24–48), which still assumed, for example, that Q assumed the "Gentile mission."

in communities in Syria, even in Galilee, because of the Galilean place-names of Capernaum, Chorazin, and Bethsaida. Moreover, it is increasingly clear from ancient Judean sources such as Josephus's histories that the principal conflict in late second-temple Palestine was between the Judean and Galilean people, on the one hand, and their high-priestly, Herodian, and Roman rulers, on the other, compounded by regional tensions.[32] There is simply no historical warrant for reading either "Jerusalem" or "this generation" as indicating "all Israel." At least in Q 11:49–51 "this generation" refers to the scribes and Pharisees (and others in the ruling city of Jerusalem, to which prophets were repeatedly sent). Furthermore, the comparative Judean texts used to illuminate the "coming from east and west" in Q/Luke 13:28–29, such as Ps. 106(107):3 and Isa. 43:5–6, refer not to a Gentile pilgrimage but to a gathering of previously dispersed Israelites.[33] And what must have been the concluding saying in Q, Q/Luke 22:28–30, refers not negatively to the "judging" of the twelve tribes of Israel, as traditionally translated by German and English Christian translators, but positively to "effecting justice for" the twelve tribes of Israel — just as the anointed son of David effects justice for the tribes in *Pss. Sol.* 17:28–32 and the "twelve men and three priests" of the community council at Qumran were to effect righteousness and justice in the land of Israel (1QS 8:1–4).[34] The principal conflict in Q, as in second-temple Palestine generally, lies between the people and the rulers, along with the latter's scribal representatives.[35] As noted above, most of the judgmental material in Q is directed at the Q community itself, with only one of the five judgmental clusters of sayings in Q (11:14–26, 29–32, 39–52) being clearly directed ostensibly at outsiders.

No concept has figured more decisively in attempts to discern different layers in Q than the synthetic modern scholarly construct "apocalyptic(ism)." As noted above, it is used variously: for a particular form of sayings, for a set of motifs or features, and for a kind of theology, as well as for a type of literature. Confusion surrounding the uncritical use of the term "apocalyptic" stems from the way in which modern scholars, about a century ago, constructed this highly synthetic concept from Jewish literature ranging over several centuries and diverse geographical and social locations. It has then often been assumed in scholarly discourse that if a particular symbol, motif, or form, often understood in a some-

32. Explored at length in Richard A. Horsley with John S. Hanson, *Bandits, Prophets, and Messiahs* (1985; reprint, Harrisburg, Pa.: Trinity Press International, 1999); Richard A. Horsley, *Jesus and the Spiral of Violence* (San Francisco: Harper & Row, 1987); idem, *Sociology and the Jesus Movement* (New York: Crossroad, 1989); and idem, *Galilee: History, Politics, People* (Valley Forge, Pa.: Trinity Press International, 1995).

33. Richard A. Horsley, "Social Conflict in the Synoptic Sayings Source Q," in *Conflict and Invention: Literary, Rhetorical, and Social Studies on the Sayings Gospel Q*, ed. John S. Kloppenborg (Valley Forge, Pa.: Trinity Press International, 1995), 37–52, esp. 46–47; Dale C. Allison Jr., *The Jesus Tradition in Q* (Harrisburg, Pa.: Trinity Press International, 1997), 176–86.

34. Horsley, *Jesus*, 200–206.

35. Richard A. Horsley, "Q and Jesus: Assumptions, Approaches, and Analyses," *Semeia* 55 (1991): 195, 199–202; idem, "Social Conflict in the Synoptic Sayings Source Q," in Kloppenborg, *Conflict and Invention*, 37–52.

what literalistic way, has been identified as typical of apocalyptic, it carries with it and indicates an apocalyptic theology wherever it occurs. Determinative for twentieth-century interpretation of Jesus and the Gospels, the highly influential work of Johannes Weiss and particularly Albert Schweitzer persuaded many in the scholarly guild that the worldview, the teaching, and even the practice of Jesus were basically apocalyptic or "eschatological" (e.g., in expecting an imminent end of this world in a cosmic cataclysm). Their influence was compounded by that of Bultmann, which decisively shaped both the method and the theology of the field of New Testament studies. When Q began to receive more attention as a document or source in its own right after midcentury, it was understood as the principal document of Jesus' (or the early church's) apocalyptic or eschatological teaching. Finding the key in Q's apocalyptic christology, German New Testament theologians stressed that while Jesus had expected the Son of Man as a figure other than himself (Bultmann's view), the Q community identified Jesus with the Son of Man and proclaimed his imminent parousia.[36] In his widely used introduction to the New Testament, Norman Perrin treated Q as the principal example of "apocalyptic Christianity," believing that he was representing a scholarly consensus.[37] Much of the recent critical discussion of Q has focused on the "apocalyptic Son of Man sayings" that appear to play such a prominent role in Q.

It has been confidently assumed and repeatedly asserted that "Son of Man christology" was the focus of, perhaps even distinctive to, Q and the Q community.[38] " 'Son of Man' is the only christological title found in Q and was both fundamental to the community's confession of Jesus and the cause of its persecution."[39] Ironically, while investigations of the phrase "the son of man" have been recognizing that there is no basis in contemporary Judean texts for the modern concept of the apocalyptic Son of Man, particularly as a title, something similar is still being read into Q texts. It is still assumed that the phrase "the son of man" in certain texts (esp. Q 12:8-9; 17:24, 26, 30) refers to a *figure* coming in eschatological judgment and that this is understood by Q as the risen or exalted Jesus in his parousia. This image of Jesus returning as the eschatological judge is then also placed in the broader context of the modern scholarly composite apocalyptic

---

36. For example, Ernst Käsemann, "Die Anfänge christlicher Theologie," *ZTK* 57 (1960): 161–85; Eng. trans.: "The Beginnings of Christian Theology," in *New Testament Questions of Today* (London: SCM, 1969), 82–107; Heinz E. Tödt, *Der Menschensohn in der synoptischen Überlieferung* (Gütersloh: Gerd Mohn, 1959); Eng. trans.: *The Son of Man in the Synoptic Tradition* (London: SCM, 1965); Lührmann, *Redaktion der Logienquelle*; and Paul Hoffmann, *Studien zur Logienquelle*, NTAbh NF 8 (Münster: Aschendorff, 1972).

37. Norman Perrin, *The New Testament: An Introduction* (New York: Harcourt Brace Jovanovich, 1974). Cf. H. C. Kee, *Jesus in History* (New York: Harcourt, Brace, 1970), chap. 3, who argued that Q consisted largely of "eschatological materials," although he did not use the term "apocalyptic."

38. The scholarly foundation for this was laid by Tödt, *Son of Man*, 232–74, esp. 269; cf. Hoffmann, *Studien*, 82–158.

39. M. Eugene Boring, *Sayings of the Risen Jesus*, SNTSMS 46 (Cambridge: Cambridge University Press, 1982), 141; cf. Frans Neirynck, "Recent Developments in the Study of Q," in *Logia: Les paroles de Jesus*, 69–74.

scenario replete with "the delay of the parousia," the "nearness of the end," and "the impending catastrophe."[40]

The whole discussion of "the apocalyptic Son of Man" and "Son of Man christology," however, has projected a combination of the modern scholarly construct of "apocalyptic" and the theological concept of "christology" into Q, which attests neither the phrase "Son of Man" as a title of an eschatological figure nor the concept of the parousia of Jesus. In Q material, Jesus frequently uses the phrase "son of man" in reference to himself. Whatever one's conclusion about the scholarly debate concerning whether the generic use of the Aramaic phrase *bar (e)nash(a)* ("a human being" or "anyone/someone") provides a basis for a circumlocution for the speaker's self-reference ("I/me"), "the son of man" would appear to be used in the latter sense in Q 6:22; 7:34; 9:58; and 11:30. Similarly, in the light of those passages, and since Matthew 10:32 has (the emphatic) "I" in his parallel to Luke 12:8, the most obvious way to understand "son of man" in Luke 12:8–9 is as another self-reference: Jesus anticipates that he will appear as an advocate for his faithful followers in the eschatological court of judgment.[41] In Q/Luke 17:24, 26, 30, the stereotyped phrase "the day(s) of the son of man" appears as a symbolic reference to the judgment. This appears somewhat similar to, but also distinctively different from, the appearance at the divine judgment of the beastly empires of "one like a son of man" ("a human-like figure") in the dream vision of Daniel 7, where it is interpreted to mean "the people of the saints of the Most High," who are finally awarded their own sovereignty, that is, the restoration of an independent Judea/Israel. The "son of man" in Q 12:40 may be a similar symbolic reference to the judgment. Thus there is nothing in either Q 17:24, 26, 30 or in Q as a whole to indicate that "(the day of) the son of man" referred to a particular individual agent of redemption or judgment. When Jesus refers to himself with "the son of man," it is not a title. When Jesus refers to "the day of the son of man" (also not a title), it may not refer to himself. Moreover, there are also "no indications that Q represented itself to its intended audience as oracles of the Exalted Lord."[42] Since it is Matthew who introduces the concept of the "coming" of the "Son of Man," therefore, there appears to be no basis whatever in Q itself for positing the concept of "the parousia" in Q, let alone to believe that two whole sections of Q (12:39–59; 17:23–37) deal with it.[43]

Rather than question "apocalyptic" and other standard synthetic concepts inherited from previous generations of scholarship, recent studies have instead critically chipped away at the characterization of Q as apocalyptic. This enterprise, moreover, appears to be part of a general scholarly tendency in the last several decades to rescue Jesus and at least some Gospel materials from their im-

---

40. E.g., Kloppenborg, *Formation of Q*, 152–53, 162–64.

41. See now James M. Robinson, "The Son of Man in the Sayings Gospel Q," in *Tradition und Translation: Zum Problem der Interkulturellen Übersetzbarkeit religiöser Phänomene: Festschrift für Carsten Colpe zum 65. Geburtstag* (Berlin: Walter de Gruyter, 1994), 315–35.

42. Kloppenborg, *Formation of Q*, 322.

43. See ibid., 102, 150, 152, 153, 157, 163, 165.

prisonment in the modern scholarly construct of ancient Jewish apocalypticism, with which contemporary scholars are uncomfortable.

One way of critically chipping away at the previous understanding of Q as apocalyptic has been to notice more critically than before that little of the material in Q actually fits the typical features that constitute the synthetic scholarly construct of apocalyptic. In one of the most discerning examples of this approach, Kloppenborg lays out a catalogue of the "characteristic features" of "apocalypticism," in a way long since standard in the field, and then checks Q materials for their appearance.[44] He then finds that "much of the specialized vocabulary of apocalypticism and even some of its central presuppositions are absent from large portions of Q" and that "in those sections which do reflect apocalyptic idiom" Q is restrained and selective.[45] Even continuing to work with such a synthetic concept of apocalypticism, however, such findings are a considerable understatement of how completely Q lacks apocalyptic features. The distinctively Pauline and Matthean notion of the parousia is missing in Q[46] — and questionable as a standard feature of apocalypticism. It is also difficult to find "apocalyptic" features such as "historical determinism" in a text such as Q 10:23–24 or "the catastrophic destruction of the world by fire and flood" in texts such as Q 3:9, 17; 12:49 (in Q?); and 17:29.[47] With respect to the quest for different layers in Q, if even "those sections of Q that supposedly do reflect apocalyptic idiom" are restrained and selective and the nonapocalyptic "sapiential" sections of Q are also pervaded by an "eschatological tenor,"[48] it would seem that precious few apocalyptic forms and motifs remain as the differentiating features.

Reading such texts as Q 3:9, 17; 10:23–24; and 17:29 apocalyptically, however, almost certainly results from the way in which the composite concept of apocalypticism, constructed a century ago, has shaped our discernment. Instead of measuring Q materials against a list of "characteristic features" of "apocalypticism," we should question the standard procedure of categorizing materials by such broad synthetic concepts in the first place. Indeed, it is not clear that Judean apocalyptic literature itself would measure up to the synthetic scholarly construct. A more appropriate procedure would be to compare Q as a whole or particular coherent sections of it with particular Judean apocalyptic documents prior to or contemporary with Q, such as sections of Daniel, sections of 1 Enoch, or the Testament of Moses. Were we to proceed in this way, for example, it would not be

---

44. John S. Kloppenborg, "Symbolic Eschatology and the Apocalypticism of Q," HTR 80 (1987): 294–95.

45. Ibid., 292, 296–303. Arland D. Jacobson, "Apocalyptic and the Synoptic Sayings Source Q," in The Four Gospels 1992: Festschrift for Frans Neirynck, ed. Van Segroek et al. (Leuven: Leuven University Press, 1992), 403–19, goes even further in questioning the presence of "apocalyptic" elements and perspective in Q, yet still allows passages that are "arguably apocalyptic in outlook and formulation," and still applies the concept of "parousia" despite the absence of the term itself.

46. Once it is recognized as Matthew's reformulation of "Son of Man" sayings in Q/Luke 17:23–37; cf. Kloppenborg, "Symbolic Eschatology," 296, 300, 302.

47. Cf. ibid., 296; on "cataclysmic destruction," see John S. Kloppenborg, "The Sayings Gospel Q and the Quest for the Historical Jesus," HTR 89 (1996): 339.

48. Kloppenborg, "Symbolic Eschatology," 291–92.

surprising that in Q there is "only passing reference to the motif of cosmic transformation" because such motifs do not occur with "high frequency" in Judean apocalyptic literature, especially not in documents prior to the time of Q.[49]

The more prominent way of critically chipping away at the understanding of Q as apocalyptic — which is often also a way of attempting to save Jesus from perceived imprisonment in a seemingly fanatical ancient worldview — has been to establish the apocalyptic or judgmental features of Q as secondary to the original nonapocalyptic Q or Q material. Some of Bultmann's influential students insisted, contrary to Schweitzer's and Bultmann's view, that Jesus' teachings had been nonapocalyptic and that only the post-Easter experiences of Jesus as the exalted Lord had introduced the fervent apocalypticism that led to "the beginnings of Christian theology."[50] While Jesus had preached the kingdom of God, moreover, the expectation of the coming Son of Man (identified with Jesus), the central apocalyptic element in Jesus traditions, arose among his followers after his crucifixion-resurrection.[51] Several redactional studies then offered various hypotheses of how collection(s) of Jesus' sayings behind Q had been edited with a focus on apocalyptic judgment pronounced on Israel[52] and/or the expectation of Jesus' parousia as the judgmental Son of Man.[53] Koester's and Robinson's analysis of Q combined this distinction between nonapocalyptic materials in Q and their apocalyptic redaction with a suggestive thesis about the formative genre of Q, a combination upon which Kloppenborg built his grand hypothesis of Q layers (discussed further below).

This line of analysis, however, continued to use, indeed reinforced, the synthetic scholarly construct of "apocalyptic," now placing it in dichotomy with a similarly synthetic construct of "wisdom." A key paragraph from this approach articulates the conceptual dichotomy that has come to inform much of dominant American discussion of Q. When one tries to determine the literary genre of Q,

---

49. Cf. ibid., 299–300. Kloppenborg's passing reference to "a coherent scenario of imminent cosmic transformation" that can be deduced from Mark 13 (ibid., 304–6), in which he must have in mind the reference to "natural disasters and astral events" (Mark 13:8, 24–25; Rev. 6:12–17; Did. 16:6), provides a good illustration of the perpetuation of the synthetic modern construct. Upon close examination of these texts, however, it is difficult to find "cosmic transformation." Mark 13:24–25, which alludes to Isa. 13:10, picks up Israelite prophetic traditions about how awesome will be "the day of the Lord" in judgment. This tradition was continued in certain Judean apocalypses, such as Testament of Moses 10, where again it refers to the awesome theophany of God coming in judgment, but is hardly meant to be taken literally as "cosmic catastrophe." Didache 16:6 refers to "the sign spread out in heaven" but not to any "cosmic transformation." And as a note on Rev. 6:12–14 in the New Oxford Annotated Bible explains (apparently in attempting to "deconstruct" the old synthetic construct), "the cosmic catastrophes are not to be understood literally, but represent social upheavals and divine judgment on the Day of the Lord (Isa. 34:4; Joel 2:30–31; Amos 8:9)." It is thus difficult to understand exactly what it is in Q that constitutes "the apocalyptic language of Q" or "Q's apocalypticism."

50. Käsemann, "Beginnings of Christian Theology," 82–107.

51. Philipp Vielhauer, "Gottesreich und Menschensohn in der Verkündigung Jesu" (1957); and idem, "Jesus und der Menschensohn" (1963), both reprinted in Aufsätze zum Neuen Testament (Munich: Kaiser, 1965), 55–91, 92–140.

52. Odil Hannes Steck, Israel und das gewaltsame Geschick der Propheten, WMANT 23 (Neukirchen-Vluyn: Neukirchener Verlag, 1967); Lührmann, Die Redaktion der Logienquelle.

53. Hoffmann, Studien.

On the one hand, wisdom materials are obvious. In addition to proverbs and rules for right conduct, there are I-sayings in which Jesus speaks in the first person with the voice of Wisdom (Matt. 11:25–30) and even a quotation from wisdom material (Luke 11:49–51). On the basis of such materials, the *Synoptic Sayings Source* would have to be identified as a wisdom book, comparable to such works as the Wisdom of Solomon. On the other hand, a number of sayings reveal a very different theological orientation which is more clearly evident in the sayings about the coming Son of Man (Luke 17:22–32). This eschatological expectation has its ultimate origin in the Book of Daniel. It appropriately dominates the Synoptic Apocalypse (Mark 13). Among the wisdom sayings of the *Synoptic Sayings Source*, it is a foreign element. If the genre of the wisdom book was the catalyst for the composition of sayings of Jesus into a "gospel," and if the christological concept of Jesus as the teacher of wisdom and as the presence of heavenly Wisdom dominated its creation, the apocalyptic orientation of the *Synoptic Sayings Source* with its christology of the coming Son of Man is due to a secondary redaction of an older wisdom book.[54]

The label "apocalyptic" is no longer being used as a conceptual umbrella that includes most Q materials. Yet the conceptual confusion that results from perpetuation of such broad synthetic constructs to describe theologies and christologies as well as literary forms and motifs, compounded by the dichotomizing between "apocalyptic" and "wisdom," is immediately evident from a comparison with Kloppenborg's hypothesis of the Q layers. The supposed quotation from wisdom material (Q 11:49–51), the other explicit reference to Wisdom (Q 7:35), and the other texts where Wisdom supposedly speaks (Q 13:34–35) constitute key components of the secondary apocalyptic stratum. On the other hand, the saying where Jesus supposedly speaks with the voice of Wisdom (Matt. 11:25–27 // Luke 10:21–22), which is located squarely in the sapiential layer, displays the most explicitly apocalyptic language in Q, with Jesus giving thanks that God has "hidden these things" specifically from "the wise"! If Wisdom appears in "apocalyptic" or prophetic sayings and "sapiential" sayings use apocalyptic language against the sages, then the criteria of categorization require critical attention.[55]

In a number of important respects, analyses of Q in recent decades have repeatedly peeled away or broken through standard theologically determined concepts, rooted in a simpler older paradigm of how Christianity emerged from Judaism, to discern a distinctive aspect of Q or Q materials. No longer viewed as a catechetical supplement to the Pauline crucifixion-resurrection kerygma and the Gospel of Mark, for example, Q could be seen as a document from a distinctive community with its own distinctive views of Jesus. Once it was recognized that Q made no mention of the crucifixion or resurrection, there was no reason to view Q materials as the sayings of the risen Jesus / exalted Lord. That same breakthrough should lead to the recognition that the concept of the parousia, found

---

54. Helmut Koester, "Apocryphal and Canonical Gospels," *HTR* 73 (1980): 112–13.

55. The confusion that results from the use of such vague dichotomized concepts can be further illustrated from Robinson's recent survey of Q scholarship, "The Q Trajectory," 188: "For Lührmann, the sapiential layer responsible for the genre *logoi sophon* was the latest layer, for here Sophia christology is presupposed (Q 7:35; 10:21–22; 11:31–3, 49–51; 13:34–35)."

only in Matthew's version of certain sayings, is inappropriate to Q. It should now be possible, similarly, to cut through other aspects of the standard older paradigm of "Christianity's" origin and break from "Judaism" and recognize, for example, that Q does not refer to or presuppose a Gentile mission, indeed that Q remains within Israelite tradition, with no distinctively "Christian" features, since Christianity could not be said to have come into existence yet historically. The Christian theological concept of christology may be inappropriate to Q, especially insofar as it has connotations of a "Messiah" or "exalted Lord" or "Son of Man" and other traditional concepts or titles that were included in that synthetic Christian construct. Similarly, it seems appropriate to abandon standard synthetic scholarly constructs that have become problematic, such as "apocalyptic" or "sapiential." Certainly it seems inappropriate to allow such concepts to become determinative or definitive in historical analysis. Such vague concepts, whose referents are various and uncertain, may well block more than they facilitate insight and discernment.[56]

Considerations of Genre

Discovery and intensive study of the Gnostic Gospels from Nag Hammadi strongly reinforced the tendency to drive a wedge between the "apocalyptic-judgmental" and the "sapiential" materials in Q. Insofar as the *Gospel of Thomas* provided an actual document presenting a random collection of the sayings of Jesus, only some of which were paired or grouped by form or *Stichwort*, it reinforced the treatment of Q as a collection of sayings. More decisively, the *Gospel of Thomas* was also construed as a model according to which a formative "sapiential" layer in Q could be differentiated from a later, "apocalyptic" redaction.

In his influential essay "LOGOI SOPHON: On the Gattung of Q," Robinson took his cue from the occurrence of *logoi* in the opening clause of the text and again in sayings 1, 19, and 38, apparently in reference to the contents of the document.[57] Accepting this as an indication of the genre of the *Gospel of Thomas*, he named it *logoi sophon*, "sayings of the sages" or "words of the wise." He then suggested that the genre has a Gnostic tendency on the basis of the occurrence of "secret sayings" as self-designations in certain other Gnostic documents from Nag Hammadi, such as the *Book of Thomas the Contender* and *Pistis Sophia*.[58] Noting that *logoi* is used in various early Christian literature for collections of Jesus' sayings as well as

---

56. Tuckett, *Q and the History of Early Christianity*, esp. 330–37, points out that some of the most prominent interpretations of Q materials as sapiential have devoted little attention to defining wisdom / sapiential. He voices similar reservations about recent discussions of apocalyptic or eschatological aspects of Q. I am suggesting that it makes no sense to perpetuate a scholarly procedure that classifies sayings, motifs, or ideas according to such synthetic and vague concepts as apocalyptic / ism or sapiential / wisdom. Rather, specific comparisons of particular documents or texts can be made with other particular documents or texts, with both evaluated critically in their respective historical social contexts.

57. Robinson, "LOGOI SOPHON: On the Gattung of Q." Despite the subtitle, Robinson's agenda was as much or more focused on the *Gospel of Thomas* and scholarly debate about it as on Q itself, as he explains retrospectively in his foreword to Kloppenborg, *Formation of Q*, xii–xiii.

58. Robinson, "LOGOI SOPHON," 76–85.

individual sayings,[59] he also suggested that the genre of sayings of the sages was already well-established in Jewish wisdom literature, as is evident particularly in the collection of sayings by sages and early rabbis in the Mishnah tractate *Abot* and in the *Testaments of the Twelve Patriarchs*, seven of which are referred to as *logoi* (indicating the overlap with the genre of testament), as well as in the earlier collections that constitute the book of Proverbs.[60]

In a groundbreaking study of the newly discovered *Gospel of Thomas* and its seeming parallels with the recently rediscovered Q, Koester, who was well acquainted with the recent German discussion of the coming Son of Man as the distinctive apocalyptic christology of Q, used the *Gospel of Thomas* as a model for distinguishing a formative collection in Q from its later apocalyptic redaction.[61] The *Gospel of Thomas*, which conspicuously lacked apocalyptic Son of Man sayings, provided a secure written case of the genre *logoi sophon*, in which wisdom sayings were supposedly typical. Koester argued that it represented an earlier stage in the development of the collection of Jesus' sayings than that represented by Q, in which the apocalyptic Son of Man sayings are prominent.[62] Given the typical wisdom character and Gnostic tendency of the genre, as illustrated by the *Gospel of Thomas*, Q apparently represented the attempt to block that tendency by framing it with an apocalyptic Son of Man christology.

Koester's discussion of the *Gospel of Thomas* and the "original" Q as examples of *logoi sophon*, however, involved some significant shifts in the original hypothesis of the genre. Robinson assumed that Q represented an earlier stage than the *Gospel of Thomas* in the use of the genre in the collection of Jesus' sayings. Correspondingly, he also apparently thought that because of "the wisdom implications" of the genre taken by Q, the direction of development went from "the apocalyptic context that may have predominated in Jesus' sayings" (through the stage of a collection of "words of wisdom") "to a wisdom context predominating in the sayings in Matthew," which has close affinities with the genre, and eventually toward Gnostic wisdom.[63] Koester imagines rather that "wisdom sayings" were "typical" in the very formation of Q, which he calls a "wisdom gospel,"[64] with apocalyptic sayings, particularly of the Son of Man, having been superimposed to effectively block its movement toward the Gnostic tendencies of the genre.

---

59. Ibid., 85–103.

60. Ibid., 105–10.

61. Koester, "GNOMAI DIAPHOROI," 135–40; and esp. idem, "One Jesus," 166–87.

62. His own construal of the *Gospel of Thomas* is virtually the only criterion Koester used for distinguishing earlier and later parts of Q. In retrospect, Tuckett comments that in Koester's "appeal to GTh he appears to assume what perhaps needs to be proved, i.e., that GTh is both independent of the synoptics and is also a pure form of the genre to which Q is supposed to belong . . . before being secondarily adulterated" (*Q and the History of Early Christianity*, 67–68). Also in "Q and Thomas: Evidence of a Primitive 'Wisdom Gospel'?" *Ephemerides theologicae lovanienses* 67 (1991): 346–60, Tuckett reviews critically Koester's recent restatement of his thesis that the *Gospel of Thomas* represents an earlier stage in the development of Jesus' sayings than Q, concluding that in the key parallels, *Thomas*'s version appears to be secondary to the critically reconstructed Q version.

63. Robinson, "LOGOI SOPHON," 112.

64. Koester, "Apocryphal and Canonical Gospels," 113.

As he explains in his introductory chapter, Kloppenborg[65] built his fully developed hypothesis of Q strata on the groundwork laid by Robinson in defining the genre *logoi sophon* and by Koester in using the *Gospel of Thomas* as a comparative model of that genre to distinguish the formative document of Q from its later, redactional edition. Kloppenborg's understanding of the genre *logoi sophon* as a written document and as consisting almost completely of wisdom sayings also involves a shift from Robinson's understanding of the genre as functioning at the stage of oral transmission and as comprised of a wide range of sayings materials that developed in the wisdom direction because of their inclusion in the genre.[66] Kloppenborg's hypothesis of strata in Q depends upon wisdom sayings being sufficiently incompatible with apocalyptic and prophetic judgmental sayings that they can serve as distinguishing features of the separate strata. Robinson, on the other hand, apparently thought that the movement he imagined from the apocalyptic context of Jesus' sayings to the wisdom context dominating Matthew was intelligible "in view of the emerging scholarly awareness that apocalypticism and wisdom, rather than being at almost mutually exclusive extremes within the spectrum of Jewish alternatives, share certain affinities and congruencies that encourage a transition from one to the other."[67]

A critical review of the evidence on the basis of which Robinson posited the genre *logoi sophon* and of the way in which Koester used it in interpretation of Q and the *Gospel of Thomas*, however, suggests that it does not provide a solid enough foundation to support the elaborate superstructure of Q strata erected upon it. This conclusion arises from several observations.

First, all but one of the many Christian and Jewish texts cited as illustrations or indications of a genre *logoi sophon* contain only the term *logoi*. The only occurrence of the combination *logoi sophon* comes in the Septuagint version of the superscription to the collection of sayings in Prov. 22:17–24:22. In naming his "Gattung" *logoi sophon,* Robinson evidently took his cue not necessarily from Prov. 22:17 but from Bultmann's designation of the synoptic tradition of "*logia* in the narrower sense [as] wisdom sayings."[68] If we look at the actual contents and forms of the sayings included in collections of or references to *logoi* / "words," however, it is evident that the term "words" was inclusive of a far broader range of materials than merely proverbial wisdom sayings. For example, among the documents listed as examples of "Jewish wisdom literature" are the sections of *1 (Ethiopic) Enoch,* usually classified as apocalyptic literature, and the "testaments" that constitute the *Testaments of the Twelve Patriarchs*. All but one of the six originally independent works that comprise *1 Enoch* are usually classified as apocalypses in literary genre.[69] The "words of wisdom" in the Book of Watchers (*1 Enoch* 1–36) and in the Similitudes (*1 Enoch* 37–71) focus on visions, heavenly journeys, angels, and

---

65. Kloppenborg, *Formation of Q.*

66. Robinson, "logoi sophon," 102–3, 112.

67. Ibid., 112.

68. Ibid., 71–74.

69. John J. Collins, "The Jewish Apocalypses," *Semeia* 14 (1979): 31, 32, 37–40, 45.

eschatological judgment and salvation. Even the exhortations of the Epistle of Enoch, which is the section of *1 Enoch* closest to Q in form and content, are framed by and inseparable from eschatological woes, judgment, and promises of rewards and punishment. Similarly, the *logoi* in the *Testament of Levi* include "a heavenly journey (chaps 2–5), which contains an eschatological prophecy of judgment and salvation (chap 4), and a vision of the heavenly temple and the Most High on a throne of glory (chap 5)"; and the *logoi* in the *Testament of Judah* contain "both ex-hortation of a proverbial wisdom type (chaps 13–19) and apocalyptic eschatology (chaps 24–25)."[70] It is thus not an accurate representation of Jewish documents that refer to themselves as "sayings" to designate them more narrowly as examples of *logoi sophon*, "sayings of the sages," if that implies that they have "wisdom implications" or that proverbial wisdom sayings are "typical" of the supposed genre. The designation *logoi* / words / sayings also referred to what has standardly been classified as apocalyptic disclosures, exhortations, and judgmental materials.

Second, to label the supposed genre *logoi sophon* is also inaccurate, even mis-leading, with regard to the uses of *logoi* in early Christian literature as a designation for Jesus' sayings. *Logoi* refers to Jesus' sayings in the context of the traditional Jewish covenantal "two-ways" teaching in *Did.* 1:3, to Jesus' covenantal discourse in the Matthean sermon (Matt. 7:28), and to Jesus' apocalyptic sayings and ex-hortations in the Matthean eschatological discourse in Matthew 24–25 (Matt. 26:1). In *1 Clement* the *logoi* of Jesus are covenantal teaching in 13:1–2 and pro-phetic threats and woes in 46:7–8 (similar to those in Q!). Justin Martyr uses *logoi* frequently as a virtual quotation formula for prophetic sayings from the Jewish Scriptures (*Dial.* 31.2; 39.4; 62.3; 79.3) and for a sequence of sayings of Jesus, similarly understood as prophecy (*Dial.* 76.5). He also uses the similar term *logia* for sayings of Jesus quoted in a sequence of prophetic *logia* (*Dial.* 18.1). Judging from the material included in these references to collections of the *logoi* of Jesus, a supposed genre would have to be called "covenantal-prophetic sayings," not "sayings of the sages."

Indeed, third, an analysis of the contents and types of sayings included in the *Gospel of Thomas* leads to somewhat the same conclusion. Although Koester, perhaps influenced by the designation *logoi sophon*, asserts that "wisdom sayings" were typical of the genre, his original survey of the sayings included in *Thomas* by standard form-critical types suggests that the materials were quite diverse.[71] His more recent review of materials in *Thomas* then reinforces the impression that, if anything, prophetic sayings and parables and community rules were more promi-nent in the sayings tradition leading to *Thomas* than wisdom sayings proper.[72] Of the 114 *logia* in *Thomas*, around twenty (plus or minus, depending on individ-

---

70. Adela Yarbro Collins, "The Son of Man Sayings in the Sayings Source," in *To Touch the Text: Festschrift for Joseph A. Fitzmyer, S.J.*, ed. M. P. Horgan and P. J. Kobelski (New York: Crossroad, 1989), 372.

71. Koester, "One Jesus," 167–86.

72. Helmut Koester, *Ancient Christian Gospels* (Philadelphia: Trinity Press International, 1990), 80–128.

ual classification) consist of proverbs and other wisdom sayings. Prophetic and apocalyptic materials, however, including kingdom sayings and parables and the other, largely prophetic parables taken together, comprise nearly half of the contents of *Thomas* as a whole. "I-sayings" and what in pre-*Thomas* tradition were "community rules" have roughly the same frequency as wisdom sayings, and what are apparently "Gnostic" materials are more extensive than the wisdom sayings. Among the "prophetic and apocalyptic" materials that dominate the collection, moreover, are several that are apocalyptic in motif or could be classified as "apocalyptic" sayings, even when we are careful to follow Bultmann's more restrictive usage of that category.[73] Thus although *Thomas* lacks "apocalyptic Son of Man" sayings, it includes sayings that are reminiscent of motifs otherwise distinctive of apocalyptic literature proper, concerning the heavens passing away or being rolled up (11, 111), speculation about the fate or end of the dead and the new world (e.g., 18, 51; cf. 19, 85), and elements known through Paul (17; cf. 1 Cor. 2:8–9). Indeed, although *Thomas* lacks "apocalyptic Son of Man" sayings, it contains more apocalyptic material and more vividly apocalyptic material than does Q (on the more critical reading by comparison with Jewish apocalyptic literature suggested above).[74] Most prominent of all the materials in *Thomas* — more "typical" — appear to be the prophetic sayings, particularly those that have parallels in Q, and a remarkable number of parables, particularly parables of the kingdom and/or those with parallels in Mark.

Fourth, the prophetic sayings also appear to be more important than the wisdom sayings in discerning the "hermeneutics" of the *Gospel of Thomas*. Meaning in *Thomas* does not appear to lie in the composition of the document, the ordering of materials seeming somewhat random. It is apparent, moreover, that *Thomas* does not assume that each saying has meaning in itself. The sayings require reflection or pondering to penetrate their meaning, as indicated in the very first saying: "He who finds the meaning of these words shall not taste death." To help the seeker of "life," the composition has at points included clues in the form of brief additional phrases (compare saying 16 with its parallel in Q/Luke 12:51–53, and saying 78 with its parallels in Q/Luke 7:24–25). Koester finds *Thomas*'s distinctive understanding of self and the world not in its wisdom sayings but in its specially interpreted apocalyptic and prophetic sayings such as 3, 51, and 52, or in sayings with affinities to Johannine materials such as 29, 49, and 50.[75]

---

73. As suggested above, in some scholarly discourse, "apocalyptic sayings" has become a rather vague and loose category. Koester, "One Jesus," 168–75, 213–19, appears to be using Bultmann's collective "apocalyptic and prophetic sayings," sometimes without closely distinguishing prophetic from apocalyptic sayings.

74. That these apocalyptic sayings were reinterpreted in the *Gospel of Thomas* as we have it does not undermine but rather underlines the point. It means that what are properly categorized as apocalyptic sayings and motifs remained integral components of the tradition leading to *Thomas* and were adapted rather than eliminated in *Thomas* itself. It is further indicative of the hermeneutics of *Thomas* that what appears to be a typical apocalyptic motif of the end being the same as the beginning (18) and a statement of seemingly "realized eschatology" (51) and a saying that rejects apocalyptic-style calculations (113, parallel to Luke 17:20–21) can stand in the same collection of sayings.

75. Koester, *Ancient Christian Gospels*, 82–83, 124–26. Also more important than the wisdom say-

Moreover, fifth, Koester's recent review of sayings materials in both the *Gospel of Thomas* and Q suggests that the earlier claim that *Thomas* provides a basis for discerning a formative wisdom collection underneath a later redacted document may be questionable. Koester's recent review also suggests that the supposedly separate layers in Q cannot be characterized simply as "sapiential" vs. "apocalyptic." If we do not count passages which were not clearly included in Q, then thirty-eight or thirty-nine sayings or passages in Q have parallels in *Thomas*. Of these, by Koester's classification, fourteen (or fifteen) are wisdom sayings or proverbs, twelve (or thirteen) are prophetic sayings, seven are community rules, and five are parables. When we examine how these parallels fall relative to Kloppenborg's assignment of Q sayings to the respective "sapiential" and "apocalyptic / judgmental" strata, however, no striking distinctions emerge. The quantity of parallel material in *Thomas* falls fairly evenly between "Q1" (roughly seventy-five lines of Coptic text) and "Q2" (roughly eighty-five lines), with virtually every cluster in both hypothetical strata having one or two parallels and the large clusters having the most (the thirty verses in Q/Luke 6:20–49 having twenty-eight lines parallel in *Thomas*, while the eighteen lines in Q/Luke 12:39–59 have twenty-four lines parallel in *Thomas*). Moreover, the clusters of the "sapiential" layer include prophetic (five) as well as wisdom sayings (eleven) among *Thomas* parallels, while the "apocalyptic" stratum includes wisdom sayings (three) as well as prophetic sayings (seven) among *Thomas* parallels — just as particular *Thomas* logia include both. The parallels of parables and community rules are also distributed across the hypothetical layers of Q. The presence of apocalyptic materials (although not apocalyptic Son of Man) in *Thomas* appears to eliminate the basis on which Koester and Kloppenborg posited a formative collection of sayings featuring wisdom antecedent to the final form of Q. Koester's recent review of the parallel sayings in Q and *Thomas* indicates further that there is nothing in the character or distribution of the *Thomas* parallels (such as a strikingly greater number of *Thomas* parallels to the hypothetical sapiential layer) that would support the hypothesis of separation of Q into different layers.

Sixth, despite his ostensible adoption of the redactional hypothesis of Lührmann and Kloppenborg, Koester's interpretive comments on Q materials repeatedly qualify or even undermine that "stratigraphy" of Q in such significant ways as to call it into question.[76] The inaugural sermon, "a mixture of wisdom

ings for discerning *Thomas*'s hermeneutics are the interpretations of the many "community rules" (127–28). Corresponding to the esoteric theology of coming to know one's true self in the symbolism of realizing "the kingdom" and attaining "rest" or "wealth" or being a "solitary one" is the rejection of ordinary social and familiar bonds, as can be seen in *Thomas*'s transformations of certain "community rules" in sayings 6, 14a, 95, 110. What Gerd Theissen, *Sociology of Early Palestinian Christianity* (Philadelphia: Fortress, 1978), and others have been saying about the "radical" lifestyle supposedly espoused in Q had long since been seen by Koester in the *Gospel of Thomas* (see Helmut Koester, "One Jesus and Four Primitive Gospels," originally published in *HTR* 61 [1968]: 229).

76. Koester, *Ancient Christian Gospels*, 134–35, 149–50. Koester's qualifications of and chipping away at the secondary "apocalyptic / prophetic" stratum as delineated by Kloppenborg thus undermine the overall hypothesis of strata in a way parallel to those of Burton L. Mack, *The Lost Gospel: The*

and prophetic sayings," is not so much a "sapiential speech" as a "prophetic . . . announcement of the presence of the rule of God."[77] The second speech assigned to the "sapiential" layer, moreover, stresses the urgency of the mission to spread "knowledge of the present eschatological fulfillment."[78] Further, taking *Thomas* parallels as his cue, he suggests that Q/Luke 7:24b–26, 28; 12:(39–40), 49, 51, 52–53, 54–56, in speeches assigned to the "apocalyptic" layer, belong to "the original version of Q" because they point basically to the fulfillment of prophetic longings, the presence of the kingdom in Jesus and his preaching.[79] Finally, he cautions that although Q at points expresses a sense of persecution (6:22–23; 10:16), it articulates no rejection of "Israel" or "the Jews," as often claimed for the "judgmental" layer.[80] That is, besides the keynote speech of the supposedly sapiential layer really being a prophetic announcement, significant blocks of sayings assigned to the supposedly apocalyptic stratum really belong with the formative speeches which are more prophetic than sapiential, representing Jesus as a prophet of the new age, not a sage.[81] Thus Koester's recent analysis of *Thomas* and the "Synoptic Sayings Source" Q as "collections of the sayings of Jesus" characterizes the sayings materials in both documents in ways that make both of them seem to fit the genre *logoi sophon* much less than originally claimed and that make Q seem prophetic throughout rather than divisible into different "sapiential" and "apocalyptic" layers.

In an attempt better to understand the genre of Q's formative layer Kloppenborg explored a wide range of ancient comparative literature in connection with his elaborated hypothesis of strata in Q. He argued that "the formative stratum has the strongest generic contacts with the genre of 'instruction,'" whose many examples in antiquity he explored.[82] Yet that stratum's "two notable departures from the typical form of instruction" would appear to constitute decisive differences. In contrast to the instructional genre, the sapiential speeches in Q do not take the form of parental instruction. Even more important, "in contrast to the generally conservative comportment of the instruction, Q presents an ethic of radical discipleship which reverses many of the conventions which allow a society to operate."[83] The explanation? "Q has moved towards the form of gnomologium." And "although Q infuses the form with new content, and al-

Book of Q and Christian Origins (San Francisco: HarperSanFrancisco, 1993), and Leif Vaage, *Galilean Upstarts: Jesus' First Followers according to Q* (Valley Forge, Pa.: Trinity Press International, 1994), as pointed out by James M. Robinson, "The History-of-Religions Taxonomy of Q: The Cynic Hypothesis," in *Gnosisforschung und Religionsgeschichte: Festschrift für Kurt Rudolph*, ed. T. Schweer and S. Rink (Marburg: Diagonal, 1995), 261–65, and Tuckett, *Q and the History of Early Christianity*, 369–73.

77. Koester, *Ancient Christian Gospels*, 137–38.
78. Ibid., 158.
79. Ibid., 139, 147, 150–55.
80. Ibid., 161.
81. Ibid., 160.
82. Kloppenborg, *Formation of Q*, 317.
83. Ibid., 318.

though it shifts from a presupposition of this-worldly order to eschatological order, the basic hermeneutic of the instruction is preserved."[84]

Yet not only is Q's hermeneutic significantly different from that of "instructional" literature; indeed, Q's hermeneutic matches none of the three hermeneutical modes of gnomological literature.[85] A hermeneutic of "penetration and research" fits the Gospel of Thomas, but not the sapiential speeches of Q. That of "fittingness" fits Q even less. The third hermeneutical mode, of "obedience and assimilation," might seem more appropriate to Q. But whereas gnomologia require study, reflection, and interpretation toward the attainment of a perfect and untroubled condition of the soul (again suitable to Thomas), "sapiential" Q requires obedience to a new social order that entails conflictual social interaction ("love your enemies"; being sent out "as sheep in the midst of wolves"; "do not fear those who [only] kill the body"). In the concerns of Q sayings for the basic human necessities of food and shelter (Q 6:20–21, 27–36; 10:5–8; 11:2–4; 12:22–31) one detects a different social location from that presupposed in gnomologia, which require study and reflection. The hermeneutic of the "sapiential" layer of Q, some of which is not sapiential instruction anyhow, is simply not that of an assimilation of a wisdom ethos — not in 6:20–49, concerned with community interaction; nor in 10:2–16, concerned with mission to village communities; nor in 11:2–4, 9–13, concerned with prayer for the economic necessities of "bread" and "cancellation of debts"; nor in 12:2–12, concerned with political struggle; nor in 12:22–31, concerned with anxiety about food and clothing.

•

Considered on the basis of its own stated criteria and procedures standard in the field of New Testament studies, the most influential hypothesis of different strata in Q does not stand up to critical scrutiny. The criteria that supposedly distinguish the secondary apocalyptic layer from the supposedly formative sapiential layer fail to appear in its component clusters. Correspondingly, the supposedly common features of the sapiential layer do not appear consistently across its constituent clusters. The concepts used to distinguish between the hypothetical layers, derived from modern New Testament studies, turn out to be highly problematic when measured against particular Q passages and closely related comparative texts. Moreover, the characterization of the genre of Q, like the supposedly similar collection of sayings in the Gospel of Thomas, as logoi sophon reduces the wide range of materials referred to as logoi in ancient Jewish and Christian sources to the single type of sapiential sayings. Such logoi could as easily be characterized as logoi prophētōn. Thus the way Q is understood and interpreted in recent scholarly analysis, particularly in American academic circles, appears highly problematic even when examined on its own terms.

---

84. Ibid., 319, 321.
85. A discernment that Kloppenborg himself sets up, ibid., 301–6.

Much more serious questions about the recent enterprise of Q studies arise once the standard assumptions and procedures of modern biblical scholarship come into question. For example, from emerging critical perspective on the determinative effect of the invention of the printing press, recent Q studies appear to be a perfectly "logical conclusion" of print culture. As Werner Kelber points out, "it makes sense in typographic culture to visualize texts as palimpsests, with layer superimposed upon layer, and stratum superseding stratum, building up to layered edifices."[86] The stratigraphy of Q, moreover, is an impeccable product of the logic of modern science. Kelber's critique of standard scholarly procedure on Jesus' sayings pertains as much or more to Q studies:

> Confronted with a multiplicity and multiformity of phenomena, logic administers ...organizing principles. Words are sequestered and regrouped by virtue of resemblances.... Words must be categorized so as to be apportioned to divisions of "classification" such as "stratification."[87]

No matter how limited it is to the concepts of modern theology, the assumptions of print culture, and the logic of scientific method, however, the work of Kloppenborg, Koester, and Robinson on Q and related material such as the *Gospel of Thomas* leads to other possibilities for a more appropriate understanding of Q in the ancient historical context and communication forms of eastern Mediterranean society.

Q as a Sequence of Discourses

An Alternative Approach

The compositional analysis that begins with the individual component sayings has, ironically, been one of the factors leading to recent recognition that Q is not a collection of sayings but a collection of speeches. Analysis that begins with categorization and characterization of individual sayings by form or motif, however, can lead only into the cul de sac of clusters of homogenous sayings (e.g., sapiential or apocalyptic). As Bultmann and other pioneers of form criticism recognized, "form" implied and included function and context. "The literature in which the life of a community...has taken shape springs out of quite definite conditions." Because of the typical life-situations in which Jesus traditions functioned, "the literary 'category' or 'form'...is a sociological concept and not an aesthetic one."[88] From the outset Bultmann declared that his own procedure "from the analysis of the particular elements of the tradition" and Martin Dibelius's reconstruction of "the history of the synoptic tradition from a study of the community and its needs" were "mutually complementary and corrective work."[89] Thus, although Bultmann offered little or no discussion of the *Sitz im Leben*, for example, of the

---

86. Werner Kelber, "Jesus and Tradition," 141.

87. Ibid., 144.

88. Rudolf Bultmann, *The History of the Synoptic Tradition* (New York: Harper & Row, 1963), 4.

89. Ibid., 5.

logia and prophetic sayings of Jesus, he called for "complementary and corrective" analysis of community contexts in which Jesus traditions functioned. The form criticism that became dominant in New Testament studies, however, tended to follow Bultmann's approach almost to the neglect of the "corrective" work pioneered by Dibelius. Correspondingly, most analysis of Q materials has not only begun with individual sayings but has focused on literary-aesthetic formal characteristics without attending to "form" as "a sociological concept." Even the recent composition criticism of Q begins with categorization and characterization of individual sayings; then notices the order, method, and theme by which they were juxtaposed or added to one another; and, only when compositional layers have been secured, proceeds to look for evidence of social context and community formation.

As evident in recent disagreement about how to categorize many sayings in Q, however, characterization of individual sayings in fact depends ultimately on their larger literary context. Indeed, as form criticism originally understood, the form and function (as well as the meaning) of Jesus traditions cannot be discerned apart from their social context (*Sitz im Leben*), for the discernment of which we are dependent on its literary context. It is impossible to start with characterization of individual sayings basically because individual sayings do not in and of themselves constitute intelligible units of communication. It is becoming increasingly clear, precisely from the analyses of Kloppenborg and others, that individual sayings are intelligible only in larger groupings or discourses that constitute the units of communication in Q. In order to begin to understand the form, function, and significance of particular sayings, we must start with the units of communication in which they now stand and then understand their functions in typical community contexts. This would ultimately mean beginning with Q materials as used and embedded in Matthew and Luke. By comparison and contrast with their use in Matthew and Luke it would then be possible to discern and analyze the units of communication in Q in their historical social context.

Besides such comparisons with their later uses by Matthew and Luke, comparisons with the parallels to Q in the *Gospel of Thomas* can help us discern the units of communication in Q. Despite the intense comparison of Q with the *Gospel of Thomas* in the last generation, little attention has been given to the differences between them in internal structure. Both have been understood as collections of sayings and the now-dominant hypothesis of strata in Q is heavily invested in their generic similarities. Yet if we think in compositional terms rather than in terms of types of sayings, a major difference between Q and *Thomas* is immediately evident. In Q the sayings are formed into larger clusters or discourses. In *Thomas*, on the other hand, although a dozen or so of the 114 sayings could be described as brief clusters or discourses and more than twenty take the form of brief dialogues (with another dozen in the form of parables), the vast majority of the material — more than seventy of the *logia* — stands in fragmentary units of single sayings, sets of two or three parallel sayings, or short sequences of two or three sayings. *Thomas* parallels provide striking contrasts with some of the Q clusters.

Thomas offers perhaps the most parallel material to the large cluster comprised of Q 12:39–40, 42–46, 49(-50), 51–59. Of the parallel *logia* in *Thomas*, 16 joins the same two sayings as stand in Q 12:51–53; but the parallels to Q 12:39 and 12:49 are isolated in *Thomas* 103 and 10, respectively, and the *Thomas* parallel to Q 12:56 is the answer to a question of Jesus' identity in *Thomas* 91. Thomas also offers several parallels to the materials in Q 6:20–49, the largest discourse in Q. One could argue that *Thomas* 45, parallel to Q 6:43–44, constitutes a brief discourse, discussion, or argument. Most of the parallels to other parts of the "sermon" in Q, however, are again isolated sayings, in 54, 69b, 68 = 69a, 95, 47a–b, and 34 (following the order of the material in Q). As illustrated by the Q clusters that have the most parallel material in *Thomas*, the relatively large clusters of sayings or speeches in Q form a distinctive contrast with the appearance in *Thomas* largely of brief units of single, double, or triple sayings with no apparent overall sequence of arrangement. Perhaps *Thomas* can be appropriately characterized as a collection of sayings. Q, however, is not a collection of sayings but a sequence of speeches or discourses. This difference between the internal structure of Q as clusters or discourses and the apparent lack of any corresponding internal structure in *Thomas* suggests an approach to understanding the character and composition of Q as a whole document quite different from, and no longer dependent on, categorizing the forms and motifs of individual sayings and sets of sayings. That is, if Q is composed almost entirely of larger or smaller complexes of sayings, then the composition, character, and function of those clusters may be the key to understanding Q as a whole.

The Form-and-Function and the Structure of Q as a Sequence of Discourses

This conception of Q as a collection of discourses or speeches is not unprecedented, as noted in chapter 1.[90] In the first book-length study of Q at the beginning of this century, Adolf von Harnack concluded that it was a collection of discourses. Once the field tended more and more to focus on individual sayings, partly under the influence of form criticism, it was inevitable that the understanding of Q as sayings (the "Synoptic Sayings Source," "Sayings Gospel") would dominate discussion. Yet despite the continuing predisposition of many to focus on individual sayings, references to Q as a collection of discourses or speeches have become increasingly frequent in recent years.[91] Outlines and divisions of Q read as more than a collection of individual sayings have been proposed with increasing specificity, but they have been basically topical or thematic labels or sequential indicators.

We may get further by investigating the functions, the possible purposes, and the effects of the various complexes that comprise Q. A clue to what these may be can perhaps be found in the "hermeneutics" implicit in the Q discourses. Again

---

90. The next two sections depend partly on Horsley, "*Logoi Prophētōn?*" 195–209.
91. Kloppenborg, "The Sayings Gospel Q," 35–74; Horsley, "Q and Jesus," 175–209.

the comparison with the *Gospel of Thomas* may be helpful. The latter specifies its hermeneutics in the very first saying: "He who finds the meaning of these words shall not taste death." That is, the sayings require study or pondering by an individual in order to penetrate their meaning. To help the seeker of "life" the composition of *Thomas* at points adds clues in the form of brief additional phrases (cf. *Thomas* 16 and 78 with their parallels in Q 12:51–53; 7:24–25), some of which also make explicit that the collection is for individuals who may come to know their true self in the symbolism of realizing the "kingdom" or "wealth" or "rest" or "the solitary one" and in the rejection of ordinary social and familial bonds (e.g., 6, 14, 95, 110). By contrast, the hermeneutics implicit in Q is primarily straightforward exhortation of a community of people regarding social-economic-political interaction sanctioned by prophetic threats of reward and punishment (e.g., Q 6:20–49; 12:2–12, 22–31). Insofar as Q is structured into discernible discourses or speeches, therefore, we can investigate the purpose of particular discourses. The procedure would be analogous to form criticism's analysis of the function of particular sayings and stories in the life of the early church, only now focused on the function of whole discourses in the life of the Q community or movement.

In a few discourses, the functions are transparent. Q 10:2–16, the contents of which do not fit what is normally understood as sapiential admonitions, is instruction regarding mission, the sending of envoys to preach and heal and generally spread the movement village by village while based in households. Q 11:2–4, 9–11 offers instruction and encouragement about prayer. The Q material behind Luke 17:23–37, exhortation on preparedness in the face of the suddenness of judgment, apparently functioned as the sanction on the whole of Q, somewhat similar to the way Q 6:46–49 serves to sanction the exhortations in 6:27–45.

Functions of other discourses are not difficult to discern. Q 6:20–49, often referred to as Jesus' inaugural "sermon," is a long set of opening admonitions that corresponds to the set of sanctions with which Q ends in Q 17:23–37. More precisely, however, as can be determined from the contents of such admonitions as 6:27–38, it appears to be intended as instruction on social-economic relations within the community and not merely as religious teaching to individuals. The discourse as a whole, moreover, has a fairly clear structure: the initial blessings set the stage for the exhortations regarding social-economic interaction, which are followed by sanctioning sayings that reinforce motivation to observe the preceding injunctions. Q 7:18–35 deals not merely with Jesus, John, and "this generation" but with the significance of what is happening with John and Jesus, the fulfillment of expectations and prophecies of personal and societal renewal. Q 11:39–52 condemns some of the principal opponents of the Q movement. Although the parameters of the discourse are difficult to identify, the Q materials in Luke 13:28–30, 34–35; 14:16–24 appear to be components of another cluster directed against opponents of the Q movement, in this case the Jerusalem rulers. The fragments of Q used in Luke 14:26–27, 34–35; 15:4–7; 16:13, 17, 18; and 17:1–6 would all be intelligible as parts of a cluster of stringent demands for community discipline with the appropriate encouragement, although this material could also be viewed as two shorter clusters divided on either side of 16:13. John's speech on the crisis of impending judgment and deliverance, Q 3:7–9, 16–17, and Jesus' declaration about the restoration or liberation of Israel in Q 22:28–30, finally, function as the opening and closing, respectively, of the whole sequence of speeches that comprise Q.

Less evident yet nevertheless intelligible are the division, coherence, and functions of the remaining materials, mainly of those in Q 12. Q 12:2–12, which evidently came immediately after a discourse that condemned the Pharisees and scribes, exhorts the Q people to be confident and bold when brought before the authorities, with the promise of vindication or the specter of judgment by the heavenly court. Q 12:22–31 (33–34) addresses the Q people's anxieties about necessities of life, which will take care of themselves if the faithful are single-minded in pursuit of the kingdom. Q 12:39–40, 42–46 could be sanctions on the previous exhortation or part of a larger set of sanctions addressed to the Q community. Q 12:49–59 proclaims the disruptive, conflictual effect of Jesus' practice or movement, with a challenge lest addressees not respond to the crisis (i.e., that presented by the very appearance of Jesus and his movement). Q 13:18–21 presents two parables indicating the amazing expansion of the kingdom (as manifest in the Q/Jesus movement?).[92]

The principal, unifying theme of the whole document is clearly "the kingdom of God." Featured prominently at crucial points in most of the speeches (6:20; 7:28; 10:9, 11; 11:2, 20; 12:31; 13:18–21, 28–29; 16:16; 22:28–30), the kingdom of God is virtually assumed or taken for granted as the focus of Q discourses as well as the comprehensive agenda of preaching, practice, and purpose in Q. The kingdom of God, moreover, is double-edged, with positive, salvific benefits for those who respond to its presence but negative, judgmental implications for those who do not (see esp. 10:9[11]; 11:20; 13:28–29). Kingdom sayings and parables are also scattered throughout the *Gospel of Thomas*. But they do not play the same role in providing a unifying theme in that collection of short units without any discernible sequence or other internal structure that corresponds to the series of discourses in Q.

Indeed, partly by focusing on the dominant kingdom theme, we can discern how the various discourses may cohere in sequence as a whole document. Q 3:7–9, 16–17 and 22:28–30 provide, respectively, a promising as well as a threatening opening and a highly positive, anticipatory ending, in which the kingdom clearly means the renewal of Israel. Jesus' long opening speech in 6:20–49, after

---

92. With or without the exhortation to bold confession when under persecution in 12:2–12, the four or five smaller clusters just discussed could be taken together as one long discourse that offers positive encouragement followed by two sets of sanctions and rounded out by two encouraging parables of the kingdom's growth. The resulting long speech could then be understood as parallel, and roughly comparable in length, to 6:20–49. That is, the Q material behind Luke 12:22 through 13:21 addresses particular understandable anxieties of Q people with appropriately sharp sanctions, while 6:20–49 addresses intracommunity relations with less ominous sanctions.

announcing the kingdom for the poor, presents fundamental instruction for inter-action in the kingdom community(ies). It is followed in 7:18–35 by a discourse that affirms the fulfillment of age-old longings now happening with Jesus and the kingdom. The two closing discourses, which include the fragments utilized in Luke 14:26–27, 34–35; 15:4–7; 16:13, 17, 18; and 17:1–6 and the mate-rials behind Luke 17:23–37, articulate (respectively) the stringent demands of community discipline and admonition about preparedness in the face of sudden judgment that provides sanction for Q as a whole. That these discourses may lack the kingdom theme (depending on how Luke 16:16 is placed) makes sense inso-far as the kingdom does not have negative implications for those who respond, that is, those who are in the movement. In between the opening programmatic discourses and the closing community-disciplinary and sanctioning discourses are several discourses whose sequence seems intelligible: instructions on the mission of spreading the kingdom movement (9:57–10:16) and on petitioning God boldly for the kingdom (11:2–4, 9–11), and the highly reassuring announcement of the kingdom's presence, along with a note of warning about movement discipline, in the Beelzebul discourse (11:14–26). Immediately after the challenge to Jesus in the Beelzebul discourse come Jesus' warning and condemnation of "this genera-tion," who appear to be identical with the scribes and Pharisees who in effect block the people's entry into the kingdom (11:29–32, 39–52). Next, in reassurance to the Q people faced with such opposition, come the exhortation to confidence in confession (12:2–12), followed by the discourse declaring that despite their poverty they need have no anxiety if they remain single-minded in pursuit of the kingdom (12:22–31). Those encouraging speeches are followed by sanctions in 12:39–40, 42–46, and then a statement of the crisis constituted by Jesus' mis-sion (12:49–59). As if expanding on how the crisis (judgment) cuts both ways, there follow first two encouraging parables of growth of the kingdom (13:18–21) that evoke trust and hope among the Q people, then a discourse in which Jesus condemns the ruling house in Jerusalem, for whom, in their presumption of their own salvation, the kingdom means condemnation (13:28–29, 34–35; 14:16–24), and finally the exhortation to the Q people to maintain group discipline men-tioned above, followed by the sanctioning discourse in 17:23–37 and the closing declaration of the kingdom of God as the renewal of Israel in 22:28–30.[93]

Throughout the sequence of discourses, the constituent sayings and motifs cor-respond to the particular function or concern of the discourse. Those addressed to community relations and discipline (e.g., 6:27–49; 12:22–31; and the pieces behind Luke 14, 15, 16, 17) utilize traditional covenantal exhortation and popular wisdom, as we might expect, given the traditional function of such materials (in contrast to the more individually addressed parental instruction of professional sages). Not surprisingly, the instructions for mission in peasant towns and villages

---

93. This tentative sketch of how the Q discourses may form a coherent sequence will be confirmed by the analysis of particular discourses in chapters 9–13, which will also show how their coherence is rooted in Israelite cultural tradition.

(not in scribal schools) and prayer by those who are hungry and in debt (not by professional sages-scribes) do not correspond to conventional forms of scribal-sapiential instruction. Prophetic forms come to the fore in the discourses directed to the community as sanctions (e.g., 17:23–37) as well as in the speeches against the scribes/Pharisees and Jerusalem rulers, again not surprising considering the traditional function of prophetic woes and laments. Also not surprisingly, the motif of the killing of the prophets occurs in the two prophetic discourses addressed ostensibly to the Pharisees and the Jerusalem rulers (11:47–51; 13:34–35), and the polemic against "this generation" is almost exclusively concentrated in one of those prophetic speeches (11:29–32, 49–51). "The day of the Son of Man" as a symbolic reference to (the suddenness of) the judgment — which is apparently conceived as a positive, salvific, as well as negative, judgmental, event — operates in the final discourse of Q before the concluding promise of societal renewal, the discourse that sanctions the exhortation in the rest of the document.

Further comparison with the *Gospel of Thomas*, focusing on materials that function importantly in Q but are absent or transformed in *Thomas*, confirms the social or community function of many of the Q discourses. Significantly, *Thomas* has no parallels to the prophetic woes against the Pharisees (a parallel only to Q 12:52 in *logion* 39; cf. 102) or to the prophecies against the rulers in 13:28–29, 34–35. (Contrast the guarding against the "world" in *logion* 21.) *Thomas*, moreover, has no parallels to those (portions) of Q discourses that suggest a community in struggle, such as Q 7:31–35; 11:14–20; and 12:3–9. (Only the general saying in 12:2 is paralleled in *Thomas* 5 and 6.) Many of the prophetic sayings in *Thomas* have apparently been explicitly interpreted or adapted in an individualizing and/or gnosticizing manner, as can be seen by comparison with their counterparts in Q, which still have a social thrust. The effect becomes clear particularly when we consider the discourse composition in Q in contrast with the isolated sayings or sayings pairs in *Thomas*. The discourses embody a social context in which sayings have significance in Q, whereas the sayings are left without any corresponding context for interpretation in *Thomas*. For example, the saying about sending out workers into the harvest in *Thomas* 73 has no particular connotations of mission, whereas in Q 10:2–16 it functions as the very keynote to the mission of spreading the kingdom from village to village. In *Thomas* 35 the saying about binding the strong man and plundering his house has no connotations of the struggle against Satan's rule that not only has been engaged but is being won, as suggested in the Beelzebul discourse of Q 11:14–23. "Cleansing the outside of the cup" and the Pharisees' hiding the key to knowledge in *Thomas* 89 and 39, respectively, have no political-religious context at all because they are not part of a series of woes indicting the Pharisees for their detrimental effects on the people, as in Q. What is hidden and becoming revealed in *Thomas* 5, finally, gives nothing of the sense of encouragement or vindication in the face of acute social conflict that it offers as part of the discourse in Q 12:2–12.

The discourses and their social function would thus appear to be the key to understanding Q and its implicit hermeneutics. The *Gospel of Thomas* is a collection of separate sayings intended for pondering and reflection, "penetration and research," with no concern for a social group and no social conflict in view, toward the goal of individual enlightenment by persons who have apparently withdrawn from ordinary social and familial interaction. The sequence of discourses that make up Q, on the other hand, is concerned not with a "radical mode of existence" for individuals but with a renewed societal order, which entails social conflict, and particular discourses focus on particular aspects of that societal renewal and social conflict.

Comparison with Other Documents Composed in Discourses

Once we recognize that Q was composed in discourses, we should compare it not primarily with the *Gospel of Thomas* but with other documents of Jesus movements or early Christianity that are also composed in discourses. Perhaps the most obvious cases would be the Gospel of Matthew, which simply took over some Q discourses and reconstituted others, and the *Didache,* the "Teaching of the Twelve Apostles."

As is commonly observed, Matthew structures his Gospel into five major sections, a discourse following narrative in each section, with the infancy narratives as the introduction and the passion and resurrection-exaltation as the conclusion. It is significant that Q provided Matthew with the basis for at least four (and perhaps all five) of his discourses, and that those four discourses stand in the same order as in Q: Matthew 5–7, the "Sermon on the Mount," which is quite explicitly a covenantal discourse, based on Q 6:20–49, which also provides the overall frame of the Matthean discourse; Matthew 10, the mission discourse, based on Q 10:2–16, which again provides the overall frame (into which Matthew conflates material from the Markan mission discourse); Matthew 18, on community discipline, based on Q 17:1–6; and Matthew 24–25, the eschatological or apocalyptic discourse, based on Q 17:23–37 (with which Matthew conflates the Markan apocalyptic discourse), to which he prefixes a discourse against the Pharisees, based on Q 11:39–52. The only question is whether the parables discourse in Matthew 13, based far more clearly on Mark 4, could also be understood as based on Q 13:18–21, which it incorporates — in which case it would be the only Q discourse used as a basis for a Matthean discourse which is out of Q order in Matthew. Into his grand structure of discourses, designed to fit an explicitly Mosaic prophetic scheme, Matthew then integrates many of the other Q discourses or parts thereof (although by no means all of the remaining discourses) into one of his own major discourses: the Q discourses on prayer and on anxiety (Q 11:2–4, 9–11; 12:22–31, 33–34) into the covenantal discourse (Matthew 5–7); the Q discourse on bold confession (12:2–9, 11–12) and part of the discourse on the current crisis (12:51–53) into the mission discourse (Matthew 10); the Q discourse on preparedness (12:39–46) into the apocalyptic discourse. Comparison of Matthew's expanded discourses with the Q material he used as a basis, particularly where the Q discourse provides the framing for Matthew's more elaborate discourse, enables us to see clearly that the Q materials he used were already structured in discourses. That is, well before Matthew, Q already manifests the composition of Jesus' teachings and prophecies in speeches focused on the principal concerns of the movement.

The *Didache,* whose superscription reads "The Lord's Teaching to the Peoples through the Twelve Apostles," also provides some striking similarities with Q in the focus and function of certain discourses, further confirming that Q was composed in discourses and was not merely a collection of sayings. The *Didache* opens with a traditional two-ways teaching in chapters 1–6 (closely related to that in *Barnabas* 18–20) that expands on the traditional Israelite summary of the decalogue and Torah ("Thou shalt love God...and thy neighbor" [1:2]), explicitly designated as "the sayings" = *hoi logoi* (1:3). The *Didache* thus opens with a lengthy covenantal discourse parallel to the first major discourse in Q (Q 6:20–49). The first major section within this covenantal discourse then happens to be a set of sayings with close affinities to Q/Luke 6:27–35 (cf. Matt. 5:38–48) and continues with other covenantal exhortations in the form "Do not...[Thou shalt not]," followed by further admonitions in the form of "parental instruction." The overall discourse is clearly covenantal in substance and form, with decalogue and decalogue-related prohibitions and "fences around" the decalogue prohibitions, and is concerned with social-economic interaction within a community. Thus *Didache* 1:1–6:2, like the even more explicitly covenantal structuring of Q material in Matthew 5, further confirms that Q 6:20–49 is a discourse concerned with social relations in a community and not simply ethical admonitions for individuals. Its size (by far the longest and most substantive discourse) and placement at the opening of the document, like the similar size and placement of the great covenantal discourse in Matthew 5–7, further indicate that it constitutes a renewal of covenant that forms the basis of the community(ies) that comprise the movement for which the document was written. Q 6:20–49 apparently constitutes the parallel covenant renewal for the communities of the Jesus movement for which Q was composed.

The *Didache* ends with an "eschatological" or "apocalyptic" discourse in chapter 16. Substantively this speech has more in common with Mark 13 and Matthew 24–25 than with Q (e.g., Q/Luke 12:35, 40) and is replete with what could appropriately be termed apocalyptic motifs (such as "the world-deceiver," "signs spread out in heaven," etc., climaxing with "the Lord coming on the clouds of heaven," reminiscent of Daniel 7), motifs that are lacking in Q. The function of *Didache* 16, as a sanction on the teaching and exhortation in the whole series of discourses, however, suggests that the terminal discourse in Q (Q 17:23–37), focused on the suddenness of "the day of the Son of Man," had a similar function as sanction on exhortations in the preceding series of discourses in Q.

The material in between these opening and closing discourses in the *Didache* are also composed in topical discourses. Many of them are devoted to issues not paralleled in Q, such as baptism, fasting, and celebration of the eucharist. But the *Didache* does provide parallel instruction on the Lord's Prayer (8:2–3; cf. Q 11:2–4) and on community discipline, which is placed immediately before the closing eschatological discourse (15:3–4; cf. Q 17:1–6). The lengthy instructions concerning the support and treatment of itinerant apostles and prophets in *Didache* 11–13 correspond to the mission discourse in Q/Luke 10:2–16, with the changes in emphasis appropriate to the later stage in the development of the early Christian movement represented by the *Didache*. The *Didache* thus has discourses parallel to five of the speeches in Q; they come in the same sequence; and they serve the same functions.

These parallels, however, do not suggest that Q was a proto-*Didache*, an early form of a community manual for the Jesus movement in Palestine. Nor do they in any way suggest a reversion to earlier treatment of Q as a catechetical document supplementary to the Gospel of Mark or other Gospels. Surely part of its purpose and function was instruction on matters such as mission and prayer. But the bulk of Q's discourses are exhortative speeches of promise and encouragement as well as of crisis and warning directed to communities of a Jesus movement: 7:18–35 about the fulfillment at hand; 12:2–12 about bold confession; 12:22–31 on not being anxious but single-minded in focusing on the kingdom; 12:49–59 on the crisis at hand; and 11:(29–32)39–52, plus the speech containing 13:28–29, 34–35, and 14:16–24, condemning the Jerusalem rulers and their representatives (in Q for the benefit of the hearers/readers). The keynotes with which the whole sequence of speeches begins and ends, moreover, are prophetic threat and promise: the "stronger one who is coming" will baptize "with holy spirit" as well as "fire" and "gather the grain" as well as burn the chaff (3:16–17), and (once we translate terms more appropriately) the Q program is to be "making justice for/liberating" (not negatively "judging") the twelve tribes of Israel (22:28–30). Jesus, whose *logoi* comprise most of the contents of the discourses, finally, is fairly clearly understood as a prophet — indeed (along with John) as the culminating prophet in a long line of prophets, in 3:16–17; 7:18–28; 11:49–50; 13:34.

Thus, while comparisons with similarly sequenced and functioning discourses in Matthew and the *Didache* enable us to discern that Q consists of a sequence of discourses concerned with community life, it is also clearly a perpetuation of the prophetic proclamation of Jesus (and John), announcing the presence/imminence of the kingdom of God, which means fulfillment of traditional longings and renewal of community life in Israel for those who respond, but condemnation for "Pharisees" and Jerusalem rulers who oppose. If Q is more than a *Didache*-like manual for community order, it is much more than instruction addressed to individual disciples in the tradition of wisdom teaching evident in literature such as Sirach. The sayings tradition that culminates in the *Gospel of Thomas* does indeed focus on individual penetration and interpretation of particular separate sayings of Jesus. In pursuit of such a hermeneutic, moreover, *Thomas* must alter and adapt the dominant prophetic components in the tradition of Jesus' sayings. Q, on the other hand, is concerned not simply with the instruction of individuals but with the social relations and political conflicts of a movement. Besides including sapiential materials (of which it has more than *Thomas*) in its discourses concerned with community relations, prayer, and discipline, it utilizes whole complexes of prophetic materials as sanctions on community discipline and as polemic against the authority figures and ruling institutions that oppose the movement.

Until we recognize and understand Q as a sequence of discourses, the determination of its genre more precisely is probably not of crucial importance and is likely premature. Robinson's survey of literature designated as *logoi* turned up a great variety, some of it sections of larger wholes, some of it sapiential in character, some of it clearly understood as prophetic. With respect to documents with hermeneutics as variant as those of Q and the *Gospel of Thomas*, it is misleading to classify both under the rubric *logoi sophon*. Indeed, as indicated in the discussion above, that rubric is appropriate to neither, if judged by comparison with Sirach or *Pirke Abot*. It is possible that something in the vein of "words of the prophet(s)" (*logoi prophētōn*) would be more appropriate.[94] Precisely that designation was given to earlier Israelite prophetic documents, such as the books of Amos (LXX) and Jeremiah (Masoretic text) and Haggai (1:12), curiously omitted in Robinson's survey. Yet Q displays clear differences with these prophetic books that were composed centuries earlier and were apparently developed in stages, before being included in second-temple Judean collections of scripture. Most important at this point is to recognize that Q at the point that it was used by Matthew and Luke had the form of a sequence of discourses devoted to principal concerns of the Jesus movement in which it was developed and cultivated.

---

94. Suggested tentatively in Horsley, "*Logoi Prophētōn?*; Migaku Sato, *Q und Prophetie*, WUNT 2, no. 29 (Tübingen: J. C. B. Mohr [Paul Siebeck], 1987), even argued that Q should be seen as following "canonical" Israelite prototypes.

Chapter 5

ISRAELITE TRADITIONS IN Q

Richard A. Horsley

Recent interpreters appear to be attempting to extricate Q as much as possible from its roots in Israelite tradition.[1] Some indeed acknowledge that Q stands within Israel.[2] Yet even they repeat the claims, for example, that the Q people came into conflict with the rest of Israel, that Q pronounces judgment against all Israel (Judaism), and that Q presupposed a mission to Gentiles. Recent "stratigraphy" of Q portrays the "sapiential" layer as wisdom so general in its pithy contents that few distinctive and particularistic Israelite traditions are in evidence. The wisdom of the supposedly formative layer is characterized as "unconventional" or "countercultural," in opposition to an imagined standard "conventional" Jewish culture. Its individualistic and universalistic wisdom supposedly resembles that of Cynic philosophers. Only when their conflict with Jewish society came to a crisis did the Q people reach for Israelite traditions as weapons in their prophetic arsenal of condemnation. Thus the Israelite elements in Q are represented as negative and condemnatory, arising from resentment at rejection.

Such interpretation of Q is still captive to the conventional Christian theological paradigm of the emergence of the universalistic and spiritual religion Christianity from the particularistic and political religion Judaism. A more precise analysis of the Q discourses against a more complex and historically appropriate construction of Q's social context, however, finds no such condemnation of Israel in general but only some prophetic pronouncements against the Jerusalem ruling house and its representatives, the scribes and Pharisees, as explained in chapter 4.[3] That Q presupposes a Gentile mission is a projection from other "early Christian" literature, which leads to an inappropriate reading of Q 7:2–9 and Q 13:28–29. As noted in the previous chapter, Q uses the centurion's faith as a rhetorical

---

1. For example, Burton L. Mack, *The Lost Gospel: The Book of Q and Christian Origins* (San Francisco: HarperSanFrancisco, 1993); Leif Vaage, *Galilean Upstarts: Jesus' First Followers according to Q* (Valley Forge, Pa.: Trinity Press International, 1994); and to a lesser extent, John S. Kloppenborg, *The Formation of Q: Trajectories in Ancient Wisdom Collections* (Philadelphia: Fortress, 1987).

2. For example, Arland D. Jacobson, *The First Gospel: An Introduction to Q* (Sonoma, Calif.: Polebridge, 1992).

3. See further Richard A. Horsley, "Social Conflict in the Synoptic Sayings Source Q," in *Conflict and Invention: Literary, Rhetorical, and Social Studies on the Sayings Gospel Q,* ed. John S. Kloppenborg (Valley Forge, Pa.: Trinity Press International, 1995), 37–52.

foil in a speech pressing Israelites to repent and have faith in the presence of the kingdom of God (the renewal of Israel). The pilgrimage to the banquet of the kingdom in 13:28–29 is not of Gentiles but of dispersed Israelites returning to a renewed people, set over against the Jerusalem ruling class who presume that they are the true "sons of the kingdom."[4] Particular Gentiles mentioned in Q figure in the past and/or the hypothetical future, not in a present mission. That Q not only stands within Israel but also looks across assumed boundaries to other peoples/nations/Gentiles is clear from the passing, unpolemical, rhetorical comparisons with other "peoples" in both Q 6:33 (*ethnikoi* in Matt. 5:47) and 12:30.[5] To claim that the material assigned to the sapiential layer largely lacks (references to) Israelite traditions simply ignores their presence, in both form and substance, as we shall discuss below. And to claim that the atomized sapiential materials in Q are unconventional begs the question of what was conventional in a society characterized by considerable cultural diversity. A closer examination of Q discourses indicates rather that they are not only full of references to, but also deeply embedded in, Israelite tradition.

Survey of Q Discourses and Israelite Traditions

We must examine Q discourses for more than explicit or implicit references to Israelite traditions. More than references are evident. Many, in fact most, of the discourses in Q indicate that the speaker stands within Israelite history and society. And many of the discourses are framed or shaped in terms of traditional Israelite covenantal or prophetic forms. Analysis must explore all of these aspects.

The pronouncement by John the Baptist with which Q begins (3:7–9, 16–17) is permeated with references to Israelite tradition. Most obvious is the warning against appealing to descent from Abraham, the original patriarch from whom all Israel was presumably descended. But also the call to repentance presupposes and attempts to perpetuate the Mosaic covenant, and the harvest image for judgment draws on a rich tradition of Israelite prophets. The very form of the sayings is prophetic, as is often noted. And the speech as a whole positions itself at a crisis in Israel's history. Q thus begins with a prophetic covenantal exhortation to Israel to repent in the face of judgment, including not to trust in descent from Abraham as any guarantee of God's favor.

Jesus' testing by Satan is similarly rich in references to Israelite traditions. Besides Jesus' recitations of Deuteronomic principles (cf. Deut. 6:13, 16; 8:3), there are Satan's allusion to Ps. 90:11–12 and references to central Israelite traditions of forty days (cf. years) in the wilderness, the sites of the wilderness and the Jerusalem temple, the Holy Spirit as agent, and the "Son of God" as title. Again,

---

4. Ibid., 46–47; and Dale C. Allison Jr., *The Jesus Tradition in Q* (Harrisburg, Pa.: Trinity Press International, 1997), 176–86.

5. So also Christopher M. Tuckett, *Q and the History of Early Christianity: Studies on Q* (Peabody, Mass.: Hendrickson, 1996), 399, 402–3.

however, the rich references point to a deeper embeddedness of this dialogue in Israelite tradition. The whole is formed as a testing of an Israelite prophet being commissioned to lead the people, patterned after that of Moses and Elijah. Hence also the story presents Jesus as standing at a crisis within Israel's history.

The longest discourse, Q 6:20–49, makes numerous allusions to Israelite traditions, particularly to Mosaic covenantal laws and teachings in 6:27–36 (to Q 6:27 cf. Lev. 19:17–18; Exod. 23:4–5; Deut. 22:1–4; Sir. 29:1; to Q 6:29 cf. Exod. 22:25–26; Deut. 24:10–13; Amos 2:8; to Q 6:36 cf. Lev. 19:2).[6] The whole discourse, moreover, is framed with Mosaic covenantal components, indeed displays a structure similar to those of covenants and covenant renewals discerned in biblical texts such as Exodus 20 and Joshua 24. The discourse thus appears to be a virtual covenant renewal (as discussed at length in chapter 9).

The discourse in Q 7:18–35 proclaims that Jesus' preaching and practice are fulfilling the persistent longings of Israelites, as articulated particularly in prophecies that became incorporated into the Isaiah scroll (cf. Isa. 61:1; 35:5–6; 42:6–7), and that John fulfilled the prophecy of a messenger preparing the way of the new exodus (cf. Exod. 23:20; Mal. 3:1). The concluding sanction in the discourse alludes to the role of Wisdom in Israelite society (Sir. 4:11) or in Israelite history (1 Enoch 42 vs. Sir. 24). Again, the whole discourse is framed according to fulfillment of Israelite prophecy and assumes its stance within Israel's history, indeed at its climax. The renewal of Israel (the kingdom of God) now underway in the mission of Jesus is greater than anything in the previous history of Israel.

Judging by the allusions to Elijah and Elisha stories in its introduction, Q 9:57–60 (61–62), the mission discourse in Q 10:2–16 appears to be in service of a mobilization and renewal of Israel analogous to that spearheaded by the great northern Israelite prophetic leaders of resistance and renewal. Although other allusions in the mission discourse are not as dense as in Q 6:27–36, references to Israelite traditions are prominent: "lambs among wolves" (10:3) was a standing reference for the precarious standing of the people and their prophets under the power of their rulers (Ezek. 22:27; Zeph. 3:3); customary Israelite law (see Num. 18:30–31) provided a traditional analogy for the wages of the workers in the harvest of the mission (10:7); and previous prophetic declarations provided basic symbols for sanctioning sayings ("Sodom" and "Tyre and Sidon," "heaven . . . Hades [sheol?]," in 10:12, 13–15; see further chapter 10).

The next several discourses both make references to Israelite traditions and take their stance within Israelite tradition in ways similar to the previous discourses. Like Q 7:18–35, Q 10:21–24 contrasts the fulfillment happening in Jesus' mission with the experience of earlier generations, those of "many prophets and kings." Like Q 6:27–46, the petition to "cancel debts" in the Lord's Prayer in 11:2–4 appeals to Mosaic covenantal ideals. The Beelzebul discourse proclaims that "the finger of God" active in Jesus' exorcisms manifesting the kingdom of

---

6. See the analysis and discussion in Richard A. Horsley, *Jesus and the Spiral of Violence: Popular Jewish Resistance in Roman Palestine* (San Francisco: Harper & Row, 1987), 271–72.

God is (like) a new exodus (see Exod. 8:19; cf. 31:18; Deut. 9:10). The framing of the charge and Jesus' response appear to stand within more recent attempts by the Israelites to comprehend their struggle under imperial domination with reference to a dualism of God vs. Satan/Beelzebul (as can be discerned in the Dead Sea Scrolls, particularly the War Scroll and the Community Rule [1QM 1–2 and 1QS 3–4]). The brief discourse on the sign of Jonah in Q 11:29–32 repeats and reinforces the proclamation that decisive, unprecedented events of Israelite fulfillment are taking place in Jesus' mission in contrast to the Ninevites' response to Jonah and the Queen of the South's journey to see Solomon (and for the rhetorical "evil generation," cf. Deut. 32:5, 20).

The woes against the scribes and Pharisees in Q 11:39–52 include wide-ranging references to scribal-priestly holiness/purity codes, alms, tithing, the opposing prophetic preaching about justice and mercy (Mic. 6:8; Hos. 4:1; 12:7; Zech. 7:9), the role of Wisdom in Israel's history (again cf. *1 Enoch* 42 vs. Sirach 24), and previous generations of Jerusalem-based authorities killing the prophets, then honoring their memory. Framing all these references and allusions, however, the discourse takes the traditional Israelite prophetic form of woes against authorities (indictments, for their violation of the Mosaic covenant), followed by declaration of God's judgment (e.g., Isa. 5:18–19, 20, 21, 22–23 + 24; Amos 6:1–3, 4–6 + 7). And the discourse takes as its stance the current crisis in the history of Israel. (On "the key to knowledge, see 1QH 4.)

The next few discourses make fewer allusions to Israelite traditions and do not appear to be patterned according to traditional covenantal or prophetic forms so explicitly as many of the preceding discourses. Q 12:2–12 refers to "Gehenna," "the son of man," and "the angels of God" in a traditional judgment scenario. Q 12:22–31 refers to "Solomon in all his glory." Q 12:39–40 again mentions "the son of man." Q 12:49–59 refers to the prophetic image of the division between the generations in time of crisis (Mic. 7:6).

The traditional judgmental materials in Q 13:28–29, 34–35 (and perhaps 14:16–24) again not only make references to Israelite traditions but also have traditional Israelite forms and take as their stance the current crisis in Israel's history. The references are explicit: to the ingathering of dispersed Israelites to join Abraham, Isaac, and Jacob (and the prophets?) in the kingdom of God; to Jerusalem's historic behavior in its killing of the prophets; to the Song of Moses and the figure of the mother bird (Deut. 32:11; cf. Jer. 22:1–9); and to the psalmic phrase "blessed is he" (Ps. 117[118]:26). The traditional prophetic forms are also explicit: 13:34–35 in particular is clearly a declaration of judgment in the form of a prophetic lament (cf., e.g., Amos 5:1–3; Isa. 1:21). Equally clear is the stance taken at the crisis and climax of Israel's history. Similarly, not only do the three related sayings of Q 16:16–18 refer to the Torah/Law, but one takes the form of a law, the others prophetic forms, and the whole assumes a stance again at the crisis of Israel's history.

Finally, at the end of the sequence of discourses, Q 17:23–37 provides a sanction on all the previous covenantal, prophetic, and other discourses by comparing the future divine judgment to the suddenness with which both Noah's flood and the fiery destruction of Sodom happened when Lot escaped. Again traditional Israelite forms and a stance at the climax of Israel's history frame the allusions. The concluding saying of Q 22:28–30 refers to the twelve tribes of Israel and declares that Jesus' representatives will be "effecting justice for Israel," in the tradition of God effecting justice particularly for the widow and orphan, but also for Israel generally (as seen frequently, e.g., in the Psalms). Combined with other discourses in Q, especially the opening discourse, the renewal of covenant in Q 6:20–49, and the declaration of fulfillment of Israel's history in Q 7:18–35, this final statement in Q 22:28–30 situates Q itself at the climax of Israel's history as it declares that Israel is finally being delivered and restored.

Great / Official vs. Little / Popular Tradition

To explore these references to Israelite tradition, however, is far more complex than it has been made to appear in previous studies of "scripture / the Old Testament in Q" or in recent discussions of "intertextuality." Previous commentators on the use of "scripture" in Q have noted that only three times in Q 4 and once in Q 7:27 could Q be said to "quote" scripture.[7] As discussed in chapters 6 and 11, those may not be actual quotations of a text but references to traditions that stand "written" on sacred scrolls and hence are known to have the authority of sacred writing. Of course, whether Q ever recited a tradition from a text or not is not necessarily a decisive question since probably literate intellectuals such as scribes and Pharisees would also ordinarily have recited "scripture" from memory.

More decisive for understanding Q's relationship to Israelite tradition is its decidedly antiscribal stance. As noted in chapter 4, the Q discourses that pronounce judgment against the Jerusalem ruling house and the scribes and Pharisees were previously taken as directed generally against "all Israel" only because interpreters were still projecting Christian theological constructs onto the texts. These Q discourses should rather be understood in the historical context of their origin in late second-temple Palestine, in which the society was divided between the Roman-appointed Jerusalem and Galilean rulers and their representatives, on the one hand, and the Judean and Galilean people, on the other.[8] Q discourses reflect and express precisely such a division within the society.[9] In Q 7:24–28, for example, we detect a caustic comment about the Herodian ruler Antipas, comfortable in his luxurious palace and clothing in Tiberias, and in Q 13:34–35 we see a prophetic lament pronouncing imminent divine judgment on the high-priestly Jerusalem ruling house. The most biting rhetoric in Q is the series of woes in 11:39–52 that brings specific indictments against the scribes / lawyers and

---

7. For example, Kloppenborg, *Formation of Q*, 247.

8. Argued and documented in Richard A. Horsley, *Sociology and the Jesus Movement* (New York: Crossroad, 1989), chaps. 4–5; and idem, *Galilee: History, Politics, People* (Valley Forge, Pa.: Trinity Press International, 1995).

9. See, for example, Horsley, *Sociology*, chaps. 6–7; and idem, "Social Conflict."

Pharisees for their impact on the people, including that of their specifically scribal activity (that of their "fingers," 11:46). Thus it is not surprising that Q understands Jesus' exhortations, instructions, and prophetic pronouncements pointedly over against the scribes and other intellectual elite: "hidden from the sages and the learned and revealed to babes" (Q 10:21). Interpretation of Q, particularly of Israelite tradition in Q, needs to take into account this pointed self-distancing of the Q discourses from the culture and practice of the scribal elite.

Anthropologists and others make a distinction in the culture of traditional agrarian societies and other complex societies that may be helpful with regard to interpretation of Q in the context of a traditional agrarian society sharply divided between an urban elite and a struggling peasantry: that between the "great tradition" and the "little tradition," or what in certain societies would have been the elite and possibly "official tradition(s)" and the "popular tradition(s)."[10] The distinction between cultural traditions is solidly rooted in the political-economic-religious structural division — that between, on the one hand, the ruling elite who live in cities, operate the institutions that claim to represent the whole people or society, and are often in contact with other urban elites in parallel cities of an empire and, on the other hand, the subsistence-oriented agricultural producers (peasants) who live in semiautonomous and relatively homogeneous villages in which life is governed by local custom. The little tradition is "the distinctive patterns of belief and behavior which are valued by the peasantry"; the great tradition is the corresponding patterns among the society's elite, sometimes embodied in written documents.[11]

The popular and the official traditions are often parallel, interrelated, and interactive in various ways. The one may at points derive from or adapt or oppose the other. For example, for both the official tradition of Jerusalem written in the scrolls of the books of Moses and the popular tradition(s) behind the popular prophetic movements in late second-temple times the exodus of Israel from servitude in Egypt was a foundational event. In the promise-fulfillment theme of the official books of Moses (Genesis through Deuteronomy), however, the exodus was framed in such a way as to lead (by implication) to the establishment of the Davidic monarchy and Solomonic temple. Ironically, the histories composed and recorded in written form by the Judean elite included stories of how Israelites at points mobilized massive revolts against both David's imperial monarchy and Solomon's forced labor required to build the temple (2 Sam. 15–21; 1 Kings 11–12). The northern Israelites must have told stories about the

---

10. This distinction is applied to interpretation of the popular prophetic and messianic movements in late second-temple times in Richard A. Horsley, "Popular Messianic Movements around the Time of Jesus," *CBQ* 46 (1984): 471–95; idem, "'Like One of the Prophets of Old': Two Types of Popular Prophets at the Time of Jesus," *CBQ* 47 (1985): 435–63; idem, *Sociology*, 91–92; and Richard A. Horsley with John S. Hanson, *Bandits, Prophets, and Messiahs* (1985; reprint, Harrisburg, Pa.: Trinity Press International, 1999).

11. The theoretical and comparative study by James C. Scott, "Protest and Profanation: Agrarian Revolt and the Little Tradition," *Theory and Society* 4 (1977): 3–32, 159–210, is particularly suggestive for analysis of Q and other Jesus traditions.

prophetic heroes Elijah and Elisha, who had organized resistance to the oppressive rule of Ahab and Jezebel, stories that survive only because they were useful to the intellectual elites who composed the Deuteronomistic History. For those elites, popular opposition to what was to them an illegitimate northern monarchy was useful for retrospective self-legitimation.[12] Recent studies of narratives and other material from the Judean great tradition that are extant as biblical texts have clarified how they were composed to provide legitimation for the second temple (temple-state) and its priestly aristocracy.[13] We have little or no evidence for how ordinary Judeans responded or interacted with the narratives and litanies of the early second-temple great tradition. There was at least minimal interaction between scribal elite such as the Pharisees and the ordinary people.[14] Ben Sira urges his students to mitigate the worst exploitative effects of their patrons, the Judean magnates, on the Judean peasants. And the rulings not contained in the books of Moses that were promulgated by the Pharisees were intended for the people, as Josephus reports in his account of the squabble between the Pharisees and the Hasmonean high priest John Hyrcanus (*Ant.* 13.296–97).

In second-temple Judea, as in other agrarian societies, the great tradition was not necessarily unitary.[15] Ben Sira provides a remarkable illustration of how the Israelite tradition could be used to legitimate the dominant institutional order of the temple-state, including the incumbent high priest and Zadokite priestly aristocracy around 200 B.C.E.[16] The Epistle of Enoch (*1 Enoch* 92–105), on the other hand, a roughly contemporary scribal product, offers a sharp prophetic indictment, apparently of the same Zadokite high priesthood, by what must be an alienated scribal circle. The Qumran community and the many scrolls they left in caves near the Dead Sea provide illustrations of the extent to which a dissident scribal-priestly group shared the same basic great scriptural tradition with the high-priestly regime holding power in Jerusalem, yet insisted upon a different calendar, different interpretive practices, and different emphases.

As James Scott points out in his comparative analysis of traditional agrarian societies,

> the uniformity of the little tradition in a given society is . . . [even] more problematic. By virtue of the *relative* isolation of its carriers from one another, we may expect the little tradition to display more variety than the great tradition. [Nevertheless,] subsistence-oriented cultivators all growing similar crops, all subject to a capricious nature, and all enmeshed in a wider state with its economic and political demands may well develop similar solutions to common problems. . . . There are [thus] enough

---

12. See especially the essays in Robert B. Coote, ed., *Elijah and Elisha in Socio-Literary Perspective* (Atlanta: Scholars Press, 1992).

13. Robert B. Coote and Mary P. Coote, *Power, Politics, and the Making of the Bible* (Minneapolis: Fortress, 1990).

14. Explored with regard to the Galilean peasantry in Horsley, *Galilee*, chaps. 2 and 6.

15. Scott, "Protest and Profanation," 8.

16. See especially the paean of praise of the ancestors in Sirach 44–50, and the incisive analysis and interpretation by Burton L. Mack, *Wisdom and the Hebrew Epic: Ben Sira's Hymn of Praise of the Fathers* (Chicago: University of Chicago Press, 1985).

centripetal tendencies in peasant culture to compensate, at least in part, for the fragmented nature of peasant social structure.

Certainly compared with the recently created working class of a modern industrial society, a traditional peasantry such as the Galileans and Judeans inherited a great repertoire of "custom, community, and values which influence[d] its behavior."[17]

Scott insists that the great and little traditions are not simply variations on the same cultural tradition. Rather "each represents a *distinct* pattern of belief and practice." In the absence of the integrating factors such as mass media that we are familiar with in modern industrial societies, the popular tradition(s) of an agrarian society such as that in second-temple Palestine would have diverged considerably from the official tradition.[18] That means that it is important to investigate "just how much cultural distance separates them." To pursue this "important analytical question" Scott suggests comparisons of such matters as residence, income, consumption, language, religious practice, education, jural status, and ethnicity.[19]

In patterns of income, consumption, and residence, the high-priestly and Herodian elite were building ever more sumptuous mansions and palaces in Jerusalem, Caesarea, Sepphoris, and Tiberias in Roman-controlled Palestine, funded by the revenues they derived from the peasantry, while the Judean and Galilean villagers labored under multiple layers of economic dues, tithes, offerings, Herodian taxes, and Roman tribute.[20] Thus in late second-temple Judea and Galilee, as in other agrarian societies, "the carriers of each tradition represent classes whose interests are, in some respects, diametrically opposed."[21] The stratification by residence and consumption was reinforced by those of social-religious status, with concentric circles of priestly aristocracy, priests and Levites, and the mass of general Israelites, with those distinctions reinforced by the great scriptural tradition as interpreted by its scribal guardians and cultivators. These social-religious differences were compounded by certain other inner-ethnic differences. Galileans would have ranked below Judeans, at least in the minds of the Jerusalemites at the top, and Jewish families from the Egyptian and Babylonian diaspora brought in by Herod the Great were among the four high-priestly families that dominated Judea in the first century. Differences of language and education further reinforced the gap between the urban elite and the villagers.[22] Apparently the scribal elite still used biblical Hebrew in cultivating the official tradition, and the Herodian administrations in Jerusalem, Sepphoris, and Tiberias used Greek, while most ordinary people spoke some variant (local dialect?) of Aramaic. The scribal circles

---

17. Scott, "Protest and Profanation," 5.

18. Ibid., 7.

19. Ibid., 9.

20. Martin Goodman, *The Ruling Class of Judea* (Cambridge: Cambridge University Press, 1987); Horsley, *Galilee,* esp. chap. 6; K. C. Hanson and Douglas Oakman, *Palestine in the Time of Jesus* (Minneapolis: Fortress, 1998).

21. Scott, "Protest and Profanation," 16.

22. See the provisional sketch of the complex language situation in Palestine in Richard A. Horsley, *Archaeology, History, and Society in Galilee: The Social Context of Jesus and the Rabbis* (Valley Forge, Pa.: Trinity Press International, 1996), chap. 7.

that cultivated the great tradition presided over education of subsequent generations precisely for purposes of continued cultivation of the tradition, whereas
the popular tradition(s) would have been learned informally from household and
community practices and interactions. All of these differences suggest that there
would have been a considerable gap between the official tradition in Jerusalem
and the popular tradition in Judean and Galilean villages.[23]

In Galilee, where the Jesus movement that produced Q originated, differences
of regional history would have compounded the class differences, which created
the gap between the official Jerusalem tradition and the local popular tradition.
Scott points out that "the closeness of an elite's culture to that of its peasantry
depends, in large part, on how its great tradition developed" and its historical
relation to the peasantry and its tradition.[24] Jerusalem was originally a Canaanite
(Jebusite) city (2 Samuel 5). But, according to the Jerusalem-based great tradition, besides perpetuating standard Canaanite traditions, David and Solomon
installed or constructed Israelite institutions such as the ark of the covenant and
the temple in Jerusalem (2 Samuel 6; 1 Kings 8) and reconstrued Israel's history in such a way that it led inexorably to the establishment of the Davidic
monarchy in Jerusalem, presumably to unite Israel under their monarchic rule.
The same Jerusalem-based great tradition, not uncritical of the Davidic monarchy, includes stories of Israel's massive rebellions against David and Solomon's
successor (2 Samuel 15–21; 1 Kings 11–12).

Historically, the bulk of Israel, including the Galilean tribes, were in rebellion
against Jerusalem rule since the death of Solomon. After the Assyrian conquest
of the kingdom of Israel, moreover, the people of Galilee lived under a separate
(Babylonian or Persian or Ptolemaic or Seleucid) imperial administrative district
than did the Judeans. Not until a hundred years before Herod's death and Jesus'
birth did Galilee again become subject to Jerusalem rule. The priestly aristocracy
of the Jerusalem temple-state and their scribal circles apparently developed a rich
great tradition in early second-temple times. Yet since the Jerusalem temple-state
did not have jurisdiction over Galilee, they had no administrative mechanism by
which they could have brought that tradition to bear on life in Galilean villages
until the intensely troubled and disruptive last decades of Hasmonean rule and
the even more chaotic beginnings of Roman rule in Palestine. Josephus says that
when the Hasmonean regime took control of Galilee after 104 B.C.E., it required
the Galileans to live according to "the laws of the Judeans" (Ant. 13.318, etc.).
Since it would have been impossible to replace the previous culture and customs
of village life, that presumably meant that the relations between villagers and the
Jerusalem temple-state would have been conducted according to "the laws of the
Judeans," but that the local popular tradition(s) according to which village life was
carried on would have continued. It is conceivable that coming under Jerusalem

---

23. The historical background of these differences are explored in Horsley, *Galilee*, chaps. 1–2, 6, and summarized in chap. 3 above.

24. Scott, "Protest and Profanation," 10.

rule again after eight centuries of separation would have revived both a sense of common Israelite heritage shared with Judeans and Jerusalemites (over against imperial rulers) and a sense of a common popular Israelite heritage with Judeans over against Jerusalem rulers, their representatives, and particular features of the official Jerusalem tradition.[25]

These features of the structural and historical relations between the bearers of the official Jerusalemite tradition and the Israelite popular tradition illuminate how "the material and symbolic hegemony normally exercised by ruling institutions does not preclude, but rather engenders, a set of contrary values which represent in their entirety a kind of 'shadow society.'"[26] In Galilean village culture, as in other agrarian societies, the popular tradition(s) would have been "not simply a crude version of" the Jerusalem-based great tradition. It would have functioned also "as a symbolic criticism of elite values and beliefs... for the most part muted within a context of subordination."[27] "Under certain circumstances, however,... forms of symbolic conflict may become manifest and amount to a political or religious mobilization of the little tradition."[28] That the bifurcation of tradition is more than simply a clash of ideas or of varying versions of the same stories can be seen in the multiple popular prophetic and messianic movements that emerged from among the Judean and Galilean villagers during the generation of Jesus and that of the Jesus movement that produced Q.[29]

Thus we should be prepared to recognize in the very existence of Q the production of a movement mobilized on the basis of the Israelite popular tradition long operative in Galilee. Yet because this product emerging from the Israelite popular tradition shared both cultural roots and cultural content with the official Jerusalem tradition known in what became canonical biblical texts and because there had been generations of interaction between them, it should be possible to make useful comparisons between Israelite traditions referred to in Q and Israelite traditions appearing in biblical and extrabiblical Judean texts.

The question of textual and other sources and the relationship of extant texts to historical processes and relationships is an extremely complex one with regard to the Israelite "great" and "little" traditions in late second-temple times. Since it is almost completely oral, popular tradition leaves no direct textual evidence. Its very existence must often be deduced from the behavior and movements of ordinary people, often as portrayed in accounts of the literate elite who, feeling threatened by them, are hostile witnesses. Biblical texts and some extrabiblical Judean literature are unusual among world literatures, however, in having in-

---

25. A comment by Scott, "Protest and Profanation," 18, is pertinent to the Israelite popular tradition in its relation to the Jerusalem-based great tradition: "The little tradition's dissent may also derive from the fact that its social base, the peasant community, is both historically and functionally *prior* to cities and to the great tradition."

26. Ibid., 19.

27. Ibid., 12.

28. Ibid.

29. Horsley, "Popular Messianic Movements," 471–95; idem, "'Like One of the Prophets of Old,'" 435–63.

cluded — although often also overwritten — a great deal of popular expression. For example, some of the accounts of the exodus, the Song of Deborah, much of the material in biblical law codes, many of the fragments of prophetic oracles, and some of the stories of Elijah and Elisha appear to be popular, oral cultural expressions onto which biblical literature provides windows although not direct access. Similarly, the Q discourses incorporated into and/or adapted by Matthew and Luke and much if not most of the materials in the Gospel of Mark appear to be expressions of popular tradition. Ancient Judean literature, whether or not it became part of the biblical canon, was by definition shaped and written in scribal circles, which were ordinarily serving the interests of the temple-state and its priestly aristocracy. Much of the extant Judean literature, however, was produced by dissident scribal circles, whether it be the apocalypses included in *1 Enoch,* the *Psalms of Solomon,* or the products of the Qumran community such as the Community Rule. Because those who held power in Jerusalem claimed the parts of the great tradition that legitimated their position, it is not surprising that dissident scribal-priestly groups often reached for those parts of the great tradition that had originated in popular tradition. A clear example is the Qumran community, in literature such as the Community Rule and its interpretations of prophetic oracles, which sees itself in terms of new exodus and renewed covenant and applies prophetic oracles to its own experience of alienation and persecution. Nevertheless, such scribal literature also gives clear indications of its roots in and orientation to the great tradition, often revealing its hopes for a return to positions of power and influence (e.g., some of the Dead Sea Scrolls or *Psalms of Solomon*).

Use of such dissident scribal-priestly literature as sources for and comparisons with (admittedly often hypothesized) popular tradition must thus be critical and nuanced. It is also noteworthy that extant literature as well as archaeological excavations may provide evidence for nonliterary expressions of the great tradition, such as buildings and monuments, as well as nonliterary expressions of the popular tradition, such as popular protests and movements. And these nonliterary expressions of great and little traditions can also shed light on oral-derived texts such as the Q discourses. Although the use of sources in all these cases is problematic and requires complicated critical judgments, texts such as law codes in the Pentateuch, prophetic oracles, late second-temple period psalms, and accounts of popular movements in Josephus's histories, as well as archaeological finds, can provide windows onto how materials common to the two traditions, great and little, may have functioned at different social levels and enable us to make informed projections about the varying uses of contested Israelite traditions.

Contested Israelite Traditions in Q

Examining Q's references to and uses of Israelite tradition will thus be a complex task, which can be explored only in preliminary ways here. Given recent reticence to explore Israelite tradition in Q, part of the task is simply to identify references and allusions. Another important aspect of the task will be to identify traditional

Israelite forms operative in Q discourses. Balancing the tendency of studies in Synoptic Gospel materials to focus only on the form of individual sayings, it will be particularly important to discern broader traditional forms in some of the Q discourses. Given the class division in ancient society and the struggle between the great and the popular traditions that shared many particular Israelite traditions, we must attend carefully to indications that the traditions Q refers to were contested in the broader context of the communities Q addressed. Q's roots in and expressions of popular Israelite tradition, sometimes even pointedly over against the corresponding great tradition, are more clearly evident in some discourses than others. In most cases only comparison and contrast with scribal use of the same contested tradition will enable us to recognize the difference between the great and little traditions. Q's use of Mosaic covenantal tradition, prophetic testing tradition, and prophetic renewal tradition (particularly Elijah-Elisha) will be explored in the discussions of Q 6:20–49; Q 9:57–10:16; and Q 4:1–13 in chapters 9, 10, and 11. This chapter will focus on Q's use of the theme of Israel's renewal in its twelve tribes, its references to prophets and uses of prophetic forms, its treatment of the Torah, and its references to key figures such as Abraham and Solomon.

The Restoration of Israel (Q 22:28–30)

This concluding pronouncement in Q (22:28–30) was seriously transformed in Matthew and has been one of the key proof texts that Q proclaims judgment against all Israel. As noted in chapter 4, however, that interpretation is a projection of a Christian (supersessionist) construct of Christianity emerging from and replacing Judaism in the divine economy of salvation. The "Son of Man . . . on the throne of his glory" must be stripped away as a distinctively Matthean overlay. With or without that grand royal scenario, it is clear that Matthew understood Q in terms of the *restoration* of Israel, not its judgment, from the term *palingenesis*, which Josephus also used in reference to the historical restoration of the people not only in their twelve tribes but also in their land (*Ant.* 11.66, 107).[30] Christian Bible translations continue to perpetuate the "judgment" misunderstanding by translating *krinein* with "judging." Ironically, standard word studies have long since made it clear that the meaning here, as in Septuagint translations of *špt*, is not the negative-sounding "judge/*richten*" but the positive "establish justice for" or "deliver."[31] In Israelite tradition, God does not "judge" but "delivers" ("liberates/saves/effects justice for") the orphan, widow, poor, oppressed (e.g., Pss. 9; 10:18; 35; 58; 72:4; 76:9; 82:1–4; 94; 103:6; 140:12; 146:7), or even the whole people (Isa. 42:1, parallel with "salvation" in 49:6) and other peoples (Pss. 96:13; 98:9). However grand and unrealistic its expectation may seem to realistic modern Christian scholars and Bible translators, here in Jesus'

---

30. For this and the following points, see the fuller discussion in Horsley, *Jesus*, 199–208.
31. See, for example, Volmar Herntrich and Friedrich Buchsel, "*Krino*," in *TDNT*, 3:923–41.

final pronouncement Q was proclaiming the deliverance or renewal of Israel in its twelve tribes.

The restoration of the twelve tribes had become one of the principal images of the future renewal of Israel, in both prophetic and sapiential literature. The ways in which this image was shaped and used in literature produced by dissident scribal circles who had come from, and desired restoration to, positions of power and influence provide instructive comparison for how Q uses the image. The restoration of the tribes was a longstanding theme in Judean literature. "Second" Isaiah linked the restoration of the tribes with fulfillment of the promise to the ancestors; the servant of Yahweh is called "to raise up the tribes of Jacob" (Isa. 49:6). Ben Sira appealed to God to gather the tribes of Jacob and give them their inheritance and indicates that one of the appointed functions of the returning Elijah, the earlier restorer of Israel, will be "to restore the tribes of Jacob" (Sir. 36:13; 48:10). The inclusion of the passage on Elijah in the great hymn of praise of the ancestors (Sirach 44–50), most of whom were the illustrious high-ranking kings and high priests of Israel, is a good example of how a figure originally from popular tradition of the northern Israelite tribes had been installed firmly into the Jerusalem-based great tradition. Early Christian groups continued this standard way of symbolizing the restoration of Israel (Rev. 21:10–14; Acts 26:7; etc.).

Most important for comparison with Q is that the Qumran community, acting in anticipation of imminent fulfillment, structured its leadership in terms of twelve symbolic representatives of the twelve tribes: twelve chief priests and twelve representative Levites, "one for each tribe" (1QM 2:2–3); twelve chiefs of the twelve tribes, along with the "prince" and priestly leaders (1QM 5:1–3); twelve loaves of bread offered by the heads of the tribes (11QT 18:14–16); and a community council consisting of twelve laymen along with three priests (1QS 8:1–3). Not surprisingly for the Qumran community, the role of these twelve and three is conceived in highly scribal-sapiential as well as covenantal terms: "perfectly versed in the Torah, . . . they shall preserve faith in the land . . . and atone for sin by the practice of justice." The major differences with Q discourses are the priestly hierocracy and scribal activity at Qumran, utterly foreign to Q, and the intense apocalyptic tone and systematic apocalyptic perspective of the authors of 1QS, 1QM, and other texts, in contrast with the paucity of apocalyptic worldview and motifs in Q discourses. The Qumran War Scroll and Community Rule present a scribal anticipation of the restoration of Israel in its twelve tribes, while the concluding pronouncement of Q presents a nonscribal popular anticipation.

Psalms of Solomon 17 presents not a priestly centered but a scribal-sapiential and Jerusalem-centered vision of the restoration of Israel in its twelve tribes led by a scribal anointed son of David. As in Q, the overarching theme or symbol is the kingdom of God, although in the psalm God's kingdom has a more explicitly universal scope and certain imperial traits, whereas the kingdom of God in Q pertains directly to the people and their lives in village communities. The scribal authors, who had no political power themselves but depended on priestly or royal patrons, envision that the restoration will be accomplished "from the top down" by an anointed son of David in a somewhat imperial, albeit intellectual, royal manner, "destroying nations with the word of his mouth" (not the sword; 17:24) and subjecting the Gentiles to servitude under his yoke (17:30). His focal function is that

> He will gather a holy people whom he will lead in righteousness; and he will judge the tribes of the people that have been made holy by the Lord their God.... He will distribute them upon the land according to their tribes. (17:26–28)[32]

The most striking differences between the restoration of Israel in its twelve tribes in the *Psalms of Solomon* 17 and Q 22:28–30 are the psalm's scribal dependence on an imperial royal figure to do the work and its emphasis on his restoration of a purged Jerusalem, from which he will rule Israel as well as the nations. The psalm envisions an imperial but reformist royal messiah purging Jerusalem of corrupt officials and making it "holy as it was even from the beginning," presumably under David himself (17:30, 36; cf. 17:4). The scribal memory that informs the fantasy here is somewhat selective, forgetting the large section of the Deuteronomistic History that recounted the massive popular rebellions against David, once he assumed a fully monarchic position in the Jebusite (i.e., originally Canaanite, non-Israelite) city of Jerusalem, which he had conquered with his own personal mercenary troops as a capital from which to rule over Israel. One wonders if the descendants of northern Israelites, who rebelled successfully against the Davidic monarchy after the death of Solomon, had a better memory for how Jerusalem-based rulers treated their subjects. For Q includes an explicit prophetic lament over the imminent desolation of the ruling city (13:34–35) as well as the expectation of Israel's restoration headed not by a royal messiah but by representatives of the people themselves establishing justice for the twelve tribes (Q 22:28–30).

The *Testament of Judah*, from the *Testaments of the Twelve Patriarchs*, appears to stand somewhere in between *Psalms of Solomon* 17 and Q on a spectrum of great to little tradition. The *Testament of Judah* articulates a tradition similar to that of *Psalms of Solomon* 17, with a much less imperial role for a royal messiah and more of a role for the (rest of the) twelve, conceived as "chiefs (wielding) our scepter in Israel" (*T. Judah* 25:1).[33] In relation to Q it is surely significant that the same sentence in *T. Judah* 25:1 has Abraham, Isaac, and Jacob resurrected into the final restoration of Israel, just as does Q 13:28–29, which also focuses its expectation with the traditional eschatological banquet image, as does 1QSa. One wonders

---

32. Like those who worked on the RSV and other translators of the Gospels into English, R. B. Wright, the translator of the *Psalms of Solomon*, in *The Old Testament Pseudepigrapha*, vol. 2, ed. James H. Charlesworth (Garden City, N.Y.: Doubleday, 1985), does not follow the careful studies of the LXX and other Jewish use of *krinein* and related terms, for a people already made holy hardly requires "judging" by their messiah. "Do justice for" or "establish justice among" the tribes carries the sense better.

33. Again, to translate the preceding verse, 24:6, with "to judge" as well as "to save all that call on the Lord" does not adequately render the completely positive sense of deliverance ("to establish justice for") in this passage. See H. C. Kee, *Testaments of the Twelve Patriarchs*, in Charlesworth, *Old Testament Pseudepigrapha*, 1:801.

about the degree to which the "thrones" in Q 22:28–30 elevate representative leaders above the rest of the Q people within a movement that otherwise seems relatively egalitarian, judging from the other Q discourses.

Prophets

Perhaps the most ominous indication in Q of just how contested Israelite traditions were in late second-temple times is the reference to the contemporary building of the tombs of the prophets, followed by the accusation of the previous killing of the prophets, in Q 11:47–51. The latter charge is repeated in Q 13:34–35. Contemporary Judean literature provides some clear windows onto how the prophets were being memorialized both in the building of monuments, as charged in Q 11:47–48, and in extrabiblical literary elaboration of prophetic traditions, as will be discussed in chapter 13. The charge of killing the prophets sent by God appeared at points in Israelite tradition long before late second-temple times, and Israelite tradition included several memorable cases of rulers' killing or attempting to kill prophets. Ahab and Jezebel had attempted to get rid of Elijah (1 Kings 19), a story that would likely have been remembered in the north of Israel, where he had been active. Jeremiah had been the object of repeated persecution and attempted lynching. Another prophet who prophesied against Jerusalem was hunted down and killed by Jehoiakim (Jer. 26:20–23). Such traditions would have been all the more significant to ordinary people living out of the popular tradition at the time of Jesus and the Q people, because of the rash of prophet killings during the mid–first century c.e. The Roman governors slaughtered the popular prophet Theudas and the "Egyptian" Jewish prophet and the Samaritan prophet who led popular movements in eager anticipation of a new act of divine deliverance like those led by Moses and Joshua in ancient times (Ant. 18.85–87; 20.97–98, 169–71; B.J. 2.261–63; cf. Acts 5:36). In Galilee the recent execution of John the Baptist would have evoked memories of earlier prophets killed, as carried in Israelite popular tradition.

In the great tradition based in Jerusalem, as known from Hebrew biblical literature, the theme of the sending and rejection of the prophets appeared more frequently than the charge of killing the prophets. Many recent studies of Q have accepted, without much critical discussion, that the motifs of God's sending and the people's rejection of the prophets were parts of a larger scheme of the "deuteronomistic" view of history.[34] As presented and applied to Q, however, the

---

34. The thesis of the prominence of the deuteronomic tradition in second-temple times and its implicit structuring role in Q was developed in Odil Hannes Steck's *Israel und das gewaltsame Geschick der Propheten: Untersuchung zur Überlieferung des deuteronomistischen Geschichtsbildes im Alten Testament, Spätjudentum und Urchristentum,* WMANT 23 (Neukirchen-Vluyn: Neukirchener Verlag, 1967). Its most accessible discussion in English is Jacobson, *First Gospel,* esp. 72–76. Steck's stated approach, as explained in a recent paper by Jacobson ("Odil Hannes Steck's Contributions to the Study of the Traditions of Israel in Q," delivered at the Q Section of the SBL 1998 Annual Meeting), seems highly appropriate to the available materials and issues entailed in understanding how Israelite tradition functioned. He deals with "textual units which are dependent upon oral tradition" rather than "*literary* dependence among textual units." He focuses on "conceptual units [attested in certain texts] which

deuteronomistic tradition appears to be a rather vague and amorphous construct. Closer examination of the texts adduced as manifestations of the tradition indicates that different combinations of the component motifs appear from text to text. Rarely if ever do all the supposed components[35] appear in the texts cited. Most of the supposed examples of the deuteronomistic tradition lack the motifs of God sending and Israel (or its rulers) rejecting the prophets (e.g., Ezra 9:6–15; Neh. 1:5–11; Tob. 3:1–6; Ps. 106:6–46; Deut. 4:25–31; 28:45–68 + 30:1–10; 1 Kings 8:46–53), and many contain only the themes of Israel's general disobedience and God's punishment. The deuteronomistic view of history was clearly derived from and dependent on the Mosaic covenantal tradition (as can be seen clearly in the penitential prayers in Dan. 9:4–19 and Bar. 1:15–3:8) and is often difficult to distinguish from what are more broadly covenantal motifs and themes. About the only texts cited that mention the sending and rejection of the prophets (briefly!), in the context of a long recitation of God's deliverance and the ancestors' disobedience, followed by a brief declaration of punishment, are the covenant renewal ceremony in Neh. 9:5–37 and the penitential prayers in Dan. 9:4–19 and Bar. 1:15–3:8. If the deuteronomistic tradition had become the common property of a number of different groups by late second-temple times, then it would have been widespread in the society generally and not particularly helpful in discerning the distinctive features of a particular group or text and the tradition on which it was drawing.

It is highly questionable, furthermore, whether Q as a whole or Q 11:47–51 and 13:34–35 in particular express the deuteronomistic view of history as it is described, since the motifs of the sending and the rejection of the prophets and the resulting divine punishment occur only in Q 11:47–51 and 13:34–35, and none of the other key motifs occurs clearly anywhere in Q. Most telling perhaps, while the deuteronomistic scheme looks back on both Israel's disobedience and God's punishment as having occurred to the ancestors in the past (setting up a call to repentance or an appeal for new deliverance), the Q discourses pronounce an imminent punishment of the rulers and their representatives for present as well

---

are fairly stable, often using fixed themes and terminology." And he "also attends to the *bearers* of various traditions." (Jacobson, *First Gospel*, 4). With more than thirty years of subsequent analysis of the traditions attested in Hebrew biblical and related second-temple Judean literature since Steck's analysis, however, it is evident that the four principal streams of tradition he and others projected behind the texts — priestly-theocratic, wisdom, prophetic-eschatological, and levitical-deuteronomistic — are all rather vague general constructions abstracted from the concrete political struggles of second-temple Judea and now in need of thorough reexamination. The reconstruction of late second-temple groups on which he depended for projecting the bearers of these traditions (Steck, *Israel*, 206–9), particularly the "Hasidic movement" and its splintering, is now widely questioned. For a critical review of the whole question of the Deuteronomistic History, see Patricia Gutcher-Walls, "The Social Location of the Deuteronomists: A Sociological Study of Factional Politics in Late Pre-Exilic Judah," *Journal for the Study of the Old Testament* 52 (1991), 77–94; and Gary Knoppers, *Two Nations under God*, SBL Monograph Series 52–53 (Atlanta: Scholars Press, 1993), 1:1–56.

35. The component motifs of the deuteronomistic view of history are: (*a*) the history of Israel is recited as one of persistent disobedience; (*b*) God sent the prophets to call Israel to repent; (*c*) Israel rejected the prophets, killing some; (*d*) God (will) punish(ed) Israel; (*e*) there is a new call to repent; and (*f*) if Israel repents, (1) God will restore it, and (2) God will bring judgment on Israel's enemies.

as past violence and injustice in conjunction with the renewal of Israel already underway in Jesus' preaching and practice.

For interpretation of Q 11:47–51 and 13:34–35 in particular, the most suggestive (supposedly deuteronomistic) texts may be several from Jeremiah. They lack the motif of killing the prophets that seems central in these two Q passages. But they do exhibit the same combination of God's punishment with his sending and the rulers rejecting the prophets who called for justice. In Jer. 7:21–35, the sequence of the sending and rejection of the prophets and the prophetic pronouncement of punishment is connected with condemnation of the temple at the head of an exploitative system (7:21–22; cf. 7:1–15!). In Jer. 25:4, the sending and rejection of the prophets are mentioned in the context of destruction in punishment for refusing to heed Jeremiah's persistent prophetic protest against injustice (25:1–14). In Jeremiah's letter to that portion of the Jerusalem ruling class already exiled in Babylon, Jeremiah 29, he recites God's sending and the ruling class's rejection of the prophets as one reason for God's condemnation (Jer. 29:17–19). In Jeremiah 35, the same combination of motifs is cited in a demonstrative prophecy directed against the temple. And in a letter to exiles in Egypt, Jeremiah 44, the sending and rejection of prophets are recited in connection with the crimes of the kings of Judah that lead to God's punishment.

The penitential prayers prefatory to covenant renewal that provide the most convincing examples of the deuteronomistic tradition present fascinating case studies of the interaction between the popular and the great traditions. In any historical reconstruction of the Deuteronomistic History, its authors used Mosaic covenantal and prophetic materials based in tribal/village Israel in support of a program to centralize power in Jerusalem. After the destruction of Jerusalem and the original temple and the demise of the Davidic monarchy forced the issue, moreover, the exiled Jerusalem ruling elite acknowledged the validity of the pre-exilic prophets' insistence that their failure to observe the Mosaic covenant would result in defeat by foreign powers. In the penitential prayers in Nehemiah 9 and Baruch 1–3, the restored Jerusalem elite confess their own ancestors' disobedience of the Mosaic covenant and rejection of the prophets in petitioning God to restore their fortunes more fully, apparently in full confidence in the continuing validity of God's unconditional promise to (covenant with) Abraham. The building of monuments to the prophets, who had condemned the rulers of their own time, was a parallel "penitential" adjustment to representatives of the popular tradition by the late second-temple elite. The prophets who had sharply criticized the rulers and their representatives in a previous time were honored and incorporated into the great tradition by the very descendants of those who had castigated or persecuted them because of their criticism. That, of course, is precisely what Q 11:47–48 condemns, from the popular point of view. There is no "breakdown" in the "logic" of Q here.[36] The popular tradition and the Q people have a con-

---

36. The question of such a breakdown in Q and of its pointing to the hidden premise of the Q people being persecuted is raised by Robert J. Miller, "The Rejection of the Prophets in Q," *JBL* 107

sistent view of the consistent behavior of their rulers and the scribal elite. The monuments to the prophets and penitential prayers, however, represent an inner conflict or contradiction not in Q but in the elites' behavior and their great tradition. In honoring their fathers' victims they are indeed implicitly admitting their fathers' guilt, just as in their penitential prayers they confess their fathers' sins.

The deuteronomistic tradition as delineated in connection with Q provides little or no background for the charge of killing the prophets in Q 11:47–48, 49–51 (cf. 13:34). Only in Neh. 9:26 is it mentioned that the Israelite ancestors had killed God's prophets. Only a few cases of prophet-killing or attempted prophet-killing are mentioned in the other books that became canonical scripture: Ahab's and Jezebel's attempt to eliminate Elijah and other "troublesome" prophets of Yahweh (1 Kings 18–19); King Jehoiakim's murder of Uriah son of Shemaiah, the contemporary of Jeremiah who prophesied against the ruling city of Jerusalem (Jer. 26:20–23); and the violent treatment of Jeremiah by officials of the temple and monarchy. On the other hand, the late second-temple legends, mentioned above, reflected in documents such as the *Martyrdom of Isaiah* and the *Lives of the Prophets* attest the apparently current belief that the ancestral rulers had killed several prophets and severely persecuted others. One wonders about the degree to which such legends reflect the late second-temple experience of so many popular prophets, their movements, other popular leaders, and popular protesters being killed by the Jerusalem and Roman rulers.

Matthew's transformation of the "sign" of Jonah in Q 11:30 into an allegory for the death and eventual resurrection of "the Son of Man" conforms the overall reference to Jonah in Q 11:29–32 to the contents of the story and book of Jonah that became canonical. Josephus's account of Jonah (*Ant.* 9.206–14) concentrates on the legend of his vain flight by sea, then conforms his message to Nineveh to Nahum's prophecy of its historical defeat. The focus in Q on Jonah's preaching and the Ninevites' repentance departs more significantly from the emphasis in the book of Jonah itself. Q's reference to Jonah's preaching as a sign and the Ninevites' repentance resembles more an alternative tradition about Jonah appearing in somewhat later texts that may well build on or reflect popular tradition that directs the burden of Jonah's repentance preaching to the Ninevites back on Jerusalem. Proem 31 to *Lamentations Rabbah* attributes to Rabbi Simeon b. Yohai (second century) the declaration that the "oppressive city" Jerusalem ought to have learned from Jonah and Nineveh. "One prophet I sent to Nineveh and she turned in penitence; but to Israel in Jerusalem I sent many prophets.... Yet she hearkened not." Similarly the (late?) first-century *Lives of the Prophets* (10:10) has Jonah give a "portent concerning Jerusalem and the whole land."

(1988): 230. The parallel between the Q people's persecution and that of the earlier persecution of the prophets is not hidden in Q 6:22–23. Moreover, "violent men" were storming the kingdom of God, its original preacher, and presumably its subsequent preachers, according to Q 16:16. Q 11:47–51 thus may well reflect the Q people's experience of repression by the authorities, but there is no basis in Q for claiming that Q 11:47–51 is pervaded by "a keen sense of failure" in and "presupposes wholesale rejection" of the Q people (*pace* Miller, "Rejection," 231).

Jonah's preaching and the Ninevites' response may have had popular currency in Galilee because his memory was cultivated there among the people, and not simply as a topic in later rabbinic discussions.[37] The prophet Jonah son of Amittai came originally from Gath-hepher, which was located in Zebulun, in lower Galilee, in the traditional tribal allotment of territory (2 Kings 14:25; Josh. 19:13). Jerome attests local tradition locating the tomb of Jonah in Gath-hepher, "two miles on the road from Sepphoris, today called Diocaesarea, towards Tiberias" (*Comm. in Jonam, Prol. Patrologia Latina*, 25:1119). Rabbinic discussions also locate Jonah in Gath-hepher, which was called Gobebatha (of Sepphoris) in late antiquity. And in contrast to later Christian sources that link Jonah with a shrine near Lydda on the southwestern coast of Palestine, Jewish pilgrimage itineraries locate the tomb of Jonah near Sepphoris along the road to Tiberias.[38] What would appear to be a separate legend (attested in *Lives of the Prophets* 10), while having him originate in the south near Azotus, has Jonah active in the north and closely associated with Elijah, as the widow's son that Elijah raised from the dead (1 Kings 17:8–15).[39] Such references suggest that Jonah may have been an important prophetic hero in the popular tradition particularly in Galilee, with his memory attached to a village only a few miles from Nazareth.

Prophetic Forms

The woes against the scribes/lawyers and Pharisees in Q 11:39–52 offer an opportunity to discern how broader forms from Israelite tradition than those of individual sayings inform the Q discourses. This was ignored in previous studies because of preoccupation with Jesus vs. the Pharisees on the Law, and it has gone unexplored in recent studies because of their keen interest in the role of Wisdom in Q and in "this generation" as a key to Q's redaction. As will be explored further in chapter 13, however, the series of woes plus a statement of punishment in Q 11:39–52 takes a form familiar from prophets such as Amos, Micah, Isaiah, and Habakkuk. These prophets declared not only single woes as an in-

---

37. Jonah's connection with Galilee is rarely noticed in works on Jesus and the Synoptic Gospels, as noted by Jonathan L. Reed, "The Sign of Jonah and Other Epic Traditions in Q," in *Re-imagining Christian Origins: Essays in Honor of Burton L. Mack*, ed. Elizabeth Castelli and Hal Taussig (Valley Forge, Pa.: Trinity Press International, 1996), 134–36, who has gathered the key evidence and earlier scholarly discussions on which the following paragraph depends. Reed also recognizes the importance of shifting the focus from how Q might be using "the Hebrew Scriptures to the selection of figures, events, and places found both within, alongside, and outside the Hebrew Scriptures" (130). Also useful is the information and discussion in Anna Maria Schwemer, *Studien zu den frühjüdischen Prophetenlegenden Vitae Prophetarum* (Tübingen: J. C. B. Mohr [Paul Siebeck], 1995), 2:48–83.

38. According to Reed, "Sign of Jonah," 135, the ancient descriptions of the site "all coincide with the modern village of el-Meshhed, where to this day inhabitants will show visitors the tomb of *nebi junis*, Jonah the prophets." Surface surveys by archaeologists indicate that the site was inhabited more or less continually from the Iron Age through Persian times and into Roman-Byzantine periods. See William F. Albright, "New Israelite and Pre-Israelite Sites: The Spring Trip of 1929," *Bulletin of the American Schools of Oriental Research* 35 (1929): 8; Zvi Gal, *Lower Galilee during the Iron Age* (Winona Lake, Ind.: Eisenbrauns, 1992), 18.

39. *Midrash Rabbah, Genesis II* (London: Soncino, 1939), 959.

dictment and sentence against kings and their officers for breaking covenantal principles in exploitation of the people. They also pronounced whole series of woes plus sentence (e.g., Isa. 5:18–19, 20, 21, 22–23 + 24). And the recurrence of the same form in the Epistle of Enoch (*1 Enoch* 94–105) indicates the prophetic form of a series of woes plus declaration of punishment was still alive later in second-temple times.

Q clearly uses this form of woes against the very scribal elite responsible for the cultivation and interpretation of the official Israelite tradition in the Jerusalem temple-state. Thus the woes aimed at the guardians of the great tradition in Q 11:39–52 are apparently rooted in popular tradition. The woes pronounced by the dissident scribal group that produced the Epistle of Enoch provide an interesting comparison for those in Q 11:39–52. The content of the indictments in *1 Enoch* 94–105 are true to the prophetic tradition, castigating the wealthy and powerful "sinners" for their oppression and exploitation of the poor (as well as their persecution of the "righteous" — the self-reference by the authors?). Whereas the Q woes form part of a larger agenda of the renewal of Israel as a whole, however, the woes in *1 Enoch* 94–105 anticipate only the eschatological vindication of the "righteous" (95:3; 96:2; 98:12; 104:2, 6) who are clearly indicated at key points as the dissident scribal authors (see esp. 98:14–16; 99:2; 103:1–3; 104:1, 10–13).

For Q's use of two other traditional prophetic forms of speech we have some fragments of evidence that they were current in or near the popular level. The prophetic pronouncement over Jerusalem in Q 13:34–35 has the form of a prophetic lament (cf. the book of Lamentations, in which 2:13–17 is addressed directly to Jerusalem / Zion; for the closely related "dirge," see, e.g., Amos 2:2–3). Josephus's account of Jesus son of Hananiah allows the reader to discern that his pronouncement ("A voice from the east, a voice from the west,...a voice against Jerusalem and the sanctuary" [*B.J.* 6.300–301]) must have been a dirge or lament (or a "woe" pronouncement, discussed above). Josephus thus indicates that a "crude peasant" (*tōn idiōtōn agroikos*) was quite capable of using such a traditional prophetic form in late second-temple times. Apparently the form of "prophetic correlative" used in the "sign of Jonah" saying (Q 11:30), as well as in the discourse that appears to sanction the whole series of preceding discourses (Q 17:24, 26, 28, 30), was fairly widely employed in Judean and other Jewish circles. Originally thought to be distinctive to Q, this form can be found at many points in the Septuagint version of prophetic books. Yet it would be inappropriately labeled a Septuagintal form, since it is also attested in Judean texts from Qumran, 1Q27 1:6; 4QpsDanAa = 4Q246 2:1–2 ("As comets [flash] to the sight, so shall be their kingdom"). The latter text is not in the archaizing imitation of biblical Hebrew but belongs to a group of more popular Aramaic texts that display striking parallels to the psalms in Luke 1–2.[40]

40. See Joseph A. Fitzmyer, *A Wandering Aramean: Collected Aramaic Essays* (Chico, Calif.: Scholars Press, 1979), 90–93.

The Torah / Law

In some treatments of Q the only Q references to Israelite traditions discussed are the ostensible references to the Torah/Law. Modern Western individualism and Christian theological concepts continue to determine the categories according to which the key passages are treated.[41] Concepts such as soteriology and the individual's moral state may not be applicable to the function of Q discourses in their historical social context. Continuing to work with interpretive concepts rooted in a Lutheran/Protestant theology that pits early Christian ethical law against the supposed Jewish preoccupation with ceremonial law may simply block insight into the issues addressed in Q discourses. The most obvious appearance of the Torah in Q comes in Q 16:16–18. On the basis of Q 16:17–18 and 11:42c, recent Q interpreters suggest that Q, at least in its late "redaction," attempted to " 'rejudaize' Jesus."[42] But the interpretation of 16:16 as a relativization or supersession of the Law and 16:17–18 as a qualification or reversal of that is an imposition of a Christian theological view of the break Christianity made from Judaism centered on the Law. Apart from such a Christian theological viewpoint, in what way would Q ever have been "de-judaized" — or rather de-Israelitized?

Abandoning the Christian theological focus on ethical vs. ceremonial law enables us to recognize that the woes against the scribes/lawyers and Pharisees in Q 11:39–52 are not primarily about the Law. Rather, as noted above, they are primarily indictments against the scribes and Pharisees for the deleterious effects of their role on the people. The woes are, however, a clear window onto the conflict between the great and popular Israelite traditions. The comment about their "cleansing the outside of the cup" in 11:39 and the charge that they are "like unmarked graves" in 11:44 mock their concerns about cultic purity.[43] But purity was a matter of concern for priests, particularly the high priests who officiated in the temple cult in Jerusalem and their scribal and Pharisaic retainers. In these Q woes we see an earlier version from the popular Galilean viewpoint of the same conflict between priestly-scribal concerns and those of the ordinary people as emerges later in rabbinic comments about the boorish behavior of the am-ha-aretz, the "people of the land," who fail to observe the purity codes. In the scribal great tradition the purity codes may well have been closely related to the Torah as implementation of the distinctive concerns of the priests and priestly aristocracy. But such matters were relevant to the peasantry mainly as they im-

---

41. For example, in the articles by and debate between John S. Kloppenborg, "Nomos and Ethos in Q," in *Gospel Origins and Christian Beginnings: Essays in Honor of James M. Robinson*, ed. James E. Goehring et al. (Sonoma, Calif.: Polebridge, 1990), 35–48; and Tuckett, *Q and the History of Early Christianity*, 404–13.

42. Tuckett, *Q and the History of Early Christianity*, 418; similarly, Kloppenborg, "Nomos and Ethos."

43. Kloppenborg, "Nomos and Ethos," 42, comments about Q 11:42c (as well as 11:42ab) that it "engages in rhetorical exaggeration and caricature." Extension of that recognition to much of the rest of the woes discourse will open up fresh interpretive insights. For a reconstruction of the particular Pharisaic position to which 11:39 is apparently responding, see Jacob Neusner, " 'First Cleanse the Inside': The Halakic Background of a Controversy-Saying," *NTS* 22 (1976): 486–95.

pinged on their struggles to raise enough food to feed themselves as well as those who appropriated tribute, taxes, and tithes and offerings.[44]

Tithes, the obsession about which the woe in Q 11:42 mocks the scribes and Pharisees, were indeed an important issue in the great tradition whose cultivators lived from them, directly (high priests) or indirectly (scribes?). In most agrarian societies, however, there has been considerable resentment among the peasants about having to render up their precious produce, even to the gods — particularly when it impinges on the minimum needed for survival, to which they believe themselves entitled.[45] Thus we may well suspect that Q 11:42 expresses a long-standing Israelite popular tradition of resentment about tithes, particularly when there were other persistent demands on their crops from multiple layers of rulers, Roman, Herodian, and (high) priestly. Indeed, that seems to be the thrust of the sharp contrast between the Pharisees' concern about rigorous tithing by the peasantry and "justice and mercy" in 11:42. As already noted above, "justice and mercy" is an appeal to the rich Israelite tradition of prophetic pronouncements against the rulers and ruling institutions that drained resources from the marginal peasant producers in order to support the cultic festivals and ceremonies that God rejects (see again Hos. 4:1–3; 12:3–7; Mic. 6:8; Zech. 7:9). Such prophecies are known to us only because they were taken up into the great tradition in written form. The woe in Q 11:42, however, surely drew the resonant symbols of justice and mercy from the Israelite popular tradition, as suggested by their allusive rather than explicitly "intertextual" relationship with those prophetic lawsuits. Thus insofar as justice and mercy were the core values and social policy that observing the covenantal law would realize, the Q woe about rigorous tithing was indeed concerned with covenantal torah.[46]

In contrast with the woes discourse, the three sayings in Q 16:16–18 are concerned directly with the Torah, although not necessarily the Torah that became canonical scripture. If "the law and the prophets" in 16:16a was a standard phrase for the authoritative Israelite tradition among the people as well as in scribal circles, then Q 16:16 suggests simply that beginning with John the kingdom as the fulfillment of that tradition is suffering violence, not that the kingdom has

---

44. It is now generally recognized that the rabbinic sources that apply purity codes to Jews / Israelites generally, or at least to circles beyond the priests, for whom they were originally intended, come from a period and circumstances well after the time of Jesus and his followers who produced Q.

45. As pointed out by Scott, "Protest and Profanation."

46. Cf. Kloppenborg, "Nomos and Ethos," 42: "Neither Q's criticism of the Pharisees nor its counter-proposal is obviously nomocentric." Similarly, "that none of the extended compositions [i.e., the Q discourses] shows a tendency either to buttress admonitions by means of an appeal to the Torah or to frame them in such a way as to contrast the admonitions with the Torah" (ibid., 46) means simply that Q is not a typically scribal composition. The concept "nomistic / nomism," a Christian scholarly construct, is inappropriate to Q and probably to the Israelite popular tradition generally. But Q is solidly rooted in and presents a renewal of Israelite covenantal tradition, as will be explored in chapter 9 below. While it rejects the purity concerns and the economic claims of the great tradition, Q stands in continuity with and reasserts the values of the Israelite popular tradition. The concluding section of Kloppenborg, "Nomos and Ethos," 47–48, illustrates how careful analysis of Q in terms of Christian theological categories (e.g., viewing the Torah as a soteriological category) leads to its interpretation as Hellenistic Jewish literature like the Wisdom of Solomon.

superseded "the law and the prophets."[47] Because the kingdom of God means realization and practice of just covenantal relations, moreover, "the law" not only is of enduring validity but is the authoritative guide for societal life, as stated in Q 16:17. However, if "the law and the prophets" in the popular mind referred to the great tradition, then the saying has a polemical edge: "The law and the prophets" version of the Israelite tradition prevailed up to the point that the prophet of God's decisive new action for the people's renewal appeared; and now the kingdom — including John, Jesus himself, and the Q prophets/people — is experiencing violent opposition, apparently from rulers and their representatives. In the opposition between the poor and the rich, the people and their rulers, the statement in Q 16:16 parallels much of the rest of Q, especially Q 6:20–26; 7:18–35; 10:21–24; and 13:28–29. If "the law and the prophets" refers to the great tradition, then indeed it has been "relativized" — by the fulfillment of Is-raelite longings as articulated by the prophets (see Q 7:18–28) and the dawning realization of covenantal justice (see Q 6:27–36), as understood in the popular tradition represented by Q.

In this regard, Q offers a popular parallel to the Dead Sea Scrolls' combination of a keen sense that in God's decisive action a new era is at hand with a renewed dedication to the validity and importance of the covenantal law as the guide for societal/community life. Yet a particular Qumran parallel on the issue of marriage and divorce also illustrates the difference between Q as representative of the popular tradition and scribal custodians of the great tradition in handling the same issue. In Q 16:18 the prophet-teacher Jesus merely pronounces in a legal formulation ("everyone who") the prohibition of divorce and remarriage, in a form and style similar to that of the ancient Israelite "common law" that was included in the earliest covenantal law code (Exodus 21–23). By contrast, the scribal authors of CD 4:13–21, who take a similarly strict view that divorce and remarriage are against God's law, (re-)cite a text from either the Torah or the Prophets on every other line of the scroll. Besides illustrating the difference between scribal and popular appropriation and transmission of tradition, CD 4:13–21 also illustrates the differences that can emerge among the carriers of the "great tradition."[48] It is a sharply polemical passage, apparently directed against the community's rivals, the incumbent ruling priestly regime. And it effectively ignores or by-passes the lenient provision for divorce in a Torah text, Deut. 24:1–4. This seems surprising for a scribally authored passage otherwise so full of Torah citations, whereas it is not surprising in a statement from the popular tradition, such as Q 16:18, that it ignores the same provision in the great tradition. Mark 10:2–9 provides yet another window onto the diversity within the great tradition in this connection. In addition to those attacked in CD 4:13–21, the Pharisees were also apparently

---

47. Tuckett, *Q and the History of Early Christianity*, 407, appears to perpetuate an older Christian supersessionist view: "the era of the Law has ended."

48. Lawrence H. Schiffman, *The Halakhah at Qumran*, Studies in Judaism in Late Antiquity 16 (Leiden: E. J. Brill, 1975), has explored how the community that produced the Dead Sea Scrolls cultivated halakhah differently from the line that runs through the Pharisees to rabbinic literature.

lenient with regard to divorce, in following Deut. 24:1–4. Because of the diversity within the great tradition as well as the likely variation within popular tradition, critical consideration of the Law in Q or in other texts must be complex, including careful comparison of texts from the great tradition as well as comparison and contrast between the different levels at which Israelite tradition was cultivated.

Wisdom, Abraham, Solomon, and Jerusalem

Just as Q's understanding of covenantal Torah / Law was very different from Torah in the hands and mouths of Jerusalem scribal circles, so (the) Wisdom (of God) in its two appearances in Q is quite different from Wisdom as understood in the scribal circles who identified it with Torah as part of their devotion to and specu- lation about Wisdom. The long line of wisdom speculation that finds expression in Proverbs 8, Sirach 24, Bar. 3:9–4:4, and Wisdom of Solomon 6–10 had not only reified and personified Hokhmah / Sophia but also made her into a virtual goddess, dwelling with God since before the creation, of which she was the medi- atrix. Having sought a resting place, she "was established in Zion . . . Jerusalem," where she is identified with "the book of the covenant of the Most High God, the law that Moses commanded" (Sir. 24:7, 10–11, 23; 1:15). There the scribes / sages who have the leisure, such as Ben Sira (in contrast with peasants and artisans, Sir. 38:24–34), can "seek out the hidden meaning of proverbs" and otherwise cultivate their sapiential piety and pursue their scribal careers serving the high- priestly rulers of the Judean temple-state (Sir. 38:32–39:11). Wisdom is not only accessible but also enjoys a distinctive social location in which she plays a par- ticular religious-political role via her sapiential-scribal devotees and cultivators. Other scribal-sapiential circles, however, came to a different sense of Wisdom. She was not — or no longer — present and accessible, according to the authors of the *Similitudes of Enoch*, who would appear to be dissident sages / scribes now speaking in a more apocalyptic register. As Ben Sira had declared, indeed Wisdom had sought "a place in which she could dwell . . . with people. But she found no dwelling place. [So] Wisdom returned to her place [in the heavens] and settled permanently among the angels" (*1 Enoch* 42:1–2). Again, as with the Law and its application in halakhah, the scribal great tradition was not unitary.

Wisdom's role in Q does not seem to be derived from either of these traceable scribal traditions. She sends prophets in Q 11:49–51, and she will be vindicated by her children / works (perhaps, but not necessarily only, by John and Jesus) in Q 7:31–35. Wisdom in Q, however, does not have the functions of Wisdom in earlier Judean literature, and Wisdom's role in Q is unprecedented in earlier Judean literature and diaspora Jewish literature. "Wisdom's role as creatrix and revealer are absent from Q. Even the more mundane role of teacher of wisdom does not seem to be very significant for an understanding of the role of Jesus or John in Q."[49] Scribes / sages such as Ben Sira may have understood themselves as the interpreters and even the successors of the prophets (Sir. 24:33; 39:1), but they

---

49. Jacobson, *First Gospel*, 257.

do not articulate any notion of Wisdom as the sender of the prophets.[50] Indeed, Q takes a stance opposed to the very sages who cultivated wisdom and speculated on the figure of Wisdom: the Father has hidden (from the wise, at least) what is revealed and manifested in Jesus' message and activity (Q 10:21). In Q, Wisdom is said to send the prophets precisely in the declaration of woes and condemnation of the scribes/lawyers and Pharisees (Q 11:39–52).[51] If anything, one is tempted to speculate in the case of the role of Wisdom in Q that people working out of the Israelite little tradition appropriated a figure from the great tradition and, making Wisdom the sender of the prophets, turned the figure against its scribal-sapiential cultivators.[52]

Abraham was the progenitor of both Israel (through Isaac) and the Arabs (through Ishmael). As the original recipient of God's promises that Israel would become a great people, have its own land, and be the instrument of blessings for other peoples, Abraham was always the generative figure in the history of salvation. In its origin the theme of the promise(s) to Abraham functioned to support and legitimate the claims of the Davidic monarchy to a position of preeminence and power over Israel.[53] Abraham became an especially important symbol in official Jerusalem tradition during Hasmonean and Herodian times. We know from Hasmonean literature that from at least the time that John Hyrcanus and his sons extended their rule over Idumea and Samaria by military conquest, the Jerusalem ruling elite emphasized their descent from Abraham.[54] For example, the book of *Jubilees*, building on the tradition that Abraham, through Isaac, was the common ancestor of both Idumeans and Israelites (see Genesis 25–36, where Esau = Edom, from where the later Idumeans had moved into the area around Hebron and Marisa, south of Judah), emphasized Abraham's special love for and blessing of his "son" Jacob = Israel (*Jub.* 19:16–29; 22:10–30; 23:1–3) and expanded on Genesis 27 with an account of Jacob's sons' subjection of Esau's sons (*Jubilees* 38; cf. *Testament of Judah* 9).[55] The story of the blessing on Abraham by Melchizedek, king of Jerusalem (see Genesis 14), was claimed as authorization for

---

50. The Judean texts that Jacobson, ibid., 257, lists as attesting Wisdom as a sender of prophets (Prov. 1:20–21; 8:2–3; Sir. 24:33) do not seem to do so. In Wisdom of Solomon 7:27, Wisdom, by "passing into holy souls," makes them "friends of God and prophets." But the focus there is on the individual spiritual intimacy between Sophia and the soul, and there is no hint of prophets being sent to deliver prophecies to rulers and/or the people generally.

51. Moreover, the discourse that declares that Wisdom will be vindicated by her children/works (John and Jesus?) characterizes the nay-sayers as "sitting in the agora addressing one another" somewhat as sages/scribes would in considering a case or issue, as explained by Wendy J. Cotter, "The Parable of the Children in the Market Place, Q 7:31–35," *NovT* 29 (1987): 289–304.

52. More careful and precise analysis of the variety of wisdom traditions and their social role and location than is present in the spate of explorations of wisdom theology in Q will be necessary to explain adequately the role of Wisdom in the two Q discourses where it appears.

53. See, for example, Delbert R. Hillers, *Covenant: The History of a Biblical Idea* (Baltimore: Johns Hopkins University Press, 1969), chap. 5.

54. Doron Mendels, *The Land of Israel as a Political Concept in Hasmonean Literature* (Tübingen: J. C. B. Mohr [Paul Siebeck], 1987).

55. See Robert Doran, "The Non-dating of Jubilees: Jub 34–38; 23:14–32 in Narrative Context," *Journal of the Study of Judaism in the Persian, Hellenistic, and Roman Period* 20 (1989): 1–11.

the priests' claim to tithes (*Jub.* 13:25–27). Such reshaped and expanded tradition of the great ancestor Abraham, to whom the promises for Israel's role in history were given originally, would have served to legitimate the Hasmoneans' takeover and control of Galilee as well as their conquest of Samaria and Idumea. Herod memorialized the importance of Abraham in grand style with the construction of impressive, elaborate monuments in both Mamre and Hebron, which was the site of David's original reign as king of Judah, as well as the traditional burial site of the patriarchs and matriarchs (Gen. 23:19; 25:9; 49:31; 50:13).[56] We know from both Philo and Josephus how important Abraham was for the Jews' claim of great antiquity in the broader Hellenistic culture that laid great stock in the antiquity of historical derivation. In their attempt to affirm Israelite cultural heritage over against the recent Roman takeover from the Hasmoneans, the scribal authors of the *Psalms of Solomon* (9:9–10) insisted that God "chose the descendants of Abraham above all the nations." Thus it is not surprising that high-priestly families and others in Jerusalem placed great stock in their lineages in late second-temple times, particularly in their descent from Abraham.

The two references to Abraham in Q should be read against this backdrop. John's challenge to "bear fruits of (covenantal) repentance" and not rely on one's lineage, saying "we have Abraham as our father; for I tell you, God is able from these stones to raise up children to Abraham" (Q 3:9), would have been understood as a sharp rejection of the Jerusalem elite and other pretentious wealthy and powerful families who, in the common people's eyes, would have been the worst violators of the covenantal principles of nonexploitative economic social relations. Similarly, Jesus' prophecy about the banquet in the kingdom of God with Abraham, Isaac, and Jacob (Q 13:28–29) would have been directed against those who presumed, because of their position and lineage, that they were the premier families of Israel.

Solomon would have been another central and highly important symbol for Jerusalemites, particularly in Herodian times. Solomon had brought Jerusalem to its unprecedented ancient glories as an imperial capital. He had built the original temple. And he was the source of wisdom, the patron-author of the very wisdom that the sapiential-scribal elite perpetuated in their own teaching. Solomon's prominence would only have been intensified by Herod's royal propaganda, his extensive building programs in which the massively rebuilt temple was the centerpiece, and his corresponding munificence to foreign kings and cities, as evident in Josephus's account in *Jewish Antiquities*, Book 8. A key symbol of all this was the royal pilgrimage of "the Queen of Egypt and Ethiopia" "to Jerusalem with

---

56. "The archaeological evidence... suggests that Herod enclosed the traditional site of Mamre, just north of Hebron, with a finely dressed *temenos* wall, enclosing an area of about 150′ by 200′, with a huge oak recalled traditionally as one of the oaks of Mamre at Abraham's altar to the Lord (Gen. 13:18; 14:13; 18:1)." At Hebron, Herod built "a fine and immensely powerful structure... over the caves of Machpelah, ... enclosing what was likely an open space used for religious observances in connection with Abraham and the patriarchs" (Peter Richardson, *Herod: King of the Jews and Friend of the Romans* [Columbia: University of South Carolina Press, 1996], 60–61).

great splendour and show of wealth" to experience firsthand the renowned wisdom of Solomon (*Ant.* 8.165–75). She especially admired his buildings, in which "she saw the great wisdom of the king," the lavish daily meals and sumptuous decorum of the palace, and the impressive daily sacrifices offered to God. It is not too difficult, however, to imagine how the people who were being taxed heavily to fund Herod's and his sons' grand building programs and lavish gifts to foreign cities felt about "Solomon in all his glory." Those very economic pressures would have been a key factor for those addressed in Q 12:22–31, the discourse devoted to gentle encouragement of subsistence peasants not to be overly anxious about necessities of food and clothing, which would take care of themselves if the listeners could only be single-minded in pursuit of the kingdom of God. In this context, the reference to "Solomon in all his glory" was caustic as well as ironic. The use of Solomon and the Queen of the South for comparative purposes in Q 11:31 also has a caustic edge. The Q preachers knew only too well that Solomon was world-renowned for his wisdom and that he was touted by the elite. Solomon's fame and importance may well have been augmented in their own minds by their class as well as historical distance. But that only made it all the more dramatic and astounding that "something greater is here!"

The tone of the Q references to both Abraham and Solomon contrasts sharply with that in scribal-sapiential literature such as Sirach that stood squarely in the great tradition based in Jerusalem. Ben Sira's hymnic praise of the magnificent ancestors proclaims confidently that the blessing given to Abraham has come to rest on the head of Jacob / Israel and dwells at length on the world-famous wisdom of Solomon. The Q discourses, which stand close to the popular tradition in which they originated, proclaim that God is reconstituting Israel as children to Abraham "out of these stones" over against the aristocratic circles that presumptuously claim direct linear descent from Abraham. And Q confidently overturns the aristocratic values that gloat in Solomon's imperial glory and wisdom. It is surely significant that Q makes no reference to Davidic kingship, again in contrast with scribal literature such as the *Psalms of Solomon,* as noted above in connection with the restoration of Israel. Q is rooted primarily in the Mosaic covenantal and prophetic aspects of Israelite tradition, which were popular in their origin, over against the Abrahamic and Davidic aspects, which were elaborated in the Davidic monarchy.

Indeed, the only reference to the capital city of Jerusalem comes in a prophetic lament proclaiming its imminent desolation. Far from utilizing any temple or Zion images, Q proclaims God's condemnation of Jerusalem.[57] In second-temple times "Jerusalem" was synonymous with the ruling institution(s) of the temple and its incumbent high priesthood, just as it had earlier been with the Davidic monarchy and its attendant institution, the Solomonic temple. "House" bore connotations of

---

57. On the following, see further Horsley, *Jesus,* 300–303. In contrast to the Q discourses that he incorporated into his own longer discourses, Matthew has a considerable interest in Jerusalem / Zion and Davidic traditions.

both the ruling "house" of David and the "house" that David's "house" had built for God (see, e.g., 2 Sam. 7:11–17). It is difficult to discern therefore whether the phrase "behold your house is desolate" in Q 13:35a is an allusion to the prophecy against the Davidic ruling house in Jer. 22:1–9 ("this house shall become a desolation" [22:5]), in which the "house" of David is synonymous with the "great city" of Jerusalem, or simply a stock prophetic phrase, used in Jer. 22:5 and again in Q 11:35a. More clearly a reference to a significant piece of the prophetic repertoire in Israelite tradition is the image of the hen gathering her brood under her wing (*nossia* = the "children" of the city, i.e., the Israelite villages ostensibly gathered around and under the protection of the capital city). This alludes to the prophetic Song of Moses in Deuteronomy 32, in which God is "like an eagle that stirs up its nest [translated in the LXX with *nossia*], that hovers over its young, as it spreads its wings" (Deut. 32:11), guiding and sustaining Israel in its formative period. But the ruling house of Jerusalem refused God's motherly nurture and guidance for the people. Indeed it killed the prophets. Q's condemnation of Jerusalem, couched in the traditional prophetic form of a lament over Jerusalem's desolation as if it had already happened, is rooted in the long-standing conflict between the Mosaic covenantal and prophetic traditions (such as the Song of Moses), with which the peasantry would have identified, and the Davidic and Zadokite and other aristocratic priestly traditions that served to legitimate the power and prerogatives of Jerusalem. The respective emphases and tone of the popular tradition vs. the great tradition are rooted, as Scott explains with evidence of comparative studies of other peasant societies, in the fundamental political-economic-religious divide between rulers and ruled. Q's prophetic lament over the divinely condemned Jerusalem "is quite compatible with the perspective of villagers in agrarian societies, resentful of exploitation by the ruling elites of the city."[58]

•

These probes into how Q draws upon Israelite traditions that are contested between the people and their rulers (and does so in ways very different from the scribal elite) are merely an opening exploration of a previously unexamined set of historical social relationships. It may be sufficient, however, not only to confirm that Q discourses are deeply embedded in Israelite traditions but also to suggest that an adequate analysis must take into account the complexity of social locations and competing groups who cultivated those traditions. Clearly the historical realities awaiting analysis are more complex than can be adequately approached by the old procedure in terms of quotations of or references to "scripture" in Q.

---

58. The treatment of Q's saying on Jerusalem by John S. Kloppenborg, "City and Wasteland: Narrative World and the Beginning of the Sayings Gospel (Q)," *Semeia* 52 (1990): 155, moves along the same lines as the analysis in Horsley, *Jesus*, 301–3. I see little justification, on the other hand, for conflating the "wilderness" in which John appears in Q 7:24 with the references to Sodom in Q 17:28–30, such that "the wasteland of Sodom now threatens...the (un)holy city of Jerusalem" (Kloppenborg, "City," 157).

The difficulties of analyzing Q and Israelite tradition will be pushed even further beyond the familiar charts of standard biblical studies once we recognize in the course of the next chapter that, since communications in antiquity were overwhelmingly oral, we must face the implications that Q is an "oral-derived" text. An exploration of recent attempts to more adequately understand oral-derived texts in the following chapter, moreover, will send us back to grapple with Israelite tradition in Q as the only basis on which the sequence speeches in Q can be appropriately heard.

Chapter 6

THE ORAL COMMUNICATION
ENVIRONMENT OF Q

Richard A. Horsley _____

Biblical scholars who write mass-produced books for individual modern readers have simply assumed that biblical books were readily available, widely distributed, and easily read in the historical situation for which they were written. They even assume that the biblical "writers" they study proceeded basically as they themselves do.[1] Biblical scholars have been in good company. Not surprisingly, scholars of the "great books" have also assumed that the Greek and Roman cultures that constitute the unsurpassed sources of Western civilization were fully literate, somewhat like the elite modern schools and colleges in which they are studied. "Biblical and patristic scholars have shared with classicists the sanguine assumption that literacy prevailed in antiquity on a scale roughly comparable to literacy in modern Western societies and so have imagined that early Christianity was broadly literate."[2]

This "sanguine assumption" was seriously challenged initially by the theory of Milman Parry and Albert Lord that the *Iliad* and *Odyssey* were "composed" as they were performed orally, which they backed up from their field studies of illiterate "singers of tales" in modern Yugoslavia. The impact of their theory and investigations was reinforced by a grand theory, articulated by Walter Ong and others, of a fundamental difference between an oral culture and a literate culture and the dramatically different mentalities shaped and expressed in each. Simultaneously, Erik Havelock argued that Greece was primarily an oral society down to the time of Plato, who was pivotal in bringing about a rapid transition to a rational mentality made possible by writing. The dominant scholarly establishment, particularly Homer scholars, were unmoved. After their initial reaction they basically

---

1. See the remarkable discussion in Burton L. Mack, *A Myth of Innocence* (Philadelphia: Fortress, 1987), 321–23.

2. Harry Y. Gamble, *Books and Readers in the Early Church* (New Haven: Yale University Press, 1995), 2–3. For a sample of earlier estimates of widespread literacy in ancient Greece and the Roman Empire, see William V. Harris, *Ancient Literacy* (Cambridge, Mass.: Harvard University Press, 1989), 8–9. Susan Niditch, *Oral World and Written Word* (Louisville: Westminster/John Knox, 1996), 1–2, 39–40, points out that scholars of the Hebrew Bible/Old Testament and biblical archaeologists similarly assume widespread literacy in ancient Israel.

ignored the ongoing investigation of oral "literature" and oral-derived literature. In biblical studies, Werner Kelber, following the lead of Ong and others, proposed that after an initial phase of orality in which Jesus traditions were performed by prophets, as evident in the prophetic sayings gathered in Q, the living but unstable oral communication of the prophets was "killed" with the written narrative Gospel, as evident in Mark. His thesis about the orality of Q was far too troubling for Gospel scholars, who largely persisted in the older assumptions of literacy and written texts.[3] This should not be surprising since modern biblical scholars not only presuppose writing but also make their living as paradigmatic practitioners (and perpetuators) of print culture and approach the Bible as silent readers of printed books and attempt to interpret printed words, not audible sounds.

The "autonomous" model of orality and literacy as different technologies or "media" of communication and the respective mentalities (and theologies) that they engender, however, may not be the most appropriate way to go about a historical investigation of communication in Western antiquity. This approach looks for the general features and effects of orality or literacy and works with a rather simple theory of causation. It was claimed, for example, that the development of writing in ancient Greece produced democracy, rational thought, and historiography.[4] The understanding of literacy in this approach appears to be identical with Western culture more generally. Interestingly enough, a major study by Elizabeth Eisenstein attributed many of those same effects to the development of printing in early modern Europe.[5] Most seriously, this theory of the "great divide" between orality and literacy, as almost mutually exclusive media of communication and cultural mentalities, does not take into consideration the interaction of orality and literacy that characterizes most historical societies and the respective and possibly related uses or functions of orality and literacy in those societies.

Such historical complexities and contingencies as the interaction and relationship of oral and written communication, however, are precisely what an alternative, "ideological" approach considers.[6] During the last two decades, with increasing frequency, a number of studies of classical antiquity and medieval European materials, as well as anthropological studies of non-Western societies, have explored the fluid relationship between writing in various functions and implications of writing and the dominant oral communication.[7] Even these studies

---

3. See the reviews of Werner Kelber, *The Oral and Written Gospel* (Philadelphia: Fortress, 1983), for example, by J. D. G. Dunn in *Interpretation* 40 (1986): 72–75; and Daniel J. Harrington in *Biblica* 65 (1984): 279–81. Most studies of Q seem to have ignored Kelber's work and the work of Walter Ong and others on which it is based.

4. Jack Goody and Ian Watt, "The Consequences of Literacy," *Comparative Studies in Society and History* 5 (1962–63): 304–45; reprinted in *Literacy in Traditional Societies*, ed. Jack Goody (Cambridge: Cambridge University Press, 1968).

5. Elizabeth Eisenstein, *The Printing Revolution in Early Modern Europe* (Cambridge: Cambridge University Press, 1983).

6. Brian Street, *Literacy in Theory and Practice* (Cambridge: Cambridge University Press, 1984).

7. Michael T. Clanchy, *From Memory to Written Record: England 1066–1307* (Cambridge, Mass.: Harvard University Press, 1979); Mary L. Carruthers, *The Book of Memory: A Study of Memory in Medieval Culture* (Cambridge: Cambridge University Press, 1990); Brian Stock, *The Implications of*

generally lack analysis of the social location of orality and the uses of literacy and the power relations involved, which is necessary to accomplish anything more than an appreciation of particular literary documents of relatively high culture. Since some of the early rediscoveries of "orality" overemphasized the "great divide" between orality and literacy and because the studies of the interaction of writing with oral communication in historical societies have been relatively recent, studies of Q and other Gospel materials have not yet taken account of their findings. In moving toward a more adequate and balanced approach to Q, therefore, we must recognize (1) that very few people had even a minimal ability to read; (2) that writing functioned primarily in service of oral communication; and (3) that, given the limited availability and prohibitive usability of written scrolls such as those of Jewish Scripture, the cultivation of Israelite cultural tradition continued largely through memory and oral communication.

Limited Literacy in Western Antiquity

Literacy may have been as low as 1 percent in ancient Mesopotamia, confined to a small circle of scribes.[8] The spread of minimal literacy among the elite *hoplites* in classical Athens — supported by their economic basis in slavery and colonization — brought the figure to between 5 and 10 percent of the overall population.[9] The idea that all male citizens of a city-state should learn to read and write emerged during Hellenistic times (Diodorus Siculus 12.12–13), but there is little evidence that even elementary education became prominent — outside the family.[10] As in classical Greece, so in the Roman Empire generally, literacy corresponded to social location. A modicum of literary culture was a requisite for any aristocrat or magnate of any pretensions. Yet, while generally literate, the urban and provincial elite of the Roman Empire may not have done much reading or writing themselves. Suitably trained slaves handled correspondence and read aloud to "the respectable," which, along with the recognized role of slaves as teachers, suggests also that a certain number of household slaves were highly literate.[11]

For the Roman Empire, the best evidence comes from Pompeii and Egypt, where writing was used more than elsewhere in the empire, making it unrepresentative.[12] Evidence from Pompeii suggests that perhaps no more than two or

Literacy: Written Language and Models of Interpretation in the Eleventh and Twelfth Centuries (Princeton, N.J.: Princeton University Press, 1983); Rosalind Thomas, *Literacy and Orality in Ancient Greece* (Cambridge: Cambridge University Press, 1992); Katherine O'Brien O'Keeffe, *Visible Song: Transitional Literacy in Old English Verse* (Cambridge: Cambridge University Press, 1990); Karen Schousboe and Mogens Trolle Larsen, eds., *Literacy and Society* (Copenhagen: Akademisk Forlag, 1989).

8. Mogens Trolle Larsen, "What They Wrote on Clay," in Schousboe and Larsen, *Literacy and Society*, 121–48.

9. Harris, *Ancient Literacy*, 114; cf. Mary Beard, ed., *Literacy in the Roman World* (Ann Arbor, Mich.: Journal of Roman Archeology, 1991).

10. Harris, *Ancient Literacy*, 20–21.

11. Ibid., 248–53.

12. Ibid., 202.

three thousand of the hundred thousand residents alive in 79 had some ability to write.[13] In Italy generally, under 15 percent may have achieved the minimal literacy of writing slowly (or not at all) or of reading simple short messages.[14] In Roman Egypt, where papyri provide better evidence than is available elsewhere, most males of the "gymnasium" class, that is, substantial property owners, were literate in Greek. In the towns and villages, some artisans were minimally literate. In the villages, literacy was rare indeed, there being no requirement that village elders or even the village scribe, unique to Egypt and historically subject to an elaborate governmental bureaucracy, had to be literate. Petaus, the clerk of the village of Ptolemais Hormou, apparently never did learn to sign his name independently of copying a model.[15] Origen commented that most people — apparently meaning Greek-speaking people — were "unlettered and somewhat rustic" (Contra Celsum). Large numbers of miscellaneous papyrus documents from Hellenistic and Roman Egypt indicate explicitly that one or more of the principals was illiterate. Close studies of these papyri concluded that the large majority of male and almost all women artisans and farmers were illiterate.[16] For example, in the towns all master weavers who appear in apprenticeship contracts were illiterate.[17] While some of the indigenous Egyptian population knew minimal Greek, the vast majority, the peasants, knew no Greek and were presumably largely illiterate in their own language(s).[18]

More generally, "the classical world, even at its most advanced, was so lacking in the characteristics which produce extensive literacy that we must suppose that the majority of people were always illiterate."[19] No elaborate network of schools was developed. Nor did the structure of the ancient economy generate a need for widespread literacy.[20] In every province of the Roman Empire, indeed, the elite supported a degree of literary culture; artisans used writing in brief forms; agents of the emperor administered his property with the aid of writing; and merchants engaged in long-distance trade sent and received letters.[21] Yet even on a minimalist definition of what constitutes literacy, "The likely overall illiteracy level of the Roman Empire under the principate is almost certain to have been above 90%."[22]

---

13. Ibid., 264.

14. Ibid., 259–67.

15. H. C. Youtie, "Petaus, fils de Petaus, ou le scribe qui ne savait pas ecrire," *Chronique d'Egypte* 81 (1966): 127–43.

16. H. C. Youtie, "*Agrammatos:* An Aspect of Greek Society in Egypt," *Harvard Studies in Classical Philology* 75 (1971): 161–76; idem, "*Bradeos grafon:* Between Literacy and Illiteracy," *Greek, Roman, and Byzantine Studies* 12 (1971): 239–61; idem, "*Hypographeus:* The Social Impact of Illiteracy in Graeco-Roman Egypt," *Zeitschrift für Papyrologie und Epigraphie* (1975): 201–21.

17. Harris, *Ancient Literacy,* 277.

18. Ibid., 280–81.

19. Ibid., 13.

20. Ibid., 17, 19.

21. Ibid., 202.

22. Ibid., 22.

Recent studies of Jesus and early Christianity acknowledge the extremely limited levels of literacy in ancient Greek cities and the Roman Empire. Ironically, however, they continue to trust generalizations about high rates of Judean or diaspora Jewish literacy that preceded recent critical studies of literacy in antiquity.[23] "According to Josephus, in first-century Judaism it was a duty, indeed a religious commandment, that Jewish children be taught to read.... [R]abbinic sources suggest...there is little question that by the first century C.E. Judaism had developed a strong interest in basic literacy and that even small communities had elementary schools."[24] In fact, the Josephus passages cited indicate not that children were taught to read but that the teaching and learning of scripture / the laws were carried out by public oral recitation (at sabbath assemblies), suggesting both that the general populace was illiterate and that communication of the most important matters was oral. Indeed, the concept of writing in these contexts is magical-religious: by hearing the sacred laws taught aloud, the latter would become "engraved on [the people's] souls...and guarded in their memory" (*Ant.* 4.210; 16.43; *c. Apion* 2.175, 178, 204; cf. Philo, *ad Gaium* 115, 210).[25] The rabbinic sources cited for the ubiquity of schools not only are late but also clearly refer to a limited segment of the Israelite population, mainly rabbinic circles themselves. Rabbinic texts that have previously been claimed as evidence for the people *reading* (e.g., *m. Ber.* 4:3; *m. Bik.* 3:7; *m. Sukk.* 3:10) in fact refer to them *reciting* from memory, and with different abilities, certain psalms and prayers. Other rabbinic references often cited as evidence for general literacy refer only to rabbinic circles themselves, such as the ruling about not reading by lamplight (*m. Sabb.* 1:3).[26] In late second-temple Judea and Galilee, like the rest of the Roman Empire, literacy was concentrated in the political and cultural elite. The scribes and Pharisees and other teachers constituted the professional literate stratum of the Jerusalem temple-state. Officials in the Herodian administrations in Jerusalem and the Galilean cities were presumably literate in Greek, although probably not in Hebrew and Aramaic. A recent study concludes that in Roman Palestine, the literacy rate could have been as low as 3 percent.[27]

---

23. For example, in Martin Hengel, *Judaism and Hellenism* (Philadelphia: Fortress, 1974), 1:78–83; S. Safrai, "Education and the Study of the Torah," in *The Jewish People in the First Century*, Compendia Rerum Iudaicarum ad Novum Testamentum, sec 1.2, ed. S. Safrai and M. Stern (Philadelphia: Fortress, 1976), 2:945–70, esp. 952, 954.

24. Gamble, *Books and Readers*, 7.

25. "To learn *grammata*" in *c. Apion* 2.204, in the context of study of the Law, suggests not learning to read (so Thackeray's translation in the Loeb edition), but learning "scripture," which is done through public oral teaching, as indicated earlier at 2.175.

26. *Pace* Martin Goodman, *State and Society in Roman Galilee, A.D. 132–212* (Totowa, N.J.: Rowman and Allanheld, 1983), 72, whose discussion of "education" (71–81) does not appear to apply to village culture.

27. Meir Bar-Ilan, "Illiteracy in the Land of Israel in the First Centuries C.E.," in *Essays in the Social Scientific Study of Judaism and Jewish Society*, ed. Simcha Fishbane and Stuart Schoenfeld (Hoboken, N.J.: Ktav, 1992), 46–61.

Uses of Writing in Relation to Oral Communication

The principal uses of literacy in ancient Greece, Rome, and Israel were embedded in traditional oral forms of communication. As noted in the previous section, communication was predominantly oral, with literate aids and literacy operating mainly among the elite. Writing functioned primarily in the service of the spoken word. Insofar as various kinds of writing themselves had meaning, it was derived from traditional oral performance and oral functions and did not replace or undermine them.[28]

Magical and Symbolic Writing and Writing in Everyday Life

Magical uses of writing appeared early and continued throughout Western antiquity. In the Hebrew Bible the inscription of the commandments on stone by the finger of God (Exod. 31:18; 32:16; 34:1; Deut. 10:2) provides the most vivid example of magical writing. "Through the medium of writing, the laws shimmer with the power of the one who spoke them; through writing, God is invested in the tablets" (see also Deut. 4:13; 5:22; 9:10).[29] Magical writing even has the power to transform in the ritual imposed on the wife suspected of adultery by a jealous husband (Num. 5:11–31). A curse written on a scroll is washed into a concoction ("the water of bitterness") that she is made to drink. If she is guilty, the words she drinks are expected to effect the curse on her body in a most visceral way (Num. 5:20–22, 27). As further examples of magical writing, we may think of the incantation bowls inscribed in Aramaic and Greek magical papyri, whose scripts evoke the divine name in various soundings, and any number of blessings on amulets and curses inscribed on various surfaces in various languages. Similarly, the so-called abecedaries, lists of Hebrew letters previously taken as schoolbook exercises, seem rather to have been "of magic or religious significance."[30] Lest we imagine, as did earlier studies of such writing in non-Western societies, that this magical writing is to be dismissed as an expression of pre- or semiliterate peoples — or merely a popular phenomenon in classical antiquity — we should take note of the many public (besides the frequent private) curses inscribed on lead tablets or stone in classical Greece, writing presumably by the educated elite of cities such as Tean. Public curses served to protect the city by means of religious sanctions; inscribing them visibly on lead presumably intensified their effectiveness. In classical Athens, politicians also used private "judicial curses" against their opponents.[31] In all these cases writing was used magically to intensify oral pronouncements and make them all the more effective.

---

28. Oivind Andersen, "The Significance of Writing in Early Greece — a Critical Appraisal," in Schousboe and Larsen, *Literacy and Society;* Thomas, *Literacy and Orality,* 61.

29. Niditch, *Oral World,* 80.

30. Gabriel Barkay, "The Iron Age I–III," in *The Archaeology of Ancient Israel,* ed. Amnon Ben-Tor (New Haven: Yale University Press, 1992), 350; Niditch, *Oral World,* 45. For other such phenomena, see Bengt Holbek, "What the Illiterate Think of Writing," in Schousboe and Larsen, *Literacy and Society,* 183–96.

31. Further discussion in Thomas, *Literacy and Orality,* 78–82.

Similar to such magical uses of writing are cases of symbolic, representative writing in which a written sample of words stands for the whole, which is oral. The command that God's words be written "on the doorposts of your house and on your gates" (as well as fixed "as an emblem on your forehead") in Deut. 6:9, previously mistaken as an indication of general literacy in ancient Israel, refers to the key statement of the covenant: "The LORD is our God, the LORD alone." And it concludes the larger exhortation to "keep these words *in your heart*" and to "recite . . . and discuss" them in the home. The words written "on the doorposts" are thus a kind of "iconic" writing symbolic and/or in service of a continuing oral communication (Deut. 6:5–9).[32]

Closely related to magical writing are short messages inscribed on stones, such as epitaphs and votive offerings, aiming to perpetuate the name and fame of a person through the permanence of writing. Such writing inscribed on stone represented statements uttered aloud, usually in verse. Here writing is the vehicle of words spoken or sung.[33] Writing is added to the already existing customs of erecting tombstones or making offerings. In these practices writing seems "to be at the service of speech, repeating verse, enabling the objects to 'speak' as if they were animate, preserving and reinforcing the pre-literate habits of the society, extending and deepening the customs of poetic and visual memorials."[34] Such inscriptions exemplify how writing in early Greece was used primarily in the service of oral communication.[35] Such inscriptions on stones, monuments, and other memorials serve to externalize an event or persons symbolically.[36]

Except for the inclusion of inscriptions on civil religious monuments, writing played little role in household religion or worship at shrines and temples.[37] Epitaphs on tombs became increasingly important socially as well as religiously under the Roman empire. Since such epitaphs were inscribed by masons, however, they provide little evidence about the literacy of the family of the deceased.[38]

In the everyday social and economic life of antiquity, virtually all activities were carried out without writing, from the production or purchase of food to dirges at funerals. Throughout antiquity ordinary shopkeepers and artisans had little use for writing and peasants almost none, even in bureaucratic Egypt.[39] Nearly all buying and selling and modest transactions were done orally in face-to-face interaction.[40] Only among the wealthy and powerful Roman elite do we find use of written records and documents in the operation of their huge "households." Large-scale loans, wills, and marriage contracts were recorded in writing, partly

---

32. Niditch, *Oral World,* 70.

33. Thomas, *Literacy and Orality,* 62.

34. Ibid., 65.

35. Oivind Andersen, "Mündlichkeit und Schiftlichkeit im frühen Griechentum," *Antike und Abendland* 33 (1987): 29–44; and idem, "Significance of Writing in Early Greece."

36. Niditch, *Oral World,* 55, compares the Vietnam War memorial in our own culture.

37. Harris, *Ancient Literacy,* 220.

38. Ibid., 221–22.

39. Ibid., 201

40. Ibid., 198–99.

for control and inheritance of property. Varro (*Rust.* 1.17.4) recommended that the (slave) overseer of the slaves be literate — which also suggests that it was not absolutely necessary. Long-distance trade, basically in service to the lifestyle of the wealthy, involved considerable written correspondence and records. In economic life, islands of records and documents of the upper class float on a vast sea of direct oral interactions.

Writing in Service of the State

In both ancient monarchic and second-temple Judah and classical Greece, writing was used by the state, but in public display and decrees and the recording of laws or decrees, not in the subsequent consultation of documents as records in "archives." Virtually no evidence exists from ancient Judah of libraries or archives. The term "archives," moreover, seems inappropriate to the haphazard mix of records on wood or bronze or lead in Greek city-states, which had little use for administrative records.[41] In a passage often cited as evidence for the importance of state archives, Dio Chrysostom (31.50–53) says merely that public registration makes a contract more valid, that is, provides a guarantee in addition to the usual oral testimony. Rather than archival records, the polis produced public inscriptions of laws and decrees, primarily to memorialize rather than communicate information, broadly to lend public authority and monumental weight to the political organization emerging in Greece. Significantly, the contents of many of the individual laws inscribed on stone pertain to unprecedented matters not already commonly covered in traditional oral law: laws about procedure or laws controlling magistrates. Other inscriptions, such as dedications and curses, clearly have ceremonial, civil religious functions.[42] The Greek city-states inscribed their laws and decrees for display, to cultivate authority, and to intimidate their citizens.[43]

Writing in service of the state, however, not only presupposed an established oral political culture but was suspect to the very citizens it purported to serve. Politics was conducted orally. Official decrees were memorialized in stone, but there was apparently no sense that this fixed the text in verbatim accuracy. Copies of fifth-century Athenian decrees are notoriously variable.[44] Athenians distrusted written records, which they knew could be tampered with. Memory and oral testimony were more reliable. For all the previous scholarly claims that writing made Greek democracy possible, public inscriptions indicate that the citizens could not read the content of the inscriptions. The public curses of the city of Teos include some against political officers "who do not read out the writing on the stele to the best of their memory and power" — that is, even the officials are "reading" from memory, and the rest of the populace are dependent on their memory as well

---

41. Niditch, *Oral World*, 60–63; Thomas, *Literacy and Orality*, 129–56.
42. Thomas, *Literacy and Orality*, 71–72.
43. Ibid., 156–57.
44. Ibid., 48.

as their integrity.[45] Little wonder, then, well after the development of written laws, that Greek cities depended upon officials called *mnemones,* literally, "re-memberers," whose duties were to remember the affairs of the city, both sacred and secular, including court proceedings for which there were no written records, and whose memory was binding, in some places.[46] Not until the late fifth century B.C.E. did "unwritten law" come to be distinguished from "written law," the term "law" having previously meant customary law carried in common memory. The earliest Hebrew law code, the covenantal code in Exodus 21–23, appears to be a representative selection from Israelite "common law," which continued to function from village to village long after "codification" in writing, which the villagers could not have read anyhow.[47]

Writing was far more important in the operation of the Roman Empire than in that of the Greek city-state.[48] As in the city-state, however, writing was primarily for display rather than practical communication and keeping records that would be consulted later.[49] Imperial edicts, letters, and rescripts were commonly but not necessarily inscribed publicly and were not always preserved in archives. When three thousand bronze inscriptions on the Capitol in Rome were destroyed by fire, Vespasian had to search for other copies of the texts. Suetonius (*Vespasian* 8) names these "the imperial power's finest and oldest equipment" or "record." That such a search was necessary, however, and the very location of civic documents in prominent civil religious sites suggest that their primary or real function was symbolic as well as (or rather than) practical. The primary and traditional way of communicating with the public at large was not written but oral. Criers (*kerykes, praecones*) were ubiquitous, and were attached to Roman officers at every imaginable level, whether consuls, censors, praetors, aediles, quaestors, tribunes, or provincial governors.[50] Imperial control over the provinces, on the other hand, involved extensive correspondence, particularly with the emperor's subordinates and the army.[51] The army was the institution in which writing became most important.[52] Record-keeping expanded under Augustus, and imperial records of

---

45. P. Hermann, "Teos und Abdera im 5. Jahrhundert v. Chr," *Chiron* 11 (1981): 1–30; Thomas, *Literacy and Orality,* 69.

46. See the fuller discussion by Thomas, *Literacy and Orality,* 69–70.

47. English common law, now used in all but one of the United States, was originally customary unwritten law that varied somewhat from area to area and was collected, written, and codified over a long period of time at the instigation of English kings.

48. The primary practical use of writing was the ruling of empire, according to Pieter J. J. Botha, "Greco-Roman Literacy as Setting for New Testament Writings," *Neotestamentica* 26 (1992): 208.

49. "The Roman Empire depended on writing,... [yet] the social limits of education and literacy remained quite narrow" (Harris, *Ancient Literacy,* 206).

50. Ibid., 208.

51. Ibid., 209; on the importance of imperial correspondence, see Helmut Koester, "Writings and the Spirit: Authority and Politics in Ancient Christianity," *HTR* 84 (1991): 355.

52. Harris, *Ancient Literacy,* 217–18. It is worth noting the parallel for letter writing in ancient Hebrew. Virtually all of the relatively few (forty-eight) letters in Hebrew from 700 B.C.E. to C.E. 135 pertain to military affairs. Hebrew biblical references to letters, mostly in postexilic materials, portray them as dictated to scribes, then read aloud to the addressee — again writing functioning in an oral communications context. See Niditch, *Oral World,* 51–53, 91.

such matters as delinquent taxes and debts became symbolic objects of intense resentment. Imperial regimes even tried public burning of such books in attempts to regain at least the tacit consent of the governed.[53]

Writing was also part and parcel in the various forms of imperial political propaganda. Inscriptions on coins were the most widespread form of such symbolic propaganda in writing. Far more awesome and, presumably, effective as a written language of power were the inscriptions on massive monuments erected in the most propitious public spaces in every city of the empire. For these inscriptions that pervaded public space, practical communication of the written message was incidental to the symbolic communication of power. Previous empires had erected massive monuments, such as the pyramids in Egypt, and some, such as the Assyrians, had added inscriptions to the other impressive components such as visible portrayals of conquests. The Romans constructed them on an unprecedented scale. Whether it was Assyrian royal inscriptions or Roman imperial inscriptions, "the very alienness of this script...would have collaborated with the rest of the relief to convey the message of power, fear, and obedience."[54] The very feeling of helplessness of the onlookers facing such monuments confirmed them in their place at the bottom of the hierarchy of power. In the case of inscriptions on public buildings and imperial monuments, of course, writing was not added to and in service of oral communication, but visual-spacial communication. The point is that again writing on these monuments is not only symbolic but also secondary and instrumental to another, primary medium of communication (the text inscribed did not "stand on its own"). Closely related to the massive monuments proclaiming Rome's imperial rule, urban and provincial elites, whose position depended on their patron-client relation with the imperial family anyhow, proliferated additional, smaller monuments and inscriptions honoring the emperor, along with the glory that reflected on their symbolic homage and their own magnanimity in gifts and endowments. The imperial elite's obsession with honor became literally a "subtext" of empire in the form of honorific inscriptions.

Written Literature

Literary production was extensive in Greek and Roman antiquity. For example, orators increasingly "published" their polished speeches, usually after delivery. Yet there were no publishers and mass production as in modern print culture. Papyrus rolls were expensive, and literary works were copied by hand. With no divisions between words in the writing on the scrolls, it would have been extremely difficult to follow texts with the eyes and to locate particular passages.[55]

---

53. Harris, *Ancient Literacy*, 209–11.

54. Peter Machinist, "Assyrians on Assyria in the First Millennium B.C.," in *Anfänge politischen Denkens in der Antike: Die nahöstlichen Kulturen und die Griechen,* ed. Kurt Raaflaub (Munich: R. Oldenbourg, 1993), 101.

55. Botha, "Greco-Roman Literacy," 201. With regard to Plato's apparent inconsistency, Doyne Dawson, *Cities of the Gods: Communist Utopias in Greek Thought* (Oxford: Oxford University Press, 1992), 89, comments: "The form of the ancient book made it so difficult to look up exact references

It is often commented that reading aloud from an ancient manuscript would have required some familiarity with the content of the document. Diffusion of literature remained basically oral, through public readings or recitations at private banquets.[56] "There was no such thing as 'popular literature' in the Roman Empire, . . . Greek romances [being] the light reading of a limited public possessing a real degree of education."[57] Ordinary people could enjoy many forms of entertainment and culture without literacy. In describing the festive atmosphere in a hippodrome, Dio Chrysostom (20.20) mentions the recitation of a poem and the recounting of a history, along with singing, dancing, and flute playing. Quintilian (*Inst.* 5.11.19) portrays the uneducated as listening to Aesop's fables and other stories.

The function of written literature and its relation to the culture in which oral communication still prevailed even among the literate have been illuminated by recent studies focused on Greek poetry and other literature, studies that take the oral performance and aural hearing of literature critically into account. "Practically all ancient literature, however compressed in style (e.g., even Pindar or Thucydides), would have been heard and not read silently."[58] Drama of course was performed in a fully staged production with actors and chorus in the theater of a polis. But virtually all types of poetry, whether performed in a public venue or a private banquet, would have been chanted or sung, accompanied by music, perhaps even dancing. The words were only part of the whole composition that included music as well. Poetry (= music) of all kinds, dramas, and even history, moreover, were performed at particular occasions. On some occasions a particular kind of performance was customary: for example, wedding songs at marriages, dirges at funerals, elegies at private symposia, hymns and processionals at public religious festivals, and victory odes and encomia at games.[59]

"Written texts existed for most of the types of literature that were performed in ancient Greece."[60] The relation between text and composition and performance was necessarily a rather fluid one. For poetry, for example, the written text recorded only one facet of a complex combination of words, music, and perhaps dance. The only ancient descriptions of poets in the process of composition make no mention of pen and papyrus (Aristophanes, *Acharnians* 383–479; *Thesmophoriazusae* 95–265).[61] The written text may have been the final record made only after composition in the poet's head or in (further) oral composition in rehearsal and performance or a "transcript" of a particular performance. Moreover, "the written texts of the poetry recorded only an element of the total performance.

that authors usually relied on their excerpts, notes, and memories; and the notion of a 'book' implied not so much a fixed text as an oral presentation, sometimes with commentary."

56. Harris, *Ancient Literacy*, 223–28.
57. Ibid., 227–28.
58. Thomas, *Literacy and Orality*, 102–3.
59. Ibid., 120–23.
60. Ibid., 123–24.
61. See further J. Herington, *Poetry into Drama: Early Tragedy and the Greek Poetic Tradition* (Berkeley: University of California Press, 1985).

They were merely an *aide-memoire*, a silent record of a much richer experience, hardly something to be relished and read on their own.... [A] text was a simple memorial or words which were to be learnt by heart as soon as possible, and transmuted into a far richer experience."[62] While the words may have been transmitted with the help of written texts, the rest of traditional performance, which continued for generations and centuries, "was passed down purely through the continuity of performance, the teaching of one generation by another."[63] "The presence of writing alone does not necessarily transform the oral tradition, let alone kill it."[64] Rather, "continuity in style and methods even after the coming of writing... merely duplicated orally composed poetry rather than cutting it dead."[65] The "song-culture" of classical Greece did not die out and give way to a (supposed) "book-culture" in Hellenistic and Roman times. Even the public delivery of history did not die out with Herodotus.[66]

A suggestive recent reflection on the "forms of discourse in ancient philosophy" presents a parallel picture even with regard to the dense discourse of Hellenistic and Roman philosophy:

> More than other literature, philosophical works are linked to oral transmission because ancient philosophy itself is above all oral in character.... In matters of philosophical teaching, writing is only an aid to memory, a last resort that will never replace the living word. True education is always oral because only the spoken word... makes it possible for the disciple to discover the truth himself amid the interplay of questions and answers.... Thus for the most part the literary productions of the philosophers are a preparation, extension, or echo of their spoken lessons.... Some of the works, moreover, are directly related to the situation of teaching,... either a summary the teacher drafted in preparing his course or notes taken by students during the course.[67]

Thus whether it be poetry, drama, history, or even philosophy, the "literary" situation in the Roman Empire was not much different from that in earlier Greek city-states. "Whether or not a written text existed, oral transmission, performance, and discourse were predominant.... The evidence... shows both a sophisticated and extensive use of writing in some spheres and what is to us an amazing dominance of the spoken word.... [D]ense and complex literature was regularly heard rather than read by its public. The written word was more often used in the service of the spoken."[68]

---

62. Thomas, *Literacy and Orality*, 118.
63. Ibid., 122.
64. Ibid., 50.
65. Thomas, *Literacy and Orality*, 48–49.
66. Ibid., 123.
67. Pierre Hadot, "Forms of Life and Forms of Discourse in Ancient Philosophy," *Critical Inquiry* 16 (1990): 497–98.
68. Thomas, *Literacy and Orality*, 4.

Manuscripts and Oral Communication in Judea and Galilee

To move back in the direction of Q and its origins in a Galilean Jesus movement, it may be useful to explore the relative roles that writing and oral communication may have played in the appropriation and cultivation of cultural tradition in second-temple Judea and Galilee.

Sacred Scrolls and the Ceremonial Recitation of Torah

In second-temple Judea the use of writing developed differently from the way it did in the contemporary Greek city-states in one highly significant way: the development of scripture. Whereas in Athens new laws were inscribed on stone as memorials of the legislation and the curses sanctioning their authority, in Jerusalem the laws legitimating the temple-state were written on scrolls, apparently then housed in the sacred precincts of the temple. Such scrolls, however, were not any the less memorials than the inscriptions in Athens and were perhaps even less "legible" to ordinary Judeans than the inscriptions were to ordinary Athenian citizens. Two stories about the reading of books reveal both how dominant oral communication was in Judean society and the distinctive function of "books of the Law."

The story of the "book" or scroll of Torah "found" in the temple that became the basis of Josiah's reform in 2 Kings 22–23 indicates that written documents were highly unusual, even at the center of power in the Jerusalem temple and the Davidic court. Nothing in the story suggests that this scroll was simply an old copy of the Law that had somehow gotten displaced (or suppressed by a previous regime) from the temple library, where it would previously have been read by priests in their regular study or teaching of the people, or from the royal "archives," where such law books would regularly have been consulted by royal officials. Communications at court and in the temple, as in the society at large, were basically oral. The purpose of the (almost certainly newly produced) writing was to legitimate and authorize the centralization of political-religious power in Jerusalem, similar to the function of the "found book" tradition in other cultures that legitimates innovation in highly traditional societies.[69] The reason this worked, the explanation for the respect and awe which the people were expected to have for the recently discovered document, is that writing was unusual, not a familiar aspect of life that was simply taken for granted. Like the covenantal tablets given by God on Sinai, this *sepher* was endowed with aura and mystery. "It validates reform not only because it is written and true, but because it is unusual, mysterious, and divinely sent."[70] Inscribed with the sacred words of God, the scroll, whose contents and authority (and legitimation by the prophet Huldah) were managed by the royal scribes and priests all the way, was read aloud, "in the hearing" of the Jerusalemites and the Judeans.

---

69. Wolfgang Speyer, *Die literarische Fälschung im heidnischen und christlichen Altertum: Ein Versuch über Deutung* (Munich: Beck, 1971).

70. Niditch, *Oral World*, 104.

Ezra's "reading" of "the book of the Law of Moses" was a virtually unprecedented founding ceremonial occasion on the first day of Tishre, the first month of
the New Year, an assembly of Judean elite just returned to Jerusalem from exile in
Babylon under Persian imperial sponsorship.[71] The story in Nehemiah 8 portrays
the scroll of the Law of Moses as a numinous sacred object.[72] Ezra stood on a
platform made specially for the occasion, so that "he was standing above all the
people." "And Ezra opened the scroll in the sight of all the people . . . and when
he opened it, all the people stood up. Then Ezra blessed the LORD, the great
God, and all the people answered, 'Amen, Amen,' lifting up their hands" (Neh.
8:4–6). Ezra has "brought the Torah (= teaching) before the assembly" who *listen*
attentively from early morning until midday (8:2–3). Then named Levites "read
from the book . . . with interpretation" (8:8). The scroll is sacred, almost iconic;
the reading is oral; and the teaching must be interpreted. Interpretation may be
necessary because of a language barrier, if the assembly of those returned from
exile used Aramaic and the Torah was in Hebrew. It may also have entailed the
particular understanding that Ezra and the Levites wanted to inculcate. Given the
function of sacred scrolls ("books") in authorizing reform and innovation, however, additional factors may have been operative. The "citations" regarding the
festivals of booths (Neh. 8:14–15; and those in Ezra 9:11, 12) supposedly "found
written in the Law which the LORD had commanded by Moses" do not appear in
the received version of the Torah / Pentateuch. Like the lost scroll found in the
temple in 2 Kings 22–23, so the sacred scroll lifted and opened before the assembly in Ezra 8 serves to authorize a reform, including innovations in traditional
practices, changes of the customary (oral) laws of the people. The inscribing of
new written law in a sacred scroll as a memorial fraught with mystery and authority in early second-temple Judea parallels the inscription of new written laws
on stone as a memorial in classical Athens.

We can imagine that as actual scrolls became more familiar to Judeans, their
presentation and oral recitation by the high priests became regularly reenacted
ceremonies (Deut. 31:10; Josephus, *Ant.* 4.209; *m. Sotah* 7:8). The scrolls, however, retained their sacred aura, the mystery that surrounded their usually hidden
existence as well as their ceremonial exaltation, display, and reading — a sacred
mystery that continues in the sabbath reading in synagogues today. From at least
late antiquity, scrolls were opened and read, apparently on a weekly basis, in
many Jewish synagogue buildings. One may doubt that many Judean or Galilean
village assemblies (*synagogai*) in late second-temple times owned Torah scrolls —
or for that matter an assembly building to house them. Certainly some diaspora

71. The "documentary history" recounted in Ezra 1–6 of the Persian imperial authorization of the
rebuilding of the temple in Jerusalem illustrates both the memorial character of the Persian imperial
decrees, which prove difficult to locate in the imperial "archives" (6:1–2), and the magical-religious
function of (some of) the writing. In the decree authorizing support from the imperial revenues for
sacrifices to God and prayers for the emperor in the rebuilt Jerusalem temple, Darius also pronounces
a curse on anyone who would dare to alter his edict (6:6–12): he would be impaled on a beam from
his own house, which would be turned into a manure heap!

72. Niditch, *Oral World*, 105–6.

assemblies (synagogues) possessed copies of the Septuagint, as Philo and other sources suggest, and the presence of multiple scrolls, for example, of Exodus, Numbers, and Jeremiah among the Dead Sea Scrolls, suggests that Judean scribal groups likely possessed scrolls of both Prophets as well as Torah. But scrolls were costly, and it seems doubtful that very many village assemblies could have afforded them. Josephus's accounts of a heckler in Tarichaeae holding up a copy of "the laws of Moses" and of a scroll burned by Roman soldiers (*Vita* 134–35; *B.J.* 2.229) are strikingly unusual references. But they do indicate that at least some copies existed in Judean and Galilean towns in mid–first century C.E.

Oral Cultivation of Israelite Cultural Tradition

Judean literature contains a number of indications, however, in addition to the widespread lack of literacy, that appropriation and cultivation of Israelite and Judean cultural tradition were primarily by memory and oral communication. Insofar as the vast majority of Judeans and Galileans were not literate, whatever cultivation of Israelite tradition continued in village life must have taken place in oral communication. Even among the literate circles who left literary records, those very records, which provide virtually our only evidence, indicate that cultivation of Israelite and Judean cultural tradition was primarily oral.

First, several different modes of recounting Israel's history developed, some of which are discernible both in materials which were included in the subsequently defined biblical canon and in extant noncanonical literature. For example, besides the sustained, eventually canonical epic narratives in Genesis-Exodus-Numbers, one can discern two particular summary modes of historical presentation, one of which focuses on patriarchal incidents and exodus and wilderness incidents as a sequence of deliverance (and/or fulfillment of the promise to Abraham; e.g., Psalm 105; Pseudo-Philo, *Biblical Antiquities* 10), the other of which juxtaposes such incidents of deliverance with examples of Israel's unfaithfulness (e.g., Deuteronomy 32; Psalms 78; 106; Nehemiah 9; cf. 1 Cor. 10:5–11). These shorter narratives, some of them psalms of praise, are not summaries of an already existing standardized written text of Genesis-Exodus-Numbers. From late second-temple times the book of *Jubilees* (in Hebrew, copies of which were found among the Dead Sea Scrolls), the *Genesis Apocryphon* (in Aramaic, discovered among the Dead Sea Scrolls), and the *Biblical Antiquities* of Pseudo-Philo (extant in Latin; originally in Hebrew) all provide alternative accounts of Genesis history and beyond. These have been characterized as combinations of biblical accounts and apocryphal legends.[73] Other than their largely following the same sequence of events as canonical biblical literature, however, there is little evidence that they were working with a written text of Genesis. Later *midrashim* make explicit where they are (re-)citing the biblical text and where expanding and interpreting. The

---

73. O. S. Wintermute, "Jubilees," in *The Old Testament Pseudepigrapha*, 2 vols., ed. James H. Charlesworth (Garden City, N.Y.: Doubleday, 1985), 2:35–41, 48–50; Daniel J. Harrington, "Pseudo-Philo," in Charlesworth, *Old Testament Pseudepigrapha*, 2:297, 301–2.

three long alternative histories, however, are most likely separate accounts of Genesis and Israel's early history that may well know of, but do not work directly from, a written version of the books that became canonical. There is thus good evidence for the continuing composition and performance of parallel but varying accounts of Israel's beginnings that achieved written form at various points.

Second, judging from the remarkable textual plurality evident among the Dead Sea Scrolls, a stunningly rich variety of "editions" or textual traditions persisted probably until rabbinic times. The modern scholarly categories of "actual text," "paraphrase," and "reworking exegesis" may not approximate what was apparently a fluid relationship between scriptural tradition and written scrolls. In the case of such a pluriform textual tradition, it is difficult to determine what was the "original" text — or perhaps more fundamentally if the concept of an "original" text is pertinent to the way in which textual versions developed in their interaction with (memory and) oral recitation.[74]

Third, the Qumran community provides a remarkable example of a scribal community that, on the one hand, possessed scrolls, made additional copies of biblical documents, and wrote commentaries on those documents, yet, on the other hand, conducted a lively and highly disciplined community life orally. The many scrolls discovered near Qumran attest an intense scribal activity. The documents that originated in the community, however, attest the intense oral life of the community, whether in composing and reciting hymns and blessings at communal meals and meetings (e.g., 1QSa 2:21–23), composing and reciting hymns (e.g., 1QH), reciting prayers and blessings (e.g., 1QSb = 1Q28b; 4Q408; 4Q503; 4Q507–9), delivering sapiential exhortation (e.g., 4QS184–85), or rehearsing holy war (1QM). Virtually all such scrolls and scroll fragments either describe or must be written copies of (often regular) oral performances and rituals.

The Community Rule (1QS and variants) found at Qumran provides perhaps the best indication not only that the relationship between oral performance and textual record was fluid but also that the primarily oral community life would not have used its textual records regularly. It may be of special interest for Q and related material from Jesus movements since it has parallels not with previous or contemporary Judean literature but with the later Christian *Didache* and *Didascalia*. The textual tradition of the Community Rule is remarkably pluriform. The manuscript from cave 1 (1QS) bears marks of editorial modification such as

---

74. Eugene Ulrich, "The Bible in the Making: The Scriptures at Qumran," 77–93, and Emanuel Tov, "Biblical Texts as Reworked in Some Qumran Manuscripts with Special Attention to 4QRP and 4QPara Gen-Exod," 111–34, both in *The Community of the Renewed Covenant: The Notre Dame Symposium on the Dead Sea Scrolls,* ed. Eugene Ulrich and James VanderKam (Notre Dame, Ind.: University of Notre Dame Press, 1993). For the beginning step in an explanation of textual plurality on the basis of scribes living in a fundamentally oral culture, one that builds on Niditch (*Oral World*), see Raymond F. Person Jr., "The Ancient Israelite Scribe as Performer," *JBL* 117 (1998): 601–9. Some generalizations by Kelber seem applicable to the textual plurality of Jewish Scripture at this stage: "chirographs were not perceived as having firmly fixed boundaries.... Texts were viewed as constituents of a collective cultural enterprise or of a communal memory" ("Jesus and Tradition: Words in Time, Words in Space," *Semeia* 65 [1994]: 155).

corrections and interlinear additions, none of which appears in the manuscripts from cave 4. The section of the Rule in columns 8–9 of 1QS is far shorter in 4Q259. Only 4QS256 contains parallels to all sections of 1QS, while the significantly different texts of 4QS258 and 4QS259 contain only parts and differing parts of the rule in 1QS. There was thus apparently not a set "canonical" text of the Rule. Practice and performance were evolving. A reading of these scrolls quickly reveals that only the section in 1QS 10–11 is a written version (transcript) of an oral performance. Otherwise the Community Rule manuscripts are variant copies of a "handbook" or "manual" for the leaders of a priestly-scribal movement, including instructions for the initiation of new members into the renewed covenantal community, for doctrinal instruction of the initiates, and for the functioning of the community and the community council, as well as a set of laws, instructions for the master, and the master's hymn. The covenant renewal ceremony described in 1QS 1–3 would have been enacted orally whenever new members were inducted. The doctrinal instruction epitomized in 1QS 3–4 would have been delivered orally by the master. Community members already engaged in the communal life hardly needed to read the scroll to know that "they shall eat in common and bless in common and deliberate in common" (1QS 6:3). Since the master and other leaders of the community would have been performing or practicing virtually all of these matters on a regular basis, they would have known all these matters from ongoing practice or frequent repetition. The leaders of the community would hardly need to consult a "manual" very often.[75] But this was a primarily scribal community, hence in these scrolls they recorded and memorialized their ideology, constitution, practices, and procedures that continued to evolve, as evident in the corrections, additions, and variant textual versions.

The Community Rule also illustrates how the Qumran community did not treat the Mosaic Law, of which it possessed written scrolls, as textually (i.e., "literally") prescriptive for its community life but drew upon the scriptural tradition creatively as it responded to its own historical circumstances. The contents of the Rule belong solidly in the Mosaic covenantal tradition, but the fundamental frame of the Mosaic covenant as a whole, as well as component forms, have been dramatically transformed by a community that is explicitly striving to remain faithful to that tradition (see further chapter 9).

Fourth, Josephus's account of the Pharisees under the Hasmoneans suggests that their continuing extension and application of the Mosaic Torah took the form of oral formulation of additional rulings and their oral transmission to the people as well as to their own students. "The Pharisees had handed down to the people [certain / many] regulations (*nomima*) from the teaching of the fathers which were not recorded in the laws of Moses," whereas the Sadducees considered valid "only those regulations that are written [in scripture]" but not those "from the tradition of the fathers" (Josephus, *Ant.* 13.297). Nor was this a sectarian practice. As

---

75. By analogy with the *Didache*, "there is nothing in this didache that the reader does not already know" (Ian Henderson, "Didache and Orality in Synoptic Comparison," *JBL* 111 [1992]: 292).

Josephus explains, these orally formulated and transmitted laws comprised part of Hasmonean state law, both before they were rescinded by John Hyrcanus and again after his daughter-in-law Alexandra restored the regulations introduced by the Pharisees "in accordance with the tradition of the fathers" (13.408–9).[76] We may surmise that the Pharisees and other sages / teachers actually cultivated and transmitted "the laws of Moses" orally as well, although with their "scribal" skills they could surely have consulted written scrolls, assuming they had access to them.[77]

Finally, the surmise that the Pharisees cultivated Mosaic Torah orally (as opposed to regular consultation of actual scrolls) is reinforced by recent study of the rabbis, which is moving further from a textual model in reconstructing the rabbis' mode of teaching Torah. A series of articles analyzing rabbinic use of scriptural references concludes that "Biblical citation in rabbinic literature — no less than quotation from analogous classics among other literary cultures in the Greco-Roman world — testifies to the commission of the text to memory."[78] "As a cultural tradition, Scripture was at least as 'oral' a phenomenon among the Sages as a 'written' one.... And Sages' scriptural quotations are, no less than Paul's, quotations from memory in service of more ambitious rhetorical constructions."[79] Furthermore, the rabbinic compilers or earlier rabbinic traditions

> were pedagogically and ideologically committed to the oral mastery of the traditions they believed to be tannaitic. Written texts were preserved.... Yet their use in instruction was discouraged. Rather, the exposition of Sages' teachings took place in a highly ritualized setting designed to re-create and represent an original imparting of oral tradition from Moses to his disciples.... Within such a milieu, written texts enjoyed an essentially oral cultural life, subject to all the vagaries of oral transmission as they are memorized and transmitted in face-to-face performance.[80]

Scriptural References and Recitations in the Synoptic Gospels

This limited review of some second-temple Judean literature finds a number of indications that even among literate, scribal groups the cultivation of Israelite

---

76. Perhaps these oral regulations were included in what Josephus calls "the laws of the Judeans," by which the Hasmonean state ruled its people.

77. Paul Achtemeier, "Omnes verbum sonat: The New Testament and the Oral Environment of Late Western Antiquity," JBL 109 (1990): 26–27, makes the general point that since written scrolls in antiquity were so difficult to "read," given the lack of breaks between words, the lack of markings of divisions, and the cumbersome unrolling and rolling of the scroll, "references were therefore much more likely to be quoted from memory than to be copied from a source." The opening of the Mishnah tractate Abot certainly gives the impression that the rabbis believed that the tradition of (the?) Torah had been oral all along, as Moses handed it on to Joshua, Joshua to the elders, in the "chain of tradition."

78. Martin S. Jaffee, "Writing and Rabbinic Oral Tradition: On Mishnaic Narrative, Lists and Mnemonics," Journal of Jewish Thought and Philosophy 4 (1994): 126.

79. "Neither Paul nor the Sages had writings before them as they composed their discourses" (Martin S. Jaffee, "Figuring Early Rabbinic Literary Culture," Semeia 65 [1994]: 70–71). Achtemeier, "Omnes verbum sonat," 27, draws the implications for the futility of attempting to ascertain what "text" Paul may have been using.

80. Jaffee, "Writing and Rabbinic Oral Tradition," 143–44.

cultural tradition, like the conduct of their community or "academic" life, was predominantly oral. The texts they produced were transcripts and/or records or memorials of oral performances. Insofar as they consulted their own texts, it was for purposes of oral performance. If communication in general and the cultivation of Israelite tradition in particular even among literate groups were oral, then it would appear certain that the corresponding communication and cultivation of Israelite tradition among village communities and popular movements would have been oral. Some rather high estimates of the presence of writing among Galilean villagers appear in recent discussion of "orality and literacy" in "early Christianity": for example, that hearing "Scripture read aloud" was the source of Jesus' "knowledge of Scripture."[81] If "Scripture" means written scrolls, then that seems somewhat unrealistic. It presupposes both that village assemblies generally possessed scriptural scrolls and the presence of someone who could read them aloud. The only literature we have that originated in popular movements that can provide a source for investigation happens to be the documents of the Synoptic Gospel tradition, the earliest of which were presumably Q and Mark. Some Gospel passages that might provide test cases are the references to Israelite cultural traditions, many of which have previously been characterized as quotations of or allusions to scriptural (Hebrew biblical) texts.[82]

The picture in Luke 4:16–20 of Jesus in the Nazareth assembly on the sabbath, just happening to be handed the Isaiah scroll and easily finding the passage "The Spirit of the Lord is upon me" to read is now widely recognized as a Lukan projection of a more literate situation and a tailor-made christological scheme onto the launching of Jesus' ministry in Galilee. Mark's portrayal of Jesus teaching on the sabbath in his hometown assembly makes no mention of a scroll or "reading" (6:1–2). Matthew, with his explicit "formula quotations" of scripture, is recognized as a writer with some scribal training. Mark and Q, by contrast, present virtually no evidence of the use of written texts of scripture. Caution must be exercised in claiming such use, since a Markan passage referring to a scriptural tradition may have been somewhat conformed to the Septuagint text either in being placed in textual form or by an early copyist of a manuscript, and references to scriptural tradition in Q may have been conformed to the scriptural text by Matthew or Luke and/or by an early copyist. As already noted in the previous chapter, in Q "explicit biblical quotations are rare."[83] Three are concentrated in the story of Satan testing Jesus, and in the only other ostensibly "explicit quotation" (Q 7:27) it is unclear exactly what passage(s) (in what textual traditions) are referred to. Mark has more ostensibly "explicit quotations" of scripture, but closer examination raises questions about whether Mark was

---

81. Vernon Robbins, "Oral, Rhetorical, and Literary Cultures," *Semeia* 65 (1994): 79.

82. To say "Old Testament," as is often done in Christian New Testament interpretation, of course, is an anachronism, since there was no such thing yet as the New Testament.

83. John S. Kloppenborg, *Formation of Q: Trajectories in Ancient Wisdom Collections* (Minneapolis: Fortress, 1991), 247.

working with written texts. Indeed, a complete analysis of Mark in this regard may not be necessary in order to obtain a sense of Mark's apparently nontextual relation to scripture.

Some passages in Mark that scholars treat as references to scripture are not to written texts at all but to words uttered by characters in the story ("Hosanna!" [11:9–10]) or a hero in Israel's history ("David declared" [12:36]) or to what Moses himself "allowed" (10:4). The acclamation of those accompanying Jesus' entry into Jerusalem in 11:9–10 varies considerably from its ostensible source in Ps. 118:25–26. But festival psalms would have been familiar among the people from regular use and not dependent on some textual tradition. And what Moses allowed in so important a matter as divorce would have been common knowledge among the people as well as the Pharisaic guardians of the literate great tradition, encountered in Mark 10:4, with no need to consult a scroll for Deut. 24:1–4. Some "citations" of scripture in Mark are composites of poetic couplets that would have been written in different scrolls. "As it is written in the prophet Isaiah" in 1:2–3, for example, begins as a version of Mal. 3:1, with differences from the Hebrew and Septuagint texts, and continues with Isa. 40:3, with an often-noted difference from the reading of the same passage in the Dead Sea Scrolls. Such composites, in which a prophetic or psalmic couplet (e.g., from Malachi) is attributed to a different prophet (e.g., to Isaiah), may well stem from a popular tradition of Israelite culture, as discussed in the previous chapter. Some of Markan Jesus' apparent scriptural citations are of the most fundamental principles and memorable passages that would have been well known to ancient Israelites (including Judean and Galilean peasants), in the same way as the pledge of allegiance to the flag and key passages of the Declaration of Independence are easily cited from memory by a patriotic citizen of the United States. Examples of such references are those to the "commandment of God" to "Honor your father and your mother" (Mark 7:9–10), to the second half of the decalogue (Mark 10:19; but note the addition of "you shall not defraud," which points precisely to how the man could have come to have "many possessions," Mark 10:22), and perhaps to the two principles from the creation stories, recited respectively in Mark 10:6 and 8. Sometimes Mark simply alludes to an Israelite tradition, as in the messianic entry into Jerusalem on a colt (Mark 11:2–8), which Matthew (21:5) makes explicit by quotation of Zech. 9:9. As has long been recognized, the Markan "passion narrative" is replete with allusions to, but not precise quotations from, biblical traditions or passages. A telling illustration of Mark's relation to Israelite tradition may be provided by Mark 2:25–26, where Jesus' account of David and his companions varies widely from the account in 1 Sam. 22:1–6, including substituting a son for his father in the role of high priest (cf. 2 Sam. 15:35), which office did not exist yet when David was fleeing from Saul. All of these aspects of Mark's relation to Israelite traditions suggest that the author/story is working not from written texts but from memory/oral tradition, as were Paul and the rabbis when they referred to biblical traditions.

The appearance of "it is written (in the prophet)" and "scripture" (*gegraptai* and *graphe,* respectively) has often been taken as an indication of a textual quotation or a reference to an actual text. This may need reconsideration in the light of what we are learning about the function of writing, particularly of sacred writing, in ancient societies. A recent discussion of the references to "the gospel" in the *Didache* (8:2; 11:3; 15:3–4) has shown the way for the supposed "inter*textual*" relations of "early Christian" literature.[84] There appears to be no point in perpetuating the debate whether the references or appeals to "the gospel" in the *Didache* (8:2; 11:3; 15:3–4) are to a particular written text (such as that of Matthew), since "the acknowledged debt is to the gospel's authority, not its text."[85] That principle can be extended also to a reference to scripture (presumably in the Septuagint) in other "early Christian" or Jewish literature, not simply because the reference does not follow the Septuagint text exactly but also because the appeal is to the authority of scripture, which is by definition written (and could be consulted) on scrolls. Thus, for example, the term "as it is written" in the Q story of the testing (4:1–13) and the Q discussion of John the Baptist (7:27) should be understood not so much as a citation formula or reference to a particular written text as a reference to the authority of the scripture.

In that sense we can discern some further overtones of certain references in Mark, several of which are explicitly marked with "as it is written" or indicated as from "scripture." When Jesus cites Isaiah against the scribes and Pharisees (Mark 7:6) and Jeremiah and a festival psalm against the predatory rulers of the temple as "it is written" (Mark 11:17; 12:10), he throws back at the literate ruling elite the very authority that they themselves claim as legitimation for their own power and/or authority. The references in Mark 9:12–13 are similarly an appeal to the general authority of scripture (with no particular references given) over against the scribal authorities on scripture. In 10:3–5 Mark throws a citation of Moses back in the face of the Pharisees, and in 12:18–27 another citation of Moses back in the face of the Sadducees. That is, most of the references to scripture in Mark have Jesus citing it over against the rulers and their scribal representatives who claim it as the authorization of their power and privilege over the people. Only in the passion narrative does Mark appeal to the general or particular authority of the scripture as explaining the events that were difficult to accept and understand, such as the betrayal, arrest, and crucifixion of Jesus and the desertion of the disciples (14:21, 27, 49). This is similar to the way the creed Paul cites in 1 Cor. 15:3–5 refers to the general authority of "scripture" (with no particular references) to authorize the death and resurrection of Christ. Mark's attitude toward and use of scripture is thus complex, and it is clear that Israelite tradition is nothing if not contested. Mark uses it against the ruling and literate elite who cultivate it and wrap themselves in its authority. Yet Mark for his own audience/community appeals to the gen-

---

84. Henderson, "Didache and Orality."
85. Ibid., 297.

eral authority of the sacred written tradition, scripture, to interpret the events of the passion narrative that were so difficult to accept and understand, the betrayal and desertion by the disciples and the arrest and crucifixion of Jesus. Throughout, the terms *gegraptai* and *graphe* are not so much citation formulas or references to a particular written text as references to the authority of the scripture.

In summary, there is little likelihood of regular (daily or weekly) use of actual texts (written parchment or papyrus scrolls) in ancient Judea and Galilee, at least in the assimilation and cultivation of Israelite cultural tradition. Even elite literate groups such as Pharisees and the later rabbis apparently taught, learned, and recited scripture orally. It also seems evident from their ostensible citation of scripture that the earliest documents of the Jesus movements, Mark and Q, apparently cultivated and recited Israelite (including biblical) traditions in oral form.

Implications for Q

The above surveys of the general lack of literacy in Mediterranean antiquity, the largely ancillary functions of writing in the predominantly oral societies of Mediterranean antiquity, and the oral cultivation of Israelite traditions in Judea and Galilee have some clear implications for our approach to Q. These surveys lead to some fairly clear generalizations about the historical context in which Q must be understood. We may focus on three implications of particular importance.

First, as recent surveys of literacy and orality in antiquity conclude, most "texts" from antiquity are "oral-derived" literature. That is, most extant pieces of literature from the ancient Mediterranean — from poetry and speeches to history and philosophy — originated in oral performance and continued to be recited or performed after they were written down. Literary texts were written and used primarily for the purpose of facilitating oral communication. Texts were transcripts of and/or aids to oral performances. If read, they were read aloud, hence re-oralized in performance, usually before a group of people. The "hermeneutics" implicit in such oral-derived literature would thus have been oral-aural. Even after performed materials were written down, they continued to function primarily in further oral performance.[86] That Papias preferred the oral over the written gospel long after Gospels existed in written form is well known (Eusebius, *Hist. eccl.* 3.39.4).[87] As evident in the way they are "cited"

---

86. The observation by Achtemeier, "Omnes verbum sonat," 7, that "the sheer act of committing traditions to writing did not eliminate their continued transmission in non-written forms," while making somewhat the same point, is in effect an understatement, for transmission was embedded and effected in repeated performance.

87. His comments are paralleled by Seneca (Achtemeier, "Omnes verbum sonat," 10). Well into the second century, the Gospels that became canonical were not yet widely distributed (Birger Gerhardsson, *Memory and Manuscript: Oral Tradition and Written Transmission in Rabbinic Judaism and Early*

in the apostolic fathers, Jesus' sayings continued to be recited orally long after the Synoptic Gospels were written, as Helmut Koester demonstrated more than forty years ago.[88]

Since most literature from antiquity originated and continued in oral performance, and since literacy was so limited, particularly among ordinary people, then Q also must have originated and continued in oral performance. This is not to imply that Q was only a layer of oral tradition, in a way that would be threatening to those concerned primarily about the mere transmission of Jesus' sayings. The transmission of Jesus materials was ensured because they were embedded in repeated oral recitations. Moreover, that Matthew and Luke present so much of Q in verbatim parallels suggests that Q did indeed exist as a written document before it disappeared from historical view into their respective Gospels. But even after Q discourses were written down and were taken up into written copies of Matthew and Luke, they would have continued to be performed orally in communities of the Jesus movement that produced them.

That Q was an "oral-derived" text and continued to function in repeated recitation "in an environment saturated with oral sensitivities" is difficult for us to understand because we work on the assumptions of print culture and the methods of biblical studies "have instilled in us the idea of autonomous textual entities, which grew out of texts, linked up directly with other texts, and in turn generated new texts."[89] In his original presentation of Q as belonging to the genre he labeled *logoi sophōsn*, James M. Robinson assumed that Q was oral and that Q disappeared only as its context (*Sitz im Leben*) in "oral transmission of Jesus' sayings" declined.[90] Werner Kelber laid out a highly suggestive interpretation of Q sayings as oral.[91] But most studies of Q seem to have ignored his work and the provocative portrayal of orality by Ong and others on which it is based.[92] As Robinson stated recently:

> The standard Q hypothesis today is indeed that Q was a written Greek text, two copies of which existed, one in the Matthean community and one in the Lukan community. The respective evangelists used each, perhaps in a form glossed by the ongoing proclamation of Jesus' sayings in that community. Nevertheless, both Matthew and Luke relied upon copies of that one Q archetype. That archetype is

---

Christianity, Acta Seminarii Neotestamentici Upsaliensis 22 [Lund: C. W. K. Gleerup; Copenhagen: Ejnar Munksgaard, 1961], 200).

88. Helmut Koester, *Synoptische Überlieferung bei den apostolischen Vätern* (Berlin: Akademie-Verlag, 1957).

89. Kelber, "Jesus and Tradition," 141.

90. James M. Robinson, "LOGOI SOPHON: On the Gattung of Q," in *Trajectories through Early Christianity* (Philadelphia: Fortress, 1971), 102–3. Kloppenborg, *Formation of Q*, 31, however, insisted that Q was a written text. The stability of a text is essential, of course, for stratigraphic analysis to have any credibility.

91. Kelber, *Oral and Written Gospel.*

92. Kelber's thesis that Q was oral was probably threatening to biblical scholars working on the standard assumptions and procedures of biblical studies; for if Q was oral, then modern scholars could

what the scholarly community means by Q and is what the International Q Project is seeking to reconstruct.[93]

The concern that drives the project of securing the written text of Q is clearly anxiety about the transmission of Jesus materials, which seem threatened if Q "was only a layer of oral tradition." With Q secured as a written text (by the recent discovery of a "scribal error"), "the history of the synoptic tradition is no longer dependent only on the forms of oral transmission, but now was a series of written texts bridging much of the gulf back from the canonical gospels to Jesus."[94]

As the above survey of literacy and orality in the ancient Mediterranean world indicates, however, it would perpetuate a false, unhistorical alternative to argue that Q was exclusively oral or exclusively written. Q was indeed more than "only a layer of oral tradition." Q was indeed a text — an *oral-derived* text and a text that was recited repeatedly both before and after it was written down in one or more copies. Reading Q as a mere written text, however, would be like reading the words of an ancient Greek drama without reconstructing the performance situation with our informed historical imagination, or like merely reading the libretto of Mozart's *Magic Flute* instead of attending a performance. If we are interested in understanding the "historical Q," which functioned in oral performance, and understanding it with a historically informed sense of its "authentic" performance in its historical context, then we must work toward greater sensitivity to oral performance and oral-derived literature rooted in such performance. As Rosalind Thomas says about the oral-derived literature of ancient Greece, it may help "to strip away too 'bookish' an approach to the written texts, and to emphasize the value and circumstances of the performance."[95]

---

not "control" it with the standard tools of analysis premised on models of print culture. One of the only studies of Q that responds to Kelber's presentation of its orality is Arland D. Jacobson, *The First Gospel: An Introduction to Q* (Sonoma, Calif.: Polebridge, 1992), 8–12. Jacobson reasserts that "Palestine in Jesus' day was not an oral culture." He recognizes that indicators of oral composition can be found in Gospel texts (11). But that does not necessarily point to literary composition. The argument that Q was written rather than oral in Kloppenborg, *Formation of Q*, 42–51, engages primarily older studies of Q and, while not cognizant of Kelber's work, is aware of Milman Parry's argument about the oral character of Homer, based on formulaic diction (45). Ironically, three of the four arguments Kloppenborg makes for Q as written (peculiar phrases in both Matthew and Luke, agreement in order between Matthew and Luke, and doublets in Matthew and Luke [ibid., 46–50]) are just the sort of features that more recent studies of oral-derived literature suggest are indicative of oral composition behind or written down in texts. That part of Kelber's analysis that pointed to the instability of sayings material such as Q in oral tradition becomes the basis for rejecting Q speeches in oral form in Leif Vaage, "Composite Texts and Oral Mythology," in *Conflict and Invention*, ed. John S. Kloppenborg (Valley Forge, Pa.: Trinity Press International, 1995), 75–97. We should probably imagine similar explanations for why the careful suggestions by Pieter Botha ("Mark's Story as Oral Traditional Literature: Rethinking the Transmission of Some Traditions about Jesus," *Hervormde Teologiese Studies* 47 [1991]: 304–31) and Joanna Dewey ("Oral Methods of Structuring Narrative in Mark," *Interpretation* 43 [1989]: 32–44; and idem, "Mark as Interwoven Tapestry: Forecasts and Echoes for a Listening Audience," *CBQ* 53 [1991]: 221–36) that Mark displays features of oral composition have not been explored by other Mark scholars.

93. James M. Robinson, "A Written Greek Sayings Cluster Older than Q: A Vestige," *HTR* 92 (1999): 61–62.

94. Ibid., 61.

95. Thomas, *Literacy and Orality*, 104.

Second, in contrast to silent, solitary reading in modern print culture, recitation or performance in Mediterranean antiquity was usually a communal experience. The same was true even of reading from a written letter or other manuscript. "Reading was . . . oral performance whenever it occurred and in whatever circumstances. Late antiquity knew nothing of the 'silent, solitary reader.' "[96] Thus even texts functioned "as constituents of a collective cultural enterprise or of a communal memory."[97] Recitation and even literally reading from texts were therefore relational, interactive events. Of course there may well have been exceptions. Indeed the *Gospel of Thomas* would appear to be an exception that proves the rule. The *Gospel of Thomas* provided written copies of speech fragments of Jesus for solitary meditation and reflection leading to an interpretation appropriate to individual salvation, as indicated in its first *logion*. Precisely in its stated hermeneutics, however, the *Gospel of Thomas* is distinctive and decisively different from the Q discourses, as argued in chapter 4. In contrast to the sayings in the *Gospel of Thomas*, on which solitary interpreters meditated, the Q speeches, like most other oral-derived texts in Mediterranean antiquity, would have been recited in a communal hearing, a relational, interactive event. Since the words recited or texts read did not mean anything in themselves, it is inappropriate to those texts therefore to attempt to establish their meaning in themselves. A "reader response" approach moves in an appropriate direction but is premised on a modern, individualistic reader who is silent and solitary. We should be looking in a more relational way for the ways in which a performed speech and communally read texts interacted with the group(s) of hearers to whom they were addressed. Far more than a biblical scholarship focused on a solitary, silent reading of printed texts has imagined, recited discourses or communally read texts were embedded in communities and their particular historical and social circumstances.

Third, corresponding to its recitation or reading as an oral-aural and communal event, the recited Q material consisted mainly not of aphorisms or individual sayings but of discourses (as argued on other grounds, i.e., the appearance of Q material in the texts of Matthew and Luke, in chapter 4). Individual sayings do not mean anything in and by themselves. They come to have significance only in recitation in particular relational contexts. The sayings in Q are integral components of speeches focused on issues of concern to a community. "Love your enemies," for example, is the general admonition that opens the covenantal exhortation section of the larger covenant renewal speech in 6:20–49. "Seek and you will find" is part of a sustained encouragement to boldly petition God to send the kingdom (11:2–4, 9–13). "Even the hairs of your head are all numbered" is among the encouraging words given as part of a speech insisting that those called before the authorities boldly confess their allegiance to the movement (12:2–12). "Seek first the kingdom of God" concludes a speech reassuring people who have legitimate anxieties about their marginal economic situation (12:22–31).

---

96. Achtemeier, "Omnes verbum sonat," 17, vs. Havelock.
97. Kelber, "Jesus and Tradition," 155.

To highlight Q as a set of discourses, it can be contrasted with the phenomenon of the list, which Jack Goody sees as a key written genre used by many societies moving from oral communication into literacy. Lists, "characteristic of the early uses of writing," are "promoted partly by the demands of complex economic and state organization, partly by the nature of scribal training, and partly by the 'play' element."[98] Lists make possible certain classificatory schemes and presentation of bureaucratic materials that are "presented in a form which is very different from that of ordinary speech." The list "rarely occurs in oral discourse at all."[99] John Dominic Crossan, much of whose work has been devoted to making "lists" of Jesus' sayings according to occurrence and topical categories, suggests that Q is a development of the listing phenomenon. "We could imagine sayings lists developing into dialogues and discourses in which accidental juxtaposition generated meditative combination, extension, and expansion."[100] As the supposedly formative layer was expanded into the secondary layer, "the phenomenon of listing becomes more and more structured thematically." Structured thematic clusters of sayings, however, are not lists at all but speeches or discourses that present arguments (whether exhortation, consolation, or deliberation) on certain issues. The difference can be clearly discerned in a biblical book such as Proverbs. Much of Proverbs indeed consists of lists (esp 10:1–22:16; 31:10–31). Far from being collected in a haphazard manner, the individual sayings in Prov. 10:1–22:16 are "listed" by word plays, catchwords, assonance, and alliteration, and Prov. 31:10–31 in particular is an acrostic (which presupposes literacy, the alphabet, but could still be a device for memory in oral recitation). Other sections of the book, however, consist of short discourses devoted to given subjects in which nothing in particular would point to composition in writing (e.g., 1:1–9:18; and "the words of the wise" in 22:17–23:11; 24:23–34; most of Sirach/Ecclesiasticus is similar). These would appear to be (written collections of) instructional speeches composed and delivered orally (and repeatedly) by sages to their students. Moving back to Jesus' sayings, the *Gospel of Thomas* may indeed be "a perfect example of a list," as Crossan declares; the appearance of the document is somewhat like Prov. 10:1–22:16.[101] But the more discursive and thematically structured clusters of sayings in Q appear to be not a bunch of expanded mini-lists (eventually evolving in successive writings into a maxi-list) but speeches on matters of concern composed and delivered orally to communities of Jesus' followers by certain speakers/leaders. And insofar as Q takes the form of discourses addressing issues of concern to the communities of a movement, it is necessary to attempt to discern how whole discourses, not individual sayings, addressed those issues.

Q studies, indeed studies of Jesus' sayings generally, as previously constituted,

---

98. Jack Goody, *The Domestication of the Savage Mind* (Cambridge: Cambridge University Press, 1977), 108.

99. Ibid., 80, 108.

100. John Dominic Crossan, "Lists in Early Christianity," *Semeia* 55 (1991): 238. Crossan is building on Goody's observations about lists.

101. Crossan, "Lists," 237.

are not well-equipped to deal with any of these implications. Not only do Q studies and studies of Jesus' sayings generally proceed on assumptions of a textual model derived from print culture[102] and tacitly resist the suggestion that Q is an oral-derived text. But Gospel studies generally have tended to focus on the meaning of individual sayings for individuals, while openings toward consideration of whole discourses and community experiences and circumstances have emerged only very recently. What is needed is some appropriate procedure with which to approach whole discourses in a way analogous to the agenda of form criticism, which originally focused on the social context (*Sitz im Leben*) in which Gospel materials functioned. The desired procedure would approach particular Q discourses and the whole series of discourses in terms of how they functioned in communities of a movement understood in their historical social and cultural circumstances. And just as those who originally developed and pursued form criticism did, we apparently must look beyond standard biblical studies to other academic fields for adaptable approaches, analyses, and analogies.

---

102. See Kelber, *Oral and Written Gospel;* and idem, "Jesus and Tradition."

Chapter 7

RECENT STUDIES OF ORAL-DERIVED LITERATURE AND Q

Richard A. Horsley _____

> Literacy is so deeply implanted in every twentieth-century biblical scholar that it is difficult to avoid thinking of it as the normal means of communication and the sole measure of language. — WERNER KELBER

That Q may have been an oral-derived text has apparently not been considered. This should hardly be surprising. After all, it is difficult enough to demonstrate that Q was ever a text, since it is known only indirectly through the parallel non-Markan material in Matthew and Luke. Its existence depends on the two-document hypothesis as a solution to the "Synoptic Problem." And if it ever existed as a document it disappeared from history as a separate entity once it was incorporated into and overwritten by Matthew and Luke. That Q as an oral-derived text has not been examined is also not surprising given the field of the relatively few scholars who are interested in it. Biblical scholars have a professional bias toward and a vested interest in texts, sacred texts. Moreover, since Q, as the source of Jesus' sayings for Matthew and Luke, apparently originated before the great Jewish Revolt of 66–70 C.E., which supposedly precipitated the separation of Jesus' followers from nascent "Judaism," it brings the modern historian and believer a giant step closer to the circumstances of Jesus' ministry and the early stages of the movement in which the Jesus traditions took form. Thus it is important for the scholarly enterprise to have a stable text.[1]

Nevertheless, once we recognize the predominantly oral communication environment in the Roman Empire in general and in Palestine in particular, we are forced seriously to consider that Q, even if known as a written text by Matthew and Luke, was an oral-derived text whose function and hermeneutic remained oral. To consider Q as oral, however, we must review some significant new initiatives in the study of oral and oral-derived literature in which classics scholars, folklorists, and cultural anthropologists have compared notes and shared insights

---

1. The International Q Project is now publishing a critical edition of its reconstruction of the text of Q.

based on a wide variety of oral materials. These may lead us beyond the pioneering probes into the orality of Mark and Q that have been either ignored or found unsatisfactory by students of the Synoptic Gospel tradition.

Recognition of Orality in the Synoptic Tradition, Q, and Mark

Although the field of New Testament studies has been reluctant to recognize the orality of its "texts," a few pioneers have applied the developing discussion on orality and literacy in the fields of anthropology and literary studies to the pre-Synoptic tradition, including Q, and eventually to Mark. The recognition that not only Q and pre-Markan materials but also Mark originated in oral recitation has been complicated as well as facilitated by the rapidly developing theory of orality and its relation to literacy.

Form Criticism and Oral Tradition on a Model of Literacy

Martin Dibelius, Rudolf Bultmann, and other pioneers of form criticism were constrained to differentiate the Synoptic Gospel tradition from *belle lettres.* They viewed the Synoptic Gospel tradition rather as *Kleinliteratur,* that is, as arising from the anonymous matrix of *das Volk,* in the Romantic tradition of the brothers Grimm, as mediated through the work of Hermann Gunkel on oral tradition behind the "Old Testament." Form criticism (originally *Formgeschichte* = "form history") investigated the interrelationship of social setting and linguistic form — something that was subsequently neglected by scholars claiming to follow form criticism. Bultmann viewed Synoptic materials not as composed by individuals but, like communally shaped and shared folk traditions, as arising out of typical situations in the life of a religious community. Unlike Gunkel, however, Bultmann did not then engage in a study of folk traditions in order to derive a model for analysis of the Synoptic Gospel tradition. Rather he derived the tendencies that were supposedly followed by the oral Gospel tradition from the way Matthew and Luke handled Mark and Q. That is, ironically, Bultmann used the model of how literary authors handled their already written sources as a model for the tendencies of supposedly oral tradition.[2] Even perceptive critics of Bultmann considered the distinction between the oral and the written irrelevant: "The tendencies of the one are presumably the tendencies of the other."[3] Oral criticism thus paid little or no attention to oral communication because it was assumed that, in effect, it made no difference.

The theological presuppositions that determined how form criticism constructed the tendencies of the Synoptic tradition also foreclosed any attention to oral communication in a traditional "folk" society. By theological definition, form critics were dealing with material much of which had originated with Jesus.

---

2. Rudolf Bultmann, *The History of the Synoptic Tradition* (Oxford: Blackwell, 1963), 6.

3. E. P. Sanders, *The Tendencies of the Synoptic Tradition,* SNTSMS 9 (Cambridge: Cambridge University Press, 1969). See the discussion in Werner Kelber, *The Oral and Written Gospel* (Philadelphia: Fortress, 1983), 6–8.

Moreover, they believed that with Jesus Christ and his apostle Paul had come a completely new departure in the history of salvation. Indeed, the decisive event that had become the transforming or originative source for all Jesus tradition was the "Easter faith in Jesus' resurrection."[4] Jesus the messenger of the kingdom was displaced by the Christ present in the kerygma. "The proclaimer became the proclaimed."[5] Given the tendency, since the advent of printed Bibles, to read the scripture verse by verse, and the tendency of scholars trained in philology to focus on individual words and statements, it is not surprising that form critics assumed that, so to speak, in the beginning was the individual saying. That is, the Jesus tradition was assumed to have originated in separate aphorisms, many of which were somehow remembered but remained "free-floating" early in the oral tradition. The final products of the Synoptic tradition, of course, were the Synoptic Gospels, scripture of the Christian churches. It can hardly be surprising that, since the model for the growth of the Synoptic tradition was the way Matthew and Luke combined, expanded upon, and revised their sources Mark and Q,[6] the Synoptic Gospel tradition was seen to have an inherent tendency to expand by combination, analogous formation, secondary additions, and redaction in a straight-line teleological development toward the first Gospel, Mark. Form criticism, in effect, worked on a model of literary editing and composition based on available, free-floating Jesus sayings and never got around to considering how genuinely oral tradition worked in a traditional oral communication environment. It was imagined that the oral tradition of Jesus materials developed steadily in the direction of the complete written Gospels because it was understood according to a literary model.

"Orality and Literacy" Theory: Oral Tradition vs. Written Gospel

Werner Kelber almost single-handedly pioneered the effort to break through the "disproportionately print-oriented hermeneutic in our study of the Bible."[7] In the same highly innovative work, Kelber both sounded a long-overdue "wake-up call" for Gospel studies to take oral communication seriously and dramatized the difference between Q (and pre-Markan materials) as oral and Mark as written. In countering "a prevalent tendency to perceive the written gospel in continuity with oral tradition" conceived on a literary model, Kelber adapted the theory of orality vs. literacy developed by Walter Ong and others.[8] Most importantly, he replaced form criticism's literary model for the oral transmission of Jesus traditions

---

4. Rudolf Bultmann, *Theology of the New Testament* (New York: Scribners, 1951–55), 1:42–43; idem, *History*, 348.

5. Bultmann, *Theology*, 1:33.

6. Leander E. Keck, "Oral Traditional Literature and the Gospels: The Seminar," in *The Relationships among the Gospels: An Interdisciplinary Dialogue*, ed. William O. Walker Jr. (San Antonio: Trinity University Press, 1978), 108.

7. Kelber, *Oral and Written Gospel*.

8. Major works by Walter Ong are *The Presence of the Word* (New Haven: Yale University Press, 1967); *Interfaces of the Word* (Ithaca, N.Y.: Cornell University Press, 1977); and *Orality and Literacy: The Technologizing of the Word* (London: Methuen, 1982).

with an illuminating characterization of orality as a mode of communication very different from literacy.

Determinative for his contrast between the Jesus sayings in Q and the Gospel of Mark was the theory that orality and literacy constitute fundamentally different technologies or media of communication that even engender different mentalities. He followed the recently developed theory of Ong, who argued that writing is "a technology that restructures thought," that produces a "literate mentality" in contrast to an "oral mentality."[9] Adapting Ong for the theologically oriented field of New Testament studies, Kelber substituted "christologies" for "mentalities." In Mark "the new technology of writing produced a christology that was in tension with, and a replacement of oral christology."[10]

Kelber's discussion of orality focused on the remembrance and transmission of pre-Markan and Q materials. With form critics and most Q interpreters, Kelber assumed that the unit of communication was the individual Jesus saying, parable, miracle story, and so on. He agreed that Q at some point must have been written, yet insisted that it is transparently a collection of spoken sayings (in the genre of *logoi sophon*).[11] He understood Q in terms of a "Son of Man" christology. Even though Q does not deal with Jesus' death, it somehow does assume the resurrection-exaltation and imminent parousia of Jesus as the Son of Man. Indeed, since Q makes no differentiation between the historical figure Jesus and the exalted Son of Man, the individual Q sayings are understood as the living address of the living exalted one. "A separation between the words of the historical Jesus and those of his followers was thus not only blurred, but often nonexistent."[12] "The speakers of Q sayings" were speaking Jesus' words. In opposition to the notion of a passive transmission of Jesus' sayings, Kelber suggested that social context is an essential factor (thus expanding on an insight of early form criticism). Their survival depended on "their social relevancy and acceptability."[13] Kelber's enthusiastic, almost evangelical, discussion of the oral transmission of Jesus' sayings concentrated on the medium of orality more than on the concrete oral communication of Jesus' message. Indeed, the medium appears to be, even to overwhelm, the message in its soteriological efficacy:

---

9. Kelber, *Oral and Written Gospel*, 14. While he seemed to shy away from Albert Lord's presentation of the two media as "contradictory and mutually exclusive," Kelber did not explore Ruth Finnegan's insistence on the interaction of the two. He emphasized the ways in which the written word transforms the oral word. And he suggested that "oral and written compositions come into existence under different circumstances" (14).

10. Kelber, *Oral and Written Gospel*, 93.

11. Ibid., 200. Kelber (ibid.), following Helmut Koester, used the *Gospel of Thomas* as the key to understanding "oral hermeneutic." Rather than exemplifying the immediate presence of the spoken word, however, the *Gospel of Thomas* contains a list of isolated individual or double sayings for apparently silent meditation by a reflective individual interpreter who must not cease until she or he finds the "explanation" (*hermeneia*) of a given saying, as in *logia* 1–2.

12. Kelber, *Oral and Written Gospel*, 203.

13. Ibid., 24. At points, however, such relevancy seems to be a matter of individual people's "hearts and minds" apart from their concrete social circumstances.

Spoken words breathe life.... They carry a sense of presence, intensity, and instanta-neousness that writing fails to convey.... Sounded words emanate from one person and resonate in another, moving along the flow and ebb of human life.... One can well imagine Jesus' words interacting with people and their lives, an enacting pres-ence amidst hearers.... Language and being, speaker, message, and words are joined together into a kind of unity.[14]

And orality fuses soteriology with ontology: "This 'absolute proximity of voice and being, of voice and the meaning of being' links oral words with a whole metaphysics of presence and parousia."[15]

"It is this oral metaphysics of presence that is objectionable to Mark."[16] The Gospel of Mark was written as a "counterforce" to "the waxing and waning of oral life," in which the Q sayings functioned.[17] By using the medium of textu-ality "as a counterform to oral speech and not as an evolutionary progression of it," Mark created the form that was designed to silence the living Lord.[18] As perhaps the key step in his argument, Kelber found in Mark a polemic against the disciples, the family of Jesus, and early Christian prophets, supposedly the carriers of oral tradition, which he took as analogous to Plato's repudiation of the Greek poets' dependence on orality and mimesis.[19] Mark's move into textuality has transformed sayings and stories previously carried in oral transmission into a whole new mentality. They are not simply transmitted. Instead, "a novel, sys-tematic composition has emerged, governed not by the remembered stories, but by a single organizing intellect in control over them. This less mnemonic, more consciously plotted gospel raises a new world into being and implements a new state of awareness.... Bold invention is the prerogative of writers."[20]

In his breakthrough into recognition of the oral mode of communication, Kelber thus applied oral theory only to the "pre-canonical synoptic tradition." Because he was following Ong's and others' theory that understood literacy to be a distinctively different mode of communication, Kelber saw Mark, as the first written Gospel, as constituting "the break with synoptic orality and a move toward thoroughgoing textuality."[21] Kelber accomplished his pioneering breakthrough to

---

14. Ibid., 18–19, in n. 176 citing Ong, *Presence of the Word*, 114, and in nn. 178–79, citing the psychologist John Colin Carothers, "Culture, Psychiatry, and the Written Word," *Psychiatry* 22 (1959): 312.

15. Kelber, *Oral and Written Gospel*, 99.

16. Ibid.

17. Ibid., 184–85.

18. Ibid., 209–10. If we follow the short, open ending of the Gospel of Mark at 16:8, however, there are clues in the narrative (esp. 14:28 and 16:7) that Jesus would go ahead of them into Galilee and meet them there, in some sense still very much alive as the story "continues"!

19. Ibid., 95–96; and introduction, xxv, of the new edition (Bloomington: Indiana University Press, 1998); Erik Havelock, *Preface to Plato* (Cambridge, Mass.: Harvard University Press, 1963), 31, 47, 160, 165.

20. Kelber, *Oral and Written Gospel*, 114–15, citing Havelock, *Preface to Plato*, 46. An obvious issue that requires investigation is whether in oral communication a prophet such as Jeremiah or Jesus was a bold innovator, whereas those who then carried their innovative message settled into performance without innovation.

21. Kelber, *Oral and Written Gospel*, 98.

genuine orality in the pre-Synoptic tradition, however, without the benefit of recent investigations of the low degree of literacy and the predominantly oral medium of communication in antiquity. As recently as the early 1980s scholars generally assumed that orality vs. literacy corresponded to the sharp contrast between rural and urban situations. The precanonical Synoptic tradition belonged to the oral-rural matrix of the early Jesus movement, whereas Mark must have originated in the Hellenistic urban culture of literacy evident in the production and veneration of scrolls.[22]

With the advantage of hindsight — and subsequent studies of relations between writing and oral communication — it is possible to see also how certain assumptions of New Testament studies have blocked the extension to Mark of some of the insights Kelber developed, for example, on how the (pre-Markan) parables and the healing and exorcism stories functioned in oral communication. It is simply assumed, for example, that Mark was composed in writing because "redaction and literary criticism . . . have convincingly demonstrated that the differences among the gospels represent distinct theological views worked out by writers, not fluctuations symptomatic of oral transmission."[23] Thus the constructions of modes of criticism that clearly operate on the assumptions of modern textuality and print culture — including private silent readers and the reflective abstraction of (theological) ideas from both narratives and sayings materials — were accepted as definitive for the preprint culture of antiquity. In one important respect, indeed, the theory of orality vs. literacy seems to fit only too well a typical thesis of New Testament studies — that for the stability and continuity of the emergent new "religion" of Christianity it was necessary for Mark's stabilizing textual theology (of "death") to control the overly innovative free flow of the Spirit of life in unstable and destabilizing orality. An alternative historical model allows for different Jesus movements that each develop in a distinctive direction, one eventually producing Mark, another Q — and both in oral performance. Kelber asserts that "even if the gospel was meant to be recited or read aloud, its writing was nonetheless done in the absence of hearers."[24] Subsequent studies of ancient written texts as almost always dictated suggest that someone capable of composing in writing would have been rare in the Roman Empire.[25] A revived rhetorical criticism, moreover, would insist that the very purpose of composing a

---

22. Ibid., 17–18. To give an illustration of the shifting critical evaluation of evidence from antiquity: in 1983 Kelber offered the variant recensions of the Septuagint as evidence for "a developed manuscript culture," while more recently Eugene Ulrich ("The Bible in the Making: The Scriptures at Qumran," in *The Community of the Renewed Covenant: The Notre Dame Symposium on the Dead Sea Scrolls*, ed. Eugene Ulrich and James VanderKam [Notre Dame, Ind.: University of Notre Dame Press, 1993], 77–93), Susan Niditch (*Oral World and Written Word* [Louisville: Westminster/John Knox, 1996], 75–76), and others have taken variant recensions of Hebrew biblical books as evidence of the lack of concern about stable textual transmission more characteristic of predominantly oral culture.

23. Kelber, *Oral and Written Gospel*, 78.

24. Ibid., 115.

25. Given the state of research at the time, Kelber "was not fully conscious of composition in dictation," as he points out in his introduction to the new edition (xxii).

letter or a story would have been to persuade (and/or entertain, etc.) those who would hear the "text" read or otherwise performed.

It is now recognized that Erik Havelock made far too much of Plato's attack on the poets and that in fact Plato, who believed that truth is obtained in oral dialogue, was somewhat distrustful of writing, as were the ancient Greeks generally.[26] There is no indication in Mark itself that the disciples, the family, and the prophets were the primary bearers of oral tradition or that oral recitation of Jesus stories and sayings should be blocked. In his argument that Mark's passion narrative was largely built on texts, Kelber recognizes "that the multitude of scriptural references are integrated into the text with extraordinary disregard for their original contextual setting...so that there is no compositional difference between Mark's decontextualization and recontextualization of synoptic oral vs. Jewish scriptural units."[27] As subsequent studies of oral-derived literature point out, this is characteristic of traditional oral recitation and composition. The "scriptural" references were also oral-derived, and Mark's most obviously written section, the passion narrative, displays oral characteristics! As Kelber himself writes recently, "contrary to the assumptions of historical criticism, a text's substantial and multifaceted investment in tradition does not suggest intertextuality in the sense of scanning through multiple, physically accessible scrolls but, more likely, accessibility to a shared *cultural memory*. When Mark...operated with a plurality of oral and written traditions,...he was plugging into a copious reservoir of memories, retrieving and reshuffling what was accessible to him memorially."[28] But if the Gospel of Mark was not composed by an author working from scrolls, what makes us think that it was composed in writing? As evident from the survey of the relationship between manuscripts and oral communication in the previous chapter, most literature from Greek and Roman antiquity was orally composed and performed, and continued to be performed even after being written down. Because of our previous training in New Testament studies, however, we do not know how to imagine oral composition and performance. Until the advent of redaction criticism working from the model of modern textual theology and more recent literary criticism working from the assumptions of modern print culture, we could imagine the Gospel writers only as collecting oral materials, not composing. Thus, with only the small units of sayings, parables, and miracle stories in mind, it was impossible to imagine that "there exists in orality the impulse to collect material into an oral gospel of the nature and scope of the written gospel,"[29] let alone to compose a sustained performance of the scope of Mark or Q.

Although Ong was one of the principal theorists who dramatized the difference

---

26. Oivind Andersen, "The Significance of Writing in Early Greece — a Critical Appraisal," in *Literacy and Society,* ed. Karen Schousboe and Mogens Trolle Larsen (Copenhagen: Akademisk Forlag, 1989), 73–90, esp. 85–86.

27. Kelber, *Oral and Written Gospel,* 197.

28. Kelber, introduction to the new edition, xxii. Cf. the remarkably different picture imagined by Burton L. Mack, *A Myth of Innocence* (Philadelphia: Fortress, 1988), 321–23.

29. Kelber, *Oral and Written Gospel,* 77.

between the communications media, he clearly indicated that "the transition from orality to literacy was slow."[30] Indeed, in explanation of how "writing restructures consciousness," Ong discussed ways in which that slow transition takes place, with considerable dependence on M. T. Clanchy's important work on the interaction of writing and oral communication, although he overestimates how rapidly the transition took place in ancient Greece.[31] With hindsight Kelber himself, relying on Helmut Koester, now postulates "the continuation of a synoptic orality largely untouched by (narrative) gospel intervention until the middle of the second century."[32] Used as an explanation of rapid historical transitions in antiquity, the "orality vs. literacy" theory may simply block the path toward closer understanding of the oral communication and the relation between writing and oral communication.

Oral Theory and Oral-Formulaic Theory Applied to Mark

With an appreciation of just how "residual" oral communication was in antiquity, Joanna Dewey applied Havelock's and Ong's analysis of orality to the Gospel of Mark itself. Not only was the first Gospel embedded in orality and not only did it use oral materials, but it was composed for a listening audience using techniques of oral composition.[33] Keying from Ong's and Havelock's observations,[34] Dewey emphasized as particular features of oral narratives the additive content and aggregative structure (vs. the analytic and linear structure of written narrative), the agonistic tone, and especially the participatory character.[35] Mark displays the very characteristics, moreover, that Plato attacked in the mere *doxa* (opinion) of the poets' mimesis: "happenings / episodes" (in which teaching is embedded, not explicit), "the visible," and "the many" (the additive character of one episode after another).[36] Mark's numerous prospective and retrospective references that "interweave and integrate disparate and episodic" materials are also typical of the chaining method of oral narrative.[37] Dewey's illumination of the oral character-

---

30. Ong, *Orality and Literacy*, 115; idem, *Presence of the Word*, 53–87; idem, *Rhetoric, Romance, and Technology* (Ithaca, N.Y.: Cornell University Press, 1971), 23–48.

31. Ong, *Orality and Literacy*, 143–47, particularly in discussion of Hesiod and poetry (Sappho). He cites M. T. Clanchy, *From Memory to Written Record: England, 1066–1307* (Cambridge, Mass.: Harvard University Press, 1979). See also Andersen, "Significance," 77–82.

32. Kelber, introduction to new edition, xxiii.

33. Joanna Dewey, "Oral Methods of Structuring Narrative in Mark," *Interpretation* 53 (1989): 32–44; idem, "Mark as Aural Narrative: Structures as Clues to Understanding," *Sewanee Theological Review* 36 (1992): 45–56; cf. Pieter J. J. Botha, "Mark's Story as Oral Traditional Literature: Rethinking the Transmission of Some Traditions about Jesus," *Hervormde Teologiese Studies* 47 (1991): 304–31.

34. Ong, *Literacy and Orality*, 37–49; Eric Havelock, "Oral Composition in the Oedipus Tyrannus of Sophocles," *New Literary History* 16 (1984): 175–97; and idem, *Preface to Plato*.

35. Joanna Dewey, "The Gospel of Mark as an Oral-Aural Event: Implications for Interpretation," in *The New Literary Criticism and the New Testament*, ed. Elizabeth Stuters Malbon and Edgar V. McKnight, JSNTSup 19 (Sheffield: Sheffield Academic Press, 1994), 148–57; and idem, "Mark as Aural Narrative," 48–50.

36. Dewey, "Oral Methods," 34–38; drawing on Havelock, *Preface to Plato*.

37. Dewey, "Oral Methods," 39–42; idem, "Mark as Interwoven Tapestry: Forecasts and Echoes for a Listening Audience," CBQ 53 (1991): 224–25; drawing on Havelock, "Oral Composition," 183.

istics of Mark's narrative, with the help of Ong's and Havelock's reflections on oral composition and performance, suggests that some of the questions commonly asked of Mark by recent literary criticism rooted in the assumptions of textuality and print culture (e.g., about linear structure or plot) are less than appropriate to the Gospel if it is to be understood in historical context.[38]

Although Dewey gave more attention than did Ong and Havelock to the hearers' participation and reception, dependence on such studies of orality left the focus on the features and techniques of oral *composition*, with relatively little attention to meaning in context. Also pertinent to understanding the Gospel in historical context, Dewey, compared with Ong,[39] seemed to discount and downplay the political conflict and struggle in the social context of the oral composition. The conflict between Jesus and the Jerusalem rulers and their scribal-Pharisaic representatives cannot be explained simply as part of the agonistic tone of oral narrative. In fact, it happens to parallel fairly closely the conflict between other popular Judean and Galilean movements and the Jerusalem and Roman rulers, as attested in extra-Gospel sources such as Josephus's histories. Is it conceivable that this particular popular oral-derived text in its agonistic style reflects or represents the basic conflict in the society from which it comes? Contrary to the typical modern Western Christian reading of Mark, moreover, the structure of Mark's story as a whole displays conflict with and criticism of the disciples, which also cannot be dismissed as due simply to agonistic tone in oral narrative or the hearers placing themselves in the roles of all the participants.[40] If, as Dewey suggested, oral composition was done for hearing not by an individual but by a group in a particular historical context, then Jesus' conflict with the disciples, particularly Peter, James, and John, dramatized in Mark may have had reference to that historical context beyond the impact on individual hearers' "discipleship."

Although Kelber drew an implicit analogy between the assymetrical oral utterances of Jesus' sayings and lengthy performances by Balkan "singers of tales" described by Milman Parry and Albert Lord, he insisted that the latter's oral-formulaic theory could not be used "in contemplating the feasibility of an oral gospel."[41] The Parry-Lord oral-formulaic theory, with its emphasis on the formulas and themes used in oral performance, had been used often rather woodenly to test literatures from a wide variety of cultures for their oral features. Appropriately, Kelber rejected the search for "direct correspondences" between metrical oral epic poetry and the Gospels. Less appropriately, as we shall see below, he also insisted that Mark had no accumulated oral culture on which to draw, "despite the fact that the synoptic tradition relies on many ancient forms and models."[42] Pieter Botha, however, discerned the indirect applicability of oral-formulaic the-

---

38. Dewey, esp. "Mark as Interwoven Tapestry," and "The Gospel of Mark as an Oral-Aural Event."
39. Ong, *Orality and Literacy*, 43–45.
40. Cf. Dewey, "The Gospel of Mark as Oral-Aural Event," 154–56.
41. Kelber, *Oral and Written Gospel*, 30, 80.
42. Ibid., 78–79.

ory to Mark. "The true impact of the theory does not lie in testing for orality."[43] It can be used to illuminate the distinctive features of Mark as "composed and recited" "oral literature."[44] He looked not for the "formulas" ("fixed verbal and metrical combinations") and "themes" ("repeated incidents and descriptive passages") that directly match those in the *Iliad* but for those distinctive to Mark's narrative.[45] He recognized that some of the formulas in Mark do not so much "contain meaning in themselves" as "signal knowledge that is already shared" with the hearers.[46] Certain words, images, and references are used to draw on a whole range of experience shared with the hearers, who thus resonate with the message or story delivered by the performer.

The implications of Dewey's application of oral studies and Botha's application of oral-formulaic theory to Mark are suggestive for further work on Q as well as Mark. The contrast between oral tradition and written redaction or composition as separate stages and processes, as elaborated in New Testament studies, is simply unwarranted.[47] The characteristics of oral communication that Kelber discerned in pre-Markan and Q materials are also evident in Mark itself. As an oral composition or an oral-derived text, Mark stands in continuity with the oral tradition of Jesus' sayings and stories. The teachers or prophets or "evangelists" who specialized in regular performance of the Jesus traditions did not have to "memorize" them, whether exorcism stories, parables, or a longer "Gospel" narrative. They were not simply specialists in the tradition. They were organically part of it, not simply its carriers or bearers but its regular performers, composing on the basis of what was highly familiar.[48]

The scope of inquiry into oral tradition and oral-derived texts must obviously broaden dramatically. Study of the oral tradition of Jesus materials and even of the Gospels has focused narrowly on transmission and preservation. Betraying its modern assumptions about and interests in authors and individual reader response, recent study of the Gospels (including study of Q) has focused on the redactor's theology and the particular evangelist's composition. Recognition that Mark and Q may have been orally composed and performed, however, drives us into social and historical contexts and the corresponding relational considerations. Texts were read aloud or performed in communities, which had some cultural background and were involved in particular social circumstances.[49] Recently revived

---

43. Botha, "Mark's Story," 316.

44. Ibid., 307.

45. Ibid., 309, 317–22.

46. Ibid., 318; Botha anticipated what John Miles Foley calls metonymic referencing, discussed below.

47. Ibid., 306.

48. Ibid., 308.

49. Form criticism in effect fragmented the social context into particular, separable *Sitze im Leben*, one for each form, as it were, or a particular historical situation. Erhard Güttgemanns, *Candid Questions concerning Gospel Form Criticism* (Pittsburgh: Pickwick, 1979), 115–20, appropriately insists that the *Sitz im Leben* must have been a repeated, patterned social situation over a period of time.

rhetorical criticism has recognized that consideration of the rhetorical situation is essential to understanding speeches and texts. Investigation of oral communication and oral-derived texts must similarly include consideration of the social circumstances and the cultural background of the performers, the messages, and the hearers. Kelber has recently recognized at least the cultural dimension of these integral relations: "[T]he gospel composition is unthinkable without the notion of cultural memory, which serves ultimately not the preservation of remembrances per se but the preservation of the group, its social identity and self-image. Mark avails himself of a rich cultural memory."[50] But the same must be said of Jesus, the Jesus traditions, and the sequence of discourses known as Q. In an oral communication environment, cultural memory is maintained and cultivated only in and through performance. The focus of the inquiry must be broadened far beyond a concern with mere transmission of Jesus' sayings, for transmission is, as it were, simply an accident of the cultivation of cultural memory that takes place in repeated performance.

Immanent Art and Ethnopoetics

In an effort better to appreciate meaning in oral-derived texts by experimenting with a more adequate "theory of verbal art," John Miles Foley has recently attempted to bring together insights from oral-formulaic theory on the one side and the ethnography of speaking and ethnopoetics on the other. Scholars working with the oral-formulaic theory focused on the seemingly mechanical and repetitive formulas and themes as devices by which poets and singers of tales could remember their lengthy and complex narratives. Following the lead of a prominent interpreter of Old English literature, Foley focuses on how "rich and complex meanings can be expressed…*through* these conventions rather than *in spite of* them."[51] The key lies in asking "the question of *referentiality*. Instead of asking 'what' is meant by a work of art and its constituent parts, we should begin by asking 'how' that work or part conveys whatever meaning can be or is communicated."[52] The starting point must be with the seemingly obvious assumption that if traditional formulas, phrases, and narratives are conventional in structure, then they must also be conventional in their modes of meaning. The referential function of traditional units of oral communication will remain consistent — that is, they are traditional. Structural elements, such as "grey-eyed Athena," are not simply compositionally useful but command fields of reference much larger than the line, stanza, or overall epic in which they occur. Such "formulas" evoke "the fecund totality of the entire tradition" of Athena; "they bear meanings as wide and deep as the tradition they encode."[53]

---

50. Kelber, introduction to the new edition, xxiii.
51. John Miles Foley, *Immanent Art: From Structure to Meaning in Traditional Oral Epic* (Bloomington: Indiana University Press, 1991), 5, quoting Edward Irving.
52. Foley, *Immanent Art*, 5.
53. Ibid., 7.

Such a process of generating meaning is *metonymic*, designating thereby "a mode of signification wherein the part stands for the whole."[54] Meaning in traditional oral art is thus *inherent*, in contrast with the *conferred* meaning of modern literary art. In the latter, the writer individually manipulates inherited and / or idiosyncratic materials in a new direction or from a new perspective, thus conferring meaning on her or his fresh new literary creation. By contrast, the performer of a traditional work, depending on standard strategies long familiar to her or his collective audience, summons conventional connotations of conventional structures in evoking a meaning that is *inherent*. Performance of a traditional work depends much more heavily on extratextual factors as meaning is evoked metonymically from the tradition with which the listeners are familiar. In contrast with the originality of conferred meaning in modern literary texts, traditional oral performance cannot depart from tradition because it depends upon traditional references of symbols, phrases, and formulas. The traditional oral "work" can "never be wholly captured by textual fossilization."[55] Each performance causes that which is immanent to become an artistic creation in the present time, hence "re-creates" (but does not "repeat") the networks of inherent meaning.

To further illuminate traditional referentiality Foley adapts the receptionalist literary theory developed by Wolfgang Iser and Hans Robert Jauss, with its implication for the active participation of listeners in the constitution of meaning as it happens in oral performance. According to receptionalist theory, "meaning arises only from the interplay of the text and the individual reader's imagination."[56] The modern writer leaves "gaps of indeterminacy" in the text which the reader must inventively intervene to "close" or resolve. In a kind of collaboration with the author, the reader must engage in "consistency-building." In a reading appropriate to the text, the reader will fill the gaps of indeterminacy only with interpretations that harmonize with the rest of the work. Similarly, traditional oral performances of oral-derived texts imply an audience as participants in a process. Different from the modern novel-and-reader, however, the audience is already familiar with the work and the tradition out of which it resonates as it is realized in performance. The audience indeed includes many different individuals. But they are unified in their knowledge of the tradition, "for all members of the audience bring to the process of interpretation a deep knowledge of how to 'read' the text before them, how to construe the traditional signals in their full metonymic, inherent meaning."[57] The members of the audience interpret the "text" according to a

---

54. Ibid.
55. Ibid., 10.
56. Ibid., 42.

57. Ibid., 44. Or, as the sociolinguist M. A. K. Halliday says, "a text is meaningful not so much because the hearer does not know what the speaker is going to say, as in a mathematical model of communication, but because he does know. He has abundant evidence . . . from his sensibility to the particular cultural, situational and verbal context; and this enables him to make informed guesses about the meanings that are coming his way" (*Language as Social Semiotic: The Social Interpretation of Language and Meaning* [Baltimore: University Park Press, 1978], 61).

shared body of knowledge that is their cultural inheritance.[58] "What passes down through the generations is thus not simply an idiom that allows convenient oral composition [oral-formulaic theory], but the equivalent of a critical methodology, evolved and practiced by a 'school' or 'interpretive community' unified by the act of (re-)making and (re-)'reading' traditional verbal art."[59] By comparison with readers of modern literature, the hearers of performances or "readers" of oral traditional "texts" must participate far more actively in realizing the work, and far more actively than scholars interested only in analysis of an artifact. For the formulas and themes are cognitive as well as "compositional." Besides containing information, they "refer in an institutionalized way to other information and determine the perception or reception of the whole."[60]

The modern reading appropriate to appreciation of an oral-derived text or the libretto of a performance would thus appear to be becoming as far as possible the audience implied in that text. That would appear to require attaining a knowledge of the tradition in which the "text" or performance would have resonated, as deep and rich a knowledge of that tradition as possible. Only if the connection between text and the metonymically signaled references to the tradition is made or retained, can the work that depends on that connection be realized. The "reader" unacquainted with the tradition "will be unable to construe the work within the range of possibilities implied by the text."[61]

In his subsequent work, Foley emphasized even more the importance for oral verbal art of *tradition* as "the enabling referent."[62] Indeed, he recalls for the developing field of oral studies that Milman Parry's initial agenda was to recover the *traditional* nature of Homer's epic poetry. With Parry's 1930 and 1932 "Studies,"[63] the emphasis shifted to the oral, after which attention focused more and more on the density of formulaic phrases and themes. Instead of inquiring after the traditional context for an explanation of how and what the recurrent structures meant, "the textual parallax induced by focusing on visual evidence in this or that work" for formulas and themes blinded scholars to the possibility of anything more than generic meanings (Athena or Hector) for such phrases as "grey-eyed Athena" or "Hector of the glancing helm." By moving beyond the mere formal features of phrases and formulas, however, it becomes possible again to engage the extratextual tradition they evoke metonymically. "That is, the traditional phrase or scene or story-pattern has an indexical meaning vis-à-vis the immanent tradition; each integer reaches beyond the confines of the individual performance

58. Foley, *Immanent Art*, 44–45.

59. Ibid., 45, citing Brian Stock, *The Implications of Literacy: Written Language and Models of Interpretation in the Eleventh and Twelfth Centuries* (Princeton, N.J.: Princeton University Press, 1983), 88–240.

60. Foley, *Immanent Art*, 60.

61. Ibid., 59.

62. John Miles Foley, *The Singer of Tales in Performance*, Voices in Performance and Text (Bloomington: Indiana University Press, 1995), 1–7, 28, etc.

63. Reprinted in *The Making of Homeric Verse: The Collected Papers of Milman Parry* (Oxford: Clarendon, 1971).

or oral-derived text to a set of traditional ideas much larger and richer than any single performance or text."[64] Support for this conclusion can be found in anthropologists' research. For example, in stories of the Apache "features of the landscape have become symbols of and for this way of living, the symbols of a culture and the enduring moral character of its people."[65]

In close interrelationship with this rediscovery of both the audience of the performance and the tradition in which oral communication is grounded, along with the metonymic referencing by which the one is connected with the other, Foley emphasizes three other key (analytical) facets of oral performance. One is simply the basic unit(s) of communication and meaning in the "text." It is of obvious importance to determine just what this is with some sensitivity to the actual performer and audience. The South Slavic epic singers questioned by Parry and Lord insisted that their "word" was a set of lines, a speech, a scene, or even a whole song/epic, with the minimal unit being the ten-syllable poetic line (not the single word, as in a printed text). In Old English poetry as well, the "word" was a similarly larger unit of utterance, in contrast with the "word" we recognize in print. Something similar might well be said of written literature as well, since the unit of communication and meaning would not be a sentence, but at least a whole chapter or a complete argument. A performance, like other oral communication, far transcends any attempt at textual reduction, given its many paralinguistic features such as volume, voice quality, and pauses, such that the sounded, experienced event cannot (yet) be textually represented. It is conceivable that those working with oral-derived texts can appropriate from ethnographers struggling to find new ways of representing the paralinguistic features of Native American performances[66] an appropriate sensitivity to similar features in the performances long since textually reduced. Far easier would be to learn from ethnographically documented performances how a performance or even its textual transcript may have been structured into verbal patterns analogous to what we call "lines," "verses," "stanzas," "scenes," and/or "acts."[67] In chapters 8–13, Jonathan Draper and I (following mainly Dell Hymes's work on Chinook storytelling) will block out the "text" of many of the Q discourses into "measured verse" according to the "lines," "verses," and "stanzas" in which they may have been performed orally.

Foley borrowed another key aspect of oral performance from ethnopoetics and the ethnography of speaking. Performance sets up or entails "an *interpretive frame* within which the messages being communicated are to be understood,"

---

64. Foley, *Singer of Tales*, 6.

65. Keith H. Basso, *Western Apache Language and Culture: Essays in Linguistic Anthropology* (Tucson: University of Arizona Press, 1990), 129.

66. See esp. Dennis Tedlock, "On the Translation of Style in Oral Narrative," *Journal of American Folklore* 84 (1971): 114–33; reprinted with epilogue in Tedlock, *The Spoken Word and the Work of Interpretation* (Philadelphia: University of Pennsylvania Press: 1983), 31–61; see also Dell Hymes, "Discovering Oral Performance and Measured Verse in American Indian Narrative," *New Literary History* 7 (1977): 431–57; revised in Hymes, *"In Vain I Tried to Tell You": Essays in Native American Ethnopoetics* (Philadelphia: University of Pennsylvania Press, 1981), 79–141.

67. Cf. Hymes, *"In Vain,"* 3–9; Foley, *Singer of Tales*, 19–21.

and " ... this frame contrasts with at least one other frame, the literal."[68] The use of "words" or units of utterance in a particular context charges them with associative values particular to the event taking place, giving them highly focused meanings. In fact, the particular context of most communication marks or cues the discourse as a communication to be received in a particular way. An oral performance has a forum or "performance arena" distinct from those where other kinds of discourse take place and dedicated to a particular activity and channel of communication. The "performance arena" corresponds to the receptionalist "horizon of expectations" within which the text becomes the work. From their experience of previous performances of the same type, the audience recognizes the surroundings and is in a position to decode the signals of this particular event. Their familiarity with the performance arena, moreover, "places the audience in a position to bridge the gaps of indeterminacy that are the natural partners of the (now recognizable) meaning-laden signals."[69] The implications for readers / listeners unfamiliar with the society or culture from which a given performance comes are obvious: as with the tradition, it is essential to identify and familiarize themselves with the appropriate "interpretive frame" so that they can attend the performance event in the proper arena; for the metonymic referencing to the tradition will take place only in the arena in which that particular kind of oral communication is performed.

The third key interrelated aspect of oral performance is the way in which speech focuses and coheres in "an idiom redolent with preselected, emergent kinds of meaning" appropriate to the particular "performance arena" or "interpretive frame."[70] In an important methodological distinction made in sociolinguistics and ethnopoetics, "major speech styles associated with social groups can be termed *variants* [cf. dialect, in sociolinguistics], and major speech styles associated with recurrent types of situation can be termed *registers*."[71] With regard to communication generally, the sociolinguist M. A. K. Halliday defines register

> as the configuration of semantic resources that the member of a culture typically associates with a situation type [Foley's "performance arena"]. . . . The register is recognizable as a particular selection of words and structures. But *it is defined in terms of meanings*; it is not an aggregate of conventional forms of expression superposed on some underlying content by social factors of one kind or another. It is the selection of meanings that constitutes the variety to which a text belongs.[72]

Halliday conceives of the *register* as determined by three interrelated aspects of the type of situation of communication: the *field* of discourse (what is being transacted, the focal subject), the *tenor* of discourse (the relation among the

---

68. Richard Bauman, *Verbal Art as Performance* (Prospect Heights, Ill.: Waveland, 1977), 9.

69. Foley, *Singer of Tales*, 49.

70. Ibid., 47.

71. Dell Hymes, "Ways of Speaking," in *Explorations in the Ethnography of Speaking*, ed. Richard Bauman and Joel Sherzer, 2d ed. (Cambridge: Cambridge University Press, 1989), 440.

72. M. A. K. Halliday, *Language as Social Semiotic: The Social Interpretation of Language and Meaning* (London: Edward Arnold, 1978), 111.

participants), and the *mode* of discourse (aspects such as written or spoken).[73] In oral performance the register is the self-contained, institutionalized, idiomatic system of signification specifically dedicated to and the sole vehicle for a particular type of situation and communication.[74] As anthropologists have demonstrated, a particular society will have many traditional registers devoted to various activities such as puberty rites, curing and magic, or certain political activities, each marked by different forms, lexica, paralinguistic gestures, some less and others more highly focused.[75] The more "dedicated" the register, the greater will be the complexity and richness of the allusive world summoned metonymically by the forms or "words" that constitute that particular "way of speaking."[76]

All of these analytically distinct but interrelated aspects of communication conspire in emergence of meaning in oral performance. In the "performance arena," which frames the audience's "horizons of expectations," the performer performs the "text" or "word" in the dedicated "register," thus evoking in the audience by "metonymic referencing" the resonating depth of the "tradition." For oral performance and communication, far more than in reading texts, "each metonymic integer functions as an index-point or node in a grand, untextualizable network of traditional associations. Activation of any single node brings into play an enormous wellspring of meaning that can be tapped in no other way.... Much of what a register 'means' depends crucially on what is understood of its context as brought into play by the event of performance and the referent of tradition."[77] Through the activation of the register, the performance resonates or reverberates always as an echo rather than a sound never heard before and confers a permanence on the speech act in which performers and audience are engaged.[78]

Having outlined the dynamics of oral performance, Foley then focuses on how we may approach "those works of verbal art that took shape in or under the influence of oral tradition, but now survive only as texts."[79] Experienced events, of course, can never be adequately represented by textual cenotaphs. Nevertheless, "the best dictated texts are not in fact wholly without indication of the features" of oral performance.[80] The demise of the previously prominent "great divide" between orality and literacy makes obsolete the absolutist dichotomy of performance vs. document. "Text can no longer be separated out as something different by species from the oral tradition it records or draws upon." The question becomes not whether but how performance lives on in oral-derived literature. Since we do not have performances of the *Iliad* or of *Beowulf*, of course, we must make some adjustment for the ways in which the entextualization of those performances

---

73. Ibid., 31–35, etc.
74. Foley, *Singers of Tales*, 15, 50–53.
75. For example, Joel Sherzer, *Kuna Ways of Speaking: An Ethnographic Perspective* (Austin: University of Texas Press, 1983).
76. Foley, *Singers of Tales*, 16.
77. Ibid., 54–55.
78. Ibid., 56.
79. Ibid., 61.
80. Hymes, "Discovering Oral Performance," reprint, 338.

differs from actual performance, recognizing the differences and endeavoring, by informed analogical procedure, to investigate both similarities and differences without expecting absolute congruity or imputing absolute disparity. Oral-derived texts still contain enough of (Richard Bauman's) keys to performance to provide access to the implied array of associative, metonymic signification that experienced performance conveyed. As a reading audience, however, we must become "sufficiently acquainted with the signals embedded in the register to be able to summon the special, institutionalized meanings that are those signals' reason for being."[81] Although it is impossible to resuscitate textual libretti into historically reconstituted performances, "we will be derelict in our interpretive duty if we do not reach beyond the parallax induced by their textuality and release the resources of meaning that stem ultimately from the performance and immanence that still inform them."[82] As a reading audience, we must "rhetorically simulate the performance arena...on the basis of textualized cues that engage the enabling referent of tradition." Of course, the fundamental prerequisite for entry into the "performance arena" is fluency in the traditional oral-derived (and performance-derived) *register* in which the work is expressed. In this connection, special attention should be given to archaisms, special dialect, figurative language, parallelism, and the particular patterns in the text that may represent traditional oral speech (such as what Hymes discerned in transcripts of previously transcribed Chinook tales, which can be represented more adequately by attempting typographically to approximate the discerned patterns). Throughout, the reader of oral-derived texts must strive for awareness of how the formulaic system of signification is metonymically indexical of extratextual tradition. "In the end,...all will depend on the preparation of the audience and the process of reception—that is on the readers' prior familiarity with the immanent meaning" of the phrases and linguistic integers.[83]

The Theory of Verbal Art and Q

Text and Its Relation to Performance

In applying Foley's and others' theory of verbal art to Q, the first question must be what the text is and how it is related to oral performance. We have argued above that the standard view of Q as a collection of sayings is a modern misunderstanding rooted in the accidents of the historical development of Synoptic Gospel studies. Just as in Old English poetry and South Slavic epic, the basic "words" are not individual lines but set of lines, a speech, or a whole song, so the basic "words" or units of communication in Q are not individual sayings but short speeches or discourses focused on certain concerns of a movement or community. Chapter 4 includes an outline of the sequence of speeches that can be

---

81. Foley, *Singers of Tales*, 65.
82. Ibid., 66.
83. Ibid., 91–92.

discerned in the material common to Matthew and Luke that is not derived from Mark. On the basis of the work of Foley and the scholars in related fields upon whom he has drawn — work presenting a nuanced delineation of how various oral-derived texts appear related to previous oral performance — we believe it is possible to discern at least roughly the way Q is related to oral performance and the patterns internal to the speeches that comprise Q. A scholar of Anglo-Saxon poetry, A. N. Doane, advocates "making an informed, principled, definitive, and declared decision about a given text's relation to writing and orality."[84] He posits four kinds of interface between texts and oral performance: (1) the scribal transcription of a performed event; (2) the oral "autograph" poet who serves as his or her own scribe; (3) the literate poet who knows the tradition well enough to emulate an oral performance in writing; and (4) a scribe who may be thought of as composing in the oral traditional manner, as a kind of "reperformance."[85] Q would appear to be closest to a scribal transcript of a "text" that had been regularly performed in a movement or community. Matthew and Luke appear to have used the same transcribed text of Q (or very similar ones). But that transcript would have been made of one performance among many which would have varied somewhat in length and material included. Possible analogies are worth considering. The field studies of Parry and Lord found not only that different singers presented somewhat different versions of a traditional song but also that the same singer performed somewhat different versions of the song in different performances. In Lushootseed narrative (the Lushootseed are the Salish people of Puget Sound), "no one version is an isolate, either for the storyteller or the audience, but resounds against the knowledge of the collection held by each person present at the performance; no story-teller ever tells the whole collection, but she always knows more than she tells in any one performance or perhaps in all the performances she ever gives."[86] On the hypothesis that the different manuscripts of the Community Rule from Qumran are transcripts of oral material, it would be worth exploring the possibility that 1QS and 4Q258 and 4Q259 represent different performances of an oral "text" that vary somewhat in wording and contents included — thus providing a contemporary parallel from Palestine of oral material somewhat similar in form and contents to Q.

This particular (transcript of performance) relationship of the text of Q (as critically reconstructed from its reuse in Matthew and Luke) to previous oral performance is confirmed by analysis of the verbal patterning in the constituent speeches somewhat along the lines of Hymes's analysis of Chinook tales that had been transcribed by previous ethnologists. The patterns discerned bear many of the marks of oral performance, as studied from culture to culture in the last gen-

---

84. A. N. Doane, "Oral Texts, Intertexts, and Intratexts: Editing Old English," in *Influence and Intertextuality in Literary History*, ed. Jay Clayton and Eric Rothstein (Madison: University of Wisconsin Press, 1991), 76.

85. Ibid., 77–81.

86. Toby C. S. Langen, "The Organization of Thought in Lushootseed (Puget Salish) Literature: Martha Lamont's Mink and Changer," *Melus* 161 (1989–90): 6.

eration. As with Hymes's work on Chinook tales, moreover, the verbal patterns can be discerned in the transcribed text (as laid out in "measured verse" in chapters 9–13) and are not some scholarly scheme imposed upon it. As Foley suggests with reference to the Native American material analyzed by Hymes, it will be important to take the structural units of "line," "verse," and "stanzas" in Q into account as meaning-bearing, rhetorical signals in their own right.

Insofar as Q appears to have been the founding and grounding "text" of a movement or set of communities, the picture constructed by Gregory Nagy of how the Homeric epics became fixed in oral tradition is highly suggestive for what Q represents.[87] Comparison with other texts that emerged in the Synoptic Gospel tradition reveals parallels to some of the Q discourses, for example, those on mission (Q 10:2–16; Mark 6:7–13), Beelzebul (Q 11:14–20; Mark 3:23–29), and trial (Q 12:2–12; Mark 8:34–38). Thus it is evident that other branches or movements in the Synoptic Gospel tradition cultivated similar discourses on similar issues. Thus it is suggestive that, somewhat as the movement of pan-Hellenism streamlined a diverse set of Homeric traditions into an epitomized epic, so the Q movement consolidated a set of Jesus discourses that became standard, at least within that movement, and of sufficient stature that it was known to and used by both Matthew and Luke in composition of Gospels that were composites of Mark and Q, along with other materials.

In an important respect Q differs as a "text" from most of the other examples of oral verbal art discussed by Foley. While it appears to be poetic in form, Q is not narrative about a hero. It is rather a set of prophecies and prophetic discourses from the founding prophet-hero of the movement — prophecies and discourses that are re-presented or re-performed for that movement. Except for the narrative of the testing of the prophet in Q 4:1–13, the performer assumes the voice of the prophet himself. The contents, moreover, are often instructions directly pertaining to various facets of community life and relationships. Given this different kind of text and its contents, simple direct comparisons often may not be possible with the largely narrative examples of verbal art surveyed by Foley.

Context and Register

Since Q is not comparable to a work of oral art, such as a heroic epic, that might be performed in a theatrical or arena-like context, it seems less pretentious to speak of the *situation* or *context* of performance. Because Q is a series of discourses focused on concerns and relations of a community or movement, moreover, consideration of its "interpretive frame" or context is more complex than that of most other oral-derived texts. In a performance of a long, heroic epic poem, the situation remains more or less the same throughout. In Q there seems to be a double level of situation or context, that of the performance of a whole series of discourses and that of the particular discourse devoted to a particular topic or relationship.

---

87. Gregory Nagy, *Pindar's Homer: The Lyric Possession of an Epic Past* (Baltimore: Johns Hopkins University Press, 1990).

The context of performance of Q as a whole series of discourses would appear to be the periodic community or movement meetings. The typical situation signaled in particular discourses varied from speech to speech. That of Q 6:20–49 is covenant renewal, as signaled by the "blessings" (and "curses/woes") at the beginning and the many allusions to traditional covenantal teachings throughout. That of Q (9:57–62) 10:2–16 is the movement's mission, including the sending of envoys and their behavior while on mission. The situation that occasions Q 12:2–12 is the (potential) arrest and trial of community members. The situation of Q 13:28–29, 34–35 is prophesying against rulers. In the civil rights movement in the United States, the particular concerns of the movement — the mutual commitment of its members, their support and organizing activities, their behavior under repression, and their condemnation of oppressive laws and institutions — became the foci of song, sermon, and exhortation that were repeatedly performed in group rallies and mass meetings. Similarly, the Q movement would have taken its typical concerns and issues into its regular group meetings, a repetitive context in which the participants would have expected messages from their founder-prophet (through his spokespersons) on those recurrent problems and typical internal and external relations of the community. In addition, however, it seems likely that outside of the movement meetings, the particular circumstances of envoys on mission or members hauled before the authorities became the particular situations in which the appropriate discourses were performed apart from the complete sequence in Q as a whole that was performed at regular community assemblies.

As modern readers of Q, we must recognize the situation of the movement as a whole and their internal and external relations in order to attend to the discourses as a whole and to appreciate the situations to which particular discourses pertained. Form criticism was on the right track in looking for the life context of particular types of Synoptic Gospel material; it just had too narrow a view of the "church" as if it were only a modern religious meeting instead of a social movement whose concerns were political-economic as well as spiritual. Form criticism, moreover, followed by recent liberal individualist readings of Q, also focused too narrowly on individual sayings. In order to discern the situations to which the Q discourses are addressed we must attend not to individual sayings but to whole discourses as well as the whole sequence of discourses, as discussed in chapter 4.

Each Q discourse, then, is also couched in a register dedicated to a particular activity or subject and the people involved. The overall register is that of a founding prophet addressing his movement, with the performer playing the role of the prophet who addresses in succession the concerns and relations of the communities of the movement. The larger register is then divided into particular registers devoted to particular concerns and relations: Mosaic covenant renewal and covenantal teaching in Q 6:20–49; mission to other villages in Q 10:2–16; reassurance of members on trial in 12:2–12; prophecies against rulers and their representatives in 11:39–52 and 13:28–29, 34–35. In terms of the "tenor" of the context that partly determines the register, the speeches of the prophet almost all involve mainly the movement participants, to whom they are addressed.

The determining situation of some speeches involves outsiders, specifically rulers or their representatives, insofar as their actions, roles, or policies impinge on the movement participants. Thus the registers of those speeches are couched in terms of prophecies directed ostensibly against those rulers or their representatives. Within the overall prophetic address of Q we can discern some of the variety of registers in the movement to which it is addressed that anthropologists find in a given society. These registers, devoted to various activities and concerns, are each marked by special forms, language, and (probably) paralinguistic gestures, some more highly focused than others. For example, the prophetic lament of Q 13:34–35 and the prophetic woes of Q 11:39–52 are both highly focused forms in a distinctive style of speech, perhaps even with a distinctive rhythm.

Tradition and Metonymic Referencing

The most significant aspect of oral communication with regard to understanding Q as an oral-derived text is surely the way in which its verbal signals metonymically reference or index the meaning imminent in its tradition. This aspect is also the most complicated with regard to Q, for we must push not only well beyond previous habits of New Testament studies but well beyond Foley's socially limited theory of verbal art as well. Specific terms, symbols, formulas, and forms of speech all evoke or engage imminent meanings "as wide and deep as the tradition they encode." In the same way that "grey-eyed Athena" taps into "the fecund totality of the entire tradition" of Athena, so the image of being gathered for a banquet in the kingdom with "Abraham, Isaac, and Jacob" or that of "Gehenna" or "Gomorrah" would evoke a similarly wide and deep meaning from Israelite tradition.[88] Furthermore, the full panoply of covenantal components and allusions to traditional covenantal teachings in Q 6:20–49 and the pronouncement of woes in Q 11:39–52 would have resonated with deep traditions respectively of the Israelite covenant, including its breaking and its renewal, and of prophetic condemnation of those rulers who exploited the peasantry. At such points performances tap the lifeblood of generations of previous recitations and performances of psalms, prayers, epics, and prophecies.

Because of its standard assumptions about Jesus' sayings, however, New Testament studies tends to block off access precisely to the tradition with which the Jesus speeches in Q would supposedly resonate, the imminent meaning that they would reference metonymically. According to these standard assumptions, not only is Christianity a decisive departure from Judaism, especially with regard to matters such as Mosaic covenant. But Jesus, either the historical teacher or the resurrected Lord communicating through his prophets, is conceived as the

---

88. Some obvious illustrations of "metonymic referencing" from "American" civil religious culture might be the phrases "Four score and seven years ago," "Ask not what your country can do for you," and "I have a dream!" As these examples illustrate, metonymic referencing operates in print culture as well as in oral performance, although it is far more important in the latter. Those who remember the sound of "JFK's" and "MLK's" voices will have a "feel" for how *hearing* again even one familiar phrase of their famous speeches evokes a whole world of experience in one's memory.

originator of Jesus' teachings that are unusual if not unique. The field has abandoned what was perhaps the most extreme form this took, in the criterion of discontinuity for the authentic sayings of Jesus: different from Jewish teaching that had gone before and Christian teaching that came after. The residue of this sharp discontinuity between Jesus and Judaism persists, nevertheless, in much Q scholarship, which tends to look for extratextual meaning of Jesus' sayings largely outside of Israelite tradition. The Q community, moreover, is often constructed as rejected by and rejecting of "Judaism" or "all Israel." Such construction of Q and the Q community effectively cuts off the resonance of Q speeches with Israelite tradition, leaving only the short history and limited lore of the Q people themselves. In order even to begin to appreciate the ways in which verbal signals in Q refer metonymically to the richness of meaning immanent in Israelite tradition, we must cut through — or perhaps better yet, simply abandon — the theologically determined inclinations and conceptual apparatus of New Testament studies that will not allow that Jesus, his first followers, and the communities among whom Q was performed were rooted solidly in Israelite cultural traditions.

We must also complicate the analysis of the tradition with which Q's speeches resonate metonymically well beyond the ways in which Foley deals with tradition and immanent meaning. Most of the oral traditional literature he considers was produced in societies without sharp separation of ruling class and peasantry. The "Homeric" people were indeed a bunch of warlords, and aristocracies did indeed dominate the city-states that hosted the pan-Hellenism movement in which Nagy believes the Homeric epics took canonical form. *Beowulf* stems from and addresses a society in which feudal relations between lord and serf had not yet become full-blown. Although some of the folklorists and anthropologists Foley cites do consider class and imperial power relations in their analysis of contemporary oral performances, Foley does not attempt to factor such power relations into his theory. As explored in chapter 5, however, Q clearly references what must be popular Israelite tradition, over against official Jerusalemite tradition carried in protocanonical texts such as the Torah scrolls and Prophet scrolls as well as orally in the Pharisaic "traditions of the elders" and priestly and scribal oral knowledge of the "scriptures." Even in its use by Matthew and Luke, who clearly knew the Septuagint, Q's references to Israelite tradition are not cited according to any recognizable textual tradition or text-dependent form. Most references to Israelite tradition in Q discourses are to historical figures, places, and events, along with the use of traditional prophetic and other speech forms. Most telling is that Q discourses assume a stance sharply opposed to the ruling institutions and the scribal and Pharisaic representatives of Jerusalem, that is, those who cultivated and benefitted from the official Judean tradition.

While he draws upon Halliday's sociolinguistic theory in his discussion of "register," Foley does not pick up Halliday's incorporation of class differences in his consideration of "context of situation," "dialect," and "register." For Halliday, who draws heavily on the work of Bernstein on how working-class students' learning differs from professional-class students' learning in schools operated in the linguistic patterns in which the professional-class students are at home, the different linguistic "codes" into which children are socialized make a decisive difference for the "registers" they are able to command. Although evidence is limited and fragmentary, it is possible to discern how different "registers" of speech have particular social locations. Elaborated purity codes belong to the priestly and scribal circles; it seems unlikely that Judean and Galilean peasants would have been interested in them, much less conversant with them. Whereas the ruling Judean aristocracy may have held that genuine prophecy had become extinct with the last of the (now-canonical) prophets, the traditional Israelite register of prophesying continued among the peasantry.[89] The scribes and sages who viewed themselves as the heirs of the great prophets of the past continued to interpret prophecies, as can readily be seen in Ben Sira and the *pesharim* discovered among the scrolls at Qumran. Popular prophets such as Jesus son of Hananiah, John the Baptist, and Jesus of Nazareth, on the other hand, voiced God's judgment on rulers and ruling institutions in the familiar age-old forms used by the classical prophets of old. One might argue also that we can see in Judean apocalyptic literature evidence that during second-temple times an apocalyptic register had developed among scribal circles that paralleled but was distinctively different from the prophetic register still alive among the peasantry. Thus, in considering the Israelite tradition to which the Q discourses metonymically referenced, we must take into consideration the difference between the official Jerusalem tradition and the popular (perhaps also distinctively Galilean) tradition and the likelihood that verbal signals in Q resonated primarily with the latter.

The regular interaction between the great and the little traditions (see chapter 5), however, and the likelihood that those rooted in the latter had a sense of what was important in the former complicate even further the task of us outsiders in recognizing allusions, innuendos, and imminent meanings. To illustrate from Q: Abraham would have been a significant, founding ancestor for both the official Jerusalemite and the popular Israelite traditions. But if the ordinary people knew well that the Jerusalem elite had been legitimating their position of power by claiming Abraham as their special ancestor (see further chapter 5 above), then Abraham would have been an ambiguous symbol for them. They could both mock the elite for such a pretentious posture of legitimation by lineage ("We have Abraham as our Father," Q 3:8) and counter-co-opt Abraham (along with Isaac and Jacob) for themselves in a way that excluded the pretentious holders of power ("God is able from these stones to raise up children to Abraham," Q 3:8; and "Many will come from east and west and sit at table with Abraham, Isaac,

---

89. As I argued fifteen years ago, albeit without benefit of the concept of register, in Richard A. Horsley, "'Like One of the Prophets of Old': Two Types of Popular Prophets at the Time of Jesus," CBQ 47 (1985): 435–63. Of course Josephus, who may well be a unique case, appears to have viewed himself as a rather remarkable prophet, and some scholars might be inclined to view the Righteous Teacher at Qumran as fitting a pattern of a Mosaic prophet engaged in a covenant renewal of Israel. Cf. the treatment of prophecy and prophets in late second-temple times by Rebecca Gray, *Prophetic Figures in Late Second Temple Jewish Palestine: The Evidence from Josephus* (Oxford: Oxford University Press, 1993).

and Jacob in the kingdom of God, but the 'sons' will be cast out," Q 13:28–29). The people knew very well that the Jerusalem elite honored the great prophets of old, yet only long after the prophets had condemned the rulers and the rulers had persecuted and even killed the prophets. That remained a source of resentment among the people, who were not fooled in the slightest by the official honoring of the prophets, as indicated at several points (Q 6:23; 11:49–50; 13:34). It is evident that we must become more keenly aware of the very different values and implications that figures and symbols shared by the official and popular traditions would have had for their respective constituencies. In a historical context of perpetual conflict, in which the cultural tradition was constantly contested, it is crucial to understand the dynamics of cultural as well as political-economic "class conflict" and how they were embedded in historical relations of power.

As evident in the immediately preceding discussion, furthermore, the tradition we must include in considering how the Q discourses resonate with immanent meaning was far more comprehensive and complex than what Foley is considering in connection with Homeric epic and *Beowulf*. In his consideration of such cases of verbal art, he appears to be thinking primarily in terms of particular traditions of performance. In our consideration of Q, we are thinking of Israelite tradition generally. And that tradition included any and every level and dimension of societal life, usually without differentiation, from internal family relations to political-economic relations to imperial rulers, and every aspect of life, from personal relation with the divine to the physiological caloric minimum necessary for human subsistence. Besides being comprehensive, the Israelite cultural tradition was complex in an unusual way compared with the traditions of societies constructed in ethnographies. In some innovative treatments in the last decades, "early Christianity" (including the Jesus movement represented by Q) has been compared with movements among ethnographically documented African, Native American, and Melanesian societies that came into crisis when their traditions were impacted by Western imperial "contact" and conquest.[90] In those societies the "millenarian" or "revitalization" movements led by "prophets" were seen to make dramatic changes in the society's tradition, including extensive borrowing from the newly dominant culture. Israelite tradition, on the other hand, besides its origin with a people who attained independence from foreign rulers, included repeated struggles against imperial subjection as well as against domestic rulers who compromised with an imperial power and its culture. That is, the people's struggle to resist imperial and / or oppressive domestic rule was an integral part of Israelite tradition, from Moses to Deborah and Gideon to Elijah, and continuing into the early Maccabean resistance to Hellenistic rule and numerous popular movements resisting Roman, Herodian, and high-priestly domination in late second-temple times. Far from a movement such as that represented by Q being a departure or a novum in Israelite society, Israelite cultural tradition provided several histori-

---

90. For example, John G. Gager, *Kingdom and Community* (Englewood Cliffs, N.J.: Prentice-Hall, 1975).

cal cases of popular movements of renewal of Israel in resistance to oppressive imperial and/or domestic rulers.

In sum, in order to appreciate and understand Q as a libretto that was regularly performed in an early Jesus movement, we must engage in a number of interrelated analytical or investigative exercises. It is necessary first to establish the "texts" (or "words") that were being performed. Q was not a collection of sayings but a series of short speeches or discourses on subjects of concern to the movement. The *contexts* in which Q or its constituent discourses were performed were probably the regular community meetings of a renewal movement and/or the particular situations of mission or trial in which members frequently found themselves. The speech-*registers* appropriate to those situations included the general register of the founding prophet addressing the movement for Q as a whole *and* the particular registers of prophetic proclamation of new deliverance (the kingdom of God/renewal of Israel), Mosaic covenant renewal, mission to expand the renewal movement, encouragement-and-instruction for trial before the authorities, consolation and encouragement in difficult circumstances of poverty, and warning sanctions on discipline and solidarity. In order to attain a sense of how the verbal signals and symbols in all of the Q discourses would have *resonated metonymically* with Israelite popular tradition, in interaction with but over against the official tradition, it is necessary to explore the Judean biblical tradition and whatever other windows we may have onto how a popular movement of renewal may have understood its tradition. Much of the latter task will probably entail considerable comparison and contrast between the great and popular traditions operative in Israelite societies of the late second-temple period.

Chapter 8

RECOVERING ORAL PERFORMANCE
FROM WRITTEN TEXT IN Q

Jonathan A. Draper _____

Toward a Model of Oral Communication

In developing form criticism, Rudolf Bultmann and Martin Dibelius were concerned with the possibility of establishing authentic teachings of Jesus by tracing the development of free-floating units of Jesus traditions according to their particular forms.[1] Since the Synoptic Gospels had been discredited as reliable accounts for the life and teaching of Jesus, the remaining question seemed to be the authenticity of certain sayings of Jesus, held to have been transmitted independently in oral tradition. Joachim Jeremias took this to its farthest limits with his claim to be able to reconstruct the *ipsissima verba Jesu* (the very words of Jesus). However, the study of oral traditional forms of communication has become increasingly sophisticated in the past fifty years, since New Testament scholars applied the insights of Hermann Gunkel and form criticism to the interpretation of the Gospels.

The debate over oral tradition and performance has been carried out mostly in the field of classical studies, since Milman Parry and Albert Lord conducted field studies of the way in which illiterate Bosnian peasants performed their songs. They discovered the oral-formulaic character of epic poetry, which enables an oral performer to compose in the act of performance largely by putting together traditional formulaic units. Such oral poets could give impromptu performances of considerable length and complexity. On the basis of their observations in the field, Parry and Lord were able to argue convincingly that Homer's *Iliad* and *Odyssey* were originally composed and performed orally. The importance of this discovery for New Testament studies is the problematization of any idea of an original text in oral tradition, since each performance responds to a particular audience and context.

The broad thesis of Parry and Lord, namely, the possibility of oral-formulaic composition in performance, has remained unchallenged. However, it has been shown that not all oral literature is composed in this way and that there is often an

---

1. Rudolf Bultmann, *The History of the Synoptic Tradition* (Oxford: Blackwell, 1963 [1921]); Martin Dibelius, *From Tradition to Gospel* (New York: Scribners, 1935 [1919]).

interdependence of the oral and the written forms.[2] The oral medium continues to be reflected in written forms long after members of a primary oral society become literate.[3] Likewise, oral tradition continues to develop long after it is first set down in writing, and this can lead to multiple versions of the same text, which cannot be explained by means of text or redaction criticism. Part of the debate has focused on whether orality and literacy structure consciousness differently.[4] Anthropologists working with Native American oral tradition, such as Dell Hymes and Dennis Tedlock, have clarified many of the dynamics of oral performance, particularly highlighting the significance of perlocutionary aspects, such as pitch, volume, and gesture.[5]

John Miles Foley and Gregory Nagy in particular have opened up the possibility of recovering oral texts within written texts by combining the insights of the anthropologists and those of reception theorists in literary studies with the oral-formulaic theories of Parry and Lord.[6] Foley's work thus provides the basis for a new look at the orality of the Q discourses, as discussed in the previous chapter. However, there is a need to move one step back from his model for a broader framework in the social linguistic theory of M. A. K. Halliday, in order to construct a general model of communication, of which oral and literary communication are different possibilities in the same system.[7]

Language and Community

Any investigation of the dynamics of tradition and culture should begin with the role of language in community. The human individual is a social being and a social product, and socialization is effected in interaction by means of language. Language is shaped by human interaction but also shapes that interaction by opening and limiting the possibilities of communication. It is human interaction and communication which make it possible to transmit culture from one generation to

---

2. Ruth Finnegan, *Oral Poetry: In Nature, Significance, and Social Context* (Cambridge: Cambridge University Press, 1977), 71–84; Jack Goody, *The Interface between the Written and the Oral* (Cambridge: Cambridge University Press, 1987), 93–99.

3. J. Opland, *Xhosa Oral Poetry: Aspects of a Black South African Tradition* (Cambridge: Cambridge University Press, 1983).

4. Walter Ong, *Orality and Literacy: The Technologizing of the Word* (London: Methuen, 1982); contra J. P. Gee, "Orality and Literacy: From the Savage Mind to Ways with Words," in *Language and Literacy in Social Practice*, ed. J. Maybin (Clevendon, England: Multilingual Matters, 1994), 168–92.

5. Dell Hymes, *"In Vain I Tried to Tell You": Essays in Native American Ethnopoetics* (Philadelphia: University of Pennsylvania Press, 1981); Dennis Tedlock, *The Spoken Word and the Work of Interpretation* (Philadelphia: University of Pennsylvania Press, 1983).

6. John Miles Foley, *The Singer of Tales in Performance*, Voices in Performance and Text (Bloomington: Indiana University Press, 1995); Gregory Nagy, *Pindar's Homer: The Lyric Possession of an Epic Past* (Baltimore: Johns Hopkins University Press, 1990); Wolfgang Iser, *The Act of Reading: A Theory of Aesthetic Response* (Baltimore: Johns Hopkins University Press, 1978); H. R. Jauss, *Toward an Aesthetic of Reception* (Minneapolis: University of Minnesota Press, 1982); Milman Parry, *The Making of Homeric Verse: The Collected Papers of Milman Parry* (Oxford: Clarendon, 1971); A. B. Lord, *The Singer of Tales* (Cambridge, Mass.: Harvard University Press, 1960).

7. M. A. K. Halliday, *Language as Social Semiotic: The Social Interpretation of Language and Meaning* (Baltimore: University Park Press, 1978).

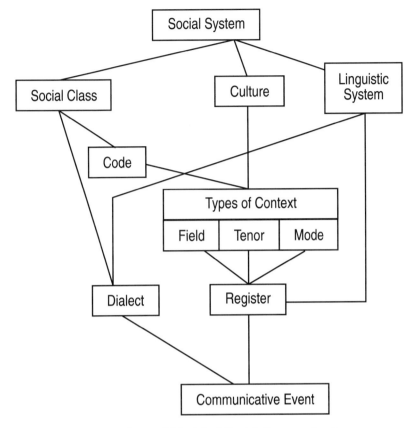

Figure 1. General Model of Social Communication

another.[8] We learn to speak a specific language in specific behavioral contexts which inculcate the norms and traditions of our particular society. Language socializes us into the value systems and behavioral patterns of that society as a basis and precondition for communication.[9] Language also socializes us into social hierarchy and social class and marks out our social status in terms of the language we speak. Thus communication is an interaction between three interlocking factors: linguistic system, culture, and social structure / class (used broadly here to designate the location of the individual within power relations and hierarchies).

In this respect, one model of communication suffices for all forms of communication, whether oral or written. This model (fig. 1), which is based on and simplified from that proposed by Halliday, is an analytical representation of the

8. Ibid., 18.
9. Ibid., 23.

multiple factors involved in the process of communication leading to an actual communicative event; it is not a representation of content.[10] The focus for our purposes is not on the linguistic, grammatical, and semantic aspects of the model. Here it is simply important to note that although the linguistic system is a dimension of the social system as a whole, and to that extent has a social dynamic, it is not directly affected by class. The dialect and register of the marginalized and dominated classes are every bit as logical and coherent as those of the dominant class.[11] Written and oral communication essentially represent different registers within the same communicative process, rather than different cognitive processes (as has been suggested by those who exaggerate the difference between oral and literate cultures). The difference is especially a factor of the code and type of context, especially mode, as we shall see.

Social Structure and Social Location

Social structure and social class are inherent factors in language as a medium of socialization. They affect communication in two fundamental ways. First, dialect is an important feature of structure and class. While different dialects usually develop in different geographical regions, they become implicated in the maintenance of social status and structure. The dialect of the dominant geographical region becomes the standardized written and spoken language of the center of power in a given society, or even if it did not originate in that way, the standardized dialect becomes the language of the elite. Since every oral communicative event will be couched in a particular dialect (whether that of the ruling elite or the dominated and marginalized), class potentially affects every oral exchange. Second, as Basil Bernstein has shown, communication is also affected by a socially determined code.[12] Bernstein's empirical research into the practice of middle-class and working-class parents has shown that children are socialized differently in terms of language use, in what he characterizes as elaborated and restricted codes.

The elaborated code is marked by the way in which communication is logically, semantically, and structurally elaborated and explicit: parents socialize their children by explaining everything in terms of connections and implications. The restricted code is marked by an authoritarian insistence on implicit rather than explicit reference, which is received on authority and is traditional in nature: rather than explaining why, parents socialize their children simply to accept that this is the way things are. It seems that these two codes correlate to a remarkable (but not exclusive) extent with oral and literate registers. The written register makes possible a focus on explicit formulation, precision, and elaboration in expression, whereas the oral register depends on implicit meanings and reference within contexts familiar to the parties to the act of communication. Foley has

---

10. Ibid., 69.

11. Ibid., 185–86.

12. Basil Bernstein, *A Socio-Linguistic Approach to Social Learning* (Middlesex: Penguin, 1965); idem, "A Socio-Linguistic Approach to Socialization," in *Directions in Socio-Linguistics*, ed. J. Gumperz and Dell Hymes (New York: Holt, Rinehart and Winston, 1970).

placed great emphasis on the metonymic reference of oral performance. In what he terms the performance arena of oral communication, language is characterized by expressions which in the literary register would appear repetitive and otiose, but in the oral register play an important role in bringing to bear the whole social world of the community, *pars pro toto*. Homer's "wine-dark sea" or "rosy-fingered dawn," for example, are not just metrical fillers but metonymic markers, signifying something beyond their semantic reference in context. This is very much the nature of the restricted code as observed by Bernstein and Halliday. Inasmuch as people are familiar with both codes and their social referents, it is possible for them to "switch codes" from one to the other, depending on context (and particularly on field and tenor, as we shall see). Nevertheless, we should assume that illiterate communities would communicate largely in the restricted code and that metonymic referencing would be the norm in facilitating "communicative economy."[13]

Since interpreters of the New Testament have generally not paid attention to social location, it is important to recognize this emphasis that modern linguistic theory places on class and status as factors in communication. In fact the Gospels give clear indications that Jesus and his followers were members of the underclass: peasant cultivators, laborers, and fishermen. They were Galileans with a distinctive social dialect. The dialect of Galilee would have been every bit as grammatically and semantically coherent and developed as that of Jerusalem; perhaps, given the influence of first Babylon and then Hellenism on Jerusalem, the dialect of Galilee even represented a more conservative and hence purer form of Aramaic, the dominant spoken language in Roman Palestine. However, its use in Jerusalem is remarked and disparaged (Mark 14:70; cf. Acts 4:13). The Galilean peasant social location of Jesus and his followers would have affected more than simply the content of his teaching; it would have determined and channeled the whole communicative process.

Culture

Edward Said has pointed out the way in which modern scholarship creates cultural constructs like "orientalism" and then reifies them, so that it no longer recognizes their artificial nature.[14] We are apt to understand the culture of a particular society in this monolithic way. In New Testament studies scholars have long spoken in broad terms of Judaism and Hellenism, as if there was one homogenous culture we could call Jewish. Recent scholarship has pointed out that while the term "Jewish" has come to signify some kind of ethnic and religious unity, in the first century the Greek term *ioudaios* referred to the geographical region of Judea and

---

13. Foley, *Singer of Tales*, 53.
14. Edward W. Said, *Orientalism* (New York: Vintage, 1978); idem, *Culture and Imperialism* (New York: Vintage, 1993).

its inhabitants and sometimes, more narrowly, its rulers.[15] Thus, as explained in chapter 3, most Galileans at the time of Jesus were apparently not Judeans. This has important implications for communicative events between Jesus and the Jerusalem retainer class usually designated as the scribes and the Pharisees. The latter represent a literate class skilled in the interpretation of texts, and thus characterized by expression in the elaborated code. Since they are described as "coming from Jerusalem" (Mark 3:22; 7:1), they would have spoken in the elite Judaean (Jerusalem) dialect, which also represented the hegemony of the center over the periphery.

A second important proviso in the model of communication is provided by the work of James C. Scott. In two different but related conceptual frameworks, Scott speaks of the "great tradition" and the "little tradition" in a society, and also of the "public transcript" and the "hidden transcript."[16] This great tradition, controlled by the elite, has normally been presented as the culture of a particular society, so that deviations from this culture are seen as aberrations or moral failure. Scott points out, however, that while the rulers and the dominated share a common set of cultural referents, the latter understand and utilize the same cultural heritage in a little tradition resistant to the hegemonic claims of the elite (discussed in chapter 5). It is a mistake to ignore the oral cultural tradition of the peasantry of Galilee and focus only on the literate cultural tradition of the Jerusalem elite. Communication within a peasant movement in Galilee would have reflected and mediated the culture of the little tradition, whereas the scribes and Pharisees would have reflected and mediated the culture of the great tradition of Jerusalem. When Jesus and his movement are seen interacting with the scribes and Pharisees, then this will represent a particular dynamic within the communicative model we are presenting, in which code and dialect and culture operate conflictually.

In his second model, Scott emphasizes the power dynamics implicit in communication between the ruling elite and the masses. The elite control the public expression of culture: they articulate the official transcript which is operative in public life and maintain it by force if necessary (though it is designed to render force unnecessary by internalizing the structures of domination). Writing and literacy as control of the written (controlled) word are important aspects of domination and control of the masses by the ruling elite, as summarized hyperbolically by Claude Lévi-Strauss's celebrated dictum that "the primary function of written communication is to facilitate slavery."[17] However, the dominated do not simply accept their own oppression, even if they are forced by their own powerlessness to participate publicly in the terms dictated by their rulers. They have their own

---

15. Richard A. Horsley, *Galilee: History, Politics, and People* (Valley Forge, Pa.: Trinity Press International, 1995); idem, *Archaeology, History, and Society in Galilee: The Social Context of Jesus and the Rabbis* (Valley Forge, Pa.: Trinity Press International, 1996).

16. James C. Scott, *Moral Economy of the Peasant* (New Haven: Yale University Press, 1977); idem, *Domination and the Arts of Resistance: Hidden Transcripts* (New Haven: Yale University Press, 1990).

17. Claude Lévi-Strauss, *Tristes Tropiques* (London: Cape, 1973), 300; cf. W. V. Harris, *Ancient Literacy* (Cambridge, Mass.: Harvard University Press, 1989), 38.

discourse off-stage, which represents a counterculture or hidden transcript, which they express among themselves and seek to insert surreptitiously into their discourse with the elite as much as possible. It represents a form of safe resistance. Nevertheless, in rare instances when the pressure of domination becomes unbearable or when there is a power vacuum, they challenge the official transcript publicly. This "breach of the official transcript" is likely to be met with brutal repression, but nevertheless alters the balance of power by inserting the "hidden transcript" into the public arena.

These two linked insights and models presented by Scott clearly have major implications for a model of communication. They are especially important for analysis of oral communication in ancient Palestine, where the dynamics of domination are central.

Register

The register of a communicative event is the configuration of language appropriate to the particular type of situation or context. Recognition of its register is fundamental to effective communication: "A text is meaningful not so much because the hearer does not know what the speaker is going to say, as in a mathematical model of communication, but because he does know. He has abundant evidence, both from his knowledge of the general (including statistical) properties of the linguistic system and from his sensibility to the particular cultural, situational and verbal context; and this enables him to make informed guesses about the meanings that are coming his way."[18] We understand what is being said because we know what is happening, or alternatively we recognize what is happening because we understand what is being said. On the one hand, if we see a young man and a young woman courting, then we know what language to expect (many plays exploit the comic effect of inappropriate language in such a situation, which requires a prior understanding and expectation in the audience). On the other hand, if we overhear the same kind of conversation without seeing the couple, we can almost immediately figure out what is going on even if we do not already know (again a rich source of comic confusion in plays). A failure to recognize the context of communication will result in a failure of communication, often with comic or tragic effects.[19] A lack of attention to the context of communication has bedevilled interpretation of the Jesus tradition and has led to misrecognition and misinterpretation. Recognition of the type of context is especially important in oral peasant communication, which utilizes the restricted code of communication. In elaborated code communication the potential for misrecognition is still there but is less overwhelming. However, when we come to a saying like "Leave the dead to bury the dead!" we are facing a major misrecognition if we treat it as disembodied wisdom of the elite rather than first seeking to understand its context of communication within the restricted-code oral communication of the peasant.

---

18. Halliday, *Language as Social Semiotic*, 61.
19. Foley, *Singer of Tales*, 30–32.

The register appropriate to each particular type of communication has three variables, according to the model of Halliday: field, tenor, and mode.[20] It is important to consider each of these in reconstructing the register of an oral communicative event. Field represents what is taking place and where it is taking place. It refers to the event which occasioned the communication and its setting. Tenor represents the relational aspect of communication: who is speaking to whom, the class dynamic, and the aspect of domination. Mode represents the means of communication (what channel of communication is adopted, such as oral or textual), genre, and form. For instance, if Jesus tells the parable of the wicked tenants in the presence of and directed at the ruling elite, then we have to take into account the aspects of field (class conflict and resistance), tenor (communication between elite and dominated classes), and mode (parable, which, because of its ambiguity, is an ideal form for the insertion of the hidden transcript of the oppressed into public discourse). In this case, the communicative event will be multilayered, communicating one thing to his followers and another to their rulers, even though there will be common elements in the cultural register which make the communicative event significant and therefore explosive.

Communicative Event

All of these aspects are implicit in a communicative event. We have used the expression "communicative event" rather than "text in situation" because the word "text" has implications of literacy not intended by Halliday, for whom it refers to any verbal articulation. Since the communicative event is a social interaction, it involves both speaker and hearer(s) in the articulation of the process described by our model. Since the configuration of class, culture, code, and dialect will differ from person to person, there will obviously be gaps of understanding. Oral communication depends especially on shared experience and expectations, since it is heavily metonymic and functions primarily through the restricted code. Successful communication will depend on efficient and appropriate filling of the gaps in the register. Foley proposed that study of oral communication should take into account the balance between intratextual signifiers which create an "implied reader" and the gaps in signification, which must be filled by the "real reader" in a process of "consistency building" by which the text (oral or written) is appropriated by the individual.[21] This seems to be a helpful tool for considering the way oral communication operates. It accounts for the continuity in oral communication, since the shared cultural experience of the participants in an oral performance will enable them quickly and efficiently to decode the metonymic reference of the speaker but will also draw them into the performance as participants in filling the gaps and creating the text through consistency building. The process is both repetitive and creative, allowing both continuity and development to occur in the transmission of tradition.

---

20. Halliday, *Language as Social Semiotic*, 33.
21. Foley, *Singer of Tales*, drawing on the literary theory of Wolfgang Iser and Hans Robert Jauss.

On the one hand, this suggests that the thesis that some of the sayings of Jesus were created entirely de novo, as proposed by several scholars, conflicts with the process of oral transmission. Such entirely innovative "words of the Risen Jesus" are inherently unlikely. On the other hand, the words of Jesus would have been repeated by himself and his followers on innumerable occasions, always in varying forms, and so it is inappropriate to speak of an original form of a saying (since it would have had no original form but only an original "shape")[22] or of ipsissima verba (since the words would have changed in each performance even on the lips of Jesus himself). Yet since they would have had an intimate metonymic reference in the register of his own community, they would have been repeated after his own death in the same way in the same type of context. When they were taken out of this type of context in his own peasant Galilean community, however, and inserted into new (e.g., urban or Hellenistic) types of contexts, they would have taken on a new reference. Change of register would have led to change of the nature of the communicative event. Thus we would expect the Jesus tradition as it is mediated within oral tradition to reflect both continuity where the register remains constant and the tendency to develop in new ways in new types of contexts.

Oral Communication Surviving in the Written Medium

It has become clear that the relationship between the oral and the written media is complex and interrelated, rather than a matter of simple alternatives. In societies where writing is known, it exercises an influence even on those who are illiterate. They will be aware of the ability of written texts to stabilize the tradition in an authoritative form, for example, in sacred texts and legal documents. It is likely that sacred texts will have a numinous signification, even for those who cannot read. Illiterates may themselves have the possibility of hiring a scribe from the city to write something for them or to read it (e.g., a marriage contract or deed). Likewise, the oral medium may continue to influence those who are literate, who may utilize oral forms of communication (perhaps using written notes as an aide-mémoire) and imitate the oral register in written form.[23] Emerging gaps and conflicts between the written tradition and the continuing, developing oral tradition would lead to periodic revision of the written text by the literate elite.

Nevertheless, the difference between the literate and oral registers is fundamental and identifiable. Hymes and, following him, Foley have argued for the possibility of identifying oral performances surviving within written texts. This is clearly of considerable importance for the study of Q, since it is widely recognized that this material originates from early oral tradition in the Jesus movement. Fo-

---

22. See Albert Nolan, *God in South Africa: The Challenge of the Gospel* (Grand Rapids, Mich.: Eerdmans, 1988), 7–30.

23. Cf. Ruth Finnegan, *Literacy and Orality: Studies in the Technology of Communication* (Oxford: Blackwell, 1988), 161; Opland, *Xhosa Oral Poetry*, 231.

ley argues that the oral context of an oral performance fixed in written text can be reconstructed, since it survives in rhetorical form:

> In simplest terms there no longer exists an actual, tangible "place" devoted to this function, no locus defined temporally and spatially, but then such tangible locations were never more than sequel concretizations of the performance arena, nominal instances of an intangible "place" or "moment" that harbored much wider and deeper implications. Thus transition from a series of nominal instances to a rhetorical function independent of concretizations does not represent as severe a shift as might first be imagined. In both cases the experience of performance, real or projected, energizes the relationship between performer, now rhetoricized as well, and the audience/reader. In both cases entering the arena means designating a preselected and dedicated channel of communication, with all of the limitations and advantages that channel entails.[24]

Since it is written in the oral register, such a text can only be fully understood if its oral "context of situation" is reconstructed. This means above all attempting to recognize and become fluent in the register of the text, so that its metonymic clues resonate and convey their appropriate force. The reader has to become as nearly as possible a hearer listening to an oral performance in a particular context.

The key indicators of oral performance in literature are alliteration, assonance, rhyme, tonal repetition, parallelism, and rhythm. All of these aid in memory and in fluent performance by the speaker. Repetition of all kinds is important, whether of content, syllables, verses, or lengthy passages. This is because redundancy enables the hearer to remember what is being said, since something said only once is quickly forgotten. Archaic language, formulas, imagery, and symbolic language all are found in oral texts, as aspects of metonymy. Other aids to oral composition, most of which are lost in written transmission, are singing, intoning, instrumental accompaniment, dramatization, dialogue, and audience response.[25] They may, nevertheless, leave traces in the text. Foley has argued convincingly for the importance of metonymic reference as a marker of oral performance. As we have seen, this is the result of the use of the restricted code of language which predominates in oral societies. The metonymic referencing will be culturally determined, and a single word or phrase will often summarize in telescoped form a whole aspect of the culture and tradition of the people. Recovery of the oral register thus requires a sensitivity to the metonymic valence of key words and phrases obtained by careful comparison with the body of tradition which forms the context of the particular performance, taking due account of the social location of the tradition.

In the case of the Jesus tradition due account will need to be taken of its location in the hidden transcript and of the little tradition. Care will also have to be taken in being sensitive to the Galilean dialect and tradition behind the Greek. In the writings of the Hebrew Scriptures and related texts we have a large repository of Israelite culture. Of course, most of this represents the great tradition

---

24. Foley, *Singer of Tales*, 138.
25. Finnegan, *Literacy and Orality*, 88–122.

of the elite, but it enables us to reconstruct, at least tentatively, the shadow little tradition of the ordinary people. For example, as noted in chapter 5, the five books of the Torah contain the covenantal legal tradition of the elite, but it is related in a fundamental way to the tradition and practice of the ordinary people of Israel, which it codifies and develops. The Israelite people of Galilee were for the greater period of their history not administered from Jerusalem, and we have only a shadowy picture of their traditions and culture. It cannot be assumed that the Torah accurately represents the culture and tradition of the people of the land in Galilee. Yet it must also be acknowledged that there will be a wealth of common tradition relating to the basic common culture of the Israelite people. The case must be argued for each metonymic referent.

Foley argues for close attention to multiple performances of the same unit and for differentiating where possible in terms of dialect and idiolect (the idiosyncrasies of the individual performer). In the Gospels and other early texts (e.g., *Gospel of Thomas, Didache, 1 Clement*) we do indeed have multiple performances and can compare them in our reconstruction and analysis.

While some anthropologists, for example Tedlock, have been reluctant to allow that the oral performance of a people can be reconstructed from written accounts, others, such as Hymes, have shown that it is possible. Indeed Tedlock himself has undertaken a similar project with Mayan culture by comparing written historical accounts with the contemporary descendants of the Mayans. Hymes has shown how oral performance can, to some extent, be represented in text by marking it out in "measured text," breaking the "typographical monopoly." Attention to textual signals like conjunctions and particles, distribution of finite verbs and sense units, can enable us to simulate the rhythm and pauses of the oral performance. While writing out an oral text as if it were a block of undifferentiated prose would be destructive and misleading, measured verse enables us to be keyed in visually to the oral patterns of performance.

A particular aspect of this reconstruction is the recognition that oral material is not transmitted as floating wreckage of the past in isolated units. It is structured in larger blocks of tradition appropriate to particular types of context, which we may term "speeches" or "discourses." Essentially this means that on particular occasions, an oral performer would recite a block of connected material relating to a particular situation to which it was appropriate. The audience would be familiar with the conventions of the particular occasion, that is, the register associated with it, so that the performer could rely on a rich field of metonymic reference mutually understood by himself and his audience.[26]

In the reconstruction and analysis of the Q material, which has survived as the material common to Matthew and Luke but which is not found in Mark, we are handicapped by the lack of a text. It should always be borne in mind that Q does

---

26. An isolated saying outside of a particular context would mean nothing and convey nothing, or perhaps more accurately it could convey anything and mean anything, so that its ambiguity would not communicate in such a setting.

not exist except as a hypothesis, however plausible that hypothesis may be. Since it is a reconstructed text, we are unable to know what has been omitted or effaced by the redactions of Matthew and Luke. Nevertheless, we can discern the broad shape and extent of an underlying tradition, and the extracanonical witnesses also give us some assistance. What remains of Q does seem to form a coherent body of discourses. Our analysis will show that Q has all the characteristics of oral communication and that due account of its oral nature should be taken in its interpretation. In particular, a full consideration of the types of context in which the material was performed and the register of the discourses will prove essential in decoding and interpreting this early body of tradition from the Jesus movement in its Galilean setting.

Toward Hearing Q Discourses in Measured Verse

The Theory of Measured Verse

As primary oral cultures have receded in the face of the inexorable intrusion of modernity and literacy, anthropologists and students of oral literature have shown increased interest in written remains of oral tradition. While insisting strongly on the reservation of the term "oral" for what is performed and observed, Tedlock has attempted to recover the oral pattern of the transcribed Popul Vuh text on the basis of observation of modern performers among the Popul Vuh.[27] Tedlock is attempting to find ways of transcribing the paralinguistic features of oral performance, like gesture, pause, tone, and volume, which are lost once an oral performance is transcribed.[28] Yet for transcribed oral texts from long-dead cultures, there seems no alternative to risking reconstruction without the benefit of these features, inferring pause and emphasis from the text itself. Here the work of Hymes is of particular significance, since his painstaking analysis of transcriptions of oral performances of Native American narratives and verse has demonstrated the way oral performance is structured into remarkably constant performance patterns and discourse features which can be reconstructed.[29] Foley has drawn attention to the relevance of Hymes's theory of measured verse for ancient texts deriving from oral tradition.[30]

Hymes proceeds on the basis of two principles: first, that a consistent structure exists in oral literature which can be identified by careful analysis; and, second, that the structure can be seen in "form-meaning covariation," which must be given equal weight.[31] He finds different levels of organization of text, from the

---

27. Dennis Tedlock, "Hearing a Voice in an Ancient Text: Quiché Maya Poetics in Performance," in *Native American Discourse: Poetics and Rhetoric,* ed. Joel Sherzer and Anthony Woodbury (Cambridge: Cambridge University Press, 1987).

28. Dennis Tedlock, "On the Translation of Style in Oral Narrative," *Journal of American Folklore* 84 (1971): 114–33.

29. Hymes, *"In Vain I Tried to Tell You,"* 142–83, 309–41.

30. Foley, *Singer of Tales,* 17–28.

31. Hymes, *"In Vain I Tried to Tell You,"* 151.

basic unit of the line, through verse, stanza, scene, and act, utilizing the terminology of dramatic performance. While there is inevitably a measure of uncertainty in this process of analysis, since a mechanical formula is not available or effective, "one is not free to make ad hoc decisions as to the status of a feature; an apparent exception must be explained in a principled way, or a broader, more adequate hypothesis of structure found."[32] The gradual breakthrough to an understanding of the structure of the text is a process of trial and error. Hymes notes in Chinook oral literature that verbal repetition within verses and stanzas provides internal cohesion, as does parallelism and patterning of lines and verses in sets of three and five.[33]

Of particular interest for our purposes is that Hymes finds that the major transitions in terms of content are determined not by relation to time or place (as in modern written literature) but by relations between participants.[34] The larger units — stanzas, scenes, and acts — are all built upon the division into lines, which is basic and depends on the presence of a verb, patterns of repetition, parallelism, repetition, and numerical sequences:[35]

> In sum, no single criterion enables one to identify lines in the material. A variety of intersecting features and patterns contribute to their recognition. The lines are derivative of the patterning of the narrative as a whole, for the most part. Strictly linguistic criteria (presence of a verb, presence of certain elements initially) go far toward a provisional segmentation, but it is the patterning of the whole that gives some confidence in the result.[36]

It is interesting to note that some of the patterns he discovers in Chinook can also be discerned when the performer operates in English. The measured-verse analysis enables the reader of a text to obtain something of the nature and experience of the oral performance.

Problems of Imagining Q in Measured Verse

There are a number of problems connected with our proposed attempt to apply Hymes's theory of measured verse to the reconstructed text of Q. The first and most obvious problem is that the text of Q reconstructed by the International Q Project is not a transcription of a performance. It is a modern scholarly reconstruction. Nevertheless, on the hypothesis that Q consisted of orally performed discourses which have been separately inscribed in text by Matthew and Luke, it seems to us legitimate to look at a reconstructed Q, based on what is common to Matthew and Luke, to test the hypothesis of an oral-derived text that can be imagined in measured verse.

Second, while what we have through Matthew and Luke is a Greek text, with no possibility of reconstructing an underlying text in Aramaic (the language

---

32. Ibid.
33. Ibid., 150–65.
34. Ibid., 171.
35. Ibid., 176.
36. Ibid., 177.

probably spoken by Jesus), it is possible that certain patterns derived from Galilean Aramaic discourse have influenced the koine Greek of Q discourses. However, we are assuming that koine Greek is the language of Q as we have it and are not speculating in any way about some Aramaic substratum. We are simply attempting the modest experiment of an initial segmentation of the Q text, mainly following its reconstruction by the International Q Project, into measured verse, to discern oral patterning.

A third problem is that the process of reconstruction adopted by the International Q Project often leaves us with a bowdlerized text. When the redactional work of Matthew and Luke are removed by scissors and paste, it is inevitable that many traces of the characteristic linkages and particles of the oral performance will be lost. This does make our reconstruction more arbitrary in places than Hymes's work on transcriptions of Chinook oral performance, where he could refer to the field notes of the transcriber as well as the published text.

Oral Features of Q

Even with all of the difficulties and uncertainties, the work of segmenting Q into measured verse reveals patterns and features of oral performance which have survived its incarceration in text. Much of the text of Q falls neatly into couplets and triplets as the basic units of lines and verses. Stanzas likewise seem to fall preferentially into sets of three to five, though here the division is more difficult. Most of the Q materials in Matthew and Luke fall into intelligible larger divisions that we are referring to as speeches or discourses.[37] This analysis of the oral patterns discernible in the Q discourses serves to confirm the impression of a coherent sequence of discourses as the overall structure of Q.

In the blocking of various Q discourses in chapters 9, 10, and 12, stanza is indicated by a capital letter, verse by a numeral, and line by a lowercase letter, so that patterns can be easily detected. Component units within lines are separated to highlight stresses and parallelism of patterns and sounds. Lines have been strictly determined by the presence (or implied presence) of a finite verb, by connective particles where appropriate, and also by their sense. It becomes clear that the Q tradition is couched in simple, unsubordinated sentences arranged in parallel lines, especially couplets and triplets, though with longer sequences for emphasis. There are extensive verbal repetition and parataxis. Sections of the material are arranged in repeated formulaic structure, for example, the woes, the oracles, and the blessings. Even the narrative sections have these characteristics. It is this consistent patterning, which has seemingly survived even the literary redactions of Matthew and Luke and the vagaries of scholarly reconstruction, which convinces us that the reconstructed text of Q has retained many of the features of its originally oral performance.

---

37. Hymes calls the larger divisions of the narratives he analyzes "scenes" and "acts," which emphasizes the drama of the narratives.

For the purposes of reconstruction, we shall use the text of Q reconstructed by the International Q Project and set it out in the manner pioneered by Hymes. We have used square brackets [and] to point to difficulty in the reconstruction of the Q text as indicated in the International Q Project. The angle brackets <and> are used to indicate the hypothetical emendations of the International Q Project, where the text is not found in either Matthew or Luke. We have used curly brackets {and} to show where we have adopted text excluded by the International Q Project, usually because the text makes no sense without choosing something similar to either the Matthean or Lukan version. And we have used double curly brackets {{and}} to indicate that text included by them should, in our opinion, be excluded. Other markers of the International Q Project are omitted here to simplify the presentation.

Analysis

The number of stanzas in a discourse depends on the length or scope of the discourse. While some stanzas have four or more verses, around half have three and many have two or only one. The arrangement is thus largely into triplets and couplets. Similarly, the verses in Q discourses consist largely of couplets (especially) and triplets, with some quartets and longer elements. The couplet is clearly the favorite arrangement for lines, with triplets popular and quartets also common. It could be asked whether the occurrence of variants to the couplet-triplet pattern does not mark out textually the equivalent of a pause, a gesture, a change of volume, or another paralinguistic marker in oral performance. This clear patterning of the material on the basis of triplets and couplets throughout the Q text, both in the macro and the micro plane, reflects an oral mnemonic patterning, which eases the performance and the reception of the material. It is so regular that it cannot be coincidence.

Application of the Model: Q 12:49–59 in Measured Verse

As we have seen, it is possible to begin to re-create the oral register of oral material, which has been fossilized in text, by careful observation of the model of communication we have constructed. We shall leave aside for the moment the question of the location of Q 12:49–59 within the overall text of Q and consider it as a self-contained discourse within the general context of Q. This will involve following the steps set out in the model, beginning with the re-creation of measured text structuring the oral communicative event. After this, attention must be paid to recognizing and reconstructing the register of the text, in terms of its metonymic reference within a particular type of context.

This measured text immediately indicates that this is the residue of oral performance. First, the discourse is structured in three stanzas, each composed of three parallel couplets. The only exceptions are A3 and C2. The three lines in A3 may have been dictated by the underlying metonymic reference to a pro-

Q 12:49–59: Transliteration in Measured Verse Blocked for Hearing

A 1a {Pur elthon balein epi tēn gēn
   b   kai ti thelō ei ede anēphthe.}
  2a [dokei] te hoti elthon balein eirēnēn epi tēn gēn
   b   ouk elthon balein eirēnēn alla machairan.
  3a elthon gar dichasai [huion] [kata] patr[os]
   b   [kai] thugatera [kata] te[s] metr[os] autes
   c   [kai] nymphen [kata] te[s] penthera[s] autes.

B 1a [opsias genomenes] legete [eudia
   b   purrazei gar ho ouranos
  2a kai proi sēmeron cheimon
   b   purrazei gar stugnazon ho ouranos.]
  3a to prosopon tou ouranou [oida] te [diakrin]ein
   b   ton kairon de ou [dynasthē]?

C 1a [heos hotou] meta tou antidikou sou en tē hodō
   b   dos ergasian apellachthai ap' autou
  2a mēpote se parado [ho antidikos] tō kritē
   b   kai ho kritēs tō huperēte
   c   kai [ho uperētes se] b[a]l[ei] eis phylaken
  3a lego soi ou me exelthes ekeithen
   b   heōs ton eschaton kodranten apodos.

---

phetic tradition, found in Mic. 7:6, though A3b and A3c could be read as one line. This tight structure serves both for mnemonic fluency and order. Couplets and triplets are favored oral devices. Parallel construction is a well-known feature of Hebrew culture.

Second, the couplets and verses are constructed on the basis of parataxis and linkage, which are also favorite oral devices. There are no subordinate clauses or complex logical constructions, such as are found in literate texts composed in writing. The favorite connective is simply the additive *kai* or the purposive *gar*. A chain of interlinking words and phrases threads the composition together: *elthon / balein* connect all three verses of the first stanza, while *eirene* and *epi ten gen* connect the first and second verses. The first stanza is connected to the second with the reference of *pur / purrazei*, which also connects the first and second verses of the second stanza. All three verses of the second stanza are linked by *ouranos*. The second stanza is connected to the third stanza by the juridical reference of *diakrinein / antidikos / kritē*, which also link together the three verses of the third stanza. All three verses of the third stanza are linked together by *dos / paradō / apodōs*. The tight coherent structure we have traced in this short passage cannot

Q 12:49–59: Translation in Measured Verse for Hearing

A 1a {I came to cast fire on the earth
  b   and how I wish it had already been lighted!}
  2a [Does it seem] that I came to cast peace on the earth[?]
  b   I came to cast not peace but a sword!
  3a For I came to divide son [against] father
  b   [and] daughter [against] her mother
  c   [and] bride [against] her mother-in-law.

B 1a [When it is evening] you say, "Fair weather!"
  b   for the sky burns red.
  2a And early in the morning, "Today stormy weather!"
  b   for the sky burns darkening red.
  3a You know indeed how to judge the face of the sky
  b   but [can you] not {judge} the time?

C 1a [While] you {are} with your accuser on the way
  b   give exertion to be reconciled with him.
  2a Lest [the accuser] gives you over to the judge
  b   and the judge to the officer,.
  c   and [the officer throws you] in prison
  3a I say to you, you will not come out of there
  b   until you have paid the last penny!

---

be accidental. It represents the basic framework of the oral discourse which has been fossilized in text.

Code / Metonymic Reference

Since we are no longer privileged to be present at the actual communicative event underlying this text, we need to reconstruct the register. We have already argued that in an oral culture, the use of the restrictive code means that the reference is metonymic, *pars pro toto*, to the culture as mediated through a particular social class.

The first and most conspicuous metonymic expression is *elthon balein [anephthe] pur / eirenen / machairan epi ten gen.* A prima facie assumption must be that this is an expression relating to warfare or its absence. However, an examination of the use of this kind of language in the Hebrew Bible / Septuagint shows that (apart from some obvious but inappropriate verbal parallels concerning the three victims in Daniel!) this expression relates to God's response to the breach of the Mosaic covenant in Israel. A good example would be Psalm 78 (LXX 77), which specifically describes itself as the traditional covenantal law to be handed on to the next generation (78:18), so that they should not be disobedient like the wilderness generation. Curses follow disobedience to the covenant (Lev. 26:14–22). The consequence of their covenantal disobedience in the wilderness is that fire was kindled against them (Ps. 78:21, 62–63). This refers to Yahweh's holy war turned against Israel rather than its enemies because of its breach of the covenant.[38] Especially suggestive are the prophecies of Jeremiah, Lamentations, and Ezekiel (which are rendered mostly in the Septuagint by the expression *anapso / anapto pur* [Jer. 11:16; 17:27; 21:12, 14; 27:32 (LXX); Lam. 2:3; 4:11; Ezek. 21:3] or variations of *ana / kata kaio pur*). Fire unleashed against Israel or occasionally its enemies is described approximately sixty times. It is anthropomorphically understood as an outpouring of God's fiery wrath which burns up the wicked (Jer. 15:14; cf. Jer. 4:4, 26 [LXX]; Lam. 2:3; 4:11; Ezek. 36:5). The prophet Jeremiah experiences this fire of God's anger as a fire within himself which is expressed in prophetic words which kindle and burn (Jer. 5:14; 20:9; 23:29). In this way, the prophet is an agent in God's unleashing of the fire of judgment. Likewise in Ezekiel, the prophet's actions in burning his own hair are envisaged as unleashing fire on the city of Jerusalem (Jer. 1:10; Ezekiel 5). This act of the prophet is mirrored by the way the man dressed in linen takes coals from the altar fire of God's presence and casts them out over the city to inaugurate its burning (Ezek. 10:2, 6; 15).

The metonymic reference of *eirene* is the opposite of that of burning / sword (the prophetic announcement of war against a disobedient nation). It represents the state of blessedness which comes from obedience to the covenant, living out the conditions of the covenant:

> If you follow my statutes and keep my commandments and observe them faithfully, I will give you your rains in their season, and the land shall yield its produce, and the trees of the field shall yield their fruit. Your threshing shall overtake the vintage, and the vintage shall overtake the sowing; you shall eat your bread to the full, and live securely in your land. And I will grant peace in your land (*dōsō eirēnēn en tē gē hymōn*), and you shall lie down, and no one shall make you afraid; I will remove dangerous animals from the land, and no sword shall go through your land. (Lev. 26:3–6)

According to Jeremiah (17:58), it is the task of the prophet to pronounce the blessings or curses of the Lord, according to the obedience or disobedience of the people. False prophets have pronounced blessings, saying to the people: "You shall not see the sword, nor shall you have famine, but I will give you true peace in this place" (Jer. 14:13). God confirms the falsity of this prophecy and instead pronounces that sword and famine will indeed strike the land, beginning with the false prophets (14:15–16).

---

38. J. A. Draper, "The Development of the 'Sign of the Son of Man' in the Jesus Tradition: Its Roots in the Old Testament Holy War Tradition," *NTS* 39 (1993), 1–21.

Similarly, the reference to the weather in the context of prophetic oracles, as in the third stanza of Jesus' discourse, is found in Amos 8:12 (cf. Mic. 7:1), where the basket of summer fruit shows that the time is ripe for judgment. Drought was a sign of God's judgment just as rain was a sign of blessing. Such imagery is tied to the understanding of the land: its fruitfulness depended on obedience to the provisions of the covenant (cf. the interplay of these concepts in Isa. 45:8). That the weather can give a sign of the time of judgment (Amos 8:11) is dramatized still more into signs in the sky in Joel 2:2, 30–32 (but notice again the context of actual drought [1:4, 11–12]). The reference to being reconciled to the accuser on the way is addressed to the unjust rulers. It refers to the tradition of God summoning the wicked to argue their case in court with him (e.g., Isa. 3:13–15; Hos. 12:2; Mic. 6:12). The prophet's warning is an opportunity for the wicked to turn away from their violation of the covenantal precepts before it is too late (Jer. 4:12; Hos. 14:1–2; Amos 5:14–15).

Similar metonymic reference to divine wrath, fire, covenant, and fruitfulness also occurs in the preaching of John in Q 3:7–9. Unless the people bear fruit for God, they will be like a tree cut down and thrown onto the fire. The coming one will baptize with Holy Spirit and fire (3:16). He will sift the wheat and burn the chaff with fire (3:17).

To summarize: the metonymic reference of this discourse is not apocalyptic, as has sometimes been argued, but prophetic-covenantal. Jesus feels compelled, like Jeremiah and Ezekiel, to pronounce the fire of God's wrath in judgment because of disobedience to the provisions of the covenant. He makes a reference to a tradition we find also in Mic. 7:6, Micah being a prophet who denounces the false prophets of peace as savagely as Jeremiah (Mic. 3:5–7). Jesus sees himself called instead to pronounce judgment with a spirit of power which brings the prophecy to pass (Hos. 12:10; Mic. 3:8). The breach of the covenant declared by Micah concerns oppression of the poor by the rich and powerful. For them the judgment brings confusion and division: "For the son treats the father with contempt, the daughter rises up against her mother, the daughter-in-law against her mother-in-law; your enemies are members of your own household" (7:6). Jesus, in his turn, pronounces that the injustice and oppression visited on the poor by their rulers (in Jerusalem? in Sepphoris and Tiberias?) will bring confusion and disaster and understands his word to effect that judgement (*elthon balein pur / machairan*). He stands squarely within the tradition of covenantal prophecy in Israel.

Register

The metonymic referencing in Q 12:49–59 indicates that the type of context envisaged prophetic denunciation of covenantal injustice by the rulers against the poor. This draws on a fundamental cultural paradigm in Israel, its understanding of itself as a people dedicated to Yahweh and its land as held in covenant under Yahweh's protection. The field, what is happening and where, is that of the suffering and oppression of the poor under the weight of taxation and loss of land, into which the prophet speaks words of judgment against the oppressors. The tenor, who is speaking to whom, determined by Jesus' social location among poor Galilean peasants, is one of hope: God has not forgotten their affliction and is about to execute judgment. The mode of the discourse is clearly that of the prophetic oracle, familiar to us from the Hebrew Scriptures. The oral pronouncement of the oracle is a word of power, effecting what it pronounces.

Chapter 9

THE COVENANT RENEWAL DISCOURSE: Q 6:20–49

Richard A. Horsley _____

The Coherence and Covenantal Character of the Discourse

Recent interpretation of Q 6:20–49 rests on two key assertions that are not sub-
stantiated by argument and evidence. First, apparently on the assumption that
Jesus' sayings existed originally as separate aphorisms and admonitions, it is asserted that the component sections of Q 6:20–49 such as 6:27–36 or 6:39–45
were "clearly" constructed from "several originally independent sayings."[1] Second, surveys of the individual sayings of Q 6:20–49 conclude that the contents
"are overwhelmingly sapiential."[2] Ironically, the very compositional analyses that
contain these assertions also include observations about the integral connections between the sayings and supply evidence that the contents are not typically
sapiential.

With regard to the first assertion, compositional analyses of Q "clusters" or
collections find all sorts of "connections" between the sayings both within and
among these sections of 6:20–49. For example, besides the "catchword" connection between "when they hate you" in 6:22 and "those who hate you" in
6:27, substantive parallels are detected between 6:22–23 and 6:29, 30, 31, so
that 6:20–23b and 6:27–35 must have formed units before being joined. Then
it is discerned that 6:37a, 38c "further develops the preceding speech on love of
enemies and...explicates the programmatic injunction to imitate divine mercy
(6:36)."[3] Such observations, however, suggest that neither the individual sayings
nor the sections of 6:20–49 are all that independent and separate.

Several other factors confirm this suspicion of how the sayings in this discourse
cohere in an overall unity. Many of these sayings from across the sections into

---

1. John S. Kloppenborg, *The Formation of Q: Trajectories in Ancient Wisdom Collections* (Philadelphia: Fortress, 1987), 173–74, 182. Again in this chapter as in previous ones, I make frequent
reference to Kloppenborg's compositional analysis because it has been so influential in American
Q studies (including my own explorations of Q) and not to argue specifically with his particular
interpretation.
2. Ibid., 187, 189.
3. Ibid., 178, 181.

which Q 6:20–49 is divided by modern readers were recited together in clusters in Christian literature that is not dependent on either Luke or Matthew. *Didache* 1:3–5 (in parallel constructions suggestive of oral derivation) has variant versions of the sayings in Q 6:27–28, 32, 29a (Matt. 5:41), 29b, 30b, and 30a, in that sequence, ending with a reference to the Father, as in 6:36. Reciting "the words of the Lord Jesus," *1 Clement* 13:2 (in simple parallel lines that suggest oral derivation) includes different versions of "be merciful" in 6:36, "forgive and you will be forgiven" in 6:37c, the "golden rule" in 6:31, and "give and you will be given" in 6:38a, "judge not . . ." in 6:37a, "give . . . " in 6:30, and "the measure you give . . . " in 6:38c, in that sequence. Polycarp's *Letter to the Philippians* 2:3, after exhortation against "rendering evil for evil, etc." parallel to Q 6:27–30 (and in parallel construction suggesting oral derivation), recites the Lord's teaching with variant versions of sayings parallel to Q 6:37a, 37c, 36, 38c, 20b, and 22a (Matt. 5:11), in that sequence (and again in parallel construction suggesting oral derivation). The *Didache* parallel suggests that (most of) the sayings in Q 6:27–36 were recited together, and the other two parallel passages suggest that the sayings in Q 6:37–38 and the beatitudes also were recited together with those in 6:27–35.[4] We may begin to doubt that all these sayings were originally independent.

Close compositional analysis of three sections of 6:20–49 (along with other clusters of sayings in Q), moreover, finds both considerable coherence within those sections and clear links among them. Q 6:37–42 is one coherent collection of sayings, not two separate ones. "Leading" in 6:39 "is parallel in thought" to "judging" in 6:37–38, and 6:41–42 resumes the theme of "judging" and applies it to critical attitudes.[5] Besides this section's internal coherence, it is clearly connected with the preceding section and the subsequent one. The command about not judging is a further aspect of the command to love, and the application of 6:43–45 to the life of the community links it with 6:37–42.[6] Literary and compositional analyses have, in fact, already done much to demonstrate the extent to which Q 6:20–49 is a coherent discourse, not a cluster cobbled together by a intricate series of decontextualized addings and couplings. What Ronald A. Piper observes about Q 6:37–42 and 43–45 and other "collections" in Q might be said about Q 6:20–49 as a whole: "These are not haphazard collections . . . ; they display a design and argument unique in the synoptic tradition."[7]

The beatitudes (and woes) section might appear to be an exception. It is difficult to find a compositional analysis that suggests a way in which the fourth, which is longer and takes a different form, can be read as integral with rather than as an evident secondary addition to the first three, which are clearly parallel in form. If the standard procedure were widened, however, both from focus on

---

4. See Helmut Koester, *Synoptische Überlieferung bei den apostolischen Vätern*, TU 65 (Berlin: Akademie, 1957), for how these sayings were carried in oral tradition.

5. Ronald A. Piper, *Wisdom in the Q Tradition*, SNTSMS 61 (Cambridge: Cambridge University Press, 1989), 40, 43.

6. Ibid., 44, 51, 71.

7. Ibid., 64.

individual sayings to broader rhetorical patterns and from focus almost exclusively on Q itself to other Jewish and Christian literature, the beatitudes could be appreciated as a unitary step in the wider discourse. Perhaps the broader pattern of beatitudes in both the *Acts of Paul and Thecla* 5–6 and *2 Enoch* 42:6–14 was not taken seriously because it comes from somewhat later literature. Both works contain a long sequence of shorter beatitudes which all take the same form concluded by a much longer one that has a somewhat different form, with a double or elaborative motive or reward clause. A document is now available from Qumran that dates this rhetorical pattern as already standard well before the time of Jesus. In 4Q525, a series of five (or possibly more in a preceding column) two-line "blessings" is present in the plural, followed by a much longer final blessing that is singular and ends with an apparently long "for…" clause.[8]

With regard to the second assertion, that the sayings included in Q 6:20–49 are overwhelmingly sapiential, recent compositional analyses repeatedly make qualifications or provoke critical scrutiny and further investigation. The form of the beatitudes

> is common in sapiential literature. But…the beatitudes of Jesus are not simple moral or religious exhortations of wisdom; they are proclamations of eschatological salvation. And unlike both sapiential beatitudes and the majority of those found in apocalyptic books, the Q beatitudes do not function as conditions of salvation or admonitions concerning how one ought to act; instead they pronounce blessings upon a group defined by social and economic circumstances: poverty, hunger, sorrow and persecution. In Q they pronounce blessing upon the community.[9]

In this regard the Q beatitudes have the form and function of covenantal blessings, not sapiential macarisms, as we shall explore below. Sapiential parallels for the conclusion of "the sermon" in Q 6:46–49 are offered from the occurrence of the figure of a ruined house or description of rewards at the end of many wisdom collections.[10] All but one or two of the thirteen cases listed, however, are not particularly clear or not good parallels. The most interesting case, Prov. 2:20–22, concluding 2:1–22, is potentially pertinent to Q 6:46–49 not because it closes a sapiential speech but because it takes the form of a covenantal two-ways scheme in a collection of wisdom (Proverbs 1–9) clearly influenced by covenantal Torah and its forms. Thus the beginning and closing of the speech in Q 6:20–49 are not sapiential in character, but if anything covenantal.

---

8. Translation from Geza Vermes, *The Complete Dead Sea Scrolls in English* (London and New York: Allen Lane, 1997), 424–25.

9. Kloppenborg, *Formation of Q*, 188. The Q beatitudes oppose the conventional wisdom that the affluent and comfortable are blessed, suggests Hans-Dieter Betz, *Essays on the Sermon on the Mount* (Philadelphia: Fortress, 1985), 17–36. If the Q beatitudes are thus "not typically sapiential in content," it is unclear how frequent addition of the adjective "radical" somehow justifies their characterization as sapiential after all — *pace* Kloppenborg, *Formation of Q*, 189.

10. Arland D. Jacobson, "Wisdom Christology in Q" (Ph.D. diss., Claremont Graduate School, 1978), 110; idem, *The First Gospel: An Introduction to Q* (Sonoma, Calif.: Polebridge, 1992), 96 n. 85; Kloppenborg, *Formation of Q*, 186.

Critical review of the arguments for the sapiential idiom of the admonitions in Q 6:27–45 suggests similar results. "Imitation of the divine virtue" is indeed a common topic in Hellenistic philosophy, and Hellenistic Jewish texts speak specifically of God's mercy (e.g., *Pseudo-Aristeas* 208). God's mercy and the call for people to imitate it, however, constitute a prominent, even central, theme in the Hebrew Bible, especially in covenantal contexts.[11] Leviticus 19 provides a window onto explicitly covenantal teaching framed by a "programmatic injunction to imitate the divine," teaching with other parallels to Q 6:27–36, as we shall see. Argument for the sapiential character of Q 6:27–36 rejects covenantal Torah as a possible background with the observation that only the Matthean redaction (with the formula "you have heard that it was said in ancient times") brings the Torah reinterpretation to the fore.[12] As discussed in chapters 5 and 6, however, the "Torah" functioned in multiple versions and at different social locations in late second-temple times.[13] It is difficult to understand the claim that the more discursive formulations about meeting an enemy with good rather than evil or turning enemies into friends found in sapiential sources and Hellenistic philosophy are much closer in form and content to the commandment to "love your enemies" than is the command to "love your neighbor" in the wider covenantal context of Lev. 19:18.[14] The sayings that refer to concrete social interaction — and specifically Israelite tradition — can be excised to make the remaining cluster of Q 6:27–28, 32–33, 35a, c, appear more sapiential in sentiment. The sayings cited as sapiential parallels (Sir. 4:3–5; 4:10; Tob. 4:7–8), however, turn out not only to be addressed to scribes / sages who stand in a mediating position between the people addressed in Q and their potential oppressors but also to be central covenantal teaching in their contents and literary context (Sir. 3:30–4:10; Tob. 4:5–19!). Although it appears only at the very end of Luke 6:45 in a saying not paralleled in Matt. 12:35, the issue of speech is taken as the concern of Q 6:43–45, a reading that fits the program of finding sapiential characteristics in the "sermon." Q 6:43–45, however, with its emphasis on the source of behavior, "is not typical of general sapiential teaching on speech" such as Prov. 14:1–4 and Sir. 28:13–26, which focus on the results of careless speech.[15] Thus when Q 6:20–49 does appear to have topics in common with sapiential literature, it treats them in a nonsapiential way. More striking yet, however, is that in Q 6:20–49 and the other supposedly sapiential "collections" in Q "many themes popular in sapiential instruction are completely absent."[16]

Finally, the overall structure of 6:20–49 that is supposedly "paralleled in many wisdom collections" turns out to be difficult to find in the two examples given,

---

11. Cf. the discussion in Kloppenborg, *Formation of Q,* 180–81, with citations.

12. Ibid., 178–79; cf. Piper, *Wisdom in the Q Tradition,* 74–75.

13. See esp. pp. 99–104, 114–17, 136–38.

14. *Pace* Dieter Zeller, *Die weisheitliche Mahnsprüche bei den Synoptiken* (Würzburg: Echter, 1977), 104–6, with multiple citations from sapiential and philosophical sources.

15. Piper, *Wisdom in the Q Tradition,* 50.

16. Ibid., 71.

Proverbs 1 and 3:13–35. Careful comparative scrutiny of all three texts finds no such parallel structure and organization. "The collection [Q 6:20–49] opens with a programmatic statement in the form of four beatitudes; the body of instructions consists of sapiential admonitions..., and it closes with a typically sapiential warning."[17] But with regard to Q 6:20–49 itself, it is unclear that the beatitudes are programmatic for what follows, and the sapiential parallels offered for the closing warning turn out to be unconvincing, as noted above. More problematically, however, neither Proverbs 1 nor Prov. 3:13–35 fits into such a structure. Prov. 1:2–7 appears to be the "programmatic statement" for the whole collection of Proverbs 1–9 rather than just for Proverbs 1. The rest of Proverbs 1 consists of two separate units, a fatherly warning addressed to "my child" about greed for gain in 1:8–19, and Wisdom's own prophet-like harangue against those who reject her counsel in 1:20–33. Proverbs 1:32–33, or rather 1:31–33, then forms the closing only to Wisdom's harangue, with verse 33 providing a surprising positive twist at the very end. Prov. 3:13–35 also appears to fall into (two) separate units. The first begins with a beatitude, 3:13–14, continues with a praise of Wisdom even for her role in creation in 3:15–20, and closes with an exhortation to "my child" not to let Wisdom escape from his/her sight in 3:21–26. The second unit consists of a series of prohibitions in 3:27–31 focused, interestingly enough, on typical covenantal concerns to aid and not take advantage of the needy, to which 3:33–35 forms the closing sanction, again in the covenantal terms of the Lord's "blessing and curse" on the respective houses of the righteous and the wicked. Only one of these five units or speeches in Proverbs 1 and 3:13–35 turns out to have a three-part structure, and except for the opening beatitude, that structure (praise of Wisdom and address to "my child") is not at all similar to the structure of Q 6:20–49.

Indeed, it has proven difficult to find any clear parallels in Jewish wisdom literature to the pattern of argument that can be discerned in parts of Q 6:20–49 and in other Q discourses.[18] The closest possibility, the exhortation against adultery in Prov. 6:25–29, is difficult to isolate as a unit from its literary context of Prov. 6:20–35. The few possibilities in Sirach seem "remote." And "no comparably constructed sections are evident in...Wisdom of Solomon, Tobit, the *Testaments of the XII Patriarchs* or *1 En.* 91ff.... It was [not] common for aphoristic traditions to 'grow together' into such a pattern.... [In Q] one is dealing with highly individual style of argument, rather than one which can claim to have many parallels in tradition."[19] It is surely significant, however, than in arguments for the sapiential character of Q 6:20–49, covenantal references, contents, and forms keep forcing their way to the surface despite attempts to suppress their relevance. These should clearly be explored rather than suppressed, and explored in their broader structure as well as particular forms and contents.

---

17. Kloppenborg, *Formation of Q*, 189.

18. "It is significant that relatively little can be found in the way of parallels to this structure in the Jewish wisdom literature" (Piper, *Wisdom in the Q Tradition*, 66).

19. Ibid., 68.

That Q 6:20–49 not only is decidedly different from sapiential instruction in substance and tone but is also rich in distinctively covenantal forms and teachings goes unrecognized for several reasons. One is that biblical scholars have been oriented to the written text of the Torah / Law and not cognizant of the oral cultivation of Torah and the variant traditions of covenantal teaching that prevailed in second-temple times. Matthew's reshaping of Q 6:20–49 and other Q materials into his "Sermon on the Mount" is recognized as a covenant renewal — or even the giving of a new law — because of the explicit recitations of commandments from the decalogue ("you have heard it said of old"). Another reason that the covenantal form of Q 6:20–49 goes unrecognized is the lack of attention to the structural features of Q discourses. Yet it is surely significant that the structure of Matthew's recognizably covenantal sermon follows the structure of Q 6:20–49 to a remarkable degree, with the same opening (the beatitudes from Q 6:20–23), the same closing (the double parable in Matt. 7:24–27 from Q 6:47–49), and the same set of admonitions in between (the "love your enemies" set of sayings from Q 6:27–36). The structure of Matthew's "sermon" which is acknowledged to be covenantal was already present in Q 6:20–49. It seems likely, further, that Luke as well as Matthew understood this Q discourse as a covenant. Parallel to Matthew's introductory statement about Jesus going up onto the mountain where he delivers the long covenantal speech — reminiscent of Moses on Sinai — Luke has Jesus go "out to the mountain to pray" just before he delivers the parallel speech to the disciples (Matt. 5:1; Luke 6:12).

The most obviously covenantal contents in Q 6:20–49, even by traditional scholarly criteria, are the teachings in 6:27–36. Even to the eye focused narrowly on scriptural texts, "Be merciful, just as your Father is merciful" clearly alludes to the opening summary statement in the covenantal teaching in Lev. 19:2, "You shall be holy, for I the LORD your God am holy." Indeed, the whole central section of the Q discourse (6:27–42) appears to have been formulated with reference to traditional covenantal teaching along the lines found in Lev. 19:17–18: "You shall not hate your brother in your heart, but you shall reason with your neighbor, lest you bear sin because of him. You shall not take vengeance or bear a grudge against the sons of your own people, but you shall love your neighbor as yourself." The formulation of the love command with reference to the enemy also alludes to traditional covenantal teaching, such as that in Exod. 23:4–5 and Deut. 22:1–4. The issue of lending generously (and without interest! Exod. 22:25; Lev. 25:35–38) was a central concern in covenantal teaching, and symbolically taking (and then immediately returning) the creditor's outer garment as a pledge for a small-scale local loan was, of course, a well-known practice (Exod. 22:25–26; Deut. 24:10–13; cf. Amos 2:8).[20] It is surely significant that what has long been recognized as basically the same set of sayings occurs in a clearly covenantal context

---

20. These and other covenantal passages as the background to Luke 6:27–36//Matt. 5:38–48 were noted in Richard A. Horsley, *Jesus and the Spiral of Violence: Popular Jewish Resistance in Roman Palestine* (San Francisco: Harper & Row, 1987), 265–73.

of "two-ways" teaching in *Did.* 1:3–5, where it is paired with another set of sayings (*Didache* 2) derived largely from the decalogue and concluded by a shorter combination reminiscent of "love your enemies" in Q 6:27–28.

In order to explore the covenantal character and structure of Q 6:20–49, however, we must focus on the concern and function of the whole discourse for a community; that is, we must investigate the *register* in which the discourse was recited. And since New Testament scholars tend to underestimate the presence and importance of the ancient Israelite covenantal tradition, it is necessary to explore that *tradition* in order to appreciate both the context in which a speaker would utilize such a register and the way in which Israelites would resonate to that tradition when hearing such a covenantal speech.

The Continuing Importance of Covenantal Patterns and Teaching

Mosaic covenantal forms and teachings are prominent in much of the Hebrew Bible, and they continue their central role in extra- and postbiblical Judean literature. Focus here must be first on the basic biblical texts of covenant-giving and covenant renewal and then on Qumran documents that exhibit covenantal forms and teachings functioning actively closer to the time of Jesus and Q.

Covenantal Form and Covenant Renewal in Israelite Biblical Tradition

The Mosaic covenant appears to have been central to the life of Israel. Indeed it would appear to have functioned as the unwritten (and later written) "constitution" that provided principles of unity and social policy that held Israel together as a society of semiautonomous local village communities. The Mosaic covenant, particularly as it plays over against the Davidic and Abrahamic covenant(s), is so prominent in the Hebrew Bible[21] as to have become the organizing principle even for Protestant "theologies" of the "Old Testament."[22] Comparative study of ancient Near Eastern international treaties in the 1950s and 1960s aided the clearer discernment of the distinctive structure of the Mosaic covenant and its constituent components as it was elaborated and deployed in materials incorporated into the Hebrew Bible.[23] Treaties given by the Hittite emperors to their subject kings appeared to have six (or seven) components: the name of the emperor giving the treaty; a historical prologue recounting the favors that the great king and his ancestors had done for the vassal king and his ancestors; a list of

---

21. Of course since we can no longer assume that scripture was already set, accepted, and ubiquitous in late second-temple Judea and Galilee, we must treat texts such as Exodus 20; 21–23; Deuteronomy, and the holiness code in Leviticus as examples of or windows onto the kind of covenantal patterns, codes, and exhortations that would have been cultivated in the Israelite great and little traditions.

22. For example, Walther Eichrodt, *Theology of the Old Testament* (Philadelphia: Westminster, 1961).

23. See George Mendenhall, *Law and Covenant in Israel and the Ancient Near East* (Pittsburgh: Presbyterian Board, 1955); Klaus Baltzer, *The Covenant Formulary* (Philadelphia: Fortress, 1971 [1964]).

stipulations undertaken by the subject king, basically concerning exclusive loyalty to the great king and mutual relations among the subject kings; a provision for periodic recitation of the treaty text; a list of divine witnesses; and blessings and curses upon the vassal(s) for keeping or not keeping the stipulations, respectively.

The key biblical texts of the Mosaic covenant appeared to have the same basic structure.[24] In the covenant given on Sinai in Exod. 20:2–17 (repeated in Deut. 5:6–21), the name ("I am Yahweh your God") has been conflated with a brief historical prologue about God's deliverance of the people from Egypt ("who brought you out of…the house of slavery"). The "decalogue" then gives ten fundamental stipulations, four covering relations between Israelites and Yahweh (20:3, 4–5a, 7, 8–10) and six concerning key aspects of social-economic relations among Israelites (20:12–17), with a blessing- and curse-like sanction inserted into the second stipulation (20:5b–6, and perhaps also into the fifth, 20:12b). Literarily, the original giving of the covenant in Exodus 20 is followed by a covenantal "law code" of "ordinances" in Exodus 21–23 that apply the basic principles of social policy in the decalogue to social-economic life, and the whole is framed by covenantal ceremonies in Exodus 19 and 24. The same structural components can be discerned in the covenant renewal ceremony in Josh. 24:1–28. Following the lengthy historical prologue reciting what Yahweh has done for Israel (24:2–13), comes a call and commitment to exclusive service to Yahweh (24:14–28) that involves obligation to observe "statutes and ordinances" (24:24–26), along with the writing of the statutes (for future recitation, 24:26), the people witnessing against themselves and a large stone as witness (24:22, 26–27), and the threat of punishment for violation of the stipulations (24:19–20). The book of Deuteronomy as a whole is structured according to these same components. Most of the book consists of covenantal statutes and ordinances along with plenty of covenantal preaching in a long speech by Moses, prefaced by a giving of the decalogue and interspersed with references to witnessing (Deut. 4:44–26:19). Not surprisingly, the book begins with a long historical review that now interweaves God's deliverance of the people with Israel's grumbling and rebellion and a reassurance of God's mercy (Deut. 1:6–4:43). The book then ends with an exhortation to write the "words of this law" on large stones (for periodic reading) and two ceremonial series of "(blessings and) curses," Deuteronomy 27 and 28. Moses' third speech in Deuteronomy 29–30 is yet another recitation of the Mosaic covenant, with emphasis on a reminder of God's deliverance and remembering the blessings and curses.

It is not difficult to discern the interrelated functions and dynamics of the covenantal components within the overall covenantal structure. The purpose of

---

24. The details of the extent to which Hebrew biblical materials parallel the pattern of ancient international treaties have been widely debated. Moreover, Baltzer includes a "statement of substance" as a separate component prior to the "stipulations" or "covenant teachings/laws" in the overall covenantal structure. The point to be gleaned here is discernment of the fundamental components and structure of the Mosaic covenant that persist through much Hebrew biblical literature and later Judean texts.

the structure as a whole is for the people to observe the stipulations. The historical prologue reciting God's gracious deliverance of the people lays the basis of their obligation to keep the stipulations. The periodic recitation, witnesses, and particularly the blessings and curses serve to motivate observance of the stipulations. Considering that the exclusive kingship of God demanded in the covenantal stipulations meant that Israel would have no central government enforcing the covenant, Israel's spiritual-historical relation to God, particularly in its memory of God's deliverance and the shaping of its desire for future well-being, was instrumental for its obedience to the covenantal principles.

Given the centrality of the Mosaic covenant, its structural components and substantive teaching, it should not be surprising that both covenantal recitation and covenant renewal persisted in biblical history, particularly at points of historical crisis for the people of Israel or Judah. The overall plot of the biblical narrative places the covenant renewals in the book of Deuteronomy and in Joshua 24 at crucial points when the people are about to embark on their life in the land. Subsequent covenant renewals still follow the same basic structure, while adapting the structural components and changing their contents to new historical circumstances. The structure appears to be simplified into the two or three basic components of historical prologue of what God has done for the people, God's stipulations or the obligations of the people, and a promise of reward (blessing) for keeping and punishment (curse) for not keeping the covenantal stipulations. In Nehemiah 9–10, for example, an elaborate historical prologue, no longer stated by God in the first person but in a prayer to God, begins with creation and Abraham and (like Deuteronomy 1–4) recounts extensively Israel's apostasy and God's continuing patience and deliverance (Nehemiah 9). The "commandments . . . and ordinances and statutes" of God that the people vow to observe focus on support of the temple and the priesthood, with little attention to the original Mosaic principles (Neh. 9:38–10:39).

Covenantal teaching was also continued in other forms. Already in the formation of Deuteronomy the presentation of Mosaic covenantal materials was couched in terms of two ways, the way of life and the way of death (Deut. 30:15–20). In this two-ways form the "blessings and curses" became the rewards or punishments that would result from choosing the way of life or the way of death, respectively. In a closely related development, as scribal circles identified more closely with the Mosaic covenantal materials incorporated into the books that became the Torah, they identified the wisdom that they had traditionally cultivated with the Torah. Both of these developments are presupposed in the collection of sapiential discourses comprising Proverbs 1–9, and the identification of Wisdom as a personified heavenly figure with the Torah is dramatically portrayed in Sirach 24. Sayings that might be formally classified as "sapiential," therefore, might well be sapientially shaped covenantal teaching. Sirach 29:1 ("The merciful lend to their neighbors; by holding out a helping hand they keep the commandments"), for example, presents an illustration of sages' perpetuation of the central Mosaic covenantal theme (Exod. 22:25) of mercy manifested in local economic relations.

With regard to the contents of the covenant, biblical scholars have had trouble recognizing the extent to which it concerns social-economic-political affairs, largely because they are embedded in modern Western cultures that consign to separate spheres, even separate institutions, the economic, political, and religious dimensions of life that are inseparable in traditional agrarian societies such as ancient Israel and second-temple Judea and Galilee. Along with the people's exclusive loyalty to God, the basic concern of the covenantal stipulations is social-economic life. Three of the ten commandments (you shall not covet, steal, or bear false witness) deal directly with economic life, and three others (no murder, no adultery, and honor father and mother) include the economic dimension of a society in which the patriarchal household was the fundamental unit of production and consumption. This becomes all the more evident when we attend to the "statutes and ordinances" through which the commandments are applied to concrete social interaction. Killing or maiming a person or even a farm animal required economic compensation because it limited the family's ability to maintain economic subsistence (Exod. 21:22, 35–36; 22:1, 5, 6, 14, 16–17).

Given the importance of economic life in the fundamental principles of the covenant, it is not surprising that the covenantal "statutes and ordinances" and other biblical covenantal teachings include elaborate provisions for maintaining the economic viability of each family/household in the village community that constituted the fundamental social unit of Israel. The land was understood as belonging ultimately to God, who had granted each family some land as an inalienable ancestral inheritance (Lev. 25:23–24; 1 Kings 21:1–4). Given the unpredictable contingencies such as weather, however, a harvest sufficient to support a peasant family in a subsistence economy was always uncertain. In order to avoid some taking advantage of others in such situations, Israel developed mechanisms to maintain the economic viability of each family on its ancestral inheritance. That these interrelated mechanisms are included in several different covenantal "law codes" indicates just how basic they were to the society and its covenantal tradition. Israelites are to give or lend to their unfortunate neighbors or brothers and are to lend without interest (Exod. 22:25–27; Deut. 15:7–11; Lev. 25:35–38). The purpose of allowing the land to lie fallow every seventh year, according to the earliest law code (Exod. 23:10–11), is "so that the poor may eat," although in the holiness code this shifts to "rest for the land" (Lev. 25:2–7). The poor also had rights to glean from the produce left in the field after harvest (Deut. 19:20–22; Lev. 19:9–10). For more serious difficulties of spiraling indebtedness and enslavement for debt, Israelite covenantal economic policy declared the cancellation of debts and the release of debt slaves every seven years (Exod. 21:2–6; Deut. 15:1–5, 9, 12–18; Lev. 25:39–43). For the loss of the inalienable family inheritance, there was provision for redemption of the land by the next of kin (Lev. 25:24–28, 48). If all else failed there was, finally, the clearly idealized declaration of the "jubilee" in the fiftieth year (after seven sevens) in which all would return to the ancestral land (Lev. 25:8–24), although there are serious doubts whether this provision was ever implemented. In its concern to maintain the economic rights and viability of a free peasantry, the Mosaic covenantal tradition of ancient Israel resembles many more recent peasant societies in which the economic rights of the people are protected by time-honored customs that discourage the exploitation of some by others or by outside landlords and rulers.[25]

The covenantal materials that comprise much of the second half of Exodus, much of Leviticus, and most of Deuteronomy, of course, cover many more issues and contingencies than the economic rights and relations of the peasantry. Deuteronomy includes laws or instructions on matters such as tithes and offerings to the Jerusalem temple and the obligations of pilgrimage festivals (Deuteronomy 12; 14:22–29; 16), the Levitical priests and dues to them (Deut. 18:1–8), and the administration of justice (Deuteronomy 17 and 19), with only one brief paragraph on the king (17:14–20) that restricts his power and privilege and requires him to study torah and adhere to the covenantal commandments! The legal material in Deuteronomy expands on the potential contingencies that accompany typical legal cases. The holiness code in Leviticus 17–26 includes much cultic material within the framework of covenantal law and teaching. Leviticus 19, which will be of particular pertinence to Q 6:20–49, is specially interesting in its inclusion of admonitions against holding grudges, harboring resentment, and allowing hate to simmer (Lev. 19:17–18). This covenantal exhortation goes beyond case laws for concrete occurrences of violence and injury to the social tensions and conflicts that fester in social relations and that might lead to violence.

Mosaic covenantal recitations, law codes, and exhortations were not simply patterns and ideas articulated in biblical literature. Numerous biblical and other references indicate that the Mosaic covenant was operative in the life of Israel. Indeed, its functioning in village life appears to be presupposed by the periodic prophetic protests about its violation by the ruling elite. Jeremiah provides a window onto how the Davidic monarchy found it expedient suddenly to observe the release of debt slaves in the midst of a siege, only to revert to its exploitative practices once the crisis was over (Jeremiah 34). It is surely noteworthy that the account presents both the covenant God made with Israel after the deliverance from slavery in Egypt and the covenant Zedekiah made with the wealthy Jerusalemites not only as implying but as consisting in liberation from slavery: covenant means, or rather is, liberation from slavery (34:8–10, 13–14). Violation of the covenant, moreover, entails a punitive sentence (34:17–22). Jeremiah himself exercised the next of kin's right of redemption, partly as a symbolic action in the face of the imminent Babylonian devastation of Judea (Jeremiah 32). In another significant case, it is necessary for the Persian governor to force the Jerusalem elite to cease charging interest from, to cancel the debts of, to release the debt slaves among, and to restore the lands of the Judean peasants who have been forced to borrow in order to meet their obligations for temple dues

---

25. See esp. James C. Scott, *The Moral Economy of the Peasant* (New Haven: Yale University Press, 1976). Judging from the striking parallels Scott presents of the "moral economy" of other peasant societies, the original covenantal policies in early Israel aimed at maintaining an egalitarian social-economic order with each family viable on its land as an inalienable right.

and imperial taxes (Neh. 5:1–13). These accounts of the concrete functioning of covenantal provisions in the history of Israel, along with the many indictments by the prophets particularly of the rulers and their officers for specific violations of covenantal prohibitions, allow us to discern that the Mosaic covenant did occasionally function in political-economic relations between the peasants and the rulers, precisely when the latter became overbearing in their exploitative practices. That it could ever function effectively in this way suggests that the Mosaic covenant was solidly rooted in village life, in the popular tradition, from which position the prophets raised their indictments and the peasants their protests.

Covenantal Forms, Covenantal Teachings, and Covenantal Ceremony in Qumran Texts

Most important for analysis of the covenant renewal discourse in Q are the explicitly covenantal texts found among the Dead Sea Scrolls at Qumran, especially the Community Rule and the Damascus Document. For modern interpreters the most fascinating features of the Community Rule (1QS) were the sweeping dualistic world-historical perspective and the eschatological intensity evident in the opening of the text. All history is ruled by the two conflicting spirits, the Prince of Light and the Angel of Darkness, who thus also control individual behavior and determine membership among the "sons of light" (the community itself) and the "sons of darkness." Despite God's creation of the two spirits in the first place, God, in his glorious wisdom, has ordained an end for injustice and will finally bring back the conditions of the original Edenic creation (1QS 3:13–4:26). Also striking was the detailed and intense rigor of the community's rules, which make previous Christian constructions of Pharisaic legalism pale by comparison. While heavily adapted to suit the apocalyptic perspective and rigorous discipline of the community, the Community Rule from Qumran (1QS and parallels from 4Q) not only includes basic Mosaic covenantal material; the document is also a renewed Mosaic covenant in form. And it includes instructions for the ceremony of covenant renewal. It has been clear since the document was first examined that it contains numerous striking covenantal motifs. It is far more significant that the document as a whole follows the basic structure of the traditional Mosaic covenant and its renewal and that it adapts that traditional structure in ways that are highly suggestive for analysis of the covenant renewal discourse in Q 6:20–49.

Shortly after key Dead Sea Scrolls such as the Community Rule became available, Klaus Baltzer pointed out the covenantal structure of the section in 1QS 3:13–4:26.[26] The "dogmatic section" with which it begins (1QS 3:15–4:1), despite focusing on God's creation and human destiny instead of God's historical actions, still functions as a prologue. The "ethical section" (1QS 4:2–6, 9–11), keyed by the reference to the two "ways," transforms the earlier stipulations guiding social relations into a "catalogue of virtues and vices" characterizing human dispositions, yet still expresses the covenantal obligations for community life and

---

26. Baltzer, *Covenant Formulary*, 99–107.

their opposite. The "blessings and curses" (4:6–8, 12–14) that follow the list of "virtues and vices," respectively, more clearly continue the form as well as the substance of the sanctioning component of the covenantal structure.

Covenantal components, forms, and overall covenantal structure, however, are not confined to 1 QS 3:13–4:26. They virtually pervade the Community Rule as a whole. The section in 3:13–4:26 not only includes the three key structural components of prologue, stipulations, and blessings and curses; that section also constitutes the historical prologue component in the wider covenantal pattern that structures the Community Rule as a whole. Indeed, 1QS 3:13–4:26 is a sustained instruction by the "master" for "the sons of light" covering the four-fold subject matter indicated at the outset (3:13–14), incorporating the three covenantal elements and, as a final step, God's final termination of injustice (that the struggle between the two spirits "explains"). This complete fourfold instruction, then, provides a grand review of what God is doing in history as a whole, as the prologue to the remainder of the document, the rule proper, that consists of laws and procedures to be followed in the community, respectively, by the community in general (5:1–6:23), by community courts (6:24–7:26), by the council of the community (8:10–19), by the community members generally (8:19–9:11), and by the master (9:12–10:5 or 9:12–11:24). Traditional Mosaic covenantal components and structure, moreover, are further evident in the opening instructions for admission of members into the covenant that constitutes the community. In the opening instruction on induction of members, the priests and Levites, respectively, are to recite God's mighty deeds of redemption and the iniquities of Israel (1QS 1:19 — 2:1), then to pronounce blessings on the insiders and curses on the outsiders (2:2–11), followed by curses on those who enter but fail to keep the rigorous discipline required (2:12–19). Throughout it is assumed that those entering the covenant are undertaking to "obey all [God's] commandments" (1:17–18).

The Damascus Document, known prior to the discovery of the Dead Sea Scrolls and now supplemented by variations from Qumran, appears to follow the same broad covenantal structure as the Community Rule. It begins with a lengthy "historical prologue" in 1:1–6:11 ranging from Abraham to the present, including Israel's transgression of the covenant (cf. Nehemiah 9) and particularly the group's own history in the recent past (3:13–6:11). A brief section of stipulations for the group in 6:11–7:4 is then followed by declarations of long life and God's salvation for those who keep the covenant and retribution for those who do not (in 7:4–6, 8–10 and recension B, 2:28–36).[27] It would also be possible to take the laws and instructions for community life in the rest of the document as the stipulations section of an overall covenantal structure, somewhat as Exodus 21–23 extends into laws the more fundamental stipulations in Exod. 20:3–17.

The presence of covenantal component forms in the Qumran Community Rule and the covenantal structure of the major sections of the rule indicate both that Mosaic covenantal forms were alive and well in second-temple Judean society and

---

27. See further ibid., 112–17.

that those forms were adapted in response to new historical crises to which Judean groups were responding. Equally if not more significant for assessing covenantal forms and materials in Q, moreover, are four further facets of covenantal forms and teachings in the Community Rule.

First, most striking in the covenantal material and structure of 1QS is that in both the opening instructions and the longer covenantal instruction the function of the blessings and curses has changed from what it was in the original structure of the Mosaic covenant. In the latter, both blessings and curses were called down upon the Israelites as a motivation to keep the covenantal principles in their exclusive loyalty to God and their social relations among themselves. In the opening instructions of 1QS, the blessings and particularly the curses upon potentially backsliding brothers (1QS 2:2–4, 11–19) still function as sanctions on maintaining the covenantal commandments. But the paired blessings and curses (1QS 2:2–4, 5–10) now apply respectively to the "men of the lot of God" and the "men of the lot of Belial." That is, the blessings and curses now distinguish the insiders from the outsiders and reassure the members of the group of their own specially favored standing with God, their own favored election and redemption by God's gracious will. In the longer covenantal instruction that follows, the blessings and curses no longer function as closing sanctions motivating covenant-keeping by the members of the community. They have now been completely taken up into the declaration of God's deliverance. World history, and thereby the covenantal community's own situation, is explained in terms of the struggle between the Spirits of Light and Darkness. Incorporated into the explanation of the community's own beleaguered situation and God's imminent termination of the reign of the Spirit of Darkness are the respective "visitations" of those who live under the power of the respective spirits. For those who live by the Spirit of Light, it will be the traditional covenantal blessings of "long life and fruitfulness, together with every everlasting blessing and eternal joy." For those under the Spirit of Darkness, the visitation will be the traditional covenantal curses of mourning, misery, and shameful destruction of their lineages (1QS 4:2–14). Thus in the Qumran Community Rule, the covenantal component of blessings and curses that had traditionally functioned as a motivating sanction on keeping the rules and ordinances is (incorporated) transformed into (part of) the historical prologue that constitutes the basis of the people's obligation to maintain the rules. A declaration of God's deliverance in the present and/or future complements or replaces that of God's deliverance in the past as the basis of the people's exclusive loyalty and commitment to God and their maintenance of covenantal social relations.

Second, in connection with the blessings and curses being transformed in placement and function to (part of) the prologue that declares God's present and future salvation of the addressees in the Community Rule, it is significant that the equivalent of the blessings and curses component in the Damascus Document is a declaration of salvation for covenant-keepers and destruction for covenant-violators without the explicit language of blessing and curse. The same is true of the corresponding component in the *Epistle of Barnabas* (21:1), an early Christian text also structured according to the threefold covenantal form (and the same is apparently also true in *Did.* 6:2).[28] Qumran covenant renewal texts thus attest both the transformation of blessings and curses into a new declaration of deliverance and the covenantal declaration of final salvation and punishment without the explicit terms of "blessings" and "curses."

Third, also noteworthy in the Community Rule is that the opening instructions are explicitly for ceremonial procedure, and other passages indicate that oral presentations were a regular feature of the community (1QS 5:6–11; 6:14–16). We could not have clearer and more explicit evidence that renewal of the Mosaic covenant was ceremonially enacted. And that indicates that covenantal instruction was delivered orally to the covenantal community by the master and/or priests and Levites. "All those entering the Covenant" were literally entering the covenantal community in a ceremony of induction. The priests and Levites were literally "blessing" God and ceremonially "blessing the men of the lot of God" and literally pronouncing "curses on all the men of the lot of Belial." The renewal of the covenant was an annual performance, enacted with ritual processions and pronouncements (1QS 2:19–22). The literate scribes in the community behind 1QS and other scrolls discovered at Qumran have written all this down, but the written form of covenant renewal and instruction was instrumental (or was it incidental?) to regular oral performance in and by a community.

Fourth, a number of themes and particular features of the covenantal teachings in the Community Rule invite comparison with those in the Q covenant renewal discourse. The "prologue" proclaims "an end for injustice" (1 QS 4:18–24; cf. the blessings in Q 6:20–21). The community that holds fast to the renewed covenant "shall practice . . . justice and uprightness and charity and modesty, . . . [and] no stubbornness of heart" (1 QS 5:4–6), and the community members "shall love each man his brother as himself; they shall succor the poor, the needy, and the stranger" (CD 6:20–21; cf. 1Q 6:27–39). No one is to "address a companion with anger or ill-temper" or "hate him, . . . but [is to] rebuke him . . . [and] admonish him in the presence of witnesses" (1 QS 5:25–6:1; paralleled in CD 7:2–3; 9:2–5; cf. Q 6:37–38; and the closely related Q 17:1–4).

This brief review of covenantal form and teachings in Hebrew biblical passages and particularly the examination of the adaptation of the covenantal form by a roughly contemporary covenantal community should provide the appropriate tradition with which the Q covenantal discourse would have resonated.

The "Text" of Q 6:20–49

Most texts in Greek, Roman, and Jewish antiquity were embedded in an oral communication environment, as discussed in chapter 6. Even when poetry or narrative or a philosophical discussion had been written down on parchment or papyrus, it

---

28. Ibid., 126–27, 129; see further below.

was still ordinarily recited or "performed" orally before a larger or smaller group of people. The discourses that comprise Q as an oral-derived text from antiquity display many characteristics of their oral origins and continuing oral recitation. As explored in chapter 7, we believe that theory of oral performance being developed among anthropologists and others can be adapted for interpretation of the Q discourses. This entails investigation of several key interrelated aspects of an oral-derived text such as Q 6:20–49 as a performance. The oral-derived text itself must be explored in its sounds, rhythms, pauses, emphases, dramatic movement, tone, and overall structure, in order to appreciate its register, particularly its mode. In order adequately to appreciate the register of a performance we must also determine its occasion or context.[29] Q itself offers an example of the failure to appreciate the register and context of Jesus' (and John's) prophetic performances in their program of the renewal of Israel:

> We played the flute for you, and you did not dance;
> We wailed, and you did not weep. (Q 7:32)

In order then to appreciate how the recitation of the oral-derived text would have meant something to the hearers in the performance context we must attempt to understand as much as possible about the tradition with which the performed "text" would have resonated. Understanding the tradition is also probably the key to determining the register and the performance context, which is always specific to a given society. Thus attempting to gain as much familiarity as possible with a society's tradition(s) is the most important task for biblical interpreters who are located in a very different society and social location and who work from very different cultural presuppositions.

In its overall structure the discourse in Q 6:20–49 develops in five steps. The speaker first declares that the present political-economic order is being turned upside down in a series of four blessings and four woes (6:20–26). In the second step she/he gives a series of admonitions regarding economic relations in the local community (6:27–36), and in the third she/he gives a parallel set of commands regarding social relations in the community (6:37–42). The fourth step explores the inner motivation of the good behavior commanded for economic and social relations (6:43–45). Finally, the double parable serves as a sanction enforcing the commands given in steps two and three (6:46–49). The exploration below of how the structure of the "text" resonates with Israelite tradition will confirm what seemed relatively clear on the surface of the discourse when compared with relatively familiar Mosaic covenantal material from the Hebrew Bible: the blessings serve as the "historical prologue" or declaration of deliverance in the standard Israelite covenantal structure, the series of admonitions in

---

29. As mentioned in chapter 7, this concept is similar to the old *Sitz im Leben* of form criticism, only for Q it would be the context of performance of a particular discourse and/or of much or all of the sequence of discourses. For the context appropriate to a given performance, Foley uses performance arena, a more grandiose term more appropriate perhaps to an official public performance of a Homeric epic or a play by Aeschylus in classical Athens.

steps two and three, "love your enemies" and "do not judge" are the covenantal stipulations or teachings, and the double parable at the end replaces the older blessings and curses as the sanction on keeping the covenantal teachings. The proverbs about the trees and their respective fruit could be seen as further covenantal teaching or taken together with the double parable as part of the closing sanction section.

The following transliteration of the oral-derived Greek text, along with a correspondingly blocked translation, is presented for readers / hearers without knowledge of Greek so that they can appreciate something of the parallel lines, the repetition and rhythm of sounds, and the movement characteristic of an oral performance. The blocking of the text is an experimental attempt to make parallels and repetitions of sounds and verb forms visible to the reader, who is expected to become also a hearer by sounding out the "text" orally in order better to appreciate those parallels and repetitions of sounds and rhythms of speech. For the most part, the "text" below follows the reconstructed text of the International Q Project, blocking out that text in "measured verse," as explained in chapter 8 above. At points it presents an alternative reconstruction that seems more appropriate to what must have been the oral derivation of the Q text behind Matthew and Luke. Uncertainties in the reconstruction of the Q text by the International Q Project are indicated by square brackets [ ]; alternative reconstructions are indicated by curly brackets { }. Simple parentheses ( ) indicate words necessary for clarity in the English translation that have no corresponding word in the reconstructed Greek text.

The blessings consist of three parallel statements in the pattern "blessed are those who + for you (pl.) shall," followed by a much longer one more directly addressed to "you" (pl.). They resemble a common rhetorical pattern observable in near-contemporary texts (e.g., the "beatitudes" in 4Q525). The corresponding set of four woes has the same pattern of three parallel statements followed by a longer one.[30]

The second step of the discourse, 6:27–36, focused on local economic interaction, is framed by the same command at the opening and closing ("love your enemies"), with the golden rule at the center and several sets of parallel couplets. The opening four commands are structured in alternating four and five word units, with each set of four + five words in parallel construction of second plural imperative + those who do x + to you. We can still sense something of the parallel lines in a somewhat literal translation. The next four commands reverse the grammatical order, in two parallel lines with the pattern of to the one who does x to you + imperative; and from the one who does x to you + negative imperative. After the "golden rule" in 6:31 come three parallel rhetorical questions that

---

30. On the inclusion of the woes in this Q discourse, see the summary of arguments in Kloppenborg, *Formation of Q,* 172 n. 4; John S. Kloppenborg, *Q Parallels: Synopsis, Critical Notes, and Concordance* (Sonoma, Calif.: Polebridge, 1988), 26; and Christopher Tuckett, "The Beatitudes: A Source-Critical Study," *NovT* 25 (1983): 196 n. 12, 199.

Q 6:20–49: Transliteration in Measured Verse Blocked for Hearing

Step I: Blessings and Curses (6:20b–26)

A. 1. Makarioi   hoi ptōchoi,   hoti humetera estin   hē basileia tou theou.
   2. Makarioi   hoi peinōntes   hoti chortasthēsesthe.
   3. Makarioi   hoi [klai]ontes   hoti gelasete
   4. Makarioi   este hotan   oneidisōsin   hymas
                             kai [eip]ōsin…ponēron… [kath'] hymōn
                             heneken   tou huiou tou anthrōpou
   5. Chairete   kai [agalliasthe]
     hoti ho misthos hymōn polus   en tǭ ouranǭ
     houtōs gar   epoioun   tois prophētais   [tois pro hymōn]
B. 1. {Ouai   hoi plousioi   hoti apechete   tēn paraklēsin hymōn.
   2. Ouai   hoi empeplēsmenoi   hoti peinasete.
   3. Ouai   hoi gelontes   hoti penthēsete [or: klausete].
   4. Ouai   hotan hymas   kalos eipōsin   pantes
   5. kata ta auta gar epoioun   tois pseudoprophētais.}

Step II: Covenantal Teaching (Economic Relations; 6:27–36)

A. 1. Agapate   tous echthrous   hymōn,
   2. {kalos poieite   tois misousin   hymas.
   3. Eulogeite   tous kataromenous   hymas,}
   4. proseuchesthe   peri tōn epēreazontōn   hymas.
B. 1. {Hostis} hrapizei se eis ten siagona   strepson {ʔautǭ} kai ten allēn,
   2. kai {   }   sou to himation   {ʔaphes} {ʔautǭ} kai ton chitōna
   3. To aitounti se   dos,
   4. kai apo danisamenou   mē apaitei.
C. 1. Kai kathōs thelete   hinapoiosin hymin   hoi anthrōpoi,
     houtōs   poieite   autois.
D. 1. [Ei] agap[a]te   tous agapōntas   hymin,   tina misthon echete?
     ouchi kai hoi telōnai   to auto [poiou]sin.
   2. Kai ean {agathopoiēte   tous agathopoiountas} hym{as,}   [tina misthon echete?]
     ouchi kai hoi [ethnik]oi   to auto poiousin
   3. {Kai ean danisēte   par' hōn elpizete   labein,   ?}
     {   kai hoi…   oi…   }
E. 1. {Plen agapate   tous echthrous hymōn   kai agathopoiete   kai danizete
     kai estai   ho misthos hymōn   polus.}
   2. {Hopos} {gene}sthe   huioi   {tou patros hymōn}
     hoti {autos   chrēstos estin}   · epi {tous acharistous   kai} ponērous
   3. [Gin]esthe   oiktirmones   hōs ho patēr hymōn   oiktirmōn estin.

---

repeat the themes of love, do good, and lend, with which the preceding commands begin and end, in 6:27a, b, and 6:30. "Love your enemies, do good, and lend" in 6:35 then repeats the three basic commands from 6:27ab and 30, which the rhetorical questions took up again in 6:32–34. "Your reward will be great" in 6:35 echoes "your reward is great in heaven" in 6:23. "Be merciful, even as your Father is merciful" then both links the covenantal teaching of 6:27–35 to that

Q 6:20–49: *Translation in Measured Verse Blocked for Hearing*

Step I: Blessings and Curses (6:20b–26)

A. 1.	Blessed are	the poor,	for yours is	the kingdom of God.
2.	Blessed are	those who hunger,	for you shall be filled.	
3.	Blessed are	those who mourn,	for you shall laugh.	
4.	Blessed are	you when	they reproach	you
			and speak evil	against you
			on account of	the son of man.
5.	Rejoice and	[be glad]		
	for your reward	is great	in heaven.	
	For so	they did	to the prophets	[before you].
B. 1.	{Woe	to those who are rich,	for you have received	your consolation.
2.	Woe	to those who are full,	for you shall go hungry.	
3.	Woe	to those who laugh,	for you shall mourn.	
4.	Woe	when all people	speak well	of you,
5.	For so	they did	to the false prophets.}	

Step II: Covenantal Teaching (Economic Relations; 6:27–36)

A. 1.	Love	the enemies	of you(rs),	
2.	{do good	to those who hate	you.	
3.	Bless	those who curse	you,}	
4.	Pray	for those who abuse	you.	
B. 1.	To the one who strikes you	on the cheek	turn	also the other.
2.	And [from the one who takes]	your coat	[offer]	also the tunic.
3.	To the one who asks from you		give,	
4.	And from the one who borrows		do not ask back.	
C. 1.	And as you wish	that people	would do	to you,
	thus		do	to them.
D. 1.	And if you love	those who love	you,	what credit is that to you?
	For even the toll-collectors	do the same.		
2.	And if you do good to	those who do good to	you,	what credit is that to you?
	For even the Gentiles	do the same.		
3.	{And if you lend to	those from whom you hope to receive,	what credit is that to you?}	
	{Even…	lend to…	}.	
E. 1.	But love	your enemies,	and do good,	and lend,
	and your reward	will be	great.	
2.	And you will become	sons	of your Father,	
	for he is	kind	to the ungrateful	and the evil.
3.	Be	merciful,	as your Father	is merciful.

in 6:38–42 and ties it to the beatitudes of 6:20–23 that have pronounced God's free grace to those who did not think they deserved it by calling the hearers to imitate God's mercy.[31] Except for the golden rule, these are not separate sayings

---

31. Given the way this saying ties the preceding and succeeding sections of covenantal exhortations together, it could easily be viewed as the "statement of substance" in Baltzer's reconstruction of the

Step III: Covenantal Teaching (Social Relations; 6:37–42)

A. 1. kai mē krinete   [kai ou] mē krithēte

   { . . . .   }

  2. Hō gar metrō   metreite   metrēthēsetai hymin.

B. 1. Mēti dynatai   tuphlos   tuphlon   hodēgein?

       ouchi   amphoteroi   eis bothunon   pesountai?

  2. Ouk estin   mathētēs   hyper   ton didaskalon

      [katērtismenos de   pas estai]   hōs ho didaskalos   autou

C. 1. Ti de blepeis   to karphos   to en to ophthalmō   tou adelphou

                tēn de dokon   tēn en to {idio} ophthalmō   ou katanoeis?

  2. Pōs [dynatai   legein]   tō adelphō sou:

       aphes ekbalō   to karphos   ek tou ophthalmou sou,

       kai   idou   hē dokos   en tō ophthalmō sou?

  3. Hypokrita.

       Ekbale prōton   tēn dokon   ek tou ophthalmou sou,

       kai tote diablepseis

            ekbalein   to karphos   ek tou ophthalmou   tou adelphou sou.

Step IV: Motivation (6:43–45)

A. 1. Ouk estin   dendron kalon   poioun   karpon sapron

       oude palin   dendron sarpon   poioun   karpon kalon.

  2. Ek gar tou karpou   to dendron   ginōsketai

       mēti sullegousin   apo akanthōn   suka

       a   ek batou   stafulēn

B. 1. Ho agathos anthrōpos   ek tou agathou thesaurou   [ekball]ei agatha

       kai ho ponēros   ek tou ponērou   [ekball]ei ponera.

  2. Ek gar perisseumatos   kardias   lalei   to stōma.

---

that circulated independently and were then joined together in various stages, but a unitary section of a unitary oral recitation that repeats the basic points / themes in different forms to drive home the message.

The third step in the discourse, Q 6:37–42, shifts the focus to local social tensions, conflictual interactions that may well be rooted in the economic conflicts addressed in 6:27–35. In a structure parallel to that in 6:27–35, 6:37–42 begins with a general admonition on not judging one another (37–38), moves through rhetorical questions exemplifying the kind of cases that might be involved (39, 41–42a), and concludes with a more precise admonition that specifies an example of how the general exhortation against judging one another applies to the hearers' social interaction (42b). Luke 6:40, which has a very different context in Matt. 10:24–25 from Q 6:39//Matt. 15:14, seems to be an intrusion into the Q discourse at this point.[32] Q 6:37–38 consists of two sets of parallel admonitions with

covenantal structure, as suggested by Ellen Aitken, "The Covenant Formulary in Q 6:20b–49," unpublished paper delivered at the "Q Section" of the SBL, 1992 Annual Meeting

32. See, for example, Piper, *Wisdom in the Q Tradition.*

Step III. Covenantal Teaching (Social Relations; 6:37–42)

A. 1.	And do not judge		and you will not be judged	
	[for with the judgment	you judge	you will be judged,]	
2.	for with the measure	you measure	it will be measured to you.	
B. 1.	Can a blind person	guide	a blind person?	
	Will not both	fall	into a pit?	
2.	A disciple	is not above	his teacher	
	but everyone well trained	will be like	his teacher.	
C. 1.	Why do you see	the speck	in the eye	of your brother,
	but	the log	in your own eye	you do not notice?
2.	How [can you say] to your brother,			
	"Let me remove	the speck	from your eye,"	
	and behold,	there is a log	in your own eye?	
3.	Hypocrite!			
	Remove first	the log	from your own eye,	
	and then you will see (clearly)			
	to cast out	the speck	from the eye	of your brother.

Step IV: Motivation (6:43–45)

A. 1.	There is no	sound tree	which bears	bad fruit,
	nor again	a bad tree	which bears	sound fruit.
2.	For from the fruit	a tree	is known:	
	They do not gather	figs	from thorns,	
	or	grapes	from a bramble bush.	
B. 1.	The good man	from the good treasure	brings forth	good (things).
	The evil man	from the evil (treasure)	brings forth	evil (things).
2.	For from an overflow	of the heart	speaks	the mouth.

---

the same verbal constructions (imperative + aorist subjunctive passive; imperative + future passive) and clear repetition of sounds evident to the ear even in English translation. The admonitions are followed by a motive clause, remarkable for its repetition of sounds, referring to an abundance of grain the hearers will receive and appealing to the poor who are ever hungry and yearning for an abundance just for once in their lives. In 6:39–42, the parallelism disappears briefly in the first rhetorical question but resumes in the second and third. Note also the chiastic structure of the last rhetorical question and the concluding admonition, the second part of which also breaks the parallelism as the point is completed.

The fourth step of the discourse, Q 6:43–45, which probes the inner wellspring of behavior, is constructed in parallel lines and parallel sets of lines (again as we might expect in oral recitation). It also begins with a threefold repetition of the Greek word for "fruit," *karpos*, that resonates with the threefold repetition of *karphos*, the Greek word for "speck" in the previous step of the discourse. The images of the "tree," "bearing fruit," and "good fruit" also resonate with the same images in John the Baptist's opening sayings in Q 3:8–9, where they are metaphors for covenantal behavior.

Step V: Sanction (6:46–49)

A. 1.	Ti	m[e kalei]te:	kyrie, kyrie,
	Kai	ou poieite	ha legō.
B. 1.	Pas	ho[ ] akou[ōn]	mou t[ōn] log[ōn] kai poi[ōn] autous
2.	Homoios estin	anthrōpō,	
	hos [ ] ōkodomēsen	{autou tēn} oikian	epi tēn petran.
3.	Kai . . . kai . . . ho . . . potamo . . . prosepes . . . n		tē̬ oikia̬ ekeinē̬,
	kai ouk [epe]sen,	tethemeliōto gar	epi tēn petran.
C. 1.	Kai [pas] ho akouōn	mou t<ōn> log<ōn>	kai mē poiōn [autous]
2.	Homoios estin	anthrōpō	
	hos ōkodomēsen	{autou tēn} oikian	epi ten ammon.
3.	Kai , , , kai ho . . . potamo . . . prose[kops] . . . n		tē̬ oikia̬ ekeinē̬,
	kai epesen,	kai ēn [hē ptōsis] autēs	megalē̬.

In the concluding sanction of the discourse, 6:46–49, part of the effectiveness of the double parable is the repetition of the same circumstances and same phrases and sounds, the only variations being "practice vs. not practice," *phronimō* vs. *mōrō*, and *petran* vs. *ammon*, that is, opposites with similar sounds or endings in Greek.

Q 6:20–49 as a Covenant Renewal Discourse

With the oral-derived text of Q in mind, it should now be possible to discern how its performance would have resonated with the hearers through the metonymic referencing of the rich tradition of covenantal form and teachings surveyed above.

Both the structure and the contents of the discourse in Q 6:20–49 stand in the tradition of Mosaic covenantal teaching. This was the tentative conclusion in the introduction to this chapter, where critical examination of the claim that the component sayings are sapiential in form and idiom kept turning up covenantal forms, themes, and patterns. The most obviously covenantal contents are the admonitions on economic interaction in 6:27–36 that make multiple allusions to similar teachings in covenantal law codes such as Exodus 21–23, Leviticus 19, and Deuteronomy 22. More thorough examination of the rest of the discourse will reveal just how completely covenantal the material is in both substance and structure.

The acknowledged covenantal structure of Matthew's "Sermon on the Mount" is evident in the Q discourse that he drew upon for the three structural components of this covenant renewal: the opening blessings, the renewed covenantal instruction, and the sanctioning double parable. To take the more obvious ending first, "hearing my words" and (not) acting upon them in Q 6:47–49 performs the same function in the Q covenantal discourse as did the blessings and curses in the archaic Mosaic covenant, as evident in Deuteronomy 27–28. Perhaps if it is heard in isolation the double parable of the houses built respectively on the

Step V. Sanction (6:46–49)

A. 1. Why	do you call me,	"Lord, Lord,"
and	not do	what I tell you?
B. 1. Every one	who hears my words,	and does them
2. is like	a man	
who built	{his} house	upon the rock.
3. And <the rain came down>	and the river beat upon	that house,
and it did not fall,	for it had been founded	on the rock.
C. 1. And everyone	who hears my words	and does not do them
2. is like	a man	
who built	{his} house	upon the sand.
3. And <the rain came down>	and the river beat upon	that house,
and it fell	and its [fall] was	great.

rock and the sand sounds simply like another piece of wisdom. In the Q 6 discourse, however, it is framed as a simile to "doing my *words*," a term used traditionally for the basic covenantal commands, and it is located structurally as the sanction standing at the conclusion of covenantal teaching (6:27–42) in the tradition of Exodus 21–23, Leviticus 19, and Deuteronomy 15. Both the Damascus Document found at Qumran and the *Epistle of Barnabas* (along with Deut. 30:15–20), moreover, provide examples of the sanction component of the Mosaic covenantal structure that pronounces salvation and punishment without the explicit language of "blessings and curses." Thus Q 6:46–49 can be discerned as the concluding sanction of a covenantal structure, the equivalent of the original blessings and curses component.

Since "blessings and curses" originally formed the sanctioning closing step of the Mosaic covenant, it may be more difficult to discern that they have been transformed into the opening declaration of God's deliverance in the Q covenant renewal discourse. Even those who insist on classifying the beatitudes at the opening of the discourse in Q 6:20–49 as sapiential macarisms often acknowledge that they are not typically sapiential in content or function (as noted above). A principal argument for taking the woes in Luke 6:24–26 as part of Q is that they would unlikely have functioned by themselves in isolation from the parallel blessings. The Qumran Community Rule, moreover, provides a clear example of how the blessings and curses component of the traditional Mosaic covenantal (renewal) form could be relocated and transformed into (part of) the prologue as a declaration of God's present or future, not past, deliverance. This appears to be precisely how the blessings and woes function in the Q 6 discourse, which can then be seen to follow the traditional three-part covenantal structure.

That Q's Jesus, in 6:20–49, pronounces blessings and curses before rather than following the covenantal teaching in the middle may be the key to understanding how Q's Jesus is drawing on and transforming the covenantal tradition as he renews it. In the original structure of the Mosaic covenant, the declaration of

God's deliverance preceded the presentation of the principles of social-economic relations (and the application in statues and ordinances). In early Israel, God's deliverance of the people from bondage in Egypt and other situations of oppression formed not only the basis of the Israelites' obligation to keep the stipulation; it also provided them with the independence and other prerequisites for the creation and maintenance of a just (and egalitarian) social order. As adapted by the organizers of the temple-state under the Persian Empire in Nehemiah 9–10, the covenantal structure could also be used in connection with the centralization of religious-economic power. The Judean and Galilean peasantry, however, would presumably have continued to cultivate the Mosaic covenantal forms and teachings that served their interests in maintaining Israelite families as economically viable on their ancestral land and members of local village communities.

At whatever social level the covenantal structure operated, the original function of the blessings and curses was to motivate the observance of the covenantal requirements and ordinances. As can be seen in so-called deuteronomistic theology in general and the long prologue in the covenant renewal in Nehemiah 9–10 in particular, however, the blessings and curses were also used in interpretation of the people's subjection to foreign rulers and other suffering as well as their own rulers' disobedience of the covenantal requirements. The people's historical defeat and subordination were God's just punishments for having broken the covenantal stipulations. The controversy story in Mark 2:1–12 provides a window onto how this use of the curses component of the covenantal structure had come to affect the ordinary people. They had come to interpret their sickness, suffering, and misfortunes as due to their own or their parents' sin. The story in Mark 2:1–12 also indicates that, among the people, the blaming of the people for their own sickness and misfortune was associated with the scribes. In a well-intentioned attempt to encourage the people's keeping of the covenantal Torah, the scribes apparently pointed to the people's own suffering as evidence of their previous disobedience.[33] The Matthean additions to the beatitudes also indicate the effect of this use of the curses in interpretation of the people's circumstances as due to their own sinfulness: "You are the light of the world!" and "You are the salt of the earth!" are addressed to people who blame themselves, who think of themselves as insignificant and unworthy. Their situation is hopeless. Only God can forgive sin, and God is obviously not about to do that, as evidenced in their own miserable circumstances of hunger and sickness, which in turn is evidence of their own sinful failure to keep the covenant.

The covenantal discourse's opening with Jesus' declaration of blessings and curses would have resonated with just such people who believed their situation hopeless because they were suffering under the implementation of the covenantal curses. "Blessed are you poor, . . . you who hunger, . . . you who weep." Jesus

---

33. The previous story, in Mark 1:40–45, moreover, illustrates that among popular circles there was resentment at the mechanisms by which the great tradition of the temple-state attempted to exploit this self-blame in its provisions for sin-offerings and other devices that offered forgiveness of sin for a price.

proclaims precisely to those who believe themselves unworthy, "Yours is the king-dom of God." Q 6:20b–21 is indeed "addressed to a rather wide group of socially and economically disadvantaged persons."[34] Peasants generally are subsistence producers. Subjected as they were to multiple layers of rulers all pressing their demands for revenues (particularly Antipas's demands to fund his city-building), the Galilean peasants would have been under unusually heavy economic pres-sures — poor and becoming poorer. Other Q passages also address people who are desperately indebted, hungry, and worried about bare subsistence, passages in which again the kingdom of God is offered as the deliverance from their plight (Q 11:2–4; 12:22–31). As noted in the review of the contents of covenantal provisions and ordinances, a basic concern of the covenant was for the economic viability of each family in the village communities that constituted Israel.[35] Cor-responding to the blessings on the poor, Q's Jesus pronounces against the rich,[36] who were presumably blessed in their plenty and happiness, the very covenantal woes or curses that the people believed applied to themselves. In this redeploy-ment and transformation of the traditional covenantal structural form of blessings and curses, Jesus declares God's new action in the present or imminent future to deliver the poor and hungry and sorrowful from the effects of their oppression, to restore justice. This pronouncement of God's certain, imminent restoration of justice then provides the basis for the renewed covenantal demands that follow in 6:27–42.

The fourth blessing and the fourth woe require special comment because they have been taken as somehow narrowing the application of the blessings and woes in two ways: from the general situation of the people to the particular conditions of the "Christians" or Q people and / or from a general group of disadvantaged people to "Christian" preachers or disciples.[37] The "persecute you" in Matt. 5:11 appears to have suggested such a narrowing to some interpreters. Yet even persecution should suggest no such narrowing, since movement members as well as leaders would have been vulnerable. If we think of a concrete communication situation, it is unclear what the difference might be between 6:20b–21 and 6:22–23 or between 6:24–25 and 6:26. Whether in the situation of the continuing recitation of Jesus' speeches in the Q movement or in the earliest situation in which Jesus' preaching evoked a response among Galilean hearers, the poor who responded to the recitation of Jesus' speech would have been the same as those who would

---

34. Kloppenborg, *Formation of Q*, 173; but these Q blessings do not address "the general human conditions of poverty and suffering," as clear from the woes which follow and the mocking of wealth and privilege elsewhere in Q, as in 7:24–45.

35. This is evident not simply in the custom of a sabbatical for the land, so that the poor could gather the produce (Exod. 23:10), and gleaning rights for the poor (e.g., Lev. 19:10; 23:22), but also in the basic commandments not to covet, steal, or witness falsely and the extensive mechanisms to cancel debts and release debt-slaves every seven years.

36. *1 Enoch* 95–104 exemplifies rather vividly how series of curses were coupled with series of blessings (or their equivalents) in second-temple Judean literature. While the woes in *1 Enoch* 95–104 are directed against the wealthy (at least partly because of their exploitation of the lowly), the blessings are primarily upon the righteous whom the wealthy and powerful were persecuting.

37. Kloppenborg, *Formation of Q*, 173, provides a concise statement.

(potentially) have been reproached. With regard to the woes in particular, we should keep in mind the rhetoric and rhetorical situation involved here. The woes are only ostensibly addressed to the rich but are actually being heard by the poor. The woes in effect reinforce their hearing of the blessings given to themselves and also reinforce their solidarity: they would surely not want to be among the upper crust where (other) wealthy people would speak well of them. Nor does the reference to the prophets suggest a narrowing of the reference to a smaller number such as the disciples or other leaders of the movement. All who participated in such a movement, one that saw itself in continuity with the prophetic tradition, would have been vulnerable to reproach, and all would have identified (themselves) with the prophetic tradition (cf. such traditions as Jer. 20:8).

The sayings beginning with "love your enemies" in Q 6:27–36, the first of two sections of covenantal exhortation, focus on local economic relations.[38] These sayings have often been taken as a teaching of nonresistance to a foreign enemy, in this case the Romans who had conquered Palestine, and/or as a general teaching of nonretaliation or nonviolence. They can be read this way, however, only by taking them out of literary and social context. Neither in Q nor in Matthew and Luke do these sayings deal with violence.[39] The slap on the cheek in 6:29a is an insult, not a physical attack. The enemies, as usual in the Synoptic Gospels, are local enemies (e.g., one who could sabotage a neighbor's crop, Matt. 13:25, 28). Indeed, the *context* of the interaction envisaged is clearly indicated in the *content* of several of the sayings, such as the insult by one villager to another and the seizure of the garment in 6:29 or one villager begging another for a loan in 6:30 or the command to lend in 6:35. These sayings all deal with local economic interaction, such as the making of and foreclosing on loans, and the social tensions and conflicts that such economic interaction entails and produces.

Although these admonitions stand in the tradition of covenantal exhortation, they are not commandments, as they might be made to appear by Matthew's juxtaposition of Jesus' teaching with covenantal commandments in Matt. 5:20–48; nor are they laws, as can be seen by contrasting them with some of the covenantal laws that they allude to, such as Exod. 22:25–26; rather, they are more in the vein of covenantal teaching such as appears in Deut. 15:1–11. The exhortation begins with general admonitions in 6:27, moves into particular exemplary cases[40] of typical local economic interaction in 6:29–30, and concludes with a repetition of the principal admonitions in 6:35. Although the focus of this set of sayings as a whole is local economic relations, as can be seen in the examples given, the rhetorical questions, and the concluding admonition (6:29–30, 32–34, 35), the opening admonitions address hostile social relations. The latter,

---

38. The following discussion draws heavily on my more extensive analysis of this passage in idem, *Jesus*, 259–73.

39. See ibid., 261–64.

40. See the discussion of such teachings by Robert R. Tannehill, "The 'Focal Instance' as a Form of New Testament Speech: A Study of Matt. 5:39b–42," *JR* 50 (1970): 377–82.

like the local tensions addressed in the subsequent section, 6:37–42, can easily be understood as arising from the difficult economic circumstances into which the local village "enemies" have come, in which they are mutually indebted and resentful at not being paid back and/or being pressured to pay up. Such local squabbles are endemic to village society[41] but are exacerbated in unusually diffi-cult economic circumstances such as those apparently addressed in Q 6:20–21, 27–36 (and Q 11:2–4; 12:22–31).

The "love your enemies" section of the discourse stands clearly in the tradition of Mosaic covenantal teaching and resonates with it intensively. Most obvious is the reference in 6:29b to the outer garment taken in pledge for a loan in the covenantal law code: "If you take you neighbor's cloak in pawn, you shall restore it before the sun goes down; for it may be your neighbors only clothing to use as cover; in what else shall that person sleep?" (Exod. 22:26–27a; Deut. 24:10–13). But that reference would have opened up a whole range of other associations and references in covenantal provisions and ordinances regarding borrowing and lending in the interaction of local villagers. An example, in the immediate context in the covenantal law code, is Exod. 22:25, 27b: "If you lend [goods] to my people, to the poor among you, you shall not deal with them as a creditor; you shall not exact interest from them. . . . And if your neighbor cries out to me, I will listen, for I am compassionate." As noted above, most of the economic provisions of the Mosaic covenant, its law code, and ongoing covenantal teaching evident through the materials taken up into the books of Deuteronomy and Leviticus were concerned with the plight of the poor. Thus, in Deut. 15:7–11: "Do not be tight-fisted toward your needy neighbor. . . . Willingly lend enough to meet the need, whatever it may be. . . . Give ungrudgingly" (cf. Sir. 29:1 for a scribal-sapiential version of the same tradition). The admonitions and closely related rhetorical questions in Q 6:29–36 stand directly in this tradition, build on it, and renew it, and they would have called the whole range of such covenantal teaching to the minds of the listeners.

However innovative it may be, the opening command to "love your enemies, do good to those who hate you" stands in and resonates with the same tradi-tion of covenantal teaching about local social-economic interaction. Not only was "neighbor" (or the synonym "brother") the general term for a fellow Israelite community member, but "enemy" (or "one who hates you") was a standard tradi-tional term used both in the covenantal law code and in covenantal teaching for a neighbor with whom one had developed a particularly conflictual relationship,

---

41. An early rabbinic ruling addresses typical cases of "slap on the cheek" insults in local social relations, attempting to assess damages in an unpeasant-like approach: "If a man cuffed his fellow he must pay him a *sela.* R. Judah says in the name of R. Jose the Galilean: One hundred zuz. If he slapped him he must pay him two hundred zuz. If with the back of the hand he must pay him four hundred zuz. If he tore his ear, . . . spat and his spittle touched him, . . . he must pay four hundred zuz. This is the general rule: all is in accordance with a person's honor" (*m. B. Qam.* 8:6). The general rule also suggests the values of a nonpeasant who presumes to possess some honor — although it may also reflect peasant realities, which were different from the ideal. Q's Jesus and particularly Mark's Jesus in Mark 10:35–45 articulate more the popular egalitarian ideal.

as illustrated in Exod. 23:4–5 and Deut. 22:1–4: "If you meet your enemy's ox or the ass of one who hates you lying under its burden, you shall refrain from leaving him with it, you shall help him to lift it up" (draft animals were essential to economic subsistence!). It has often been noted that in the command to "love your enemies" Jesus is creatively transforming the traditional covenantal command "to love your neighbor as yourself" in Lev. 19:18. Given the oral communication environment in antiquity and the popular cultivation of a little tradition parallel to the great tradition in which Leviticus stands, we should say rather that Q's Jesus is creatively transforming the popular covenantal tradition that likely paralleled what was developed by Levitical circles, as evident in Lev. 19:18. Finally, besides the opening "love your enemies" being a creative transformation of covenantal tradition evident through the window of Lev. 19:18, the closing "be merciful as your Father is merciful" is also a covenantal principle evident through the same levitical window, Lev. 19:2, "You shall be holy, for I Yahweh your God am holy." The next section of the discourse, moreover, has often been linked with the first half of Lev. 19:18 in 19:17, as we shall explore just below.

The covenantal creativity in "love your enemies, do good to those who hate you" that resonates deeply with Mosaic covenantal law and teaching on local economic relations is further evident in the new formulations on the basis of standard covenantal teaching. Most of the admonitions in the passage address neighbors, no doubt needy themselves, who may be called upon to aid another neighbor. The statement in 6:29, however, turns the tables, encouraging the desperate debtors, who may any day be accosted by the "enemies" (among those neighbors) to whom they are indebted to "pay up," to embarrass their creditors. In the exemplary situation or "focal instance" which a creditor might again seize the debtor's cloak (outer garment; the symbolic pledge for the loan), the debtor should simply render up his or her shift (undergarment) as well — thus standing there stark naked before the now-embarrassed creditor and any onlookers. Q's Jesus had a sense of humor! The creative adaptation of the tradition is also embodied in the rhetorical questions of 6:32–34. If "even toll collectors" (or Gentiles or sinners) love those who love them," the Q listeners must do better. In his renewal of the Mosaic covenant, Q's Jesus is demanding greater rigor in the traditional covenantal economic relations than previously evident in that tradition. But of course, the listeners had already received the blessings that "yours is the kingdom of God," surely a solid basis for such an escalation in covenantal rigor.[42]

Q 6:27–36 thus addresses and presupposes villagers who have come into severe economic circumstances. In the ancient Mediterranean, as elsewhere, peasants were always marginal producers and always subject to heavy demands from their rulers. Galilean peasants and / or Q people in nearby areas may have come under unusual economic pressure because of multiple layers of rulers and intensified

---

42. If the golden rule was actually in Q at this point (and not simply a Lukan addition here), it may have been ironic or intended to be surpassed in the demands articulated in the rhetorical questions.

demand of Roman client rulers.[43] The sayings address villagers, some of whom are already in debt, unable to repay their neighbor-creditors, and some of whom are reluctant to lend and perhaps eager to demand back what they have lent previously. Understandably these complicated and difficult economic circumstances have produced tensions between villagers, such that some are at each others' throats, resentful and hateful, ready to insult one another as "enemies." Directly out of standard Mosaic covenantal teaching, Q's Jesus addresses the circumstances, calling the people to take economic responsibility for one another in their desperate circumstances, to "do good," particularly to continue to "lend" despite their own real or anticipated shortage. They probably had little themselves, yet are to share what they have, even with their "enemies." In doing so, moreover, they are imitating their Father who, they have just heard, is mercifully giving them, the poor and hungry, the kingdom of God.

The rest of the covenantal teaching in Q 6 should probably be heard in two "paragraphs" consisting in 6:37–42 (possibly minus Luke 6:40) and 6:43–45. The "paragraph" in Q 6:37–42 continues the teachings about local interaction, shifting the focus from economic to social.[44] The sayings about the speck in the brother's / friend's eye in 6:41–42 continue the discussion begun in 6:37–38 about not judging lest you be judged. The saying in 6:39 about the blind leading the blind fits this discussion, while that about teachers and students in Luke 6:40 seems to interrupt it, hence may not have been part of Q (notice that Matthew has it in a very different location and context).[45] The whole "paragraph" of sayings, moreover, continues the exhortation begun in 6:36 under the central theme of love of neighbor / enemy that is deeply rooted in traditional covenantal teaching, as evident in the window provided by Lev. 19:17–18. The "not judging" is yet another aspect of loving one's brother in the village community. Q 6:38b (if it was in Q) appears to be a standard proverb, from the way it is used in the Mishnah (*m. Sotah* 1:7): "By that same measure by which a man metes out [to others], they mete out to him" (Neusner translation). The occurrence in later rabbinic literature of the same imagery of the "speck / mote" and the "beam" also in the context of reproof ("If one says to him, 'Remove the mote from between your eyes,' he would answer, 'Remove the beam from between your eyes'" [R. Tarfon in *b. Arak.* 16b]) suggests that the contents of the rhetorical questions in Q 6:41–42 were also common,

---

43. See the discussion in Richard A. Horsley, *Galilee: History, Politics, People* (Valley Forge, Pa.: Trinity Press International, 1995), chaps. 5–9; and idem, *Archaeology, History, and Society in Galilee* (Valley Forge, Pa.: Trinity Press International, 1996), chaps. 2–3, and chap. 3 above.

44. But note also how the economic dimension continues: in 6:38, as the motivating inducement not to judge or condemn the "enemy" or "brother" (6:27, 41–42), the "poor" and "hungry" hearer (6:20–21) is offered the reward of grain poured into the lap in a full measure (if Luke 6:38d was in Q) — which is also an indication of the agrarian village context and origin of these sayings.

45. This is debated, however, particularly insofar as interpreters take these sayings outside of any local context as general teaching to individuals. For example, Kloppenborg, *Formation of Q*, 184–85, reads 6:40 as the key to 6:39–42. Like 9:57–58 when read this way, 6:40 (and 6:39–42) fits the general model of instructional literature in which the disciple is to learn from and emulate the master. Piper, *Wisdom in the Q Tradition*, 40–43, looking for the "argument" of the section, in contrast, finds 6:40 as intrusive and possibly a Lukan insertion.

almost proverbial, in Galilean and Judean culture. Thus this section in 6:37–42, and perhaps the whole of 6:27–45, can be seen as a mixture of covenantal teaching that has specific roots in popular Israelite covenantal tradition and proverbs and other common sayings used effectively in the broader covenantal exhortation here. The internal structure or argument of this paragraph moves from the general exhortation not to judge (6:37–38a) through the two sayings that narrow the application with thematically parallel but concretely different illustrations from the measure of grain and the blind leading the blind (6:38b–39) to a pointed application to the particular social situation of the addressees in attacking others' behavior when they have not straightened out their own (6:41–42).

The next paragraph, 6:43–45, deals with the inner motives or motivation of behavior in the local social-economic interaction addressed in the previous exhortations. The trees' production of fruit is clearly used as a metaphoric comparison for the way peoples' hearts (or inner motivation) produce behavior. Bearing good fruit, moreover, is a standard metaphor for covenantal (repentance and) obedience, as illustrated already in John's speech in Q 3:7–9, 16–17. Fruit is generally a widespread image in Israelite biblical literature indicating either actions (in both the prophets and wisdom collections) or speech (particularly in wisdom collections). The argument of the paragraph moves from the general statement of 6:43–44a through the double illustration of 6:44bc to the application to human motivation and behavior in 6:45. Probing the heart as the source of behavior functions to encourage a change of heart so that one produces good rather than evil behavior. In probing the motivational roots of covenantal or anticovenantal social interaction, Q's Jesus is drawing on an already well-established covenantal tradition. Most familiar is the prophecy in Jer. 31:27–34 of the new covenant written on the heart rather than tablets of stone, so that the people would not have to teach and exhort each other but would spontaneously maintain covenantal justice in social interaction. The Qumran Community Rule and Damascus Document now provide further evidence of the importance of this concern with the inner motives of social action, the whole catalogues of virtues and vices in 1QS 4:2–7, 9–12 listing inner qualities, dispositions, or "spirits" that result in certain behavior. Also worth noting is the close linking of the discussion of inner motivation of behavior with the corresponding "visitations" (the blessings and curses component) in 1 QS 4:8–9, 12–14 parallel to the same proximate linking with the sanctioning double parable in Q 6:46–49.

The final step of the discourse, in 6:46–49, provides the sanction on the preceding covenantal teaching, according to the standard pattern of covenant renewal, as discussed above. Since the blessings and curses that often formed the closing of covenantal recitations and renewals had been creatively transformed into a bold new opening, the declaration of deliverance in the Q covenantal discourse, an alternative is necessary for the closing. The double parable of building houses on the rock and on the sand, respectively, serves the same function, offering positive results (although not exactly rewards) if the hearers do Jesus' words and disastrous consequences if they do not. The tone of the parable, however, in keeping with the highly positive, encouraging tone of the opening blessings, is far less ominous and threatening than the blessings and curses at the end of Deuteronomy, which are so heavily and sharply weighted toward the threatening curses, and the ominous warnings of the Qumran covenant renewal in 1 QS 1–4. The occurrence of a similar parable in the Mishnah (R. Eleazar b. Azariah, in *m. Abot* 3:17/18; cf. *Abot R. Nathan* A 24) suggests that Q's Jesus may here be adapting an image or parable already current in the culture:

> R. Eleazar b. Azariah…would say: "Anyone whose wisdom is greater than his deeds — to what is he to be likened? To a tree with abundant foliage, but few roots. When the winds come, they will uproot it and blow it down. As it is said: (recites Jer. 17:6). But anyone whose deeds are greater than his wisdom — to what is he to be likened? To a tree with little foliage but abundant roots. For even if all the winds in the world were to come and blast at it, they will not move it from its place. As it is said: (recites Jer. 17:8)." (*m. Abot* 3:17; Neusner translation, 681)

Comparison with the use of that same parable in Mishnah *Abot*, with its different form and function, moreover, points up how Q has formed the double parable precisely to serve as the closing sanction of the covenantal discourse.

Covenant Renewal in the Popular Tradition vs. Sapiential Covenantal Teaching

That Q 6:20–49 arises from and works creatively with popular covenantal tradition can be better appreciated when compared and contrasted with scribal covenantal teaching as exemplified in Judean sapiential literature, to which Q 6 has recently been likened.

It is ironic that, with all the claims of the sapiential (as opposed to covenantal or prophetic) character of the sayings in Q 6, little notice is taken of the ways in which earlier Judean sapiential teaching appropriated covenantal teaching and how differently the parallel covenantal traditions are handled in Proverbs and Sirach than in Q 6. We are again in the area of contested Israelite tradition. The sapiential collections in Proverbs are not especially noted for having already made much contact with, much less seriously appropriated, Mosaic covenantal structure and teaching. One of the short discourses in the relatively late collection of Proverbs 1–9, however, appears to be a sapiential development of covenantally rooted "two-ways" teaching. Proverbs 2:1–22 (or does the discourse extend through 3:4?) concludes with an exhortation parallel and similar to the double parable in Q 6:46–49 that concludes the Q covenant renewal discourse. Both function like the "blessings and curses" of the standard covenantal structure, even though they do not take the explicit form of blessings and curses, as in the older covenantal material at the end of Deuteronomy. The difference in both social location and orientation, however, is also evident particularly in the continuation in Prov. 3:1–4. Keeping the teacher's commandments thus results in a good life as well as favor with God. No dire circumstances are apparent in the sapiential discourse, and the inducement is "favor and good repute in the sight of God and of people" (3:4). The Q covenant renewal, addressed to ordinary people, proclaims the kingdom of God for the poor and is concerned with the solidarity and survival of the village community. The sapiential two-ways teaching in Prov. 2:1–3:4, addressed presumably to scribes-/sages-in-training ("my son"), discusses righteousness and justice in a more abstract sense and is concerned with the individual's good reputation.

Sirach 24 reveals that scribes/sages had personified and etherealized wisdom and fully identified wisdom with the Torah. Nevertheless, only a limited amount of strictly covenantal exhortation appears in Sirach itself, and only three passages provide teaching parallel to part of Q 6. Sirach 29:1–13 parallels Q 6:27–36 as exhortation based on and advocating observance of covenantal commands to lend and in other ways respond to one's neighbors (fellow Judeans) in their time of need. At the very beginning the discourse in Sirach 29:1–13 joins mercy closely with the exhortation to lend, which Q 6:27–36 does at the end. Much of the sapiential teaching on lending to one's neighbor and helping the poor also stands in the imperative. The stance, however, is somewhat detached from and reflective about the concrete situation of the needy neighbor, and the motives are mainly those of obligation to the commandments and prudential self-interest ("profit") in relation to the Most High, not concern for the needy themselves. Besides the abstract general statement at the outset (29:1), the reflective reservations about the typical behavior of the ungrateful "many" in reneging on their loans (29:4–7) in effect undermine the exhortation to "lend to your neighbor" as well as to repay a loan. "Nevertheless," exhorts the sage, with a touch of noblesse oblige, "be patient with someone in humble circumstances, ... help the poor for the commandment's sake" (29:8–11). The social location of the scribes-/sages-in-training was hardly that of immediate involvement in the social-economic push-and-shove of hungry and mutually indebted peasants ready to strike out at each other in their desperation. And they have nothing to offer comparable to the motives with which Jesus' covenantal exhortation is framed in Q 6:20–26 ("Blessed are you poor, for yours is the kingdom of God.... Woe to you rich...") or the direct command in Q 6:36 ("Be merciful, as your Father is merciful").

Sages such as Ben Sira did indeed complain of the predatory behavior of the wealthy and powerful, perhaps their own patrons among the priestly aristocracy or their allies. "To offer a sacrifice from the property of the poor" (taken in repayment of debts with exorbitant rates of interest?) and "to take away a neighbor's living is to commit murder" (Sir. 34:24–27). They were fully aware of the traditional doctrine that the Most High was especially concerned for the widow, the orphan, and the lowly (35:17–22). It also appears that the scribe/sage had a role in which it was possible for him to "rescue the oppressed from the oppressor" by "giving a verdict" (4:9). Doing so would make the scribe "like a son of the Most High" and elicit his love (4:10; cf. Q 6:35b). Yet when it came to observing the covenantal demand to respond to the needs of one's neighbors, the sapiential teacher seemed a bit detached from the "poor / hungry / needy / desperate" (4:1–5). The motives for "giving to the needy," strikingly individualistic in their focus, are both a prudential "atonement" for one's own sin (3:30) and an anxiety lest the desperate spurned poor persons curse one's stinginess and a sympathetic Creator "hear their prayer" (4:5–6). Apparently, when it came to aiding the needy neighbor, "the fear of the Lord" was quite literally "the beginning of 'wisdom'" for the sage.

Chapter 10

PROPHETIC ENVOYS FOR THE RENEWAL OF ISRAEL: Q 9:57–10:16

Richard A. Horsley _____

Toward Contextual Interpretation

Individual Appropriation of Isolated Sayings

Component sayings of the "mission" discourse have figured prominently, even decisively, in recent interpretation of Q and Q people. Key proof texts for the hypothesis of the homeless lifestyle of "itinerant radicalism," for the comparison of the Q addressees with ancient Cynic philosophers, and for the "discipleship" reading of Q generally have been lifted from this speech. Yet all of these overlapping interpretations are problematic insofar as they take individual sayings out of context and ignore other aspects of the discourse.

The mission discourse illustrates one of the serious flaws in recent stratigraphy of Q: the content of this sapiential discourse is not particularly sapiential. In fact, John S. Kloppenborg (along with others) never argues that it is, but rather admits that it does not fit the model of standard instructional or other sapiential literature.[1] It also poses the problem of inconsistency in application of the stated criteria for scholarly stratification of Q: the form of *chreiai* is supposedly a characteristic of the secondary layer of Q, but here are *chreiai* as prime instances of primary-layer Q materials (9:57–58, 59–60) used to characterize the original Q people as caught up in an itinerant, radical lifestyle. Comparison with standard Judean wisdom literature has the effect of driving even more of a wedge between the Q people represented in this discourse and typical sages. Insofar as Q 10:2–16 "deals with mission," it differs dramatically from sapiential instruction. Sages/scribal teachers were engaged in a sedentary teaching relationship with their students. A particularly well-placed sage, of course, might have the opportunity to travel with his patron among the ruling aristocracy, as suggested with considerable pride by Ben Sira, who had evidently been included on such a "mission" of state (Sir. 39:4). Generally speaking, the sage was busily engaged in study and reflection and occasionally "sitting in the judge's seat" and "serving

---

1. John S. Kloppenborg, *The Formation of Q: Trajectories in Ancient Wisdom Collections* (Philadelphia: Fortress, 1987), 190–202.

among the great" (Sir. 38:32–39:4) and would hardly have been traveling from town to town preaching the kingdom and healing the sick.

Some recent interpreters of Q do still treat the mission discourse as pertaining to mission. Indeed, Q as a whole has been seen as a collection for charismatic missionaries.[2] Insofar as the mission discourse and/or Q generally have been taken as instruction for mission, the mission has been understood as turning toward the Gentiles and away from Israel, even in judgment.[3] This reading of the "mission discourse" as directed to a Gentile mission construes the woes against Galilean towns in 10:13–15 in connection with other prophetic sayings in Q, such as 11:39–52 and 13:28–29, as directed against Israel generally. Accordingly, the discourse in Q 10:2–16 has been read as instructions for an "errand of judgment" (against Israel) rather than for a mission.[4] These readings of the mission discourse that key on the woes against the Galilean towns in 10:13–15 appear to be rooted in the assumption that any reference to a Jewish group or institution implicated the whole of Israel. The primary conflict in the historical context, however, was that between rulers and ruled.[5] Not surprisingly, in Q also it is principally the rulers and their representatives who are condemned. It is mainly in discourses against the scribes and Pharisees that "this generation" is used. And the saying against "the sons of the kingdom" that supposedly is both addressed against Israel in general and proclaims a pilgrimage of Gentiles into the kingdom is in fact directed against the rulers and proclaims the gathering of dispersed Israelites into the kingdom.[6] Thus there is no justification in Q itself or its historical context for either a judgment against Israel in general or a Gentile mission and conversion. The woes in Q 10:13–15 must be separated from those in Q 11:39–52 (and 6:24–26), since they are directed against specific Galilean villages and are apparently specific to the situation of a movement in Galilee, not to the broader social conflict between rulers and ruled reflected in those other Q woes.

Perhaps the most prominent general line of interpretation in recent Q studies is that the mission discourse is not (so much) about mission but about "discipleship." The discipleship reading usually focuses on individual sayings of this and other discourses, such as 9:57–58, 59–60; 10:4; and 14:26. One recent study argues that the editorial placement of 9:57–58 at the beginning transforms the whole discourse into instruction on discipleship:

---

2. Paul Hoffmann, *Studien zur Theologie der Logienquelle,* NTAbh NF 8 (Münster: Aschendorff, 1972).

3. Dieter Lührmann, *Die Redaktion der Logienquelle,* WMANT 33 (Neukirchen-Vluyn: Neukirchener, 1969), 24–48, 60, 63, 88, 93; and Risto Uro, *Sheep among the Wolves: A Study of the Mission Instructions of Q* (Helsinki: Suomalainen Tiedeakatemia, 1987), esp. 21–25, 162–73, 210–23, with summary of previous treatments.

4. Arland D. Jacobson, *The First Gospel: An Introduction to Q* (Sonoma, Calif.: Polebridge, 1992), 68, 137.

5. Richard A. Horsley, *Sociology and the Jesus Movement* (New York: Crossroad, 1989), chaps. 4–5.

6. Richard A. Horsley, "Social Conflict in the Synoptic Sayings Source Q," in *Conflict and Invention,* ed. John S. Kloppenborg (Valley Forge, Pa.: Trinity Press International, 1995), 37–52.

Q 9:57–58 programmatically conceives discipleship as imitation of the lifestyle of the Son of Man. The basis for the association of 9:57–62 with the mission sayings is presumably the similarity of this homeless and radically obedient mode of existence of the disciples to the itinerant and penniless existence of Q's envoys of the kingdom. The effect of the juxtaposition of the chriae with 10:3–16 ... broadens the original mission instruction by setting them within the more comprehensive framework of a speech on discipleship."[7]

"Discipleship" thus not only is the primary subject of the speech but also is "the more comprehensive" subject and concern in the whole discourse. Presumably some of the component material was concerned with mission prior to the earliest, sapiential layer of Q (given the parallel to Q 10:4–11 in Mark 6:8–13), but the people who produced that layer had apparently already transformed mission materials into instruction on individual "discipleship."

Like the reading of the Gospel of Mark in terms of individual "discipleship," the widespread assumption that some of the key sayings in Q 9:57–10:16 are about "discipleship" is a Christian projection onto biblical texts. It is imagined, moreover, that during his "ministry" Jesus simply called "disciples" and attracted "followers"; the "church" (community or movement) started only after the resurrection, at Pentecost. Thus, not surprisingly, one of the key "catchwords" that catches readers' attention is "follow" in Matt. 8:19, 22 and Luke 9:57, 59, 61. "Follow," however, is not a particularly prominent term in Q discourses. Besides its more literal sense in Q 7:9 (cf. possibly 22:28–30), it appears in the figurative sense only in 9:57–61 and possibly in 14:27 (Matt. 10:38). What "following" Jesus meant in these passages, however, would then depend on the broader context in this Q discourse and the whole sequence of discourses, along with whatever supplementary indications may emerge from Mark and other comparative material. It is extremely difficult to find any clear indications of individualistic "discipleship" in the early literature of Jesus' "followers," which is focused mainly on building a movement based in local communities.

In recent decades the individualistic Christian "discipleship" interpretation has further narrowed to an "itinerant radicalism" as constructed mainly in the highly influential thesis about "wandering charismatics."[8] The individualistic scholarly construct of "itinerant radicalism," however, is based on literalistic readings of individual sayings from the Synoptic Gospels as well as from Paul's letters and Acts and the "Teaching of the Twelve Apostles" (Didache). Once these sayings are taken literalistically, the construct of "wandering charismatics" is necessary to explain who could possibly have carried or transmitted such sayings about

---

7. Kloppenborg, Formation of Q, 200–201.

8. Gerd Theissen, Sociology of Early Palestinian Christianity (Philadelphia: Fortress, 1978); and idem, "Wanderradikalismus: Literatursoziologische Aspekte der Überlieferung von Worten Jesu im Urchristentum," ZTK 70 (1973): 245–71, where Theissen acknowledges that he is building on Hoffmann, Studien. Subsequent studies of Q and subsequent "liberal" studies of the historical Jesus, particularly in the United States, have enthusiastically embraced Theissen's construct.

abandoning home and property. The construct of "itinerant radicalism" of the "wandering charismatics," however, is not derived directly from those texts. It is rather borrowed from Max Weber's sociology of religion, which in turn was based on Harnack's reading of texts from the then newly discovered *Didache*.[9] Besides all the other serious problems that have been discerned in this construct and its application to Q, it founders simply on its failure to recognize the phenomena of metaphor and hyperbole in speech (or literature). Once these figures of speech are recognized, there is nothing in the individual sayings cited to indicate a lifestyle of voluntary poverty or homelessness.

In a further narrowing, the Cynic reading of Q extracts those sayings that can be made to fit the picture it constructs.[10] This reading treats Q as a mere collection of sayings that can be sorted out into homogeneous batches by form. It finds the stratification of Q into three layers useful in sifting the individual sayings into categories by likeness. But it uses the criteria of stratification inconsistently,[11] and it ignores the crucial component of the stratification hypothesis, that is, that Q consists of discernible "clusters" or "discourses," some of which are secondary and redactional but others of which are compositionally foundational. Far from interpreting Q sayings in the context of the whole discourses of which they are integral parts, the Cynic reading of Q tears the sayings out of literary (and thus historical) context. Thus isolated from their meaning context, the individual sayings can be discerned to have a meaning that resembles certain fragments from the ancient Cynic philosophers. The key saying for the Cynic reading is Q 10:4, which forbids purse, bag, and sandals on journeys, because these items are associated with Cynic preachers. Somehow the mere occurrence of these items in this one saying makes the early Q people Cynic-like. The saying in Q 10:4, however, forbids the carrying of these items that constitute the typical equipment of the Cynics. Thus even this saying, taken in isolation and compared with ancient characterizations of the Cynic philosophers, would appear, if anything, to be anti-Cynic. The Cynic interpretation also exhibits the same literalistic reading of isolated Q sayings that is practiced by the "itinerant radicalism" interpretation on which it builds. These difficulties in the Cynic interpretation of sayings abstracted from the "mission" discourse, moreover, turn out to be only some of the many problems inherent

9. See the critiques by Wolfgang Stegemann, "Vagabond Radicalism in Early Christianity? A Historical and Theological Discussion of a Thesis Proposed by Gerd Theissen," in *God of the Lowly: Socio-Historical Interpretations of the Bible*, ed. Willy Schottroff and Wolfgang Stegemann (Maryknoll, N.Y.: Orbis Books, 1984), 148–68; John H. Elliott, "Social-Scientific Criticism of the New Testament: More on Methods and Models," *Semeia* 35 (1986): 1–33; Horsley, *Sociology*, chaps. 1–3; Jonathan A. Draper, "Weber, Theissen, and 'Wandering Charismatics' in the Didache," *Journal of Early Christian Studies* 6 (1998): 541–76; and see esp. Draper's discussion in chap. 2 above.

10. Burton L. Mack, *The Lost Gospel: The Book of Q and Christian Origins* (San Francisco: HarperSanFrancisco, 1993), 114–19; Leif Vaage, *Galilean Upstarts: Jesus' First Followers according to Q* (Valley Forge, Pa.: Trinity Press International, 1994).

11. See the critique by James M. Robinson, "Building Blocks in the Social History of Q," in *Rethinking Christian Origins: Festschrift in Honor of Burton L. Mack*, ed. Elizabeth Castelli and Hal Taussig (Philadelphia: Trinity Press International, 1996), 87–112.

in the larger enterprise of the Cynic interpretation of Q sayings, as a number of critics have pointed out.[12]

From Noncontextual to Contextual Interpretation

Perhaps the most fundamental problem in the discipleship reading and particularly the "itinerant radicalism" and Cynic interpretations is their extraction of the sayings from the literary context in which they were embedded. According to the sophisticated recent composition criticism, the fuller mission discourse of Q (9:57–) 10:2–16 built upon earlier basic instructions for mission, visible in Q 10:4–11 and closely paralleled in Mark 6:8–13.[13] As can be readily discerned, the sayings in the basic unit of 10:4–11 instruct the envoys to carry out actions that do not accord with or are contrary to typical Cynic behavior: they are to spread a strange sort of peace, to stay in the same house in each town, eating what is provided (and not begging on the street), and to heal the sick. The problem, however, is more fundamental than comparability to other Hellenistic materials. As in the study of Q and other Jesus materials generally, priority is usually given to the individual saying as a unit of meaning and, presumably, communication. It is simply assumed that the meaning of an isolated individual saying can be determined and is sufficiently clear that it can stand on its own in comparison with other sayings with which it is linked in Q.

Not only those who treat Q as a collection of individual sayings, however, but even redaction critics and composition critics who recognize the existence of discourses in Q proceed on this assumption. The standard approach is to compare and contrast individual sayings, looking for inconsistencies, in order to detect what might be earlier and what later, what might be redactional and how. Then grand inferences and deductions are made on the basis of individual sayings and their juxtaposition regarding the historical situation and program of the Q community. For example, Q 10:2 is seen to have a more positive view of mission than the pessimistic 10:3; therefore, it must represent a different stage of the mission. These critics also propose that 10:2 addresses a different (more "ecclesial") audience than 10:3; therefore, its addition to the mission discourse indicates a change in the stage of the mission or even a change from "antisocial ethos" to more constructive mission. Following this approach the interpreter can find that even once a whole discourse developed, its meaning could be transformed by the simple addition of one or two sayings, whose meaning has been separately determined already by the interpreter. Thus, as noted

---

12. See the trenchant criticism by Hans-Dieter Betz, "Jesus and the Cynics: Survey and Analysis of a Hypothesis," *JR* 74 (1994): 453–75; Christopher M. Tuckett, "A Cynic Q?" *Biblica* 70 (1989): 349–76; Robinson, "Building Blocks"; and the briefer, more sociologically oriented critique in Horsley, *Sociology*, 116–18; cf. Richard A. Horsley, "The Q People: Renovation, Not Radicalism," *Continuum* 1 (1991): 49–63; and idem, "Jesus, Itinerant Cynic or Israelite Prophet," in *Images of Jesus Today*, ed. James H. Charlesworth and Walter P. Weaver (Valley Forge, Pa.: Trinity Press International, 1994), 68–97.

13. Kloppenborg, *Formation of Q*, 194–95; Uro, *Sheep among the Wolves*, 98–116.

just above, since Q 9:57–60 has been determined to be about discipleship, its juxtaposition with 10:2–16 transforms a mission speech into a discourse about discipleship.[14]

Meaning, however, is contextual, and it seems highly questionable that the modern interpreter can determine the meaning of a saying isolated from literary and historical context as well as unlikely that the meaning of an individual saying, determined prior to its consideration in context, dominates the larger context in which it occurs, rather than becoming an integral component in that larger context. Procedurally, it seems necessary to give priority not to the individual saying but to the discourse of which the saying is one component, while understanding the discourse in the context of the whole series of discourses that comprise Q. Since the significance of particular component sayings depends upon the larger context, it is only appropriate to examine the structure and argument of the discourse as a whole before exploring the function of its components.

Structure of the Mission Discourse

Even through standard literary analysis it is fairly clear, virtually on the surface of Luke's version of Q, that Q 10:2–16 is a speech commissioning envoys for preaching and healing activity village by village. The core of the mission discourse is paralleled in Mark 6:7–13, and Luke reproduces both the Markan and the Q discourses, while Matthew conflates them. The occurrence of "sending" in 10:3 and 10:16 frames the whole: the one who does the sending is also sent. Despite Mark's distinctive narrative touches at the beginning and end of the commissioning, the common structure of the basic mission discourse can be discerned. A sending or statement of sending is followed by instructions on what not to take (or to take, in Mark) for the journey (Mark 6:7–9//Q 10:3–4). Then come instructions for staying in households (Mark 6:10; and eating, Q 10:5–7), followed by instructions on how to respond to towns / places that welcome and that reject (Mark 6:11//Q 10:8–11). What was apparently part of the instructions for healing and preaching in the receptive towns in Q appears in Mark's narrative framing in 6:12–13. Whereas Mark's discourse lacks the balance of the Q discourse with both the accepting and rejecting towns, the latter expands on the judgment delivered against the rejecting towns, in Q 10:12–15. Q 10:2 is the introductory instruction to petition "the lord of the harvest," who appears to be (one of) the sender(s) mentioned at the closing in 10:16 ("me" and / or "the one who sent me"). As often in examining Q material, since we do not know just what is missing from Matthew and Luke, we cannot decisively determine the complete outline and structure of a discourse. It is thus difficult to discern clearly how 9:57–62 and 10:21–24 relate to 10:2–16. The latter could be seen as a

---

14. Kloppenborg, *Formation of Q,* 200–201.

Q 9:57–10:16: Transliteration in Measured Verse for Hearing

Part I: Prologue (9:57–62)

A. 1. Kai eipen tis autǭ:

Akolouthēsō soi	hopou ean	aperchę̄.

2. Kai [eipen] autǭ ho Iēsous:

Hai alōpekes	phōleous	echousin	
kai ta peteina	tou ouranou	kataskēnōseis,	
Ho de huios tou anthrōpou	ouk echei pou	tēn kephalēn	klinę̄.

B. 1. Heteros de eipen autǭ:

Kyrie,	epitrepson moi	prōton
apelthein	kai thapsai	ton patera mou.

2. [Eipen] de autǭ:

akolouthei mou	kai aphes	tous nekrous
	thapsai	tous heautōn nekrous.

C. 1. {Eipen de kai heteros:

Akolouthēsō soi,	kyrie,	prōton de
epitrepson moi	apotaxasthai	tois ein ton oikon mou.

2. Eipen de ho Iēsous:

oudeis epibalōn	tēn cheira	ep' apotron	
kai blepōn	eis ta opisō	euthetos estin	tē basileią tou theou.}

---

closing prayer corresponding to the opening prayer in 10:2 and alternatively could be the positive reinforcement for the envoys and the community that sends and receives them corresponding to the negative reinforcement of the curses against the rejecting towns. Q 9:57–62 seems more clearly to constitute (part of) the introduction to the mission discourse that grounds it in and authorizes it from the popular Israelite tradition, Elijah's commissioning of Elisha for prophetic mission for the restoration of Israel.

The Text of the Mission Discourse in Oral Performance

In its very use of performative language, the mission discourse is one of the clearer cases of an oral-derived speech. "Behold, I send you" constitutes the sending. "Woe to you" declares the curse. "Whoever hears you hears me" proclaims and actualizes the authority of the envoy's proclamation as Jesus' and even God's proclamation. When we block out the text as measured verse, moreover, the oral patterns ("sound map") are fairly evident to the ear — although the eye also helps those of us whose reception is so heavily determined by print culture. The accompanying heavily reconstructed "text" aims to provide "hearers" who do not read Greek a transliteration that can be read aloud in order to obtain at least a minimal sense of the parallel lines, the rhythm within and among lines, and the (underlined) repetition of words and sounds in the Q mission discourse. It follows the reconstructed Q text of the International Q Project as much as possible,

Q 9:57–10:16: *Translation in Measured Verse for Hearing*

Part I: Prologue (9:57–62)

A. 1. And someone said:

I will follow you	wherever	you go.

2. And Jesus said to him:

The foxes	have	dens
and the birds	of the sky	lodgings,
but the son of man	has no place	to lay	the head.

B. 1. {And another said to him:

Lord,	permit me	first
to go	and bury	my father.

2. But he said to him,

Follow me	and leave	the dead
	to bury	their own dead.

C. 1. {And another said:

I will follow you,	Lord,	but first
permit me	to say farewell	to those at my home.

2. But Jesus said to him:

No one who puts	his hand	to the plow
and looks	back	is fit	for the kingdom of God.}

---

but deviates at points where taking factors of hypothetical oral recitation into account might lead to a variant reconstruction (indicated by { }).

The overall structure and internal coherences of this speech can be seen and heard from reading the accompanying transliteration aloud. The prologue to the sending and instructions consists of three brief hypothetical dialogues between Jesus and a person desirous of following him (and his mission/program). All of the lines, or all but one, consist of three main terms. The third line in Jesus' first answer is elongated for emphasis. The interlocutors' statements or requests consist of one or two lines, Jesus' answer of two or three lines. Many of the lines across the three brief dialogues are parallel and/or have parallel ideas, such as the three parallel lines (the third antithetical in meaning) in Jesus' first response, the requests of the second and third interlocutors, and the house/family theme at the very end of Jesus' answer in every dialogue. A number of words are repeated, such as *akolouthein* (follow), *thapsai* (bury), *prōton* (first), *nekrous* (dead), and a number of sounds resonate between successive lines or from dialogue to dialogue (as should be evident to the eye and ear in reading the transliteration aloud).

The sending and instructions proper begin with the reflective or ponderous two lines of two terms each in the introductory appeal for "workers," presumably for emphasis on how great is the challenge. Thereafter, nearly every line has three terms, except for the pronouncement of woes, which consist of two, the woe and the place-name. The closing of the discourse, sanctioning the sending, ends with a line of four, presumably for emphasis on "the one who sent me" as

Part II: The Sending and Instruction of Envoys (10:2–16)

A. 1. Ho men <u>therismos</u>   polus,   H<u>oi</u> de <u>ergatai</u>   olig<u>oi</u>.

   2. Deēthēte oun   <u>tou</u> kyri<u>ou</u>   <u>tou therismou</u>
      hop<u>ōs</u> ekbal<u>ę</u>   <u>ergatas</u>   eis ton <u>therismon</u> au<u>tou</u>.

B. 1. Id<u>ou</u>   apostell<u>ō</u>   hymas
      h<u>ōs</u> [arnas]   en mes<u>ō</u>   lyk<u>ōn</u>.

   2. M<u>ē</u> [bastazet]e {chalkon}, m<u>ē</u> peran, m<u>ē</u> hypodēmata, [m<u>ē</u>dena aspasēsthe].

C.   {Q 10:5–6 reconstructed from Matt. 10:12–13}

   1. E<u>is</u> hēn d' an   eiselthēte   oikian
      <u>ean</u> men <u>ę</u>   hē <u>oikia</u>   <u>axia,</u>
      <u>elthatō</u>   hē <u>eirēnē hymōn</u>   ep' au<u>tēn</u>.

   2. E<u>an</u> de mē <u>ę</u>   <u>axia,</u>
      hē <u>eirēnē hymon</u>   pros <u>hymas</u>   epistraph<u>ētō</u>.

   3. {En aut<u>ę</u> de   tē <u>oikia</u>   menete,}
      {?esthi<u>ontes</u>   ?kai pin<u>ontes</u>}   [ta par' aut<u>ōn</u>]
      <u>axios gar</u>   ho <u>ergatēs</u>   tou misthou autou.

D. 1. E<u>is</u> hen d' an polin   eiselthēte,   {kai dech<u>ō</u>ntai hymas,}
      therapeuete   [tous en aute]   asthenountas
      kai legete [autois]
      ēggiken   eph' <u>hymas</u>   h<u>ę</u> basileia <u>tou</u> the<u>ou</u>.

   2. [E<u>is</u> hēn d'] an [polin   eiselthēte,   kai] m<u>ę</u> dech<u>ō</u>ntai hymas,
      exerchomenoi   [ex<u>ō</u>] [<u>tēs</u> poleōs   ekein]<u>ēs</u>
      ektinazate   ton koniorton   ton pod<u>ō</u>n hym<u>ō</u>n.

   3. Lego hymin:
      Sodomois   en t<u>ę</u> h<u>ę</u>mera   eke<u>i</u>nē
      anektoteron estai   <u>ę</u> t<u>ę</u> pol<u>ei</u>   ekein<u>ę</u>.

E. 1. <u>Ouai soi,</u>   Chorazin.   <u>Ouai soi,</u>   Bēthsaida.

   2. Hoti ei   en <u>Tyrǫ</u> kai <u>Sidōni</u>   egenēth<u>ę</u>san
      hai dynameis   hai genomen<u>ai</u>   en <u>hymin,</u>
      pal<u>ai</u> an   en sakk<u>o</u> kai spod<u>o</u> [ ]   meteno<u>ę</u>san.

   3. Plen   <u>Tyrǫ</u> kai <u>Sidōni</u>   anektoteron
      estai   en tē kris<u>ei</u>   <u>ę</u> <u>hymin</u>.

   4. Kai su,   Kapharnaoum!
      M<u>ę</u> <u>heōs</u>   ouran<u>ou</u>   hyps<u>ōth</u><u>ę</u>s<u>ę</u>?
      <u>heōs</u>   [t<u>ou</u>] had<u>ou</u>   katab<u>ę</u>s<u>ę</u>!

F. 1. Ho dechomenos   hymas   eme <u>dechetai,</u>
      [kai] <u>ho</u> eme   dechomenos   <u>dechetai</u>   ton aposteilanta <u>me</u>.

---

the ultimate authority for the whole program (as it were, by being outside the otherwise consistent pattern of three-word lines). The entry into a town and the reception or lack of reception there are precisely parallel. So also are the entry into a household and its worthiness or lack thereof, if Matthew's version is closer to Q. At several points, usually within successive lines, words are repeated (e.g., *therismos* [harvest] and *ergatai* [workers]), and at several points also sounds are repeated, those in the ending of lines in the curses on the towns being particularly noticeable.

Part II: The Sending and Instruction of Envoys (10:2–16)

A. 1. The harvest   is great,   but the workers   are few.

    2. So ask   the lord   of the harvest

      to send   workers   into his harvest.

B. 1. Behold,   I [myself] send   you

      as lambs   in the midst of   wolves.

    2. Do not carry a copper or a purse or sandals   and do not greet anyone.

C. {Q 10:5–6 reconstructed from Matt 10:12–13}

    1. If you   enter   a house

      and if   the house   is worthy,

      let come   your peace   upon it.

    2. But if   it is not   worthy,

      your peace   to you   let it return.

    3. {And in this   house   remain,}

      {?eating   ?and drinking}   [what they provide,]

      for worthy   is the worker   of his/her wage.

D. 1. Into whatever town   you enter,   {and they receive you,}

      heal   [those in it]   who are sick

      and say [to them]

      has come   upon you   the kingdom of God.

    2. Into whatever [town   you enter   and] they do not receive you

      as you depart   [out of that   town]

      shake off   the dust   from your feet.

    3. I tell you:

      For the Sodomites   on that   day

      it will be more tolerable   than for that   town.

E. 1. Woe to you,   Chorazin.   Woe to you,   Bethsaida.

    2. Because if   in Tyre and Sidon   had happened

      the wonders   which happened   in you

      already   in sackcloth and ashes   they would have repented.

    3. Indeed   in Tyre and Sidon   more tolerable

      it will be   in the judgment   than for you.

    4. And you,   Capernaum!

      Way up   to the heaven   will you be lifted?

      Down   to hades   you will be cast!

F. 1. Whoever receives   you   receives me,

      and whoever   receives me   receives   the one who sent me.

Metonymic Referencing and Resonance in the Mission Discourse

The significance of the mission discourse itself, like that of any discourse in Q, involves far more than its structure and the meaning of its sayings within the structure. Interpretation of Jesus' sayings focused on individual sayings usually strives to find the meaning of words and sayings, often with a special concern to establish the transmission of the saying. As noted above, once certain individual sayings are construed literalistically, the hypothesis of the "wandering charismatics" is used to explain their transmission. Communication, however, is far broader and deeper than mere transmission of sayings, and meaning depends upon a relational context. Shifting to a more adequate understanding of communication and meaning, we must attend to the historical social context of the hearers and to the tradition out of which they resonate with the message of the discourse as well as to the message itself. If we can begin to understand how and why the mission discourse resonated with its hearers, then we can also discern its *register* and *context* of performance, which will also explain the transmission of the discourse.

The Prologue

A sequence of three brief dialogues introduces the mission discourse. Probably the second and certainly the third allude to Elijah's call of Elisha as his assistant and successor in the prophetic renewal of Israel during the long struggle against the oppressive regime of Ahab and Jezebel (see esp. 1 Kings 19:19–21). Mark exhibits parallels to Q's reference to Elijah's renewal of Israel and his call of Elisha to advance the struggle and succeed him in it, in connection with a program of preaching that "the kingdom of God has come upon you" (Q 10:9) and a call for repentance. In Mark, immediately following Jesus' announcement of his / God's program ("the kingdom of God is at hand, repent" [1:14–15]), Jesus calls four of the principal disciples (1:16–20) and later sends them on the parallel mission (6:7–13; as well as makes explicit the parallel between Jesus and Elijah and Moses [9:2–8]). Many other passages in the Gospels indicate that the early Jesus movement(s) were keenly aware of the similarities of both Jesus and John to Elijah, the great prophet of Israel's renewal.[15]

The first brief dialogue refers to the political-economic situation of ordinary people and / or Jesus in contrast to that of beasts and animals of prey and / or people's predatory oppressors. In Israelite culture and tradition, as it comes to expression in the Hebrew Bible, foxes and jackals are destructive and repugnant creatures. They invade vineyards (Song of Songs 2:15). They prowl around and virtually repossess ruined cities (1 Kings 21:10 [LXX]; Neh. 4:3; Ps. 62(63):10; Ezek. 13:4).[16] "Birds of the sky" are also regarded as destructive and carnivorous predators. A standard image in historical and prophetic literature for disaster and / or punishment is that people's unburied bodies will be devoured by birds of prey and wild animals

---

15. The classic exploration is J. A. T. Robinson, "Elijah, John, and Jesus: An Essay in Detection," in *Twelve New Testament Essays* (London: SCM, 1962), 11–27; cf. more recently Dale C. Allison Jr., "Elijah Must Come First," *JBL* 103 (1984): 256–58; Joan E. Taylor, *The Immerser: John the Baptist within Second Temple Judaism* (Grand Rapids, Mich.: Eerdmans, 1997), esp. 281–94; and Robert L. Webb, *John the Baptizer and Prophet: A Socio-Historical Study,* JSNTSup 62 (Sheffield, Eng.: JSNT, 1991).

16. Christopher M. Tuckett, *Q and the History of Early Christianity* (Peabody, Mass.: Hendrickson, 1996), 181; Robert Doran, "The Divinization of Disorder: The Trajectory of Matt. 8:20//Luke 9:58//Gos. Thom. 86," in *The Future of Early Christianity: Essays in Honor of Helmut Koester,* ed. Birger Pearson et al. (Minneapolis: Fortress, 1991), 212; and Harold W. Hoehner, *Herod Antipas,* SNTSMS 17 (Cambridge: Cambridge University Press, 1972), 343–47.

(1 Sam. 17:44, 46; 1 Kings 12:24; 14:11; 16:4; 21:24 [punishment for Ahab!]; Ps. 79:2; Isa. 18:5–6 [with image of the harvest]; Jer. 7:33; 15:3; 16:4; 19:7; Hos. 2:14; Ezek. 34:5 [sheep scattered became food for wild animals]; 39:4). Far from a pastoral reference to benign natural creatures of the sky and field, "foxes" and "birds of the sky" refer to predators. We immediately think of Jesus' reference to Herod Antipas, who wants to kill him, as "that fox" (Luke 13:31–33). The term used for "nest" is not the standard *nossia* but the unusual *kataskenosis*, suggesting a settled living where birds "lodge" under trees (cf. Ps. 103:12 [LXX]; Dan. 4:21). The lodging of both the birds and beasts of prey is stable and secure.

By contrast, "the son of man has no place to lay his head." There is no note of rejection in this saying,[17] hence no reason to carry that over from the apparent rejection of "the son of man" in 7:34. Nor is there any reason to find a parallel here to Wisdom not finding a dwelling place among people and withdrawing to the heavens, apparently suggested to some interpreters by the occurrence of Wisdom at the close of the preceding discourse in 7:35.[18] Nor should we simply assume that the idiom "the son of man" here is a "christological title."[19] That assumption is an integral part of the standard Christian theological reading of Q, apparently strongly influenced by the Matthean reformulation of several of the key occurrences of the phrase "son of man" in other Q discourses, particularly in the eschatological scenario of "the parousia of the Son of Man" in Matt. 24:27, 37, 39. We, like the ancient Q people, are faced with a notorious ambiguity in reading / hearing "the son of man" idiom. Sufficient variety exists in the usage of the idiom in Q and sufficient confusion exists with regard to how to sort out the various uses against the background of an unclear cultural usage that we cannot determine whether the idiom in Q always refers to Jesus, hence is usually his reference to himself.[20] In Q the phrase refers sometimes to Jesus (7:34; 6:22?; 11:30?; 12:10?), perhaps once to a figure in the divine heavenly court who may be identical with Jesus (12:8–9?), once to an undefined figure that "is coming" unexpectedly (12:40), and in one discourse somewhat vaguely to the future "day(s) of the son of man" (17:24, 26, 30). Yet the idiom can also refer more generally to "humanity / people," which is apparently the meaning in Q 9:57–58, in contrast with foxes and birds. That "reading / hearing" also makes sense in the context of the mission discourse. In the broader context of Q, however, given its (self-)references to Jesus in 6:22; 7:34; and 11:30, it should perhaps be taken as Jesus' self-reference. But even then, since the phrase can mean "humanity," the two references can overlap: "son of man" suggests both Jesus and humanity or Jesus as a representative figure.

In its contrast between the secure dwelling enjoyed by predatory foxes and birds and the utter lack of house and home for people / Jesus, the saying protests a pat-

---

17. So also Kloppenborg, *Formation of Q*, 192.

18. See references in ibid., 192 n. 86.

19. Versus Kloppenborg, *Formation of Q*, 192, and many others.

20. See esp. James M. Robinson, "The Son of Man in the Sayings Gospel Q," in *Tradition und Translation: Zum Problem der interkulturellen Übersetzbarkeit religiöser Phänomene: Festschrift für Carsten Colpe zum 65. Geburtstag*, ed. Christoph Elsas et al. (Berlin: Walter de Gruyter, 1994), 315–35.

tern of gross injustice. The "homelessness" is not "elective," something expected or chosen, but something utterly unfair and unjust in the current state of affairs, evident in the very structure of the saying.[21] In a rough parallel from Roman history, Tiberius Gracchus defends his proposed agrarian legislation with a similar contrast:

> The wild beasts that roam over Italy have everyone of them a cave or lair to lurk in; but the men who fight and die for Italy enjoy the common air and light, indeed, but nothing else; houseless and homeless they wander about with their wives and children. And it is with lying lips that their imperators exhort their soldiers . . . [who] fight and die to support others in wealth and luxury. (Plutarch, *Tiberius Gracchus* 9.4–5.828c)

The parallel introductory statement to the Q mission discourse is thus certainly not a reference to a voluntarily homeless lifestyle, a counterculture to which villagers are called. Heard in connection with what follows in 10:3–10, Q 9:58 could indeed be simply an indication of how difficult the mission will be, as the envoys are called to follow in the way of their prophetic sender, with the traveling Jesus being the paradigm for his envoys who will be dependent on host households for shelter and food. Yet the Roman parallel, along with the cultural resonance of "foxes" and "birds of the air," suggests something more ominous and important. The beginning of the introduction to the Q mission discourse here calls attention to the situation addressed in the mission discourse. While the predatory foxes have their dens and the birds of prey their lodgings — and by innuendo, Herod Antipas has his palace (see Q 7:25) and the Roman eagle its imperial cities — the people and / or their prophet ("I") have no shelter, no home. The situation that the mission will address is polarized between comfortable predatory rulers and the ordinary people (of Israel). That was exactly the way the situation looked from the viewpoint of hungry and indebted Galilean villagers required to render up tax revenues to Herod Antipas, from which he had reconstructed the city of Sepphoris as "the ornament of all Galilee" and then constructed the new city of Tiberias, with his own luxurious palace on the hill above the city. Heard in this way, the introduction to the mission discourse would thus clearly echo the opening of the covenantal discourse that preceded it: "blessed are the poor, for theirs is the kingdom . . . , woe to the rich, for . . . " (6:20–26).

In the second and third brief dialogues the statements "Leave the dead to bury their own dead" and "No one who puts his hand to the plow and looks back is fit for the kingdom of God" both allude clearly to Elijah's commissioning Elisha to assist and succeed him in his struggles for the renewal of Israel (see esp. 1 Kings 19:19–21). Presumably these allusions would have evoked fuller memories associated with Elijah, including the larger numbers of prophets engaged in rallying the people over against the oppressive practices of King Ahab (see, e.g., 1 Kings 18:4).

In the second dialogue (9:59–60) it is unclear how "leave the dead" could ever have been taken so literally by modern scholarly interpreters, since the very content of the saying blocks a literalistic hearing / reading: the dead cannot bury

---

21. So also Jacobson, *First Gospel*, 135; and Tuckett, *Q and the History of Early Christianity*, 181–82.

the dead. The immediately following saying about putting hand to the plow is clearly metaphorical. Frequently in Q, John's or Jesus' sayings are clearly meant as metaphors or hyperbole (3:8, 9, 17; 11:39, 46; 12:49; 14:26). In the context of a call to prophetic mission, the dialogue in Q 9:59–60 is clearly hyperbole. It plays on a custom that was a solemn obligation throughout the ancient world, the burial of a deceased parent. In the Mishnah (*m. Ber.* 3:1), tending to the dead is declared far more important than reciting the Shema. In response to the request to first go bury a father, "Leave the dead to bury their own dead" declares that the call to mission is of such extreme importance and urgency that not even the obligation to bury one's father should delay one's answering the call. Moreover, there are precedents for this violation of the sacred obligation of attending to the dead in the Israelite prophetic tradition. In both Jeremiah and Ezekiel we catch sight of how a violation or refusal of the sacred obligation to bury the dead was used as a prophetic sign. God forbade Jeremiah symbolically to enter a house of mourning (Jer. 16:1–8) and similarly forbade Ezekiel to mourn "the delight of your eyes" (Ezek. 24:15–24) to dramatize inexpressible horror and grief over the unfaithfulness and destruction of Jerusalem. In Elijah's call of Elisha, to which the dialogue in Q 9:59–60 alludes, Elisha asked simply that he be permitted to "kiss my father and mother" before responding to the call, and Elijah allowed it. In Q 9:59–60 the prospective envoy requests time for a far more compelling filial obligation, and Jesus refuses. The more extreme reason for delay has the effect of radicalizing the mission's urgency. Jesus' call to mission — the program of preaching and manifesting the kingdom in Israel, and not a more individually conceived "discipleship"[22] — is of overwhelming importance and urgency, far more than even the filial obligation toward one's just-deceased parent.

The third dialogue also alludes to Elijah's call of Elisha, in which the latter was plowing when Elijah "threw his mantle over him" — although Q 9:61–62 transfers the plowing image from the activity Elisha left behind to the mission to which the followers are called. A number of persuasive arguments have been offered for including Luke 9:61–62 in Q.[23] In reminiscence of but in contrast to Elisha, who responded to Elijah's call, yet wanted to bid his family farewell, Jesus' followers are not even to "look back" but to be exclusively and single-mindedly dedicated to the task of "plowing" the soil for the kingdom. Jesus' call to mission is analogous to and in the tradition of Elijah's call of Elisha. The escalation of demands in Q 9:59–60, 61–62, however, dramatizes just how much more urgent Jesus' mission of renewing Israel is than Elijah's was.[24] Jesus requires total dedication to the task (9:62), despite separation from the family (9:60) and traveling without permanent residence (9:58?; 10:4, 5–7).

---

22. Versus Kloppenborg, *Formation of Q,* 191

23. John S. Kloppenborg, *Q Parallels: Synopsis, Critical Notes, and Concordance* (Sonoma, Calif.: Polebridge, 1988), 64: "Of all the Sondergut, this has the strongest probability of deriving from Q, since it is found in a Q context, the saying coheres with the preceding sayings formally, and it evinces the same theology of discipleship typical of other sayings."

24. So also Kloppenborg, *Formation of Q,* 191.

The Sending and Instruction

In an address to communities of a Jesus movement, the move from a petition to "the lord of the harvest" to send out (more) laborers in Q 10:2 to the declaratory sending of (more) laborers in 10:3 would be only appropriate if not expected. Detection of a discrepancy between these two closely related steps in the standard mission discourse is an inappropriate application of modern Western logic of literary compositional consistency and is perhaps rooted in a lack of class analysis. There is thus no need to view Q 10:2 as a redactional addition to the Q mission discourse in which the rest of the sayings framed by the "sending" in 10:3 and 10:16 form part of the instructions to those sent out and, at points, to the community also involved in the sending.

"Harvest" — repeated in this saying surely for emphasis — had long been a standard image for judgment in the prophetic tradition and continued into Jewish apocalyptic literature after the time of Jesus and Q. Its particular uses and applications were various and by no means always eschatological (as in 4 Ezra 9:1–21; 2 Bar. 70:2). The "harvest" is sometimes simply punitive judgment against (part of) Israel (Judah, Hos. 6:11), more often against oppressive imperial regimes (nations; Babylon, Jer. 51:33; the nations assembled against Jerusalem, Mic. 4:11–13; Joel 3:12–13 (4:10 [LXX]). Particularly interesting for Q 9:57–10:16 are Isa. 18:3–6, which combines an extended metaphor of harvest for judgment with the horror of being devoured by birds of prey, and the late Isaianic "little apocalypse" reference to the gathering of Israel when God "threshes" the oppressive imperial regimes (Isa. 27:12–13). Decisive for reading/hearing the harvest image in Q 10:2 is the parallel imagery elsewhere in Q discourses. The opening proclamation of the Baptist in Q 3:7–9, 16–17 uses harvest images both positively and negatively, as the wheat is gathered into the granary while the chaff and unproductive trees are burned with fire. And in the Q 11:14–26 discussion of exorcism, Jesus' activity is portrayed as "gathering." The gathering in these passages suggests also the gathering or pilgrimage of Israelites (not Gentiles!) to the final banquet portrayed in Q 13:28–29 (cf. Isa. 43:5–7; Ps. 107:4).[25] It is also worth noting that the parallel saying isolated in Gospel of Thomas 73 appears in a sequence of sayings that emphasize the few or single one among the many who will attain salvation/enlightenment/life and does not suggest (final) judgment. In the context of Q as a whole and the mission discourse in particular, the harvest would appear to be primarily the ingathering now that the right time has finally come, with the implication toward the end of the discourse that those who reject the preaching of the kingdom and the healing bring judgment upon themselves.

The saying addresses a movement or communities keenly aware that only a bare beginning has been made in the renewal of Israel inaugurated by Jesus and

---

25. As noted above, the frequent interpretation of this passage in terms of the "Gentiles'" pilgrimage to Zion at the end of days depends upon the Christian theological scheme of salvation history. The biblical and other passages cited refer rather to the ingathering of dispersed Israelites. See Horsley, "Social Conflict," 38; and Dale C. Allison Jr., The Jesus Tradition in Q (Harrisburg, Pa.: Trinity Press International, 1997), 176–86.

John. More workers are needed. "Workers" (originally those who worked the soil — farmers, peasants) was apparently a term familiar in Palestine for those engaged in expanding and building the Jesus movement(s), community by community. Paul uses the term in castigation of rival workers who seem to come from Palestine or are at least of Israelite / Jewish / Hebrew provenance in 2 Cor. 11:13 and Phil. 3:2. The "workers," moreover, are clearly parallel figures to "apostles" in 2 Cor. 11:13. The term carries the agrarian ethos from which the movement originated. The model on which this harvest is conceived is a large estate of a "master / lord" who hires and sends out laborers, as portrayed in the parable of the laborers in the vineyard (Matt. 20:1–16). There is no need to see a discrepancy between "the lord of the harvest" as God in 10:2 and Jesus as the immediate sender of the envoys in 10:3 and 16.[26] Although the majority of references to *kyrios* in Q allude to Jesus, the prayer here, as in Q 10:21–24, which immediately follows (or ends) this discourse, seems to refer to God. In any case, there is no need to imagine a significant difference, which may simply be the imposition of modern Western logic. As indicated explicitly at the close of the discourse, in 10:16 and again in 10:21–24, there is a functional equivalent between Jesus and the Father / the One who sent Jesus. In Q, God's power is at work in Jesus and the envoys, and the kingdom of God is manifested precisely in the renewal of Israel.

The mission is apparently to Israel, as suggested elsewhere in Q, such as the explicit reference to the deliverance or establishment of justice for the twelve tribes in 22:28–30 (discussed in chapter 12 below). Paul's account of his consultation with Peter and other key disciples of Jesus in Gal. 2:1–10 indicates that elsewhere in the early Jesus movement(s) as well the expansion of the movement focused on Israel, and that he and Barnabas were relatively distinctive in their expansion of the movement among other peoples. A close reading of the mission discourse itself suggests that it understands the mission as directed to Israel, with no extension to "the Gentiles." Nothing in Q 10:2 or 10:3 suggests that the one expresses a positive and the other a negative attitude toward the mission, let alone that such a discrepancy indicates a move from a failed mission in Israel to a more positive morale associated with positive response from Gentiles (again the imposition of a later Christian scheme). The fact that the towns of Chorazin, Bethsaida, and Capernaum are cursed for failing to respond indicates that the mission was directed to just such communities. The argument that "10:13–15 bases its condemnation of the Jewish towns on the predicted repentance of Gentiles"[27] is rooted in a standard Christian theological viewpoint. Q 10:13–15 speaks only of the hypothetical repentance of Tyre and Sidon, and the rhetoric depends upon the assumption among the hearers that those traditional enemy cities are to be punished severely in the judgment as a point of comparison for how much worse it will be for nonrepentant Israelite towns.

---

26. Cf. Kloppenborg, *Formation of Q,* 193.

27. As well as on the contention that "Gentile faith is interpreted as a condemnatory sign for Israel" (Kloppenborg, *Formation of Q,* 196, and many others).

In this connection it seems highly probable that Matt. 10:5b and possibly Matt. 10:6 belonged to the Q mission discourse. Matthew used only what he found in Mark and Q for his (conflated) mission discourse, *and* he did not omit any (other) piece of Q 10:2–16. Moreover, distinctively Matthean passages about "Gentiles / nations" (*ethne*) are positive and inclusive (cf. 4:15; 12:18, 21; 21:43; 25:32; 28:19), whereas the negative or exclusive references to *ethne / ethnikoi* are either from Mark or from Q (5:47; 6:7; 18:17), and Matthew has no interest in Samaritans. From consideration of Matthew, it would appear that Matt. 10:5b at least was from Q. Luke, on the other hand, had reason to eliminate the prohibition of going to the Gentiles and Samaritans and confining the mission to Israel as particularistic and / or no longer relevant. The principal arguments against the existence of Matt. 10:5b–6 in Q are rooted in a Christian theological scheme of the separation of "Christianity" from "Judaism."[28] Were Matt. 10:5b and / or 6 to have been part of the mission discourse, there would be no question but what the mission was focused exclusively on Israel, with no intention of a wider expansion.

The emphatic "I" in Matthew's parallel to Luke 10:3 (rare in Gospel sayings of Jesus) is unnecessary in Greek style, hence probably deleted by Luke, and may well indicate a prophetic form in the declaratory sending or commissioning.

"Lambs / sheep among wolves" was a standard image in Israelite tradition with which the hearers of this discourse would have resonated metonymically. In New Testament studies, which carry over into recent interpretation of Q, it is usually understood to be a reference to Israel / the Jews among the hostile Gentiles.[29] The use here in Q 10:3 is then read as an inversion of that situation by which the Q community's emissaries experience hostility from the Jews and is even taken as evidence of a supposedly "failed" mission to Israel. It is readily apparent, however, that this picture of the (proto-) Christian missionaries as innocent sheep among the hostile Jews is rooted in a Christian scheme of Christian origins from "Judaism." The texts that have been cited as using this metaphor for Israel among the Gentiles need some serious critical reconsideration apart from the old Christian view of Jews vs. Gentiles as the primary or only conflict in antiquity. In *1 Enoch* 89:13–27, the Egyptian imperial regime of Pharaoh is portrayed as wolves oppressing the Israelite sheep. The "nations of the earth" among whom the devout of Jerusalem or Israel are like lambs in *Pss. Sol.* 8:23 is part of a passage lamenting the Roman conquest of Jerusalem and leading into a plea to "bring together the dispersed of Israel." Similarly, the image of Israel as sheep at the mercy of the wolves in *4 Ezra* 5:18 is used in the context of pondering the Roman imperial destruction of Jerusalem. Thus these relatively late Judean uses of the standard image of sheep among wolves refer more precisely to the oppression of Israelites / Jews by imperial rulers. The earlier Israelite prophetic and other uses of the standard image also refer to oppressive rulers, only within Israel or Judea itself. Ezekiel 22:23–27

---

28. See further Kloppenborg, *Q Parallels*, 72; and David Catchpole, *The Quest for Q* (Edinburgh: T. & T. Clark, 1993), 165–71.

29. Tuckett, *Q and the History of Early Christianity*, 185–86, citing Hoffmann, *Studien*, 294–95.

portrays the various groups among the Judean ruling class as predatory animals: "the princes like a roaring lion tearing the prey"; "its officials . . . are like wolves tearing the prey, shedding blood, destroying lives to get dishonest gain." Zephaniah 3:1–3 uses the same stock image: Jerusalem is a "soiled, defiled, oppressing city! . . . The officials within it are roaring lions; its judges are evening wolves that leave nothing until the morning." The same stock image appears in Prov. 28:15 (where the LXX has translated with "wolves" the saying that reads in Hebrew: "Like a roaring lion or a charging bear / is a wicked ruler over a poor people").

Thus the standard image was one of oppressive, predatory rulers. And that is clearly the gist of the statement here in the Q mission discourse.[30] It fits several other statements elsewhere in Q. The Pharisees are accused of being full of extortion in Q 11:39 (following Matthean wording); violent men attack the kingdom violently in Q 16:16 (Matthean wording). Pharisees and / or Jerusalem rulers are charged with killing the prophets generation after generation in Q 11:49–51 and 13:34–35. From the perspective of the Q discourses, the situation in which their envoys operate is one of political-religious conflict, possibly repressive persecution and violence by the rulers, as apparently in Q 12:2–12 (see further in chapter 12). Indeed the concerns of the Q people were historically justified, given the references to violent repressive measures taken by Roman governors and Herodian kings against popular prophetic movements and other popular protests right around the time of Jesus and the activities of the Q people.[31] "Sheep among the wolves" is indeed a metaphor for vulnerability. But more specifically it refers to the potential political trouble that the envoys might evoke because their mission would be threatening to Roman client rulers such as Antipas who could easily take decisive repressive measures against such agitators. Although Q makes no explicit mention of it, John the Baptist had apparently been killed while imprisoned by Antipas (Mark 6:17–29; Josephus, *Ant.* 19.116–19). Furthermore, over against the unfounded thesis that a second redactional layer of Q attests a rejection of the Q people's preaching of repentance, Jesus' envoys would have been in a dangerous position not because of the rejection of their message but because of its success, through which they might come to the attention of the rulers.

The instructions on "equipment" for the road, or rather on what not to take, are baffling, or rather opaque, to modern interpreters. Perhaps that helps explain the susceptibility to the Cynic reading, which at least finds the specific items listed as characteristic of the Cynic philosophers. As commonly observed, the less stringent parallel in the Markan mission discourse allows a staff as well as sandals (Mark 6:8–9). That neither Q nor Mark, in contrast to Matthew and Luke, mentions gold or silver coins suggests that they come from communities

---

30. "Wolves in sheep's clothing" is a different image with various applications (e.g., in Matt. 7:14; John 10:12; Acts 20:29; *Did.* 16:3).

31. References to Josephus's accounts and analysis in Richard A. Horsley, " 'Like One of the Prophets of Old': Two Types of Popular Prophets at the Time of Jesus," *CBQ* 47 (1985): 435–63; and Richard A. Horsley with John S. Hanson, *Bandits, Prophets, and Messiahs* (1985; reprint, Harrisburg, Pa.: Trinity Press International, 1999), chap. 4.

that are economically quite "primitive." Even in the cities, the ancient economy was only partially monetarized. In villages and towns, most households were more or less self-sufficient, using only low-value copper coins if any. Presumably copper coins would have come in handy in traveling away from home. Mark allows such "copper" coins; Q prohibits even a "purse." But neither assumes familiarity with coins of any value. The prohibition of purse and bag / knapsack (in which one would carry food [cf. Jth. 10:5; 13:10]) makes sense in connection with the following instructions to stay in a given household, eating whatever the household can provide. The "workers" are going to be preaching and healing in village communities where, almost by definition in any traditional agrarian society, the people are subsistence farmers, usually economically marginal at best. The preacher-healers are to live among the people with whom they are working and are to have nothing beyond what is offered, being dependent on the subsistence support of hosts sympathetic to the movement. In any case, the prohibition of purse and bag here is not an indication of a general individual lifestyle of poverty but a specific instruction for how to live while on the mission of preaching and healing.

The prohibition of sandals is more of a puzzle. Sandals and a staff were standard equipment for those about to embark on a journey (e.g., Exod. 12:11). The proscription of sandals in Q 10:4 does not appear to be connected with mourning (cf. 2 Sam. 15:30). Instructions to the Q envoys are thus more severe than the practice of the Essenes (Josephus, B.J. 2.126).[32]

In 10:5–11, Q's mission discourse, while parallel to Mark's in structure, also presents a clearer sense of the concrete social forms entailed in the mission, the household, and the village. Indeed, the core of the instructions for mission are organized around these two social forms that constituted the fundamental structure of ancient Galilean and Judean society. Q 10:5–7 focuses on the household, the most basic social form on which all else depended, and 10:8–10 deals with the village or town. As the Lukan individualizing addition and adaptation in Luke 10:6 point up, the focus in Q 10:5–7 is clearly the household, not individuals within it, although the relationship is intensely personal. The envoy's blessing of "peace" comes upon the whole household. The envoy's peace is his or her personal blessing, and it is closely related to the household's supplying shelter and sustenance. If the household is not "worthy," then the peace returns to the envoy. Q 10:8–11 then give instructions for working, or not working, in a "city" (town / village), depending on its receptiveness. Q 10:8–9 indicates what is to happen as the mission strategy is implemented, 10:10–11 what the envoys are to do if the town does not welcome them. To the welcoming town, the kingdom and the attendant healings are offered; to an unreceptive town, the kingdom "comes near" rather as judgment. Wiping off the dust from the feet clearly involves calling

---

32. If a staff was also prohibited in Q, that removes the only means of self-protection that a traveler would have at hand (cf. Gen. 32:10; Ezek. 29:6–7; 2 Sam. 23:21).

down or enacting a curse against the unreceptive town. Yet while such a curse cuts off all association or community, it does not spell out the consequences.

Q 10:12 and 10:13–15 expand on what would be a weak climax, escalating the curse already symbolized in the wiping off the dust form the feet, by spelling out the consequences. Beginning respectively with "I tell you" and "Woe to," both 10:12 and 10:13–15 are traditional prophetic forms, with Jesus speaking for God. The form of the woe oracle in 10:13–14, like those in Q 11:39–52, corresponds to the *oi l-...ki-* type in Hebrew, which was conformed with the *hoti-*type in the later prophets.[33] The emphasis in Q 10:13–14, with its direct address, falls on the accusation. As in the woes in Q 11:39–52, the *hoti-* or "that..."-clause states the reason for the death and / or destruction presupposed in the cry of woe. Speaking on divine authority, 10:14 pronounces the condemnation to be implemented in the judgment. Perhaps the declaration of judgment in 10:14 stands out more prominently because it follows immediately upon the cry of woe, in comparison with 11:39–52, where the declaration of judgment comes after five or six cries of woe.

Besides being in traditional Israelite prophetic forms, both 10:12 and 10:13–15 resonate heavily with symbolic places from Israelite prophetic tradition. Sodom was not simply a standing symbol for divine judgment and destruction. It was destroyed not only because of its wickedness but also because its people did not recognize God's messengers (and give hospitality to them, as did Lot). The near contemporary *Testament of Asher* (7:1) offers a helpful parallel to Q 10:12: "Do not become like Sodom, which did not recognize the Lord's messengers and perished forever." It is often noted that Tyre and Sidon are the targets of numerous Israelite prophetic oracles (Isa. 23; Ezek. 26; 27; 28; Joel 4:4–8; Amos 1:9–10; Zech. 9:2–4). We should also notice the reasons.[34] As the historic trading cities of the eastern Mediterranean, Tyre and Sidon not only were the principal carriers of the trade in luxury goods, for which the ruling elite of Judah and Israel / Samaria paid with agricultural produce siphoned away from their only economic base, the Israelite peasantry. These cities also were principal carriers of the slave trade (Amos 1:9–10; Joel 4:4–8; Ezek. 27:13). Galileans in particular had traditionally been eyed by these cities, particularly Tyre, as a source for the agricultural products it desperately needed, given the limited agricultural resources in its immediate environs. Historical sources provide two revealing windows onto the relationship between Galilee and Tyre and Sidon. Josephus's accounts of the takeover of several fortresses in Upper Galilee in early Roman times by Marion, tyrant of Tyre, and Herod's retaking of the fortresses illustrate the periodic struggle for control of desired agricultural territory (*B.J.* 1.238–39; *Ant.* 14.297–98). The book of Acts (12:20) refers briefly to the rulers of Tyre and Sidon attempting to appease an offended Agrippa I "because their country depended on the king's country for food."

---

33. Waldemar Jansen, *Mourning Cry and Woe Oracle* (Berlin: Walter de Gruyter, 1972); and Migaku Sato, *Q und Prophetie* (Tübingen: J. C. B. Mohr [Paul Siebeck], 1988), 183–200.

34. For the following, see further Richard A. Horsley, *Galilee: History, Politics, People* (Valley Forge, Pa.: Trinity Press International, 1995), 161–63; and idem, *Archaeology, History, and Society in Galilee* (Valley Forge, Pa.: Trinity Press International, 1996), 85–86.

Thus both in the Israelite prophetic tradition and in contemporary political-economic power relations, Tyre and Sidon represented wealthy and powerful foreign cities that directly or indirectly drained the resources of Galilean peasants. Jesus' woe in Q 10:13–15 thus uses these hated symbols of exploitation against some of the very towns that would have resented those cities. The refusal of repentance is also a frequent motif in prophetic tradition (e.g., Isa. 30:15; Jer. 9:4; 15:7; Hos. 7:10; 11:5; Amos 4:6–10). Q 10:13–14 may also resonate with the traditional prophetic theme that foreign empires or rival kingdoms would be God's instruments of judgment against Judah or Israel (e.g., Isa. 5:26–29; 10:5–6; Jer. 4:5–8, and the contemporary *T. Benj.* 10:10), but presents Tyre and Sidon not as attacking Israel but as hypothetical cases of wicked cities turned repentant in order to bring shame to Chorazin and Bethsaida for failing to repent.

Q 10:16 is clearly the conclusion of the mission discourse. Far from ever having been an independent saying, its content and structure presuppose and encapsulate a sending of representatives who speak for the sender(s). The concluding statement of the mission discourse is not about hospitality but about the whole relationship between (the towns), the envoys, Jesus, and ultimately God, who, in giving the kingdom, authorizes the mission. In its antithetical parallelism, it sums up and ties together the discourse, picking up the recurrent pattern of reception and rejection in 10:5–7 and 8–11. Structurally, in this discourse this statement functions in the same way that the double parable about housebuilding, Q 6:46–49, does in the covenant renewal discourse. Q 10:16 is not concerned primarily with the envoys' rejection.[35] It rather restates their authorization in connection with articulating the intimate and direct representative relationship between Jesus and the prophetic Q envoys. In other contexts other "recitations" of this saying were used to authorize or legitimate apostles as representatives of and spokespersons for Jesus (e.g., *Did.* 11:4; Ignatius, *Ephesians* 6:1).

Function of the Mission Discourse in the Communities of the Q Movement

This discourse, along with other Q discourses, was performed to communities of a wider movement. One of the fundamental concerns of the new movement was its expansion, taking the announcement and manifestation of the kingdom of God to other villages and towns of Israel. That required both commissioning more workers as the prophetic representatives of Jesus, his message, and his healing and the support of the sending community. This mission and the workers involved in it were understood in prophetic terms, a prophetic extension of Jesus' own prophetic mission by a prophetic movement.[36] The "sending" itself that frames

---

35. *Pace* Jacobson, *First Gospel*, 146.

36. Further comparison should be made with the prophetic movement of renewal of Israel headed by Elijah, in which not simply Elisha but hundreds of *bene-nabi'im* were engaged and, similarly, experienced repression by the rulers (see esp. 1 Kings 18).

the instructions for mission in 10:3 and 16 stands parallel to the sending of the prophetic messenger in Q 7:27 that refers to the exodus and/or a prophetic figure in the future (Exod. 23:20; Mal. 3:1) and the prophets sent by Wisdom or God in Q 11:49 and 13:34. That the envoys are sent out as "lambs among the wolves," that is, on a mission that might attract repressive measures from threatened rulers, further parallels the long-standing pattern in Israel's history, for the previous prophetic messengers had been killed by the Jerusalem authorities, as in Q 11:49–51 and 13:34–35.

The allusion to Elijah's commissioning of Elisha as his assistant and successor in the introduction to the mission discourse in Q 9:57–62 placed the mission squarely in the Israelite tradition of popular prophetic movements of renewal of village Israel over against oppressive rulers taking their cues from foreign rulers. The messengers' lack of appropriate equipment for travel strongly suggests that their appearance is itself a prophetic sign that the kingdom and the movement of renewing Israel are for the poor, the villagers whose social lives were threatening to disintegrate under the extreme pressures of Roman and Herodian rule in Galilee. In sending out the messengers without bag and sandals, the mission discourse was referring back to and continuing the theme announced at the opening of the covenantal discourse: "Blessed are the poor..., hungry..., mourning..., for theirs is the kingdom." Finally, with regard to the prophetic character of the mission, that the envoys are to heal the sick (10:9) stands in the tradition of Elijah and Elisha, the great northern Israelite prophets who implemented a popularly based program of Israel's renewal.

The mission focused on village communities. Just as Mark portrays Jesus as entering and addressing village "assemblies" (Mark 1:21, 39; 3:1, etc.), so the Q mission discourse instructs Jesus' envoys' to enter towns and to heal and speak in and to towns (not to "convert" or recruit individuals). That whole towns are the objects of curses for lack of response to the mission is a further, indirect indication that towns/villages were the focus of the work of building the movement. The tactics of their mission that focused on villages and towns, of course, involved establishing themselves in a particular household as a social and economic base for their wider work in the village/town community. A concept such as "apocalyptic" or "eschatological" may not be appropriate, but the mission discourse carries a tone of urgency. "The harvest is great!" Responding to the call to mission is so very urgent as to be comparable with "leaving the dead to bury their own dead." And those towns that do not respond are simply calling down judgment on their own heads (10:13–15), for God is establishing the kingdom precisely in the mission of these envoys, who are continuing the mission begun by Jesus (10:16).

Chapter 11

THE ANNOUNCEMENT AND TESTING
OF THE PROPHET

Jonathan A. Draper ⎯⎯⎯⎯⎯⎯⎯⎯⎯⎯⎯⎯⎯⎯⎯⎯⎯⎯

Both John's preaching in 3:7–9, 16–17 and the temptations of Jesus in 4:1–13 seem awkward as integral components of Q. It seems odd that a whole series of speeches of Jesus would be prefaced by one by John the Baptist. More seriously for interpreters of Q, the "pure narrative" (despite its strong sayings components) of Q 4:1–13 makes the temptation story stand out from Q materials as a late addition if part of Q at all. In the grand stratigraphic hypothesis of John S. Kloppenborg, the temptation of narrative is the principal factor in the positing of a third stratum. This narrative aberration in Q must be a late addition at a time when the literary tendency was toward *bios*, or a life of Jesus as hero.[1] Moreover, whereas Q scholars can entertain the possibility of oral tradition of individual sayings behind other clusters or discourses in Q, they view the temptation narrative as a written composition.

The consignment of Q 4:1–13 to a late, third layer or its exclusion from Q altogether because of its purely narrative character or its written composition, however, is based on a theory of orality and literacy that is now being questioned. Even those few Q scholars who dealt explicitly with the oral vs. written question were influenced by earlier theory, which stressed too strongly the great divide between orality and textuality (see further chapters 6 and 7 above). Kloppenborg, for example, seems to assume that an oral performance means "simply a set of folk sayings of a pre-literate group."[2] Recent study of oral-derived literature, however, shows that it can have a high level of sophistication and most characteristically is performed in coherent discourses associated with particular contexts.

In fact, the presence of the temptation story in Q, with its apparent quotations from Israelite Scripture, provides an example of how oral performance and written text coexist and interact in the ancient communication context (as discussed in chapter 6 above). If Matthew and Luke had a written text of Q (or very similar written texts of Q), it was derived from an orally performed text. Even after Q was

---

1. John S. Kloppenborg, *The Formation of Q: Trajectories in Ancient Wisdom Collections* (Philadelphia: Fortress, 1987), 260–62.
2. Ibid., 90.

written down the discourses would have continued to be performed, for few people could read and oral communication was by far the dominant mode in the society in which Q was produced. Moreover, with its references to Israelite Scripture, Q 4:1–13 in particular illustrates the interaction between oral performance and written text that must have characterized most historical societies. As noted in chapter 6, written texts can have an almost magical authority among the people in historical contexts where oral communication is dominant. In this case, even or perhaps especially among ordinary people who are not themselves literate, the Israelite Scripture possessed a special authority as the immutably inscribed word of God.

Here we will first examine the oral text of each discourse in their mnemonic patterning, balance, parallelism, paratactic construction, and linkage. Then we will analyze the metonymic restricted-code referencing in each discourse as indicators of the register(s) and performance context(s), in particular the field and tenor of the performance.

The Announcement of the Prophet: Q 3:7–9, 16–17, 21–22

The text of John the Baptist's announcement of the coming one can be heard (and viewed) along the lines of Del Hymes's "measured verse." As explained in chapter 8, the performed text can be analyzed in its basic units of lines, identified on the basis of finite verbs (present or implied), connectives and linguistic markers, and sense. The lines are structured into verses, each of which contains a discrete idea, and these again into stanzas which are thematically coherent. The equivalent of the larger units of the longer narratives Hymes analyzed is the distinctive discourses in Q, each of which is focused on a particular subject. Moving from one discourse to another in Q may thus involve changes in place and time along with the change of subject. Of course there is a measure of subjectivity about the procedure, and this measured verse cannot be constructed mechanically but only by a combination of linguistic markers and sense. Nevertheless, if Q discourses are examined in this way, their coherence and consistent structure can be readily discerned.

A. 1. And he said to [the crowds] who came to his baptism:[3]
    (You) generations of snakes!
      Who warned you to flee from the coming wrath?
      Then bear fruit worthy of repentance.

2. And do not think to say to yourselves,
    "As \<our\> father we have Abraham."
      for I tell you,
      God is able from these stones to raise children for Abraham!

---

3. The text cannot be reconstructed with any certainty here; Luke's "crowds" certainly does not fit the sense, as we shall see.

3. Already the axe is laid to the root of the trees;
    then every tree not bearing good fruit
        will be cut down and thrown into the fire.

B. 1. I baptize you with water,
    but he coming after me is stronger than I,
        whose sandals I am not worthy [to remo]ve;
  2. He will baptize you with holy spirit and fire
    whose pitchfork is in his hand,
  3. And he will clear his threshing floor
    and he will gather the wheat into the barn,
        but the chaff he will burn with fire unquenchable.

C. 1. [Jesus . . . baptized by John . . .
  2. heaven . . .   opened
    spirit . . .   upon him
  3.   . . . son . . .][4]

The first stanza contains three verses of three or four lines each, with the lines being mostly triplets; the second stanza also contains three verses of two or three lines each that vary only between three and four stresses each, followed perhaps by another verse or two (four lines) in which the text is hotly debated and uncertain. All of the features of typical oral performance mentioned above, plus the parallelism of lines, the repetition of sounds from line to line, and the repetition of words across the verses and stanzas mark this as an oral-derived text. Hearing (and viewing) the text as measured verse also reveals a clear structuring in terms of oppositions. The reference to "offspring of snakes" at the beginning may well have been complemented by the emphatic voice from heaven declaring Jesus "son" at the end, in a obvious inclusio binding together the discourse as a whole. In between is the question of the true children of Abraham. Bearing fruit from trees in the first stanza is matched by the differentiation between wheat and chaff in the second stanza. The opposition signals a conflict over legitimate and illegitimate parentage and legitimate and illegitimate offspring. The second opposition is between spirit and fire, renewal and destruction, which matches the distinction between repentance (bear fruit) and refusal to repent.

It is important to examine the metonymic referencing of key words in the text, since they key us into the register. They stand *pars pro toto* for the universe of meaning in which the performance is situated. Although "wilderness" may not have been in the actual text of this discourse, it is implied in the setting (especially if "all the region of the Jordan" now in Luke 3:3 or "wilderness" now in Matt. 3:1 was part of this Q discourse). Wilderness is a key theme in Israelite

---

4. The Q text is uncertain here and cannot be reconstructed; in fact, many do not consider this part of the Q text; see John S. Kloppenborg, *Q Parallels: Synopsis, Critical Notes, and Concordance* (Sonoma, Calif.: Polebridge, 1988), 16, for the argument pro and con.

tradition. It evokes memory of the desert wanderings of the Israelites after they were delivered from Egypt. The desert wanderings also are a sign of hope for the renewal of Israel, since they represent the time of the Mosaic covenant and promise. Isaiah took up the theme of preparation for the coming of the Lord in the wilderness in 40:3–5, a reference which Matt. 4:3 and Luke 3:4–6 (following and developing the conflated quotation in Mark of Mal. 3:1 and Isa. 40:3) brought explicitly into connection with this reference in Q. The Dead Sea Scrolls made preparation in the wilderness the foundation of the Qumran community (1QS 8:12–16; 9:19–21). Several popular movements at the time of Jesus also withdrew into the wilderness to begin reenactments of Israelite liberation and / or crossing of the Jordan.[5] This reference to the wilderness thus clearly indicates that the setting is one of renewal of Israel.

The dominant theme in the discourse is that of fruit, issue, or sonship, beginning at the outset with "offspring of snakes" and moving through the "children of Abraham" to the trees which do not "bear fruit" and the "wheat." These are not separate concepts in Israelite tradition. The word *genēma* almost always refers to agricultural produce in the Septuagint (the Greek translation of the Hebrew Bible), that is, fruit, even though it technically means "progeny" in Greek. "Fruits," however, can also be used metaphorically for people's deeds (e.g., Isa. 3:10–11; Hos. 10:12ff.). Rare in Israelite biblical literature are references to snakes. The only combination of the semantic fields "offspring" and "snake" comes in Gen. 3:15, although utilizing different Greek words in the Septuagint, in reference to God's punishment of Eve and the serpent. Those addressed as "offspring of snakes" here in Q apparently presume that, having Abraham as their father, they are the "children of Abraham." As discussed in chapter 5, claims of descent from Abraham, of being the "children of Abraham," were relatively late in Israelite tradition, in this case from mainly from Hasmonean times onward (3 Macc. 6:3; 4 Macc. 6:17, 11; 18:23; cf 2 Chron. 20:7), and they apparently were made in self-legitimation by the elite. Ironically, in Israelite biblical tradition, of course, Isaac and the children of Israel who followed in the line of Jacob / Israel were children by promise, since Sarah was barren. At issue in John's prophetic harangue is who are the legitimate children of Abraham, that is, Israelites, those of the correct lineage or those whom God raises up and who produce fruit worthy of repentance.

The threshing floor, with its winnowing fork, wheat, and chaff, is a well-known symbol of judgment in Israelite tradition. The separation of the wheat and chaff especially is a common metonymic for divine judgment, particularly in prophetic tradition (Isa. 17:13; 29:5; 33:11; 41:15; Jer. 13:24; Dan. 2:35; Hos. 13:3; Mic. 4:12; Zeph. 2:2; etc.). Given the likelihood that those who presume to have Abraham as their father are Jerusalem elite, it is tempting to hear in the reference to threshing here an allusion to the story of Ornan's threshing floor (1 Chron. 21:15ff.), since it is one of the foundational legends associated with the Jerusalem

---

5. Richard A. Horsley with John S. Hanson, *Bandits, Prophets, and Messiahs* (1985; reprint, Harrisburg, Pa.: Trinity Press International, 1999), 161–72.

temple. David ordered a census, contrary to the will of God. As the messenger of God stood on Ornan's threshing floor, sword in hand for the destruction of Jerusalem, David pleaded with God and obtained a reprieve — and then built an altar on the threshing floor. "Spirit" and "fire" are references respectively to renewal of the people and judgment of injustice. "Spirit" draws metonymically on the tradition of the renewal of Israel widespread in prophetic literature (e.g., Ezek. 37:1–14; Joel 2:28–29; cf. 1 QS 3:6–9). Fire was a standing symbol of judgment in Israelite tradition.

These complex sets of metonymic referencing, the separation of the wheat from the chaff at threshing and the question of the offspring/children of Abraham, indicate that the register is that of prophetic declaration of judgment. In the "field" (what is happening) John denounces the Jerusalem rulers and calls them to account for their injustice, their failure to bear fruit worthy of repentance. Their presumption of proper lineage, of having Abraham as their father, is no defense against the judgment of God, since Isaac was the child of divine gift and not of human generation, so that what God has done before he can do again. In "tenor," the real addressees of the discourse are the ordinary people of the Q movement, who presumably have heeded the call to repentance. But their water baptism by John is only provisional, prefatory to that of the one who is coming. His baptism in the Spirit means renewal, gathering the fruit into the granary, while his baptism in fire means that the worthless chaff, parallel to the presumptuous and unjust rulers, will be burned in the fire of judgment.

Assuming that the third stanza was in Q, the coming of the Spirit upon Jesus then marks him out as the coming one, the son of God, analogous to the children raised up to Abraham, those who bear good fruit, who are to participate in the renewal of Israel. In this case, the declaration of judgment and announcement of the prophet of renewal and judgment are also the call of the prophet.

The Testing of the Prophet: Q 4:1–13

Again the discourse can be analyzed and represented along the lines pioneered by Hymes, in lines, verses, stanzas, and, in this brief narrative, even scenes. The Greek text of the introduction to the dialogue is somewhat unclear in its exact wording. Some of the key terms are clear, however:

A. 1. And Jesus was led into the wilderness by the spirit
        to be tempted for forty days by the devil.
    And [he had not eaten anything;]
        and he was hungry.
  2. And the devil said to him:
    "If you are the son of God,
        say that these stones should become (loaves of) bread."
  3. And Jesus answered:
    "It is written,
        'A human being does not live by bread alone.'"

B. 1. [The devil] takes/took him to Jerusalem
        and set him on the pinnacle/corner of the temple
   2. And said to him:
        "If you are the son of God,
            Throw yourself down.
        For it is written,
            'He will command/charge his angels concerning you.
            And on their hands they will bear you up,
            So that you will not/Lest you strike your foot against a stone.'"
   3. And Jesus answered to him:
        "It is written:
            'You shall not test the Lord your God.'"

C. 1. And [the devil] takes/took him to a very high mountain
        and shows/showed him all the kingdoms of the world and their glory.
   2. And he said to him:
        "All these I will give you
            If you worship me."
   3. And Jesus said to him:
        "It is written:
            'The Lord your God you shall worship
            And him only shall you serve.'"
        And the devil left him.

This discourse may not have all the same marks of the preceding one. Yet the parallelism, the repetition of sounds, and the linkage of terms and themes and formulas from scene to scene indicate that again it is a text of an oral performance, like the other discourses in Q.

The significance of the story of Jesus' testing, its register, and the performance context in which it should be heard depend completely on getting the metonymic references. The "wilderness" and the "forty days" set the stage for and provide the cues for the whole story as well as for the first scene. Not only was Israel prepared in the wilderness for its formation as a people or its later renewals. The great prophets of Israel's formation and renewal also were prepared or tested in the wilderness for forty days for their missions. Moses spent two forty-day fasts on Mount Sinai. In the first, before the giving of the Torah and the renewed covenant in Deut. 9:9–11, his prophetic status was confirmed and he was prepared for his authoritative presentation and interpretation of the word of God inscribed in text. Again in Deut. 9:18–19, after the disobedience of Israel with the golden calf, Moses lay prostrate and fasted for forty days and nights to avert the wrath of God against Israel. The paradigmatic prophet of Israel's renewal, Elijah, moreover, was tested and commissioned in the wilderness in 1 Kings 19:1–18. Having fled the wrath of Jezebel into the wilderness, he was starving and despairing but was ministered to by a divine messenger. This enabled him to survive a forty-day journey with no further food, until he came to Mount Horeb, where he heard the still, small voice of God commissioning him to go back to renew Israel (by opposing the oppressive current rulers). Like the exodus-wilderness material, this story had solid roots in northern Israel and would have been cultivated in the Israelite popular tradition (as discussed in chapter 5).

"Test" also has a rich metonymic reference, fundamentally to the testing of Israel during the forty years, particularly the grumbling and testing of God at Meribah. This testing is specifically associated with the gift of manna in Deut. 8:2, 16, in contrast to the usual bread the people were accustomed to. These people were starving and demanded food from the prophet, who then in turn complained to God. God gave them bread and then water miraculously in the wilderness but punished Moses for his lack of faith by refusing him entry into the land of promise into which he was bringing his people, where they would eat bread "without scarcity" (Deut. 8:7–10).

The metonymic references of "testing" in the "wilderness" thus cue us unmistakably into the deep Israelite tradition of the testing (and commissioning) of the prophet in preparation for leading the formation or the renewal of Israel. If there would indeed be a "prophet like Moses" to lead the people (Deut. 18:15–20), then presumably this prophet would also need to undergo a testing like that of Moses.[6]

The reference to the Spirit driving Jesus out to be tested resembles what in cross-cultural anthropology is often called an ordeal in the initiation ritual of a shaman. If Jesus is to succeed as a prophet, he must successfully complete the forty days of testing. Such trials represent an ordeal testing his suitability to undertake the task of prophet ushering in God's kingdom. The ordeal takes the traditional form of a contest between Jesus and the devil, somewhat like the ancient riddling contests where delivery from the hand of a cruel and terrifying foe depends on correct answers to seemingly impossible riddles. It is also somewhat like a "proverb contest," which is so common in African societies, where contestants conduct a battle of proverbial taunts in challenge and response, central to which is the demonstration of one's ability to know and apply the law of the land.[7] In these cases the proverbial material used by both contestants consists of accepted tradition of the society but is given an insulting or dangerous twist by the context in which it is used, or it may be used to settle some deep-rooted problem in the community. The material used by both Jesus and the devil is common to the tradition: it is no oddity for the devil to quote scripture, since it is not the material but the context which determines how it applies and whether it is appropriately used.

Also part of the metonymic referencing, in a most explicit way — and distinctive to this discourse in Q, except possibly for the only other reference to scripture in 7:2 — is the repeated reference to scripture in Jesus' answers. The

---

6. One could even argue that all three of the tests relate to key aspects of the life of Moses in the Deuteronomic tradition: the provision of manna and the murmuring of the people, which results in the failure to enter the land of promise; the provision of a miraculous sign which validates the claims of the prophet like Moses in Deut. 18:18; and the ascent of Mount Nebo from which Moses views the land of promise but is not allowed to enter because of his and the people's disobedience. The metonymic references of key words in the testing scene relate specifically to the testing of the prophet and the acceptance of the prophet by God.

7. Joyce Penfield, *Communication with Quotes: The Gibe Case* (Westport Conn.: Greenwood, 1983), 44–46.

formula "it is written" is far from common in the Hebrew Bible (and Septuagint). Of the eighteen occurrences, all but four refer to the Mosaic Torah, and many (nine) are vague in their reference, serving simply as a general citation, since they could be understood as referring to several particular texts or none. The book of Deuteronomy is the favorite common denominator, appearing seven times as the sole reference or in combination with other texts. The use of the formula "it is written" does not necessarily mean, however, that the speaker (or writer) is actually quoting a written text. In terms of the relation between oral communication and writing, the texts cited by Jesus in this discourse do not seem to be produced at the literary level. The order of the recitations does not follow the order of the canonical Deuteronomy, no matter whether the order of Luke or of Matthew is followed (Deut. 8:3; 6:16; 6:13 / 10:20 in Matthew; Deut. 8:3; 6:13 / 10:20; 6:16 in Luke), so that they do not form the underlying structural logic of the story. Also the wording is not the same as that of the Septuagint, despite all the pressure there must have been on scribes in early Christian circles to conform to it. The Western text (D) of Matthew has a text differing from that of the Septuagint in the first two temptations, and in the third Matthew, like Luke, has a composite quotation somewhere between Deut. 6:13 and 10:20. The most likely explanation of this is that these texts formed a part of the oral culture of the Galilean peasant community out of which the Q discourses emerged. But they were known to be written. And the fact that they had stood written, and had stood written in the sacred text since olden time, gave them a special divine authority even, or especially, for those who could not themselves write and read.

The importance of the formula "it is written" is its pointing to an authoritative cultural tradition fixed in writing, which was accepted as the basis of God's covenant with Israel and to which the people of the covenant were accountable. At one level this meant that a largely illiterate people were particularly vulnerable to literate scribal experts. Yet it also meant that their cultural tradition was not negotiable in the face of the intrusion of a foreign empire and the culture it might impose. However inaccessible to the ordinary people, sacred scrolls were the written guarantees of the covenant between God and his people, censuring the social and economic oppression suffered by peasants as a result of unjust rulers and promising hope, relief, and blessing for those who fulfilled the provisions of the covenant notwithstanding.

Jesus as the prophet of renewal needs to show his proficiency in the sacred tradition which stands written in the face of the confusing voices of the crisis engendered by the Roman intrusion and the complicity of the priestly and royal rulers who were clients of the Romans. In this connection Q offers an interesting case of oral-derived literature produced by a movement that originated in a society that possessed a written sacred tradition, even though most people in the society were illiterate and embedded in an oral communication environment. There is evidence from the modern world that the societies that best survive colonial oppression are those which have enshrined their culture in sacred texts, which can form the focus of resistance to domination, even if most of the members of those societies are illiterate (e.g., Somalia). Certainly this was the case in the colonial conquest of Africa, Asia, and Latin America in collusion with the Christian faith. Communities which were entirely reliant on oral tradition were the least able to resist both the political and cultural hegemony of empire. There was no agreed-upon canon of sacred tradition at the time of Jesus; indeed there were competing textual traditions (cf. Qumran's) and rival great and little Israelite traditions. Nevertheless, the Torah in writing provided a scriptural reference for the people at every level of society from which to resist the incursion of foreign rule and influence, even if they did not agree on its wording or interpretation.

In the Q testing discourse, the devil offers attractive and seemingly appropriate strategies for the prophet of renewal. Yet even he must yield to what is written in Israel's Scripture, which is immutable and authoritative. It requires the skillful use of the authoritative tradition encoded in and stabilized by text in the form of law to silence the devil's voice. Although referring to what "is written," the context takes place in an oral arena and is conducted in an oral mode. In the case of Jesus, the latter is the mark of the prophet who is able to proclaim the kingdom of God in the time of crisis.

The Sequence of Discourses

Hearing both of these discourses as if in oral performance enables us also to discern that they form an intelligible sequence, in contrast to previous studies of Q as written, which find the temptation of Jesus to be a late and relatively foreign narrative in the midst of a collection of sayings. Again the metonymic referencing of the respective discourses provides the cues. The obvious ones to start with are those words or symbols shared by both discourses. In the first, the coming one will baptize with Spirit and apparently then comes upon Jesus at his baptism, and in the second the Spirit drives Jesus out into the wilderness to be tested. This is a continuity that cannot be accidental. The Spirit draws metonymically on the tradition of the renewal of Israel (again cf. Ezek. 37:1–14; Joel 2:28–29). Assuming that implicitly, if not explicitly, John's preaching and announcement of the coming one were in the wilderness of the Jordan, then both discourses also refer to the wilderness preparation and/or testing, in the one case of the whole people, in the other of the prophet who will lead the renewal of the people. The testing in the wilderness thus authorized Jesus as the prophet who will baptize with Spirit, that is, will spearhead the renewal.

The sequence of John's announcement of the prophet who will baptize with Spirit and fire followed by the testing of the prophet of renewal becomes all the more intelligible and convincing against the background of Israelite tradition when we consider what follows in the next three discourses. In Q 6:20–49, Jesus enacts a renewal of the covenant, one that begins with covenantal blessings of the kingdom of God for the poor and covenantal curses on the rich. Next comes the prophetic dialogue, demonstration, and declaration in Q 7:18–35 of how Jesus is fulfilling the age-old longings of the people for renewal and how

John marks the completion of the old era which pales by comparison with the kingdom of God. Then in Q 9:57–10:16 Jesus, acting the role of the new Elijah in relation to the new Elishas, commissions prophetic envoys of the kingdom of God. The only part of Q in the Lukan sequence that does not clearly fit into this sequence, heard in metonymic referencing to Israelite tradition, is the story of the healing of the centurion's servant. Luke and Matthew both use this story as a confirmation of the prophet who has just delivered the covenant renewal speech, which they simply make even more explicit than it was in Q, with Jesus positioned on the mountain (Matthew) or just having come down from the mountain, as the new Moses. If Luke and Matthew thus both understood Q 7:2–9 as a story providing confirmation of the prophet in a healing miracle, then perhaps we should also. In that case this short dialogue and healing miracle would also flow in the same sequence of Q discourses dedicated to different aspects of Jesus as the prophet spearheading the renewal of Israel in an easily intelligible sequence: the announcement of the prophet, the testing of the prophet, the prophet enacting the covenant renewal, the confirmation of the prophet's authority, the prophet fulfilling the age-old longings for renewal, and the prophet commissioning envoys to broaden the movement of renewal of Israel.

Chapter 12

THE KINGDOM OF GOD AS THE
RENEWAL OF ISRAEL

Richard A. Horsley _____

Explorations in chapters 9 and 10 of how the covenant renewal discourse and
the mission discourse in Q reference Israelite tradition have established two key
components of an overall hypothesis about Q's purpose and function as a sequence
of speeches. The ways in which those discourses resonate with Israelite tradition
enable us to discern that they belong, respectively, to the registers of covenant-
making and of prophetic mission for renewal of Israel. Insofar as these discourses
were both performative speech, they effected or constituted social relations in
particular ways as they were regularly performed. Not only do the covenantal
teachings in the middle of the covenant renewal discourse make it evident that
the discourse addressed social-economic interaction in a village community. But
more important, the performance of Q 6:20–49 as a whole speech in the presence
of a group of people constituted those people as a renewed covenantal community,
the speech being all the more effective and powerful because it resonated in a
rich variety of ways with Israel's tradition of being a covenanted people. The
performance of Q 9:57–10:16 in that renewed covenantal community effected
the sending of envoys to other village communities to catalyze and/or revitalize
community life there. That is, in sending out such envoys, the renewed covenantal
community was thereby acting as part of a wider movement of the renewal of
Israel, whose fundamental social form consisted of village communities.

The functions of these two speeches in performance before groups of people
thus suggest the purpose and function of Q as a whole: it is a collection of
discourses intended for regular recitation to communities of a wider movement
of the renewal of Israel. If we review the issues or topics addressed in these
discourses, it is evident that many of them can be seen as addressing precisely the
basic concerns of village communities, and some of them can be seen as addressing
problematic political-economic-religious relations in late second-temple Palestine.
The admonition to pray boldly for the kingdom of God in 11:2–4, 9–13 addresses
people who are concerned about food and debts. The reassurance about anxiety
in 12:22–31 addresses people concerned about basic necessities of life — food and
clothing. The speech in 7:18–35 expresses resentment against the wealthy and

powerful while proclaiming the satisfaction of age-old longings for restoration of the people. In 11:39–52 (the speaker for) Jesus lashes out at the Pharisees and scribes for their lack of mercy on the people, and 13:34–35 is a condemnation of Jerusalem in the form of a prophetic lament. If we consider all of the discourses in Q together while considering the particular focus of each and the concern(s) each addresses, then the whole sequence of discourses appears to be intended for (1) a movement of renewal of Israel in its village communities, (2) over against the Jerusalem rulers and their representatives, and (3) under attack from those rulers and/or their representatives. Particular discourses, or parts of them, are focused respectively on one or another of these three facets of the movement's life. Those that focused on the first and third facets will be considered in this chapter, with the Q materials that condemn the rulers and their representatives examined in chapter 13.

Other Q Discourses Addressed to the Life of the Renewal Movement

The Beginning and Ending of Q: Q 3:7–9, 16–17 and Q 22:28–30

That Q is a sequence of discourses addressed to a movement of renewal in Israel is confirmed by the remaining fragments that apparently comprised parts of the opening and ending of the sequence. The prophetic statements in 3:7–9, 16–17 are usually taken as the opening of Q because they come first in both Matthew and Luke — and because we have become convinced by repeated analysis that Luke presents Q materials in their original order, by and large. The address of John, however, is not only prophecy of judgment. The first part of John's speech (3:7b–9) is indeed a pronouncement of judgment, against those who presume that descent from Abraham is a guarantee of their blessing by God yet do not "bear fruit worthy of repentance," according to Mosaic covenantal criteria.[1] Q 3:16–17, however, is both a positive announcement of deliverance or renewal and a negative declaration of judgment. The "coming one who is stronger" than John will baptize "with Holy Spirit" as well as with fire and will "gather the wheat into his granary," not simply "burn the chaff with fire." This double side to the coming one's mission in fact fits well with the subsequent discourses of Q, some of which focus on the positive renewal aspect, others of which focus on the negative judgment, and yet others of which sanction admonitions with threat of judgment. The register of Q 3:16–17 at least is not (negative) prophetic judgment but a two-sided prophetic program of *krisis*, consisting of God's redemption and renewal for the "poor, hungry, ...," as in the opening of the next discourse, and

---

1. According to the usual criteria of reconstruction, we cannot determine how Q 3:7b–9 was introduced. Only the theme of "coming for baptism" is common to Matt. 3:7a and Luke 3:7a, but since we may well not have all of this Q discourse represented in Matthew 3 and Luke 3, it is difficult to justify taking the Lukan "crowds" as original to Q here. For Q 3:7b–9, in fact, the Matthean "Pharisees and Sadducees" or a variation on it would fit better, although for Q 3:16–17 the Lukan "crowds" makes more sense.

threatening judgment against "the rich, well-fed rulers and their representatives," as in Q 13:34–35 and 11:39–52.

Q 22:28–30 appears to be the closing statement in Q, again because we have come to trust that Luke reproduces the order of Q, and this is the last fragment of Q in Luke with a parallel in Matthew. However, since we have so little remaining of whatever fuller complex this was part of in Q, and since Matthew and Luke use this fragment in very different contexts and each gives it a distinctive twist, it is virtually impossible to make an adequate reconstruction of the text. The projection into the text of "you who have [followed me]" in Matt 19:28 follows what is clearly the distinctively Matthean setting, where "who have followed me" simply picks up on Peter's question in 19:27, which came from Mark (10:28), where following Jesus is an important theme. Following Jesus, however, is not a significant theme in Q. Following Jesus occurs only in the prologue to the mission discourse (9:57–62; cf. the literal following in 7:9). Nor do the twelve disciples crop up anywhere (else) in Q. There is thus no reason to take Q 22:28–30 in connection either with following Jesus or with the twelve or the disciples. On the one hand, the reference to "eating and drinking at my table" is Luke's way of assimilating the Q fragment into his context, toward the end of the scene at the Last Supper (Luke 22:1–38). On the other hand, the image of "sitting at table in the kingdom (of God)" could well have been part of the saying in Q 22:30, since it occurs elsewhere, in Q 13:28–29. The fragment would have included at least:

> You will sit on seats establishing justice for the twelve tribes of Israel.

That this fragment appears to have been the closing of Q, corresponding to the opening announcement of deliverance and judgment in 3:7–9, 16–17, offers a significant clue about how it was heard. To pursue that clue, however, it is first necessary to strip away some unjustified assumptions that have affected standard translations and interpretations of this fragment. "The renewal of all things" in the NRSV is an unwarranted translation that continues older scholarly interpretation of *palingenesia* in Matt. 19:28 as referring to some sort of regeneration of the cosmos, for example, as discussed in ancient Stoic philosophy. Matthew's contemporary, the Jewish historian Josephus, used the term for a historical renewal or restoration of Israel in its land, one that he portrays also in terms of the twelve tribes (*Ant.* 11, 66, 107). This suggests that in transforming the Q fragment about the twelve tribes of Israel, Matthew understood it to be about an eschatological renewal of the people, not some cosmic regeneration.[2] Similarly, the "Son of Man sitting on the throne of his glory" is Matthew's addition, not part of Q, which has the very different image of "the day(s) of the son of man" as a symbol of the time of judgment in the discourse of Q 17:23–37.

---

2. For a more historical-eschatological reading of what has been misunderstood in terms of a cosmic catastrophe in the apocalypticism of the Synoptic Gospels, see Richard A. Horsley, " The Kingdom of God and the Renewal of Israel: The Synoptic Gospels, Jesus Movements, and Apocalypticism" in *The Encyclopedia of Apocalypticism*, vol. 1, ed. John J. Collins (New York: Continuum, 1998), 303–44.

Most important to recognize is that the translation of *krinontes* as "*judging* the twelve tribes of Israel" in Q 22:30 is not consistent with the usual understanding of *krinein* in the Septuagint and the corresponding term *shapat* in the Hebrew Bible that it translates. The continuing translation of Q 22:30 in terms of Jesus' followers "judging" Israel appears to be a continuation of the Christian conception of Israel being judged for having rejected Jesus and his message.[3] The term *krinein* does indeed mean "judging" elsewhere in the Synoptic Gospel tradition, including Q (e.g., Luke 7:43; Q 6:37; 12:57). In much of the biblical tradition, however, particularly in instances where God or a prophetic leader is the subject/actor and Israel in general or the oppressed, such as the orphan, widow, or the poor, the object, *shapat/krinein* must be translated not with "judging" but rather in the highly positive sense of "liberating/delivering/saving/effecting justice for" (see, e.g., Judg. 2:16; 3:10; 4:4; Psalms 9; 10:18; 35; 58; 72:4; 76:9; 82:1–4; 94; 103:6; 140:12; 146:7 [Septuagint numbering of Psalms is one lower]).[4] The statement in Q 22:30 thus refers not to the condemnation but rather to the deliverance of and/or effecting justice for the twelve tribes of Israel. As noted in chapter 5, moreover, near-contemporary texts such as *Pss. Sol.* 17:28–32, 1 QS 8:1–4, and *Testament of Judah* 24–25 provide windows onto the widespread tradition of the future renewal or restoration of Israel in its twelve tribes that Q 22:30 was referencing and with which its hearers would have resonated.

Thus, taken together with the John's opening speech announcing the prophet of judgment and deliverance (Holy Spirit and fire) and the long covenant renewal discourse of Q 6, this closing statement reassuring the hearers of the current or imminent renewal of Israel suggests that the context of those discourses and of Q as a whole was the renewal of Israel (movement) underway. Q is a sequence of discourses addressed to and repeatedly performed for communities of a movement of renewal of Israel.

The Fulfillment of the People's Longings in Jesus' Mission and the Kingdom of God: Q 7:18–35

The "text" of this discourse is clearly connected with that of John's announcement of the prophet of deliverance and judgment with which Q opened, in 3:7–9, 16–17. As we shall see, it is also linked with the covenant renewal in 6:20–49. In 3:16–17, John proclaimed the "one coming after me stronger than I, ... who will gather the wheat ... but burn the chaff." In 7:18–19, through his disciples he asks whether Jesus is "the one coming." In the intervening discourse, 6:20–49, Jesus establishes a renewal of the covenant, and 7:18–35 confirms that John's prophecy is being implemented.

---

3. Which, as noted repeatedly above, has played a considerable role in Christian reading of other Q texts as well, such as Q 11:49–51; 13:28–29, 34–35, as referring to the judgment of "all Israel."

4. See further the older word study, often ignored, on *krino* (Herntrich) in *TDNT*, 3:923–32; and see the fuller discussion of Q 22:28–30 in Richard A. Horsley, *Jesus and the Spiral of Violence* (San Francisco: Harper & Row, 1987), 199–208.

As in other discourses of Q, so in 7:18–35 its metonymic reference to Israelite tradition is the key to discerning the register (field, tenor, mode). The first two steps of the discourse, 7:18–19, 22–23 and 7:24–28, are rich with suggestive referencing of Israelite exodus-covenantal and prophetic tradition. The various wonders that Jesus asks John's disciples to see and hear in 7:23 may well refer to Jesus' healing and preaching activities. The focus of the list of images in 7:23, however, is not on the healing activities of Jesus in particular but on the fulfillment of age-old longings for the restoration of the people of Israel. The images of "the blind see, the lame walk, the deaf hear, the dead are raised up, the poor are given good news" reference what must have been a widespread and deeply rooted Israelite tradition of longing for God's new action to end oppression and restore Israel as a people. Several passages in different sections of the prophetic anthology that comprises the book of Isaiah indicate that the imagery in Q 7:22 was a standard repertoire used in oracles of future restoration of the people (including in connection with a new exodus). For example, Isa. 26:19 speaks of the dead rising back to life in the context of a (relatively late) prophetic psalm (Isa. 26:7–19) expressing confidence that God, the true "lord" (king) of the people, vs. the foreign "lords" who have ruled over them, will restore the people in an action of new exodus-covenant ("the way of righteousness"). The oracle of deliverance in Isa. 29:18–21 includes the images of the deaf hearing and the blind seeing and the neediest people exulting in a general prophecy of the coming of a time of justice, when people will no longer be oppressed by tyranny and manipulation of the courts by the wealthy and powerful. The (postexilic) prophecy of a new exodus in Isaiah 34 includes images of the blind seeing, the deaf hearing, the lame leaping, and the dumb singing. Isaiah 42:6–7, one of the "servant of Yahweh" songs in Deutero-Isaiah, speaking of the persistence of Israel in pursuing justice in the society, represents Israel as "a covenant to the peoples, to open the eyes that are blind..." At the opening of a general prophecy of the people's restoration (in their towns), Isa. 61:1 portrays (Israel as) a prophetic figure anointed by Yahweh, in the power of the Spirit, "to bring good news to the oppressed, proclaim liberty to the captives, and...the year of Yahweh's favor."

The second step of the discourse references the exodus-prophetic tradition in multiple images and ways, including a reference to the scriptural tradition. The first rhetorical question, about "going out into the wilderness," calls up all the memories of the escape from oppression in Egypt and the sagas of the wonder-filled way through the wilderness, a journey led by Moses, to the land that had become the people's inheritance. "The wilderness" was the place where the covenant had been given through Moses. "The wilderness" was the place of purification and preparation. It was the place where Elijah fled from Ahab's and Jezebel's death squads, only to be nourished, restored, and then commissioned by God to lead the prophetic movement of Israel's renewal against the oppression and foreign influence under Ahab (1 Kings 19). According to Josephus's accounts, several Moses-like and/or Joshua-like prophets who emerged among Judean villagers in the mid–first century, contemporary with John the Baptist and Jesus, led their followers out into the wilderness to experience the anticipated new deliverance by God (*Ant.* 20.97–98, 169–71; *B.J.* 2.261–63).[5] In "going out into the wilderness," the "crowds" would clearly have been seeing and hearing a prophet like Moses and/or Elijah, the paradigmatic founder and restorer of Israel as a covenantal society under its divine ruler whose main concern was to free them from unjust and oppressive human rulers. After the second rhetorical question leads the hearers to remember that the one they went out to see was no "reed shaken by the wind" but a powerful prophetic voice of judgment and deliverance (as in 3:7–9, 16–17), the third rhetorical question makes vividly explicit the stark opposition between the prophet-and-crowds, on the one hand, and the wealthy rulers with their "soft clothing" and palaces, on the other. The hearers may well have thought of Antipas and his recently built palace in Tiberias (which "the Galileans" from the villages and the lower class in Tiberias looted and burned in 66, Jos. *Vita* 64–65). Such popular resentment, however, was rooted in memories of previous kings and their luxury, such as "Solomon in all his glory," to visit whom the "Queen of the South" had undertaken a famous expedition (Q 11:31; 12:27).

The statement that the crowd had gone out to see "a prophet, indeed more than a prophet" (7:26), declares in insistent terms what was already implicit in "going out into the wilderness." John was surely a prophet, but far more than a prophet, which the explicit recitation of the scripture then explains:

> Behold, I am sending my messenger in front of you,
> who will prepare your way before you.

This is a recitation of Exod. 23:20 from the "covenant code" in Exodus 21–23 appended to the Mosaic covenant. The "messenger of the covenant" had long since played a role in prophecy of renewal. Early in the second-temple period, Malachi had announced the coming of God's messenger of the covenant who was drawing near in judgment on those who violate the covenantal principles against oppression (Mal. 3:1–5).[6] All of this metonymic referencing to wilderness and prophets of covenant and restoration of Israel, along with judgment against oppression, serves to build up the unprecedented historical importance of John. And John as the greatest figure in history, in turn, is used to dramatize just how great is the kingdom of God that is manifested in Jesus' program of renewal of Israel (7:28).

The register of the discourse in 7:18–35, framed at the outset as a dialogue, is prophecy of the renewal of Israel. And while it is difficult to discern the particular (typical) occasion for this speech, the general context of Q as a sequence of discourses, that is, meetings of communities of the renewal movement, would appear

---

5. For analysis of the popular prophetic movements, see Richard A. Horsley, "'Like One of the Prophets of Old': Two Types of Popular Prophets at the Time of Jesus," *CBQ* 47 (1985): 435–63.

6. Note also, at the end of this prophetic sequence in Malachi 3(–4), the admonition to "remember the teachings of Moses, the statues and ordinances" of the covenant on Horeb/Sinai, and the announcement of sending "the prophet Elijah before the great and terrible day of the Lord comes" as the agent of societal restoration, Mal. 4:4–6 (3:22–24). In the book of Malachi, these prophecies are parts of a wider program of restoring the temple-state, but on reformist Mosaic covenantal terms.

Q 11:2-4, 9-11: Transliteration in Measured Verse for Hearing

Proseuchesthe:

A. 1.	Pater,			
	hagiasthētō	to onoma sou,		
	elthetō	hē basileia sou.		
2.	Ton arton hēmōn	ton epiousion	dos hēmin	sēmeron
3.	Kai aphes	hēmin	ta opheilēmata	hēmōn,
	hōs kai	hēmeis	aphēkamen	tois opheiletais.
4.	Kai mē	eiselegkēs	hēmas	eis peirasmon.
B. 1.	legō hymin,			
	aiteite	kai dothēsetai	hymin,	
	zēteite	kai heurēsete,		
	krouete	kai anoigēsetai	hymin.	
2.	Pas gar ho aitōn	lambanei.		
	kai ho zētōn	heuriskei.		
	kai tō krouonti	anoigēsetai.		
C. 1.	Tis estin	ex hymōn	anthrōpos,	
	hon aitēsei	ho huios autou	arton,	
	mē lithon	epidōsei	autō?	
2.	Ē kai ichthun	aitēsei,		
	mē ophin	epidōsei	autō?	
D. 1.	Ei oun hymeis	ponēroi ontes	oidate	
	domata agatha	didonai	tois teknois hymōn,	
2.	Posō mallon	patēr	[ho] ex ouranou	
	dōsei	agatha	tois aitousin auton.	

to be the appropriate context for this discourse. The communities hear (again) the proclamation of the unprecedented movement in which they are involved.

Prayer for the Kingdom: Q 11:2-4, 9-13

The "text" of the discourse on prayer, when heard in "measured verse," is striking for its parallel lines (of two, three, or four components) and repetition of words and sounds (underlined) — evident in translation and even more so in transliteration.

The context of this discourse is a gathering of a community of the movement; the register is that of prayer. If the Kaddish, a prayer used regularly in local village assemblies (= synagogues), predates Jesus, then this particular prayer for the kingdom of God would have referenced a tradition of longing and petitioning for the kingdom as renewal of the life of the whole people of Israel. The Kaddish says:

> Magnified and sanctified be his great name in the world that he has created according to his will. May he establish his kingdom in your lifetime and in your days and in the lifetime of all the house of Israel, even speedily and at a near time.

In comparison with the Kaddish and particularly with parallels in the *Gospel of Thomas*, however, the Lord's Prayer and the accompanying exhortation to

Q 11:2–4, 9–11: Translation in Measured Verse for Hearing

Pray:

A. 1. Father,

Let your name	be sanctified,		
let your kingdom	come.		

  2. Our bread — for the day — give us — today

  3. And release — for us — the debts — of ours

    just as also — we — release — those indebted to us.

  4. And do not — lead — us — into the test.

B. 1. I tell you:

	Ask	and it will be given	to you,
	seek	and you will find,	
	knock	and it will be opened	to you.

  2. For everyone — who asks — receives,

    and the one — who seeks — finds,

    and to the one — who knocks — it will be opened.

C. 1. Which person — is there — of you,

    if his son — asks — for bread,

    will give — him — a stone?

  2. Or if he — asks — for a fish,

    will give — him — a snake?

D. 1. If you — who are evil — know

    to give — good gifts — to your children,

  2. how much more — will the father — from heaven

    give — good (thing)s — to those who ask him.

---

petition God boldly for the kingdom are strikingly concrete, focused on economic necessities. Parallel to and specifying the meaning of the kingdom of God are the petitions for provision of bread, the staple of the peasant's diet, and cancellation of debts, which threatened the very survival of the peasant household in a traditional agrarian society. In the prayer itself, woven into the petition for cancellation of debts, moreover, is the people's vow that they have herewith canceled each others' debts, which must be related to the covenantal teaching in Q 6:27–36. And the following exhortation offers the most basic of foods around the Sea of Galilee as illustrations, a loaf of bread and a fish.

In the *Gospel of Thomas* 2, 92, 94, by contrast, the seeking-finding and knocking-opening are in the abstract, isolated from concrete objects as well as from God, and are focused on revelation and spiritual enlightenment. Such sayings in *Thomas* do seem appropriately taken as specifically religious teachings for an individual to ponder in order to find an appropriate spiritual interpretation. The Q discourse on prayer, however, is instruction of whole communities to petition God, in precisely the short prayer in 11:2–4, to effect the kingdom by providing for the most concrete concerns of villagers: food for subsistence and the cancellation of debts, which threatened the viability of the peasant household in the moral economy of the peasantry. In this sense the prayer in 11:2–4, like the admonitions in 6:27–35, also references explicitly the Israelite covenantal tradition of economic principles ("thou shall not covet, steal, bear false witness") and mechanisms (sabbatical cancellation of debts and release of debt slaves) intended to keep Israelite families economically viable on their land as members of the village communities in which Israel was constituted.

Anxiety about Subsistence and Single-minded Pursuit of the Kingdom: Q 12:22–32

Therefore I tell you:

A. 1. Do not be anxious	about life,	what you shall eat,	
	nor about body,	what you shall put on.	
2. Is not life	more than	food,	
	and the body	(more than) clothing?	
B. 1. [Look at]	the ravens;		
they neither sow	nor reap		
2. and yet God	feeds	them.	
Are you not	of more value than	the birds?	
C. 1. And who of you	by being anxious	is able	
to add	to his life-span	a {single} cubit?	
D. 1. And why are you anxious about clothing?			
Consider	the lilies,		
they neither toil	nor spin.		
2. Yet I tell you,			
even Solomon	in all his glory	was not arrayed	like one of these.
3. But if the grass	in the field,	which is there today	
and tomorrow	is thrown	into the oven,	
4. God	clothes	thus,	
[will he not] much more (clothe) you,		persons of little faith?	
E. 1. [Therefore] do not be anxious, saying,			
What shall we eat?	or What shall we drink?	or What shall we wear?	
2. For all these things	the (other) peoples	seek;	
for your Father	knows that	you need them.	
F. 1. But seek	his	kingdom,	
and these things	shall be added	to you.	
2. {Do not fear	little	flock,	
for the Father	is pleased	to give you	the kingdom.}[7]

This discourse has a clear structure focused on the statement (in A1–2) and repetition (in C and E1) of the admonition, reinforced by the rhetorical question,

---

7. The International Q Project text does not include Q 12:32. Judging from other discourses, the closing statement in this discourse also could well have been one "verse" (12:31). But either the Matthean version, Matt. 12:34, or the Lukan version, Luke 12:32, would provide an intelligible parallel to Q 12:31. The Lukan version of two lines, included in the translation above, is preferable to the Matthean version of three lines, because it provides an elongated line for emphasis at the close of a section, as at other points in Q discourses. Both Matthew and Luke may have had a version of Q that added Q 12:33–34 to this discourse. The reconstruction of these verses by the International Q Project is highly speculative, following Matthew's version, which differs dramatically from Luke's.

not to be anxious about basic necessities of food and clothing. In between are two parallel illustrations (B and D) that form the basis of reassurance of the anxious hearers by comparison with how God cares for the ravens and lilies. The conclusion (F) presents a powerful motivating sanction: single-minded pursuit of the kingdom, which the Father is graciously giving the people, will result in provision of the necessities about which they are worried. The repetition of words as well as themes (e.g., "anxious," "life/body," "eat," "clothing/wear") is evident even in the translation. The repetition of sounds and/or verbal forms, while not as striking as in the prayer discourse, is evident in the Greek of this speech as well (e.g., the second plural -*ete* and third plural -*ousin* verbs at the beginning in B1 and D1; the five successive -*on* endings in D3; and the nine -*ē* sounds in the first three lines of A and fifteen -*ē*- sounds in the lines of D and E).

The context or occasion is difficult for those of us who live in relative comfort and plenty to discern simply because we have no regular experience of being economically marginal, of economic insecurity. Nor were those who left the literary sources on which we depend, that is, the comfortable elite of ancient societies, familiar with such circumstances. Thus we are not familiar with anything comparable to what might be a register appropriate to such a context. This should make us all the more cautious about being influenced by Luke's appropriation of this Q discourse, as having to do with "possessions" and "giving alms" from them (as in 12:32). Contrary to recent readings of Q in terms of "itinerant radicalism," there is nothing in the discourse to suggest "voluntary poverty."[8] The ravens, which neither sow nor reap nor "gather in to barns," and the lilies, which neither toil nor spin, are not presented as paradigms to be imitated. They are rather presented as illustrations of how God feeds and clothes the other, lesser creatures. The discourse is not a call to voluntary poverty but a reassurance to those who are so poverty-stricken that they are obsessed with anxiety about whether they can feed or clothe themselves. The general life situation addressed is the same as that of the people addressed by the beatitudes that open the covenant renewal discourse ("blessed are you poor . . . , you who are hungry!") and those instructed to petition God for the kingdom ("give us bread . . . and cancel our debts") and those who are at each others' throats because of mutual indebtedness (6:27–35).

The similarity to the Q covenantal discourse in the general situation addressed may be the clue to how to hear this discourse addressing the people's anxieties about the necessities of life. In the covenant renewal discourse, the declaration that God is now effecting the kingdom for the poor and hungry (6:20–21) provides the basis for them to restore the mutual local cooperation of Mosaic covenantal principles and to overcome the simmering hostilities rooted in old local conflicts and resentments (6:27–42). Similarly, in 12:22–31, 33–35, the poor and hungry worried about necessities are reassured and called to focus single-mindedly on the

---

8. Voluntary poverty is simply projected onto these sayings. It is curious that Q interpreters cite Gerd Theissen in this connection, since he read this whole passage through Matt. 6:34, which was almost certainly not part of the Q discourse (see Theissen, *Sociology of Early Palestinian Christianity* [Philadelphia: Fortress, 1978], 13).

"kingdom of God," which symbolizes the renewal of Israel precisely in its basic social form, the village community. If the hearers are focused on the kingdom God is now effecting for them (6:20–21) and are regularly petitioning God in bold persistence to send the kingdom, which means bread and cancellation of debts (as they themselves mutually cancel each others' debts) then the results of their solidarity in the covenantal program of the kingdom will see them through.

Q Discourses Addressed to Communities of a Movement under Attack

Besides its declaration of prophetic woes and laments against the Jerusalem ruling house and its representatives, Q includes material that indicates a community under attack, apparently by those it condemned. An intensity of political-religious conflict with the rulers and/or their representatives can be heard in several discourses. It is conceivable that the vehemence of Jesus' condemnation of the scribes and Pharisees in the woes of 11:39–52 derives from resentment at their surveillance or attacks. Certain other passages indicate more clearly that the Q people were feeling pressure from the Pharisees. Matthew, following the Markan (3:22) parallel to the "Beelzebul" discourse, attributes the accusation that Jesus exorcizes demons in the power of Beelzebul to the Pharisees. Luke has merely "some (people)." The "Beelzebul" discourse in Q 11:14–26, however, appears to be linked with the two following clusters of 11:29–32(–36) and 11:39–52, both of which address (ostensibly) "this generation," which appears to be synonymous with "the Pharisees (and scribes/lawyers)" in 11:39–52. As is known from comparative historical materials, such as the witch-hunts in early modern Europe, moreover, it is a typical tactic of the political-religious power-holders to demonize popular healers who threaten their grip on the people. Given the political-economic-religious structure of the temple-state centered in Jerusalem, the Pharisees would have been the obvious ones to level such a charge against Jesus, whether articulated from a distance or on the scene, during the lifetime of Jesus himself or in the next few decades. The third step in the discourse in Q 7:18–35 appears to reflect a parallel attack on Jesus and/or his movement. The scene of Jesus' words against "this generation" (which is identical with the Pharisees and scribes in 11:39–52) is the town square (*agora*), where public activities such as assemblies and courts took place. Jesus compares "this generation" to "children." Yet instead of running about, they are formally "seated," as in a court making a judgment, and they are not "calling to" but formally "addressing" one another.[9] Those who accuse John and Jesus in such completely opposite terms, "having a demon" and "a glutton and a drunkard," appear to be the Pharisees. And this Q discourse as a whole portrays a situation in which attacks simply accompany the program of fulfillment that John prepared and Jesus was implementing.

---

9. Wendy Cotter, "The Parable of the Children in the Marketplace, Q 7:31–35," *NovT* (1987): 295–302.

Bold Confession When Brought to Trial: Q 12:2–12

Only the discourse in 12:2–12 deals directly with attacks on members of the movement and how they should deal with being put to the "test" (cf. 11:4). The "text" of this discourse is difficult to reconstruct in 12:5, 8–9, and 11–12, although Matthew's and Luke's texts have more in common at those points than indicated by the text of the International Q Project.

A. 1 (2)	Nothing is covered	which will not	be revealed		
	and (is) hidden	which will not	be made known.		
2 (3)	What I tell you	in the darkness	speak	in the light,	
	and what you hear	in your ear	proclaim	upon the housetops.	
B. 1 (4)	And do not fear	those who kill	the body		
	but (who) the soul	are not able	to kill.		
2 (5)	Fear	rather	the one able		
	both soul and body	to destroy	in Gehenna.		
C. 1 (6)	Are not two	sparrows	sold for	an *asserios*?	
	And one of them	will not fall	to earth	without God.	
2 (7)	Even the hairs	of your head	all	have been numbered.	
	Do not fear,	you	are worth more	than many sparrows.	
D. 1 (8)	Every one	who confesses	me	before people,	
	also the son of man	will confess	him/her	before the angels of God.	
2 (9)	But whoever	denies	me	before people,	
		will be denied		before {the angels of God}.	
E. 1 (10)	And whoever	speaks a word	against the son of man	will	be forgiven;
2	but whoever	blasphemes	against the holy spirit	will not be forgiven.	
F. 1 (11)	{When} you	are delivered up	do not be anxious about	what you will say;	
2 (12)	for {it will be given	to you}	in that hour	what you will say.	

As in the other discourses, the pattern of parallel lines (including antithetical as well as synonymous parallelism), consisting mostly of pairs of four terms/stresses (A2; C; D; E) varied by what appear to be pairs of three (A1; B), can be discerned even in translation. More than in most other discourses the repetition of words, phrases, verbal forms, and syntactical forms can also be recognized in the translation blocked into measured verse. Where the repetition does not occur in successive or alternative lines, the reader/hearer may have to look more closely, as in the repetition of the theme "not to fear" (B1; B2; C2). What is not evident except in the Greek is the further repetition of sounds and verbal forms (e.g., the ending *-esthai* at the end of the two lines of A1; that of *-ate* in A2; that of *-etai* in E; and that of *-ete* in F). The structure of the speech is easily discernible. It moves from a bold and reassuring declaration of the broad revelatory situation and, in that context, a corresponding command to boldly proclaim Jesus' message; to admonition not to fear those who might kill; to a reassurance based on a comparison with God's close watch over the sparrows and a combination insistence on bold confession of association with Jesus in the face of judgment; to a final assurance that the Q people need not worry about situations of being brought to trial ("testing" [cf. Q 11:4]).

Just as laws that prohibit certain actions suggest that such actions are taking place, the admonition, "do not fear those who kill the body" (12:4) suggests that there are reasons to expect that "those . . . " may well attempt to kill. As indicated in 12:11–12 (cf. Mark 13:9–11), Q people faced the possibility of being "delivered up" to the authorities who would place them on trial, apparently on some charge for which they could be killed. The expanded forms of this saying in both Luke 12:11–12 and Mark 13:9–11 indicate that rulers were envisaged (*archai, exousiai, hēgemones, basileioi*), not local village "synagogues."[10] This is confirmed by the statement in the mission discourse (Q 10:3) that the envoys are sent out as "sheep / lambs in the midst of *wolves*," the latter being a traditional metaphor for *rulers*. The general context or occasion for this discourse was thus the Q people facing the possibility of repressive action by the rulers.

There is no reason to imagine that a Jesus movement would have been less subject to repressive measures than the many other popular movements at the time in Israelite Palestine. Best known, of course, are the popular messianic movements in Galilee, Perea, and Judea after the death of Herod in 4 B.C.E. and the insurrectionary movements in rural Judea which one by one moved into the fortified city of Jerusalem during the great revolt of 66–70. To these the Romans responded with devastating reconquests, including systematic "scorched earth" destruction of villages and their inhabitants. The Roman governors, however, from Pontius Pilate through Fadus and Florus, also took prompt military action against urban demonstrations and the nonviolent, popular prophetic movements in the countryside. The Judean priestly aristocracy even arrested the lone peasant-prophet Jesus son of Hananiah, whose offense was merely repeated delivery of an oracle of doom over Jerusalem. The Roman governor simply had the man soundly beaten. But the priestly aristocrats who were pressing for more severe punishment may have understood something of the resonance that prophetic oracles might have among a restive people. Among the early Jesus movements, if we cut critically through the accounts toward the beginning of Acts, the obvious cases in point are the high-priestly arrests of Peter and others in Jerusalem and the killing of Stephen. In Galilee itself, of course, the best-known case of repression of a prophet or a popular movement was Antipas's arrest and execution of John the Baptist. Besides Q 10:3 and 12:2–12, there are several other indications in Q discourses themselves that Q people were subjected to persecution, even violent repression, presumably by the rulers. The fourth "beatitude" in Q 6:22–23 suggests that Q people were experiencing persecution. The saying in Q 16:16, where the "kingdom of God" apparently refers to the renewal movement inaugurated

---

10. *Synagogai*, literally any sort of "assemblies," in this case would have been the judicial councils convened by rulers, not the local village form of self-governance, on which see Richard A. Horsley, *Galilee: History, Politics, People* (Valley Forge, Pa.: Trinity Press International, 1995), chap. 10.

by Jesus suggests that the Q communities were subjected to violence. And the saying in Q 14:27, "Whoever does not take his cross and follow after me is not worthy of me," seemingly full of hyperbole, may well have been rooted in several generations of popular experience under the Romans, the Herodians, and other client rulers.

It would even appear that the speech in Q 12:2–12 is couched in a register developed by just such renewal or protest movements for just such circumstances of repression in which they were typically placed by anxious rulers.[11] This is suggested at the two points at which the discourse makes explicit metonymic references to Israelite tradition of judgment against oppressive (indigenous and/or foreign) rulers. The first, Gehenna (Greek transcription of the Aramaic Gehinnam or the Hebrew Ge-hinnom, the "Valley of Hinnom" south-southwest of Jerusalem), because of its earlier association with sacrifice of children by passing them through fire and into the hands of the god Molech or Baal (Jer. 7:31; 19:4–5; 32:35; 2 Kings 16:3; 21:6), came to symbolize the place of fiery judgment of the wicked in later Judean apocalyptic literature and rabbinic literature. Starting at least with Jeremiah in the prophetic tradition and continuing into Judean apocalyptic literature (*1 Enoch* 26–27; 54:1–6; 56:1–4; 90:24–27), "Gehenna" was understood as the fiery place of judgment particularly appropriate for oppressive domestic or foreign rulers (some of this connotation is evident still in Matt. 13:42, 50; 23:15, 33). Q people hearing this symbol in a situation of possible trial and execution by their own rulers would have been reassured more than threatened — assuming they expected to remain steadfast in their loyalties even when brought to the test — for Gehenna was what awaited the unjust and wicked in God's justice.

The second important metonymic reference, 12:8–9, imagines a heavenly judgment scene that mirrors a human judgment scene. Such scenes had developed out of the Israelite prophetic visionary experiences in which political interactions in history were seen to be mirrored and anticipated or determined by deliberations in the heavenly court of God (e.g., 1 Kings 22; Isaiah 40). Judean scribes/sages involved in resisting either their own rulers or repressive imperial rulers drew upon this tradition in resolving the problem of what would happen to those who steadfastly resisted even to the point of being martyred — before the time of God's resolution to the historical crisis in judgment of the oppressive rulers and restoration of the people.[12] The solution was vindication in the heavenly court, possibly simultaneously with or immediately after their martyr-

---

11. John S. Kloppenborg, "Literary Convention, Self-Evidence, and the Social History of the Q People," *Semeia* 55 (1991): 83, considering 12:2 as a wisdom saying by itself, reads it as belonging to the register of "research and discovery," which then carries over programmatically to the rest of the process of preaching the kingdom and the opposition it evokes. Correspondingly, he and other recent Q interpreters view the Q people as engaged simply in countercultural instruction at the stage of the hypothesized formative layer of Q.

12. For the threefold general agenda of Judean apocalypses as God's judgment against the oppressing rulers, restoration of the people, and vindication of the martyrs, see Horsley, "Apocalypticism."

dom. The scene portrayed in Q 12:8–9 drew on and referred to this tradition, although not in its more elaborate scribal form (e.g., Dan. 7:9–14, 26–27; 11–12), regardless of how we construe the reference to "the son of man."[13] It would be hard to imagine that the appeal to the divine judgment scene as a consolation for and sanction on faithful resistance to repression by the rulers would have been confined to the apocalyptic literature written by Judean scribes / sages. In fact, it was mainly peasants caught up in popular movements in Judea and Galilee, not scribal circles, who persistently offered resistance to the Roman and / or Jerusalem rulers and were killed in repressive moves by the rulers. Indeed, the most vivid example in ancient Jewish and Christian literature of the tradition of appeal to the divine court for vindication of a martyr comes from Israelite popular tradition, from another Jesus movement parallel to the one that produced Q: the martyrdom of Stephen in Acts 7.[14]

The discourse in Q 12:2–12 calling for bold confession when brought to trial has implications for critical judgment about when and where the Q discourses took definitive form. Was the context of the performance of this discourse merely a community remembering past circumstances in which its predecessors had faced hostility and persecution from the rulers? Considering the tone of the discourse and the other evidence of repression against Jesus' followers, it seems difficult to conclude that the trials anticipated are utterly imaginary. The situation of the community hearing this speech appears to be one of actual repression or the threat of repression. It may be significant, given the numerous parallels to particular Q sayings in the *Gospel of Thomas* (which are spiritually interpreted) and to Q topics in the *Didache*, that the only saying from this discourse that either of those documents parallels is Q 12:10, about a word against the Holy Spirit — suggesting that the threat of repression was so distant for them that the pertinent sayings from the prior tradition were no longer relevant and no longer needed to be reinterpreted or reapplied. This speech calling for bold confession when facing the "test" suggests that the situation in which the speech took more or less its current form was one in which the community was still engaged in a struggle for the renewal of Israel over against the rulers.

---

13. "The son of man" in this discourse is one of the more puzzling cases in a very confusing area of scholarly investigation and debate. The term "the son of man" would appear to belong to the text of Q at this point: Matthew would have changed it to "I," since he consistently identifies Jesus with "the Son of Man" as a title. For Luke, "the son of man" would be a more "difficult" reading than the divine passive in Q 12:8. And the appearance of the term in 12:10 depends upon its previous appearance in 12:8. In Daniel 7, the term "one like 'a son of man' " appears as a symbol for "the people of the saints of the Most High" or, a close variation, for a divine angel / figure (Michael) who in turn represents Israel, to whom sovereignty is restored in the divine judgment scene. In Q 12:8–9, where Jesus seems to be referring to himself, "the son of man" is rather an advocate or accuser before the divine court at the judgment. But in Q 17:24, 26, 30, more of the Danielic sense may be present in the phrase "the day(s) of the son of man" as a reference to the future time when the judgment will occur.

14. It is worth noting that " 'the son of man' standing at the right hand of God" in the judgment scene in Stephen's visionary experience is identified as Jesus not in the saying itself (Acts 7:56) but in the literary context.

Q Discourses That Sanction Discipline and Solidarity in the Communities

Not all of the Q materials that were classified as apocalyptic or prophetic as opposed to sapiential were directed ostensibly against outsiders. In some cases there is no question. Q 11:39–52 is clearly a condemnation of the Pharisees, and 13:34–35 laments the desolation of the Jerusalem ruling house, as explored in the next chapter. Other "apocalyptic" or "prophetic" materials, however, appear rather to be directed to the Q communities themselves. In the case of some of this material, such as Q 12:39–40, 41–46, it is difficult to discern clearly the contours of the discourses that it may have been part of. Only the Q material behind Luke 17:23–37 and its Matthean parallels seems clearly to have constituted a discrete discourse, on the suddenness of the judgment.

The "text" of this discourse must be reconstructed critically without incorporating what are clearly Matthean or Lukan twists projected back into Q — for example, the parousia, or the heavenly figure of the Son of Man coming in judgment. Because of the lack of Matthean parallel to Luke 17:28–29, the International Q Project excluded the illustration from "the days of Lot" from the Q text. On criteria of oral performance, however, it would have been more satisfactory to have two illustrative examples, one from "the days of Lot" and one from "the days of Noah," as in the double illustration from the Queen of the South and Jonah in Q 11:39–42. In terms of genre, Q 17:23–37 is commonly labeled an "apocalypse," in comparison with seemingly similar material and patterns in Mark 13 and *Didache* 16, with which it also appears to share a common function toward the end of a whole document. The similarity of function in the overall documents seems clear enough. But the concept "apocalypse" has connotations that should not be imported into Q 17:23–37, which lacks many of the particular features of Mark 13 and *Didache* 16 as well as of longer Judean documents that are more properly called apocalypses.[15] Whatever label is placed on its genre, the register in which this discourse speaks is certainly prophetic warning about the coming judgment.

The metonymic reference to Israelite tradition is unusually rich in this discourse. In the illustrations from "the days of Noah" and "the days of Lot," however, the emphasis is not on the destruction of the world, the modern scholarly fantasy of a "cosmic catastrophe," but on the destruction of the unsuspecting people.[16] In fact, the destruction of the world was not the message in the biblical stories of either Noah or Lot. The problem in both cases was wicked people, not the creation itself. Nor does prophetic or apocalyptic literature use images such as a "new heaven, new earth" in literalistic ways but rather as hyperbolic and metaphoric language (e.g., Isa. 65:18–25). In the Q discourse, as different from Matthew's or Luke's use of the Q material, the speech is focused not on "the Son of Man" as

15. Horsley, "Q and Jesus," *Semeia* 55 (1991): 196.

16. John S. Kloppenborg, *The Formation of Q: Trajectories in Ancient Wisdom Collections* (Philadelphia: Fortress, 1987), 155–66.

a figure coming in judgment but rather on the time of judgment, symbolized in the term "the day of the son of man."[17] This is similar to certain later rabbinic literature where interest focuses not on "the Messiah" as a figure but on "the days of the messiah" as the time of future salvation. Since extant texts containing the phrase "son of man" are so unclear and inconsistent as to what the phrase means, leading us to conclude that there was no standard reference to a figure called "the Son of Man" until later Christian texts such as Matthew, it seems best to take the "text" of Q 17:24, 26, 30 as referring to the future judgment with the phrase "the days of the son of man," without attempting to become more specific. The emphasis in Q 17:23–37 is clearly the suddenness of the judgment, symbolized by "the day(s) of the son of man." And this message of the suddenness of judgment is directed to the Q people themselves as a sanction to maintain their community discipline and dedication to the purposes of their movement in the renewal of Israel, most obviously in their own community life.

---

17. See further the critical discussion of the "son of man" in Q by James M. Robinson, "The Son of Man in the Sayings of Q," in *Tradition und Translation: Zum Problem der interkulturellen Übersetzbarkeit religiöser Phänomene: Festschrift für Carsten Colpe zum 65. Geburtstag,* ed. Christoph Elsas et al. (Berlin: Walter de Gruyter, 1994), 315–35; and Horsley, "Q and Jesus," 196.

Chapter 13

THE RENEWAL OF ISRAEL
OVER AGAINST ITS RULERS

Richard A. Horsley ─────────────────────────────

Several passages and at least one clearly delineated discourse in Q are directed ostensibly against Jerusalem rulers or their scribal representatives. As noted above, these have been interpreted to mean that Q and the Q people were calling down judgment against "all Israel."[1] That interpretation, however, besides ignoring the diversity in contemporary Judea and Galilee, which were dominated by a fundamental political-economic divide between rulers and ruled, is determined by a standard old scheme of the origin of Christianity from Judaism that has been superseded by a far more precise sense of historical developments. The prophetic materials against the Jerusalem ruling house and Pharisees, furthermore, have been taken recently to indicate that the Q people's attempt at "reform" of Israelite society had been a failure, after which they lashed out in resentment against the rest of Israel, which had rejected their reform and its teacher. That, however, is a modern hypothesis with no clear indicators in the Q material. Now that we are much more fully aware of the general dissatisfaction in Palestine with the high-priestly aristocracy and of the historical regional differences as well as the political-economic-religious structural divide between Jerusalem and Galilee, where Q materials originated, Q's prophetic materials against the Jerusalem ruling house and the scribes/lawyers and Pharisees can be "overheard" with more of their prophetic overtones.

The survey of Israelite tradition in Q in chapter 5 turned up a significant difference between a scribal vision and a popular vision of the restoration of Israel. Both feature the symbol of the twelve tribes and focus on establishing justice in the society. The vision articulated at the end of Q (22:30), however, has what appear to be popular leaders seated on chairs establishing justice for the twelve tribes, whereas *Pss. Sol.* 17:26–32 pictures "a righteous king over them." There could not be a more striking and telling difference between the Israelite "great

---

1. For example, John S. Kloppenborg, *The Formation of Q: Trajectories in Ancient Wisdom Collections* (Philadelphia: Fortress, 1987), 119, 120, 125, 127, 167, 169, 236–37, 238; Christopher M. Tuckett, *Q and the History of Early Christianity* (Peabody, Mass.: Hendrickson, 1996), esp. chaps. 6, 9, 12, 13, is much more nuanced.

tradition" and the Israelite "popular tradition," as they embody the visions that express the fundamental interests of the Jerusalem elite and the Israelite peasantry, respectively. A critical reading of the complexly layered Hebrew Bible suggests that ever since their origins as a free, independent peasantry gave way to a monarchy and then a temple-state in Jerusalem, the Israelite villagers longed for the time when they would be free again to operate their own communities according to the Mosaic covenantal principles. The same critical reading of the Hebrew Bible, along with sapiential books such as Sirach, indicates that Jerusalem kings or high priests and their scribal "retainers" such as the Pharisees saw their own position and function as central and essential. Their responsibility was to rule and establish justice for the people. From the popular viewpoint, however, the rulers and their representatives not only were unnecessary but were the agents of injustice.

Thus it is not surprising that prophetic declarations against the Jerusalem ruling "house" and their scribal retainers, the Pharisees, are an integral part of an overall series of discourses devoted to the renewal of Israel. John the Baptist declares that the "one who is coming" is to baptize with Holy Spirit and with fire. The baptism of Holy Spirit is manifest in the renewal of covenant and the fulfillment of longings for wholeness and the mutual cancellation of debts among the people (Q 6:20–49; 7:18–35; 11:2–4). The baptism of fire, while always a sanction on the Q communities' own behavior, is envisaged as directed primarily against the rulers and their representatives, whose position and role in the society stand in the way of entry into the kingdom of God, that is, the desired renewal of Israel that would finally be free of unjust rulers.

The prophetic condemnations against rulers for their injustices toward the people are thus also not intrusive elements in a series of discourses otherwise devoted to community affairs. Evidence for historical political-economic-religious relations in ancient Palestine suggests that the various layers of rulers, Roman, Herodian, and Jerusalem high-priestly, placed burdens on village and family life, threatening its very viability. The seemingly simple petition of "cancel our debts" included in the Lord's Prayer illustrates precisely the way in which villagers, unable to feed themselves after rendering tribute, taxes, and tithes, would fall into debt to those in command of resources (usually wealthy and powerful representatives of the rulers), debt that could mean loss of ancestral inheritance and membership in the ancestral village community. Thus the woes against the Pharisees for their "extortion" and advocacy of tithing (Q 11:39, 42) are integrally related to "cancel our debts" and "love your enemies... and lend" (11:4; 6:35). It is significant to note that literature from the Qumran community includes sharp curses against the "sons of the pit" and the "wicked priest" in the same documents that contain materials dedicated to the internal life of the community (e.g., the curses at the opening of 1QS).

We noted above that some of the materials devoted to concerns internal to the movement, such as the covenant renewal and the mission discourses and the Lord's Prayer, are performative utterances, speech that enacts or effects what it pronounces. If we take seriously the traditional Israelite prophetic forms in which they are orally recited before communities of Q people, the woes against the Pharisees in Q 11:39–52 and the prophetic oracles against the Jerusalem ruling house in Q 13:29–28, 34–35 are also apparently performative utterances, speeches that effect the condemnations they pronounce.

Against the Jerusalem Rulers: Q 13:29–28, 34–35, 14:16–24

The text of the Q material directed against the Jerusalem ruling house has been difficult for modern scholarly eyes to discern. No satisfactory proposal has yet been suggested for how to reconstruct intelligible clusters or discourses from Q materials underlying Luke 13–16 and their parallels in Matthew. Ironically, Kloppenborg's proposal that views Q 13:24–30, 34–35; 14:16–24, 26–27, 34–35 as one of the "sapiential" discourses also finds that prophetic materials inserted into the discourse later far outweigh and dominate the supposedly original sapiential framing.[2] It makes far more sense to view those prophetic sayings and parable, Q 13:28–29, 34–35; 14:16–24, as having formed a long prophetic discourse or a shorter prophetic discourse followed by a semiseparate but parallel prophetic parable directed ostensibly at the Jerusalem rulers.[3] Significantly, John Kloppenborg's observations regarding the form and composition of these prophetic materials fit this hypothesis well, particularly the reconstruction of Q 13:29–28 following Matthew's wording but Luke's sequence of Q materials. Since it is not obvious on the surface that the prophecies in 13:29–28, 34–35; 14:16–24 belong together in a coherent discourse, it seems best to treat them separately, allowing their possible coherence to emerge from the material itself heard in the appropriate context and register and in its reference to Israelite tradition.

The "text" of the prophetic lament Q 13:34–35 is secure from the almost verbatim versions in Matthew and Luke. The oral pattern of this relatively brief prophecy seems to be, after the mournful repetitive address, two parallel lines with two stresses, each expressing parallel sounds and ideas, followed by two parallel lines with four stresses, each expressing an analogy between God and a mother hen, ending with a pointedly brief two-stress line that uses the same verb for Jerusalem's refusal as for God's will:

A.1. Jerusalem,	Jerusalem!		
2. Killing	the prophets		
and stoning	those sent to you!		
3. How often	did I want	to gather	your children
in the same way	as a hen (gathers)	her brood	under her wings,
4. and you	did not want (it).		

---

2. Kloppenborg, *Formation of Q,* 223–37.
3. Richard A. Horsley, "Q and Jesus," *Semeia* 55 (1991): 195–96.

B. 1. Behold   forsaken to you   is your house!
    2. I tell you,
       You will not see me   until [it comes when] you say,
       "Blessed   is the one who comes in the name   of the Lord."

Theologically oriented interpreters have regularly taken this and other prophetic statements in an inappropriate register. Just as the Declaration of Independence of the thirteen colonies against the English monarchy in 1776 was not a treatise in the philosophy of history, so Q 13:34–35 and 11:49–51 were not reflective "interpretation of history." As discussed in chapter 5, these passages do not fit the "deuteronomistic" interpretation of history as reconstructed by modern biblical scholars.[4] The register of such Q material is, rather, prophetic pronouncement of God's judgment against oppressive and exploitative rulers. The form of 13:34–35 in particular, again as noted in chapter 5, is a prophetic lament the performance of which assumes and announces that the person (institution) is already dead or destroyed (from the viewpoint of God's imminent judgment). To understand the context (occasion) for repeated performance of such prophetic speech as Q 13:34–35, we must recognize that the Q people's movement of renewal of Israel focused on village communities was simultaneously a rejection of the ruling institutions and their incumbents in Jerusalem. The context for performance of such prophetic speech against the Jerusalem ruling circles would thus have been the regular meetings of Q communities in which, as part of their celebration and reaffirmation of their movement of renewal of Israel over against its Jerusalem ruling institutions, they heard prophecies of God's condemnation of rulers they viewed as unjust and oppressive. This becomes clearer when we review the tradition referenced in this prophetic speech — and compare it with the closely related Israelite tradition referenced in other Q speeches.

The prophetic lament in Q 13:34–35 references Israelite tradition in many richly interconnected ways. In this prophetic lament, as in most oracles of the "classical" Israelite prophets, the prophet is the mouthpiece of God. This is unusual in Q discourses, where Jesus ordinarily speaks in his own voice, although other prophetic pronouncements in Q, particularly 11:29–32 and 11:39–52, come close, as we shall see below. As in earlier Israelite oracles pronounced upon rulers and their officers, the prophet speaks from the viewpoint of God, who has seen the injustice they have perpetrated and has already pronounced their sentence. In the actual oracles the "sentencing" can take the form of a prediction ahead of time, the very speaking of which in "the word of the Lord" makes the sentence effective, or an announcement of a decision already taken in the divine court, or a lament or funeral dirge as if the destruction had already taken place. The same

---

4. For the deuteronomistic view of the interpretation of history, see especially Odil Hannes Steck, *Israel und das gewaltsame Geschick der Propheten*, WMANT 23 (Neukirchen-Vluyn: Neukirchener Verlag, 1967); and Arland D. Jacobson, *The First Gospel: An Introduction to Q* (Sonoma, Calif.: Polebridge, 1992).

pronouncement of judgment against the ruling city in the different "tenses" can be seen in oracles of Amos. In 5:16–17, the prophet as the mouthpiece of God declares mourning and wailing in the future:

> Therefore thus says the LORD, the God of hosts:
> In all the squares there shall be wailing;
> and in all the streets they shall say "Alas! Alas!"
> ...Those skilled in lamentation to wailing...

In Amos 5:2–3, the prophet as the mouthpiece of God simply sings the dirge as if the city has already been defeated:

> Fallen, no more to rise is the maiden Israel;
> forsaken on her land with no one to raise her up.

Resonating with this tradition of prophetic dirge and lament, Q 13:34–35 speaks from the viewpoint of a caring God who laments the ruling "house" now desolate — "O Jerusalem, Jerusalem!" — that reluctantly had to be destroyed because of its persistent oppression and repression.

The indictment of the Jerusalem ruling house for "killing the prophets" referenced a long and deep tradition in Israel and one increasingly prominent in cultural memory at the time, as noted in chapter 5. Ahab and Jezebel, perhaps the most notorious monarchs of Samaria, had sent the "death squads" out after Elijah, that "troubler of Israel" (1 Kings 19; 18:17). And as is known from the attempts of the Davidic and temple officials to kill Jeremiah because of his persistent prophecies against monarchy and temple for breaking the principles of the Mosaic covenant, another prophet who prophesied against Jerusalem, Uriah son of Shemaiah, was hunted down in Egypt, where he had fled, and was viciously killed by King Jehoiakim (Jer. 26:7–23). When we finally have sources again, that is, for the time of Jesus and the Q people, it is clear that nothing had changed. Popular prophets declaimed — or anticipated God's action — against rulers and ruling cities, and rulers killed prophets. Roman governors quickly slaughtered figures such as the "Egyptian" Jewish prophet and his followers on the Mount of Olives, from which they expected the walls of Jerusalem to fall in the anticipated divine deliverance (Josephus, *Ant.* 20.169–71; *B.J.* 2.261–63). The priestly aristocracy arrested Jesus son of Hananiah and sought his execution by Albinus, the Roman governor, who merely had him severely beaten again. Most ominous for Jesus and the people who produced and heard Q, of course, would have been John the Baptist's execution by Antipas. Given such a long tradition of rulers killing (and attempting to kill) the prophets who delivered God's oracles against their oppressive actions, it is difficult to imagine that the hearers of Q would not have "resonated" to an indictment for killing the prophets included in a prophetic lament over the (imminent) divine judgment of Jerusalem.

The statement in 13:34b focused on the images of God's care for Jerusalem's "children" and the mother hen gathering her brood under her wings to which the former is compared references yet another long, rich, and deep-running aspect of

Israelite tradition. "Children" was apparently a standing image in the tradition for the people or villages subject to and supposedly under the care of Jerusalem as a ruling ("mother") city — just as "daughters" at a number of points in the biblical tradition refers to the villages subject to a city, and as the "sons of Jerusalem" can mean the people of Judah or Israel generally (Isa. 51:17–18). The image of God as the mother hen gathering her young under her wings alludes to and builds upon the traditional image in the "Song of Moses," where God is "like an eagle that stirs up its nest and hovers over its young, spreading its wings" (Deut. 32:11). The Song of Moses was a prominent portrayal of God's original deliverance and formation of the people of Israel as his own special people in the exodus and wilderness experience. Throughout the biblical tradition, however, as articulated particularly by the prophets, after setting rulers in charge of the people, God had repeatedly to send prophets or take action to protect the people from the rulers. Indeed, God repeatedly declared judgment against Jerusalem (or the rulers in Samaria), as can be seen in oracle after oracle of Amos, Micah, Isaiah of Jerusalem, and Jeremiah. Because the rulers have "built Zion with blood and Jerusalem with wrong, therefore . . . Zion shall be plowed as a field; Jerusalem shall become a heap of ruins" (Mic. 3:9–12). The rulers not only exploited and oppressed the people but resisted God's warnings and redemptive efforts on their behalf. To illustrate the sense that hearers at the time of Jesus and the performance and hearing of Q would have of this tradition in its various prophetic images, we need only remember the love song (turned into prophetic oracle) sung by Isaiah, centered on Israel as God's vineyard, which the wealthy ruling elite ruined with "bloodshed" instead of "justice," and a "cry of distress" instead of "righteousness" (*ze'akah* instead of *zedakah*). That is clearly the traditional image and its prophetic application that Jesus' parable of the wicked tenants of God's vineyard draws upon and references, a parable told pointedly against the priestly ruling circles in Jerusalem in Mark's Gospel (Mark 12:1–8). Referencing this rich tradition, the prophetic lament in Q 13:34–35 transforms the warrior-like God, the eagle bearing its young aloft, into a caring maternal God, the hen attempting to protect her young from the predatory Jerusalem rulers.

Finally, in this prophetic lament's referencing of Israelite tradition, the last statement (Q 13:35) recites a key line (v. 26) from Psalm 118 (117 [LXX]). This was a highly familiar psalm, being among those sung at the major festivals such as Passover. Thus the hearers of Q would have known it and would have known that the high priests and others in Jerusalem would have known it well: the next line after "Blessed is he who comes in the name of the LORD" is "We bless you from the house of the LORD." The psalm as a whole, moreover, is a thanksgiving for previous salvation and an appeal for further deliverance: "Hosanna! Save us!" (v. 25). Performances of Q 13:34–35 in communities that lived at some distance from the ruling house of Jerusalem, in both geographical and social location, were thus playing with one of the key psalms that formed part of the annual public festivals at the temple in Jerusalem: the ruling house in Jerusalem would not see God until they welcomed "the one who comes in the name of the LORD," which for Q is Jesus — but of course those who consistently killed the prophets were not about to do that, hence would not soon be seeing God's favor.

The "text" of Q 13:29–28, if heard in measured verse, with parallel lines and repetition of words and sounds, should be reconstructed somewhat differently from the International Q Project text. The pattern appears to be successive lines with three and four stresses respectively:

[Many] shall come	from the east	and the west	
and recline	with Abraham	and Isaac and Jacob	in the kingdom of God.
{And the sons	of the kingdom}	will be cast out,	
and there will be	weeping	and gnashing	of teeth.

After attaining a clearer sense of how the prophetic lament over Jerusalem would have resonated in the ears of the hearers out of the "enabling" Israelite tradition, we can discern more easily how 13:29–28(30) fits together with 13:34–35 — presumably in a longer discourse against the Jerusalem rulers. Since other possible fragments of this discourse were not used by both Matthew and Luke in the same context, we cannot presume to reconstruct the larger discourse. By itself, however, 13:29–28 is intelligible both as a prophetic oracle directed ostensibly against the aristocracy in Jerusalem and as a statement immediately preceding the lament in 13:34–35. Its context of performance, taken together with 13:34–35, was community meetings in a movement of the renewal of Israel over against the Jerusalem rulers. Again, as with 13:34–35, the oracle is in the general register of prophetic speech. And like that of 13:34–35, its referencing of Israelite tradition must have evoked a rich set of associations in the hearers, focused on images of fulfillment of Israel's longings, with the tables finally to be turned on the high and mighty.

The picture of "people / many coming from east and west (and from north and south)" would have evoked deeply rooted longings among ancient Israelites. Judging from the biblical tradition, however, those had nothing to do with a pilgrimage by Gentiles, counter to the assumption underlying the standard interpretation of Q 13:29–28. In biblical and extrabiblical literature behind Q, both the Matthean "from east and west" and the Lukan "from east and west and from north and south" find multiple prophetic precedents. All of them pertain to the ingathering of dispersed Israelites in a future restoration of Israel. God delivers or gathers the exiled people "from east and west," in some cases to Jerusalem (Zech. 8:7–8; Bar. 4:4; 5:5; *1 Enoch* 57:1). God brings the dispersed Israelites or they gather from all four directions in Zech. 2:10; Isa. 42:5–6; and *Pss. Sol.* 11:2–3 (cf. Ps. 107:3).[5] Because the prophetic saying in Q 13:29–28 references Israelite tradition, "the kingdom of God" means among other things the banquet in which dispersed Israel will finally, as prophesied again and again, come from all directions to sit at table with Abraham, Isaac, and Jacob — yet another vivid indication that the kingdom of God in Q is the renewal of Israel.

---

5. These texts are laid out systematically in Dale C. Allison Jr., *The Jesus Tradition in Q* (Harrisburg, Pa.: Trinity Press International, 1997), 178–82.

This fulfillment of age-old longings and prophetic expectations for the renewal of Israel in the banquet of the kingdom, however, differs from the picture portrayed in many of those prophecies. As we would expect, the (scriptural and extrabiblical) texts of those prophecies were written from the perspective of the scribal elite who wrote or edited them. And, since most members of the scribal circles in ancient Judea presumably lived in Jerusalem, they wrote from the perspective of Jerusalem. Thus the dispersed Israelites are expected to come to Jerusalem or be centered on Jerusalem (Zech. 8:7–8; Bar. 5:5; *Pss. Sol.* 11:2; and presumably, from wider literary context, Isa. 43:5–6). The hearers of the Q discourses would have known, again, that the Jerusalem elite knew of these prophetic expectations. Indeed, since Herod had begun his massive rebuilding of the temple, Jerusalem had already become a pilgrimage center for Jews from the diaspora with sufficient resources to afford long journeys (see, e.g., Acts 6). Two of the four major high-priestly families whom Herod left as the ruling aristocracy, moreover, had roots in the (Egyptian and Babylonian) diaspora. In diametric opposition to what was the expectation, to the elites' own program of promoting Jerusalem as a center of worldwide Jewry, and to most of the traditional prophecies, Q pointedly leaves Jerusalem unmentioned as the center of the gathering from the diaspora for the banquet of the kingdom. Indeed, the prophecy of the restoration of Israel in the kingdom in Q 13:29–28 is also a pronouncement of judgment on the Jerusalem elite. Q 13:29–28, moreover, mocks the presumption of the Jerusalem elite with the label "sons of the kingdom" and the explicit inclusion of "Abraham, Isaac, and Jacob" at table in the kingdom. The latter parallels John's harangue in Q 3:7–9, where it is apparently the Jerusalem elite who take pride in their ancestry and distinguished lineage, being secure in their position because they have "Abraham as [their] father." As a prophecy of fulfillment in the kingdom of God that is also a prophecy of judgment against the elite, Q 13:29–28 sets up the prophetic lament in 13:34–35 as the next step in a discourse condemning the Jerusalem rulers.

The parable of the "great supper" in Q 14:16–24 is a fitting sequel to the two prophetic oracles in Q 13:29–28 and 34–35, although it is difficult to discern exactly how it might have been framed or joined. The banquet image picks up the banquet of the kingdom theme. The very image of a "great banquet," moreover, evokes the wealthy and powerful ruling elite. And those invited are also clearly wealthy figures who buy multiple yoke of oxen and additional fields, in the Lukan version which is clearly closer to Q (paralleled in *Gospel of Thomas* 64, whereas Matthew has transformed the story into one about a king's wedding banquet). The parable in Q 14:16–24 thus clearly evokes the analogy of God's rejection of the wealthy elite, as "the poor and maimed and blind and lame" are gathered in. If we trust the Lukan text as closer to the Q parable, then the last statement in 14:24 constitutes an inclusio with the rejection of the elite from the banquet of the kingdom in Q 13:29–28: "I tell you, 'None of those men who were invited shall taste my banquet.'" It is pertinent to notice also that those invited from the streets and alleys in the parable are precisely those to whom the kingdom is being given and/or who are being given a new life at other key points in the Q discourses, such as Q 6:20 and 7:22.

The Prophetic Woes against the Pharisees and Scribes: Q 11:39–52

Nowhere have Christian theological assumptions played a more decisive role than in interpretation of the woes against the Pharisees in Q 11:39–52. On the interrelated assumptions that Jesus' sayings address individuals' religion or ethics and that "Jesus" articulates the views of Christianity against Judaism, interpreters find here a debate about the Law, or more particularly purity laws. More recent interpretations of these Q sayings range from a redefinition of purity in ethical terms, by taking 11:39–41 and 11:44 as the key, to a radicalization of the Law, by taking 11:42 as the key. Somehow it is not noticed that only one of the seven woes even alludes to the Torah (tithes, in 11:42) and that only two mention purity, and then only as a rhetorical device (11:39–41, 44). Again modern interpreters have been mistaking the register of Q 11:39–52. These woes do not belong to the register of theological-ethical debate between Protestant Christianity and Judaism. In recent interpretation of Q, moreover, the woes themselves have been somewhat overshadowed and obscured by the keen interest in "this generation" as the key to the redaction of Q and in the role of Wisdom in Q, for both of which Q 11:49–51 is a key text.

In the case of these woes against the Pharisees, it may not be possible to determine the "text," let alone the register of the discourse as a whole, until we can more adequately discern the register, even the particular prophetic form, taken by the material. Problems of determining the "text" are compounded by the unusual difficulty of establishing the wording of particular woes and their probable sequence, given the considerable difference between the parallels in Matthew and Luke. The "woes" discourse may well be one case in which it makes less sense to reconstruct what appears to have been the wording. It may be more illuminating to keep continually in mind the different twists and nuances on particular woes in Matthew and Luke in order to remain open to previously undiscerned possibilities of hearing them in a historically informed way. With regard to the particular form of a prophetic woe and especially of a whole series of woes, however, it may prove illuminating to review the Israelite tradition that the Q woes reference. As with the discourse in Q 6:20–49, it is necessary to discern the larger form of the whole discourse in order to understand the particular components within that framework.

Most of the examples of prophetic woes occur in the earliest layers of the prophetic books of Amos, Micah, Isaiah, and Habakkuk. The form couples an indictment for violation of a covenantal principle or law with a statement of sentence or punishment. The form is thus clearly rooted in the same covenantal traditions as appear in the covenantal law codes of Exodus 21–24, Deuteronomy, and the holiness code in Leviticus. The woes are pronounced against rulers or

their representative officers for their exploitation and manipulation of the peasants. Some are simply a single woe followed by a corresponding statement of
punishment (e.g., Isa. 5:8 + 9–10; Isa. 5:11–12 + 13; Mic. 2:1–2 + 3–5; Hab.
2:6 + 7–8). But many of the woes come in sets of two, three, or four, followed by a statement of punishment (Amos 6:1–3, 4–6 + 7; Isa. 5:18–19, 20,
21, 22–23, + 24; Hab. 2:9–11, 12, 15 + 16–17 [and another woe] 19).

Much closer to the time of Q, the Epistle of Enoch (*1 Enoch* 94–102) consists
of several sets of woes against the wealthy and powerful for their exploitation of
the poor and persecution of the righteous (the scribal authors?). In the Epistle of
Enoch they appear mostly in sets of three to eight woes, each of which combines
an indictment with a sentence/punishment (94:6, 7, 8–9; 95:4, 5, 6, 7; 98:9–
10, 11, 12, 13, 14, 15; 99:1, 2; 99:11, 12, 13, 14, 15–16; 100:7, 8, 9; note also
that after the sets of woes in 94:6–10 and 99:11–16 follow additional statements
of punishment). The Epistle of Enoch, however, also includes sequences of four
or five woes capped by a sentence or statement of punishment (94:4, 5, 6, 7,
8 + sentence; 97:7, 8, 9, 10 + sentence, followed by an additional sentence in
98:1–3, 4–8). Given these prototypes both in the original prophetic oracles and
in the later scribal use of the same prophetic form, there is no reason to continue
splitting up Q 11:39–52 into six separate woes and a separate declaration of
punishment, all of which are analyzed and interpreted separately, even set off
against one another. It is conceivable that most if not all went together as a set of
woes plus punishment, as in the prophetic prototypes. The sentence pronounced
in 11:49–51 could easily have been the completion of a whole set of woes.

Determining more precisely the form of the set of woes in Q 11:39–52 should
help clarify their function, an integral aspect of form. By cutting through the
standard Christian reading of these woes, it is possible to recognize that they
function in a way parallel to those in the classical Israelite prophets. The latter
indict the rulers and royal officers for the specific ways in which they exploit and
abuse the people, with plentiful doses of mockery and sarcasm in their rhetoric
(see, e.g., Isa. 5:8; Amos 6:1–6; Mic. 2:1–2; Hab. 2:6, 9–15). The same is true in
the Q woes against the Pharisees. Rhetorically they mock the Pharisees for their
obsession with purity and for their insistence on rigorous and precise tithing of
even "dill and cumin." But the indictments in the Q series of woes focus not on the
Torah or purity concerns but on the social function of the scribes and Pharisees.

It is most obvious in the four woes that do not mention either a Torah ruling or
a purity issue that the focus falls on the activities of the Pharisees in relation to the
people. The woe in 11:43 expresses resentment at the Pharisees' expectation of
"first seats" in the assemblies and deferential greetings in town squares. "Loading
the people with heavy burdens" in 11:46 refers to the mediating scribal-retainer
role of the Pharisees and scribes/lawyers in the temple-state, with its economic
demands on the people, not to their supposed multiplication of legalistic rules as
a mode of scribal interpretation of the Torah. "Touching the burdens with one of
your fingers" is an ironic comment that they could if they would, in their authority
as interpreters of the Law, alleviate the people's economic burden with a few

strokes of their scribal pen. The woe in 11:47–48 insists that by building memorials to the prophets the Pharisees consent to their killing (and by implication are guilty of corresponding repressive measures in the present). The concluding woe in 11:52 is a summary of the overall effect of the Pharisees' role and actions: they prevent people from entering the kingdom of God![6]

Once it is clear that the woes that do not mention the Law or purity are focused on the effects of the Pharisees' social function, it may be possible to discern the same about the woes that were previously assumed to be concerned with the Law. The first woe, in 11:39–41, does indeed begin with reference to the Pharisees' concerns about ritual purity.[7] As evident in both Matthew's and Luke's versions, however, Q quickly shifts the vessels into metaphors. As implicit in Matthew's version and explicit in Luke's, there was nothing subtle about Q's indictment: "Inside they/you [the Pharisees] are full of extortion and rapacity." The Pharisees' concerns about ritual purity veil, or at least distract attention from, the rapacious effects of their interaction with the people. The indictment covers both. Tithes, in 11:42, were a matter of taxes, not of ceremonial law. The reference to "mint, dill, and cumin," items not even certainly tithed, is hyperbole and caricature, probably full of sarcasm or ridicule. The accusation that the Pharisees were obsessed with even such minor items is "metonymic" (*pars pro toto*) rhetoric: it serves to indicate just how rigorous they were about the principal cultivated products subject to tithes, that is, the staples of wine, oil, and mainly grain that were needed by the peasants for mere subsistence. If the Pharisees and scribes, as representatives of Jerusalem, were still insisting on payment of tithes on top of the taxes that Galileans owed to Antipas or Agrippa and the tribute they were rendering to Caesar, then they were indeed neglecting justice and compassion. The accusation in 11:44, finally, that the scribes and Pharisees are like "unmarked graves" that the people walk over unawares looks like the most clever of all. Like the charge of cleansing the outside of the cup, this accusation mocks the Pharisees' concern with purity. By charging that they themselves are like unmarked graves from which people are exposed to danger unawares, however, Q's Jesus shifts the focus to the Pharisees' role or social function in relation to the people. They constitute a hidden danger to the people.

Once we recognize that the Q woes against the Pharisees continue the same form and function as those in the earlier Israelite prophets, they cannot be so easily reduced to an abstract discussion of piety and ethics. The woes against the Pharisees, particularly those in Q 11:39, 42, 44, 46, and 52, rather indict the Pharisees and scribes/lawyers for the deleterious effects of their social-political role on the people in matters such as advocating rigorous tithing and failing to use

---

6. For the woe in Q 11:52 it is worth noting that 1QH 4 from Qumran makes a less severe but parallel charge against the "smooth interpreters" (code name for Pharisees), that they "withhold from the thirsty the drink of knowledge," presumably covenantal knowledge (as in Isa. 1:3).

7. Explained in Jacob Neusner, "First Cleanse the Inside: Halakhic Background of a Controversy Saying," *NTS* 22 (1976): 486–95.

their scribal office of applying the "laws of the Judeans" to the political-economic relations between rulers and ruled.[8]

Given the previous misunderstanding of Jesus' attacks on the scribes and Pharisees in Gospel materials, it is particularly important to recognize that the Q woes are rooted in the conflict between the Galilean popular tradition and the Jerusalem scribal elite. Q's Jesus indicts the scribal elite that had been entrusted (since the Hasmoneans, according to Josephus) with the guardianship, cultivation, and interpretation of the "great" or official tradition based in Jerusalem — including that the revenues necessary to support the temple-state and priesthood were forthcoming from the peasantry — on the basis of a parallel and equally Israelite tradition cultivated in village communities. The woe in 11:42 offers a glimpse of another aspect of that tradition closely related to the prophetic woes, both of them deeply rooted in the Mosaic covenantal tradition going back to premonarchic Israel, that about justice and mercy (*mispat, hesed*). Q 11:42 does not cite any prophetic texts but alludes to and stands in a long prophetic tradition of demanding that exploitative rulers heed the covenantal principles of justice and mercy. Modern theological interpretation generalizes these as "attributes of God and expectations of humankind." In the key prophetic texts often cited, however, these terms represent central demands made on the wealthy and powerful (the rulers) in the context of what have been discerned as "covenant lawsuits" pronounced by the prophets (Mic. 6:8; Hos. 4:1–3; 12:2–7) and/or direct demands on rulers (Zech. 7:9). The woes in Q resonate with this covenantal and prophetic tradition.

The strikingly harsh condemnation in the pronouncement of sentence (11:49–51) attached to the woes indicates just how seriously the indictments were intended. The repetition of the charge of killing the prophets from the previous woe (11:47–48) that forms the bridge to the sentence — and its repetition in the prophetic lament over Jerusalem in 13:34–35 — indicates just how seriously this loomed in the Q discourses and the Q movement it addressed. In this connection, the Q indictment in 11:47–48 and sentence in 11:49–51 not only reference a long Israelite tradition, as indicated in chapter 5 and discussion of 13:34 above, but give a particular twist to an Israelite tradition being hotly contested at the time.

Judean literature roughly contemporary with Q offers some windows onto how the ancient prophets were being memorialized in both extrabiblical practices and literary elaboration of Israelite tradition. On the one hand, legends of the prophets' persecution and martyrdom under the rulers they prophesied against were cultivated, as evident in the first-century C.E. Judean text *Martyrdom of Isa-*

---

8. The Matthean sequence of these woes seems more intelligible in its gradual escalation (compared with the Lukan sequence, which is therefore the more difficult reading, hence the original Q sequence): indictments respectively for loading heavy burdens on the people, loving the place of honor, shutting off the kingdom, advocating rigorous tithing, being motivated to extortion (like unmarked graves in their own concern) being a danger to the people, and building the tombs of the prophets, followed finally by the sentence that the blood of the prophets will be required of "this generation" (Matt. 23:4, 6, 13, 23, 25–26, 27, 29–31, 34–36).

iah. Other prophets such as Micah, Joel, and Habakkuk are associated with Isaiah in their persecution, martyrdom, or exile at the hands of rulers. Included in the story are an imprisoned Micaiah and Elijah's reproof of King Ahaziah for killing prophets of the Lord. In the first-century *Lives of the Prophets*[9] five prophets are said to have been martyred under kings, three of them in Jerusalem: Isaiah, Amos, and, most significantly for Q 11:47–51, Zechariah son of Jehoiadas. Perhaps also significantly for the phrase "from the blood of Abel to the blood of Zechariah" in Q 11:51, Zechariah is the last prophet whose story appears in *Lives of the Prophets*. Moreover, the story includes the statement that "Joash the king of Judah killed him near the altar, . . . poured out his blood in front of the porch of the temple" (23:1). Rabbinic tradition adds to this that his blood seethed and bubbled on the stones in the temple court for 252 years (*b. Gitt.* 57b; *b. Sanh.* 89b; *Midrash on Ecclesiastes* 3:16 no. 1; 10:4 no. 1).[10]

On the other hand, the memory of the prophets was being cultivated in literature and in monuments constructed at their burial sites. Almost by definition this means sponsorship by the elite, which as Q notes are the descendants or latter-day equivalents of those who originally killed the prophets. The *Lives of the Prophets*, which mentions the burial place of nearly all the prophets, indicates the existence of monumental tombs or other memorials in six cases and implies memorials in three other cases (although most prophets are said simply to be buried in their own field or their own tribal territory). While three are abroad, the burial sites of the rest are spread around the land of Israel: one or two in Galilee, three or four in Samaria, one in Idumea, and three in Jerusalem. Also pertinent to Q 11:47–51 is that the *Lives of the Prophets* includes accounts of prophets who do not appear particularly prominent in the written "great" tradition that became canonical (Deuteronomic history and prophetic books) and expands the list of prophets to include figures who are hardly represented as prophets in the later canonical Law and Prophets, such as Obadiah, the royal officer of Ahab (1 Kings 18:4). The *Lives of the Prophets* reflects the keen interest in the prophets, their burial places, and the building of monuments for their memory that must have been current before the Roman destruction of Jerusalem and devastation of the Judean and Galilean countryside in 67–70.[11]

The *Lives of the Prophets* even indicates the significance of the monuments to the prophets, particularly in the case of Isaiah, who was supposedly martyred by being sawed in two. God had done the water miracle of Siloam for Isaiah's sake during a siege, so he was buried nearby "in great honor, so that through

---

9. David Satran, *Biblical Prophets in Byzantine Palestine: Reassessing the Lives of the Prophets* (Leiden: E. J. Brill, 1995), has argued recently that the *Lives of the Prophets* is a much later, mainly Christian document. Anna Maria Schwemer, *Studien zu den frühjüdischen Prophetenlegenden Vitae Prophetarum*, 2 vols. (Tübingen: J. C. B. Mohr [Paul Siebeck], 1995), esp. 1:65–71, counters with compelling arguments for dating most of the material in the document prior to 70 c.e., while recognizing what are clearly Christian additions.

10. For a survey of sources and legendary information on the martyrdom of Zechariah, see Schwemer, *Studien*, 2:283–321.

11. Ibid., 1:55–87.

his prayers even after his death they might enjoy the benefit of water" (1:8). Contemporary benefits could thus be gained through cultivation and care of his shrine. "His tomb," moreover, "is near the tomb of the kings, west of the tomb of the priests in the southern part of the city" (1:9). Moreover, Haggai, who prophesied the return of the "people" to Jerusalem and witnessed the (re-)building of the temple, "was buried near the tomb of the priests, in great honor as were they" (14), and Zechariah, also important in the restoration of Jerusalem, "was buried near Haggai" (15).

It seems likely that such building of monuments to the prophets reached its peak as part of the wider program of building under Herod and his successors. Among Herod's many extensive projects, in addition to the massive rebuilding of the temple in grand Hellenistic style, was an expensive memorial of white marble at the entrance to David's tomb (Josephus, Ant. 7.392–94; 16.179–88).[12] The ostentatious religious-cultural "renaissance" inaugurated by Herod was continued into the first century C.E., with diaspora Jews and high-ranking converts from abroad contributing.[13] Josephus's lengthy account of Queen Helena of Adiabene and her sons Izates and Monobazus concludes with the report that their bones were "buried in three pyramids that [Helena] had erected at a distance of three furlongs from Jerusalem" (Ant. 20.95), which became noted landmarks of the city's landscape (B.J. 5.55, 119, 147). Only those who commanded considerable resources could have built such monuments, whether for themselves or for revered prophets or kings of the now-glorified past. We know from archaeological excavations in Jerusalem that numerous mansions were constructed during the Herodian period, apparently by wealthy Herodian and high-priestly families. When, under Hellenistic and Roman imperial rule, Judean rulers could no longer aspire to a great monarchy or high priesthood, at least it was possible to celebrate the glories of the past and in that way preserve some semblance of cultural identity and pride amid the dominant imperial culture — as suggested by the sustained encomium on the great royal, prophetic, and priestly office-holders of the distant past in Sirach 44–50. It may be significant that Greek cities, in their rhetorical revival celebrating the glories of past heroes and almost living in the past, were taking a parallel route now that real independence and self-government were things of the past.[14] It is possible also that there was suddenly more interest in

---

12. For a survey of Herod's own building activities, see Duane W. Roller, *The Building Program of Herod the Great* (Berkeley: University of California Press, 1998); Peter Richardson, *Herod: King of the Jews and Friend of the Romans* (Columbia: University of South Carolina Press, 1996), chap. 8. An older (and still useful) survey and discussion of memorials and monuments, particularly to the prophets — done to explore the background of Luke 11:47//Matt. 23:29 — is Joachim Jeremias, *Heiligengräber in Jesu Umwelt: Eine Untersuchung zur Volksreligion der Zeit Jesu* (Göttingen: Vandenhoeck & Ruprecht, 1958). The monuments that Jeremias examines as examples of *Volksreligion*, of course, would have been sponsored by the wealthy and powerful who commanded the necessary resources.

13. Nahman Avigad, "The Architecture of Jerusalem in the Second Temple Period," in *Jerusalem Revealed: Archaeology in the Holy City 1968–74*, ed. Yigael Yadin (Jerusalem: Israel Exploration Society, 1975), 17–20, provides a brief summary of monuments excavated by that date.

14. Simon Swain, *Hellenism and Empire* (Oxford: Clarendon, 1996).

the books of the past in Roman times than earlier.[15] In the histories of Josephus we can clearly detect a competition of subject peoples centered on which ones had the more ancient and glorious history.

On the basis of such literature and later pilgrimage reports regarding tombs or graves of the prophets, it seems that Q 11:47–48 refers to actual contemporary practice. As scribal retainers in the temple-state, particularly guardians of the traditions, as portrayed both in Mark and Josephus, the Pharisees would very likely have been involved in the cultivation of such monuments. Construction and cultivation of monuments to the prophets by the Jerusalem rulers and their representatives, however, may well have seemed the height of hypocrisy to Galilean and Judean villagers of the generation of Jesus and Q. Their grandparents' generation had carried out a sustained and costly resistance to Rome's imposition of Herod as client-king, and their parents' generation had mounted extensive revolts against Jerusalem and Roman rule following the death of Herod, whose building projects they were required to support via Herodian taxation — the very kind of exploitation the prophets had protested. Contemporary with the early performance of Q discourses in mid–first century, moreover, Judean and Samaritan peasants formed a number of popular movements led by prophets — that is, Theudas and the "Egyptian" Jewish prophet, whose blood was shed by Roman governors — informed by memories of God's great acts of deliverance led by Moses and Joshua. In the early sixties, when the peasant-prophet Jesus son of Hananiah began walking the streets of Jerusalem voicing his woes against the city, the high-priestly rulers arrested him and pressed the Roman governor to do more than simply have him severely beaten. There was thus a basis in contemporary events as well as in contemporary cultivation of memorials to martyred prophets of the past for the Q woes and sentence against "this generation" in Jerusalem.

---

15. Rebecca Gray, *Prophetic Figures in Late Second Temple Jewish Palestine: The Evidence from Josephus* (Oxford: Oxford University Press, 1993), 12–14.

Chapter 14

THE RENEWAL MOVEMENT AND THE PROPHET PERFORMERS OF Q

Richard A. Horsley _____

Shift in Assumption (Oral vs. Written) Requires Shift in Approach

The drive to define and control Q as a written composition has had implications for reconstruction of the community or movement behind Q. Establishing Q securely as a written document when it was still seen as a collection of sayings led to the hypothesis that its originating genre was a collection of "sayings of the sages," and that in turn led to its comparison with ancient Near Eastern collections in the instructional genre at home in scribal and palace schools. That comparison, however, leads to a problem. Since Q clearly attacks the "scribes and Pharisees" of the establishment in the Judean temple-state (10:21–24; 11:39–52), not-establishment yet literate intellectuals must be found who could have composed the collection in the more elite instructional genre. Countercultural social critics analogous to the Cynic philosophers active in Hellenistic cities provided one attractive option. But the proof texts adduced for such hypotheses have not withstood criticism of the way they were read and used, and the presence of such vagabond, Cynic culture critics in the Galilean contexts is historically incredible.[1] A far more sophisticated hypothesis has been presented, one that attempts to tease the social solution required logically by the determinate genre from available ancient textual and inscriptional evidence.[2]

The key factor in this determination of the social location of Q's authors is not the context indicated in the content of the material but the factors operative in the selection of the instructional genre ordinarily associated with scribal schools.[3] Despite "the wealth of agricultural imagery found in Q" suggesting a peasant audience, "the selection of a relatively learned and characteristically scribal genre"

---

1. See Christopher M. Tuckett, "A Cynic Q?" *Biblica* 70 (1989): 349–76; Richard A. Horsley, *Sociology and the Jesus Movement* (New York: Crossroad, 1989), esp. chaps. 1–3 and pp. 116–19; and idem, *Galilee: History, Politics, People* (Valley Forge, Pa.: Trinity Press International, 1995), chaps. 7–12.

2. John S. Kloppenborg, "Literary Convention, Self-Evidence, and the Social History of the Q People," *Semeia* 55 (1991): 77–102.

3. Ibid., 80, 82.

requires a different social location for the document's production.[4] And despite the fact that "some of the contents of Q are not paralleled in Near Eastern instructions," the sayings are to be interpreted along the lines of the more reflective and theological sapiential piety found in Prov. 1:20–33 or Sir. 51:23–30. The beatitudes thus provide a "balanced and anaphoric synkrisis on the nature of true blessedness"; the framer of the imperative admonitions that follow "has adopted a deliberative posture"; and Q 12:2 makes preaching of the kingdom analogous to "the process of research and discovery."[5] And with some frequency sayings "idealize poverty and the simple life." Q 12:4–7 does not concern the threat of repression by the authorities who might "kill the body"; 12:22–31 does not address the concrete anxieties of destitute peasants; 14:26–27 is not a hyperbolic call to commitment despite the risks; and 16:13 is not a call to social-economic solidarity. Such sayings rather "recommend a lifestyle that does not invest in the ordinary channels of personal security. . . . These are the views of intellectuals who utilize such idealizations [of poverty and detachment] as a counterbalance to what is perceived as a bankrupt or failing culture."[6] With the sayings thus taken out of the context indicated by the content of the discourses in which they are embedded, Q can be read as similar to ancient instruction, even though "the topos of parental instruction is avoided." Logically, it is concluded that "the selection of a relatively learned and characteristically scribal genre by which to convey the sayings of Jesus does not accord well with a peasant setting."[7]

But where, in terms of social location, can a "sufficient density of scribes" be found between the peasantry, on the one hand, and the elite scribal circles such as the scribes and Pharisees, castigated in 11:39–52, on the other? Supposedly in the "petit bourgeois" of the lower administrative sector of the cities and the villages.[8] The argument, however, is utterly conjectural and involves a number of questionable assertions. The caveats turn out to be decisive against the hypothesis. The literary evidence offered from Josephus all pertains to the Herodian officials and the elite of Tiberias, hardly scribal "petty bourgeois" who would supposedly have been attracted to a Jesus movement. According to Josephus's narrative of the great revolt, these men stood in conflict with the ordinary residents of the city and the surrounding villagers. In lower Galilee itself under Antipas and Agrippa I, "the growth of independent administrative offices would probably have been suppressed."[9] The officers (e.g., *gabbaim, parnasim, rosh ha knesset = archsynagogos*) of the local "assemblies" (*synagogai*) would have tended to the local affairs of the village communities, but there is no evidence that "even these villages undoubtedly had a bureaucratic structure."[10] Some of the Greek terms used to designate vil-

---

4. Ibid., 85.
5. Ibid., 81, 82, and 83, respectively.
6. Ibid., 88.
7. Ibid., 85.
8. Ibid., 85–86.
9. Ibid., 86.
10. Ibid.

lage officials in the Hauran and Trachonitis may parallel those used for Greek city officials, but the duties of these officers indicated in the inscriptions parallel those of the leaders of local village assemblies in rabbinic and other Jewish literature (e.g., Judith).[11] The major problem with this hypothesis, however, is that evidence from Egypt indicates that even where there were local and/or lower level officers with the designation *scribes* (*grammateis*), their level of literacy was minimal, barely functional.[12] There is little or no evidence that there were "scribes" or "administrative infrastructures" in either Galilee or surrounding areas or that the village officers were literate. Even if a few had acquired "scribal technology," that hardly implies "literary technology."[13] Finally, no evidence is provided that would suggest that the hypothetical "lower administrative and scribal sectors" cultivated "instructional" wisdom. The existence of a sufficient density of lower-level scribes who were in contact with but not embedded in peasant village life and who were somehow acquainted with the instructional genre is little more than an imaginative historical conjecture. There was apparently no such social location in and around Galilee that could have been responsible for the production of Q as a literary document in the instructional genre.

The preceding chapters have argued that Q must be understood as oral-derived literature. That means that scribes are not required for the composition of Q, even when its complexity and organization are recognized. In previous analysis of Q, composition and writing are telescoped into one action, which thus supposedly "required literary (that is, scribal) technology, knowledge confined in antiquity to an elite of perhaps five percent of the population." As a product of such "scribal activity," a "collection" in the "instruction genre characteristic of Near Eastern scribal schools," Q is thus "relatively well-organized, with clearly constructed arguments and with a degree of topical organization that places it among the best organized ancient saying collections. . . . Q, then, is far from unreflective, unsystematic oral tradition."[14] Even before the intensive recent analysis of oral performance, we knew that the oral tradition is far from unreflective and unsystematic. Recent studies of oral performances in contemporary societies and of oral-derived literature are demonstrating just how complex and sophisticated

---

11. See the discussion of leaders of local village assemblies in Horsley, *Galilee*, 227–33. As Victor Tcherikover demonstrated some time ago with regard to Jerusalem, the use of standard Greek terms for urban or village officers in Judea or Syria does not mean that the structures of the Greek polis were being emulated (see Victor Tcherikover, "Was Jerusalem a Polis?" *Israel Exploration Journal* 14 [1964]: 64).

12. See H. C. Youtie, "*Agrammatos*: An Aspect of Greek Society in Egypt," *Harvard Studies in Classical Philology* 75 (1971): 161–76; idem, "*Bradeos graphon*: Between Literacy and Illiteracy," *Greek, Roman, and Byzantine Studies* 12 (1971): 239–61; and idem, "*Hypographeus*: The Social Impact of Illiteracy in Greco-Roman Egypt," *Zeitschrift für Papyrologie und Epigraphie* 17 (1975): 201–21.

13. As demonstrated by Youtie (see articles in previous note) and William V. Harris, *Ancient Literacy* (Cambridge, Mass.: Harvard University Press, 1989). Cf. John S. Kloppenborg, "The Sayings Gospel Q: Recent Opinion on the People behind the Document," *Currents in Research: Biblical Studies* 1 (1993): 25.

14. Kloppenborg, "The Sayings Gospel Q," 25. A similar dichotomy between Q as "written and not simply a set of oral folk sayings of a pre-literate group" is in John S. Kloppenborg, *Formation of Q: Trajectories in Ancient Wisdom Collections* (Philadelphia: Fortress, 1987), 90.

oral composition and oral tradition can be, as explained in chapter 6. Thus, like most other literature extant from antiquity, Q must now be understood as orally composed and only written down by means of scribal technology.

If Q is oral-derived literature, then the approach that seems most appropriate is to consider its sayings or clusters of sayings not for their meaning in themselves abstracted from their concrete communication situations but for their function or significance as communication directly in those situations, insofar as the latter are accessible and minimally intelligible to those of us outside that context. As discussed in chapters 7 and 8, this requires attending closely to key aspects of communication, particularly the communication context, the register, and the cultural tradition out of which the text can be understood. As a procedural principle in approaching the sayings of Jesus, I suggested attending to the context indicated in the content of those sayings.[15] With the help of more sophisticated theory of communication developed by sociolinguistics and studies of recent oral-derived literature, explored in chapters 7 and 8, it should be possible to give greater precision to such an approach. The key operating assumption of this approach is that in oral communication the message offered must resonate with the hearers or else it will cease being communicated. On that assumption, then, the content of the Q discourses may well contain indicators of the context of the hearers (and performers). The key to determining the situation of the people who heard and resonated to the text recited or performed is its register, analyzed according to its key features in the communication context: its field (what is happening), its tenor (between whom), as well as its mode. Attending to cues of the registers of Q discourses should enable us to obtain a sense of the more general communication contexts, such as covenant renewal and prayer. The texts of particular discourses then may provide more detailed indications of the particular situation of the Q people who heard them. By reviewing the discussion of Q discourses in the preceding chapters, it should be possible to develop a composite sketch of the situation of the Q people who listened and resonated to those discourses, before considering the performers who recited them.

The Renewal Movement Evident in Q Discourses

In the discourse in Q 11:2–4, 9–13, Jesus is giving instruction in prayer for the kingdom of God to the people ("what is happening" and "between whom," i.e., the field and tenor of the register). But the contents of the prayer and of the admonitions that follow give more precise information on the situation of the people addressed than does the Jewish prayer with which the Lord's Prayer is often compared, the Kaddish. The tone of the prayer itself in Q 11 is far more urgent than that of the Kaddish. The second and third petitions of the Q prayer, paralleling the principal petition for the kingdom of God, plead for simple subsis-

---

15. In Richard A. Horsley, *Jesus and the Spiral of Violence: Popular Jewish Resistance in Roman Palestine* (San Francisco: Harper & Row, 1987), 259–73, esp. 266.

tence bread and cancellation of debts, suggesting that the addressees/petitioners are hungry and indebted, that is, typical peasants who, ordinarily marginal economically, have come into more desperate straits. The exhortation in 11:9–13 confirms the relatively simple peasant household life indicated by the petition for subsistence bread. Indeed, the appearance of a "fish" among the illustrations indicates hearers in villages near the sea, a lake, or a stream, at least toward the origins of the discourse in oral performance.

The register of the discourse in Q 12:22–31 is more difficult to determine, given the lack of clear precedents and comparative materials, beyond "Jesus'" general encouraging exhortation to people who are in difficult circumstances. On the principle of consistency from discourse to discourse, the more precise indications in the prayer discourse (11:3–4) and the covenantal discourse (6:20–21) of poor, hungry, indebted peasants (and/or day laborers) would appear to provide the key to 12:22–31 as well. There is surely nothing in the discourse to indicate it is an exhortation to voluntary poverty. The point of the analogies of the ravens/birds and lilies is not that the people should imitate them, ceasing all their agricultural and household labor, sowing and reaping, carding and spinning; it is rather consolatory: if God cares for them, then God will care much more for you (who do labor). This discourse is thus an exhortation to those already so poor that they are worried about basic necessities such as food and clothing.

The references to Israelite prophetic tradition in the discourse in Q 7:18–35 indicate that its register is that of fulfillment of prophetically articulated longings for a new age, as noted in chapter 12 above. That biblical textual attestations of these longings appear primarily in secondary layers of the book of Isaiah, some of which were produced by prophetic spokespersons addressing the (exiled) elite, does not confine them to the great tradition. The appearance of these longings in multiple wordings in prophetic texts suggests rather that they were a tradition more widely diffused in Israelite society. The identification of John the Baptist as a prophet in pointed opposition to those who live gorgeously appareled in royal palaces in Q 7:25–27 indicates that the social locations of Jesus, John, and the hearers of this discourse all stand over against the wealthy and powerful. This discourse, along with those on prayer and the exhortations to those anxious about life's necessities, indicate that the people addressed are peasant villagers or other poor. This conclusion is confirmed by the covenantal discourse.

The Mosaic covenantal register of the discourse in Q 6:20–49 could not be clearer: "Jesus" (through the speaker) enacts a renewal of the covenant between God and the people, using a transformed "blessings and curses" as the new declaration of God's deliverance, reformulating and reinforcing principles and illustrations of traditional covenantal social-economic relations and supplying a new sanctioning motivation in the double parable at the end. Not only does the content of the covenantal admonitions indicate that local social-economic relations are at stake. These admonitions, hardly deliberative in tone, also set out illustrations basic to and typical of local village interaction governed by covenantal principles. This and other Q discourses not only are addressed to the poor ("blessed are . . . ") but are also precisely about those "rather mundane exchanges" such as small loans and small local conflicts that were the very stuff of village community life and interaction, aspects of village life that the Mosaic covenantal principles, ordinances, and teachings had traditionally governed. Moreover, the multiple references to particular covenantal rulings and mechanisms (which we recognize from biblical textual windows onto a much wider and deeper Israelite tradition, popular as well as official) suggest that the hearers must have been villagers familiar with the Israelite tradition or living in situations where they could immediately relate to them.

The covenant renewal discourse also enacts a renewal of Israel. The village was the only appropriate context for such renewal since the village community, a cooperative of many households, was the fundamental social form of Israel. The people of Israel was constituted by multiple village communities. An obvious sequel to the covenant renewal discourse in 6:20–49 is the mission discourse in Q 9:57–10:16, the register of which is the commission of prophetic envoys for renewal of Israel, as indicated by the allusions to Elijah's commission of Elisha in the introduction to the discourse in 9:57–62. In the actual text of this discourse the tenor indicates that those involved in what is happening are not just the prophet of renewal and the designated envoys but also the communities of the movement that have already joined in the renewal of Israel. They petition the "lord of the harvest" to send out (more) "workers" and by implication share in the sending as well as support of the expanding mission. Like the admonitions of the covenantal discourse, the instructions to the envoys in Q 10:8–12 indicate that the renewal focuses on village or town communities. The Q discourses are addressed to and are concerned not simply (or primarily) with individual piety and morality but with community social-economic life. Although we cannot at this point determine whether it was part of a larger discourse, the apparently concluding statement of the whole series of discourses, Q 22:30, restates the renewal in symbolic terms of "establishing justice for the twelve tribes." The communities of hearers of Q discourses apparently understood themselves as part of a larger movement of renewal of Israel.

Renewal movements, of course, do not operate in a political vacuum, and the Q people were no exception. The discourse in Q 12:2–12 speaks in the register of the eventuality about which the prayer in 11:2–4 petitioned: being led to the "test," that is, called to trial before the rulers and authorities. Thus "Jesus" admonishes those who might come before those with the power to have them executed (12:4) to fearless confession. The dynamics of oral communication of traditional material raise a significant question pertinent to the situation of the hearers of this discourse in particular. Generally speaking, what survives in continuing oral communication is what resonates with the hearers. What no longer resonates simply drops away — unless of course it is so sacred that it is perpetuated simply because of the aura it casts around the most sacred persona of its supposed originator. Would there have been any point in continuing recitation of this discourse if a threat of persecution / repression no longer existed for the

Q people? The very fact of a difference between a previous circumstance ("one who says a word against the 'son of man'") and a more recent one ("one who blasphemes against the Holy Spirit") suggests that the discourse still addressed a situation in which a test was a live possibility or eventuality.

The Q people's sense of identity and mission as communities in a movement for the renewal of Israel included their stance over against the Jerusalem rulers and their scribal-Pharisaic representatives. This is articulated particularly in the set of woes against the scribes and Pharisees in Q 11:39–52 and in the prophetic sayings of Q 13:28–29, 34–35, which may have been components of a larger discourse. In all of this material the register is that of prophetic condemnation of rulers or their officers for exploitation and oppression of the people. As with prophetic indictments and sentences available in biblical books, however, individual prophetic oracles or laments or series of woes often indicate particular behavior and abusive power relations. These sections of Q therefore require closer scrutiny than previously given to determine the particular charges made and the situation of the Q people in relation to their rulers. Redactional studies of Q, surveying Q as a collection of sayings, often claimed that Q and the Q people condemned Israel as a whole on the basis of the polemic against "this generation" in 7:31; 11:29–32, 50–51. The condemnations of the Galilean cities, Jerusalem, and the Pharisees were fitted into the same scheme: all Israel was being condemned for its lack of faith, for its rejection of Jesus and/or the Q people's message, without closer examination of who was being condemned for what reason in each particular passage. As noted above more than once, however, this reading of Q was determined by the standard Christian theological view of the separation of Christianity as a universal religion from Judaism as a parochial religion, rather monolithically conceived. If analysis focuses on a whole society with conflictual and contested power relations and if Q materials are heard or read as a series of discourses devoted to particular concerns of a movement, the same passages reveal a more complex and precise picture of political-economic-religious conflict in Roman Palestine.

In Roman-dominated Galilee and Judea, as in ancient empires generally, the dominant conflict was between the very powerful and wealthy rulers and their "retainers," on the one hand, and the ordinary people, primarily villagers, on the other. As noted in chapter 3, this usually latent but sometimes overt dominant conflict was compounded in the case of Galilee by historical regional differences and a long cultural heritage of northern Israelite conflicts with Jerusalem rule. This is the historical, political, and cultural context in which the condemnations of Jerusalem and the Pharisees in Q must be heard. In Q 13:34–35, the ruling city of Jerusalem is condemned not for rejecting Jesus or the Q people but for killing the prophets and other envoys and for preventing God from protecting his "brood" (from its depredations). Similarly in 11:49–51, "this generation" is condemned, not for rejecting Jesus or the Q message but for shedding the blood of the prophets in the past. Moreover, 11:49–51 is the sentence pronounced following the whole series of woes against the scribes and Pharisees, not for rejecting Jesus or for their lack of faith but for their extortion of and loading burdens on the people (11:39–52).

The association or inclusion of the scribes and Pharisees with "this genera- tion" and Jerusalem (building monuments for the prophets, Zechariah killed in the temple) in 11:39–52 appears to carry over in 11:29–32 as well. Some recent com- positional criticism has grouped 11:29–32 (along with 11:14–26) with 11:39–52 as one large discourse directed ostensibly against the Pharisees and "this genera- tion."[16] It is perhaps significant that asking for a sign comes from the Pharisees in Mark 8:11–12//Matt. 16:1–4, as well as Matthew's introduction to Q 11:29–32, in Matt. 12:38. The Ninevites in Q 11:30, 32, who repented at the preaching of Jonah, who was understood to come from Galilee in the Galilean popular tradi- tion, are intended to be analogous to the Jerusalemites, who apparently do not repent at the preaching of the later prophet from Galilee. The same application of Jonah's preaching to the ruling city of Jerusalem had already been made in Israelite tradition around the time of Jesus and Q, as mentioned in chapter 5. Similarly, the "something greater than Solomon" (i.e., virtually unimaginable to those rooted in Jerusalem-based tradition) is clearly over against Jerusalem, in which Solomon ruled with his unprecedented power and wisdom. In Q 7:31–32 as well, in its only occurrence outside of 11:29–32 and 11:49–51, "this genera- tion" is portrayed like scribes and Pharisees sitting and addressing one another as if in court.[17] At the conclusion of the discourse in 7:18–35, "this generation," caricatured as contentious and pretentious children, stands in opposition to the amazing fulfillment of the people's longings for deliverance in the new age, the kingdom of God. In spite of these attacks on John and Jesus, the prophets of the fulfillment now underway, (God's) wisdom will be vindicated by its children.

It should be noted that the same pattern of the fulfillment of Israel's longings and the renewal of the people is portrayed as happening over against the smug and proud Jerusalem elite, who feel secure because of their lineage and privileged position (children of Abraham, etc.) also in John's announcement that opens the series of Q discourses and again in the prophecy of the final gathering of dispersed Israel in 13:28–29. The dominant conflict in Q is between the people of Israel, in particular the Q people themselves, on the one hand, and the Jerusalem rulers and their representatives, on the other, a conflict portrayed as the renewal of Israel now underway over against the rulers and their retainers, who stand under God's condemnation for their exploitation of the people and violence against the prophets.[18]

---

16. Kloppenborg, *Formation of Q,* 121–48.

17. See Wendy Cotter, "The Parable of the Children in the Market Place, Q (Lk) 7:31–35: An Examination of the Parable's Image and Significance," *NovT* 29 (1987): 289–304.

18. In his criticism of my previous arguments along these lines, Kloppenborg ("The Sayings Gospel Q," 23–26) agrees that (as redacted) Q "uses 'this generation' and 'the scribes and Pharisees' more or less interchangeably." He attempts, however, to reestablish the older view of Q people vs. "Israel/this generation" for its "inferior faith and non-response" on a wide selection of passages taken from various points in the discourses, with the new wrinkle that "the attack is most probably directed at the influen- tial scribes and Pharisees." The conflict is both more complex and more precise, as indicated by closer

Prophetic Performers of the Q Discourses

In explorations of the oral-derived texts of the Q discourses above, the focus has been primarily on how the listeners would have heard the messages in the performance context(s) and out of the enabling tradition. We are interested primarily in the function of the Q speeches as recited to their hearers, not an imagined meaning of words and sayings abstracted from concrete contexts of communication. And insofar as we who stand outside the historical oral communication context can do little more than attempt to listen sympathetically or overhear the Q discourses, we must attempt in the first instance to identify with the listeners for whom the discourses were performed. Yet we may also want to consider the performers of these speeches; a clearer sense of their social role, as informed by their cultural tradition, may enhance our attempt to overhear the discourses they were performing.

The only appropriate starting point in considering the Q performers, as in considering the Q movement generally, appears to be the text, the Q discourses as communication. Examination of the "wandering charismatics" in what Gerd Theissen called the "sociology of literature" also started with the text. Dependent on standard biblical studies that isolated individual sayings, however, Theissen and others did not critically consider what may have been the units of communication. Nor were they interested in communication, but in the transmission of Jesus' sayings read as discrete statements. Theissen, moreover, took the sayings in a rather literalistic way, with no allowance for hyperbole and other subtle modes of meaning.[19] His interest thus focused on imaginatively constructing a composite

---

attention to the key passages read more exactly according to the principles of composition criticism: the scribes and Pharisees are condemned explicitly or implicitly only in 11:29–32, 39–52, and (possibly) at the end of 7:18–35. The Jerusalem ruling house, which could possibly include the Pharisees by implication, is condemned explicitly or implicitly in 13:24–25, 28–29. Both are condemned for actions far more ominous than "inferior faith and non-response." The latter are imported from other passages (7:2–3, 6–9, the narrative about the centurion's faith; and 10:13–15, woes against Galilean towns who reject the Q mission) and have nothing to do with condemnation of Jerusalem or the Pharisees. Apparently those who cannot accept a particular hypothesis of Q redaction "ignore the plain sense of the construction" of "units" such as Q 7:1–10, 18–35 (Kloppenborg, "The Sayings Gospel Q," 23). Because of the consistent focus on John and Jesus in 7:18–23, 24–28, and 31–35, there is general agreement among various redactional and compositional critics that these texts form a coherent and clearly defined "cluster" or discourse (see Kloppenborg, *Formation of Q,* 107–17). Partly because of the coherence of 7:18–28, 31–35, however, it is difficult to discern how the narrative in 7:2–3, 6–9 could be read as part of the same unit. Arguments for including 7:2–3, 6–9 with 7:18–28, 31–35 tend to read the story in the light of its overwriting by Matthew and/or Luke, and a key point in these arguments tends to be the combination of the centurion's faith not found in Israel and the slam at "this generation" in 7:31–32, which supposedly attest Gentile faith and the rejection of all Israel. That point, however, perpetuates an older Christian theological scheme, as discussed in previous chapters. I fully concur with Kloppenborg that it is important to distinguish the rhetorical stance of the text and the actual social situation in which it is being used ("The Sayings Gospel Q," 23–24). Kloppenborg would reduce "what is surely at stake" to "a particular view of 'Israel' and persons who are in a position to promote that view as normative." In the "performative" text of the woes in 11:39–52, however, the scribes and Pharisees are condemned not for their successful promotion of a particular view of Israel but for the deleterious effects on the people of their practice of their political-economic-religious role.

19. Horsley, *Sociology,* 43–50.

sketch of who the carriers of the sayings might have been — and, as explained in chapter 2, he utilized a selective adaptation of Max Weber's concept of charisma that was in turn dependent on Adolf von Harnack's construction of itinerant charismatics on the basis of the *Didache*. With the benefit of hindsight gained from criticism of Theissen's and others' attempts at a "sociology of literature," it is possible to devise a more appropriate approach. The units of communication in Q would appear to be individual discourses or a combination of several discourses, not individual sayings or sets of two or three sayings. Consideration of the performer as a key actor in the process of communication, moreover, should serve to keep the investigation focused on the concrete context of communication. In connection with what has been discerned about the performance context(s), register(s), enabling tradition, and hearers in the preceding chapters, therefore, we can now attempt to discern characteristics of the performers of the Q discourses.

In the Q discourses the performer is speaking for (or as) Jesus (or John). In some cases, where the discourse includes a setting, the performer also speaks about Jesus (or John). In the discourse about fulfillment of the longings of the people in 7:18–35 and the mission discourse in 9:57–10:16, the performer begins by reporting, as it were, the dialogues with which the discourse begins. But in both of these discourses, the performer becomes primarily the spokesperson for Jesus' address to the hearers. This is most dramatically and explicitly stated at the closing of the mission discourse in the statement that "whoever hears you hears me" (Q 10:16). The performer has become the mere mouthpiece of/for Jesus, and the hearers themselves, now the envoys being commissioned, in turn become the speakers of/for Jesus. The role of the performer as speaker of/for Jesus is particularly poignant in the discourses of what has been called performative speech. In the covenantal discourse, the performer speaking for Jesus enacts the renewal of the covenant in the words spoken. In the commissioning of envoys, the performer commissions new prophetic delegates ("I send you out. . . . Whoever hears you hears me"). In the woes against the Pharisees (11:39–52), with every new recitation, the performer again pronounces their condemnation before the community. With every performance of the lament over Jerusalem (13:34–35), the performer again laments the imminent desolation of the ruling city for its oppressive practices. Analogies with the reenactment of the sacrifice of Christ when the priest says Mass or the preacher's pronouncing two people married in a wedding ceremony seem apt. Even in the discourses that are less performative speech, the Q performer brings to life again the words of Jesus, for example, in admonition to bold confession when brought to the test and in exhortation not to worry about necessities such as food and clothing (12:2–12, 22–31).

We can gain a more precise sense of the Q performer as spokesperson for Jesus, bringing to life again the speech of Jesus, by comparison with earlier treatments of Jesus' prophetic sayings in Q and elsewhere as products of "early Christian prophets." As noted above, until recently Q was considered in New Testament studies as catechetical material supplementary to the Gospel (of Mark, etc.). It was simply assumed that Q presupposed the passion narrative and the resurrection of Jesus as the exalted Lord.[20] Read through Paul, Mark, Matthew, and Luke, Q's Jesus appeared to be identical with the exalted Lord, the Son of Man whose coming (parousia) was awaited. Meanwhile, Christian prophets caught up in the Spirit were supposedly receiving revelations or "words of the Lord" that were then included among the sayings of Jesus. This hypothesis is rooted in a broad synthetic construction based on wide-ranging New Testament and other sources.[21] Paul's references to his own commissioning "revelation" of/from Christ in Gal. 1:15–16 and his recitation of a "word of the Lord" regarding the resurrection of the dead at the coming of the Lord in 1 Thess. 4:15–17 are particularly paradigmatic for this picture of prophets receiving new revelations from the exalted post-Easter Jesus. The "prophet speaking in (the) Spirit" of *Did.* 11:7, for example, then appears to attest the same phenomenon of revelation of new "words of the Lord."

More recently Q has come to be understood as coming from a Jesus movement parallel to but different from the Pauline mission and the movement or community connected with the Gospel of Mark. Correspondingly, greater attention has been given to how Q differs from Matthew's and Luke's adaptation of its materials, allowing Q to stand out more clearly in its distinctive views. "Q seems curiously indifferent to both Jesus' death and a divine rescue of Jesus from death."[22] Even at the presumably late stage of its development, Q does not take the opportunity of the temptation narrative to articulate a personal interpretation of Jesus' death. Q 10:21–22 indicates Q's lack of interest in the resurrection or heavenly exaltation of Jesus, when not read through Matthew's projection of the "authority" (*exousia*) of the risen Jesus (= Son of Man) back into the ministry of Jesus (cf. esp. Matthew 24–25; 28:18) or Luke's close association of Jesus with the Spirit (cf. Luke's introduction to Q 10:21–22). The Q discourses, insofar as we can tell, simply do not include Jesus as the exalted Lord. Hence there is no basis in Q itself for imagining that its performers were receiving and delivering "words of the (exalted) Lord" in the discourses they performed.

Rather the Q performer(s) re-presented the speech of Jesus, which became present again in recitation/performance. "Lord" (*kyrios*) is not a ("christological") title for Jesus, certainly not in the same way as for Paul, for whom Jesus Christ is enthroned as the transcendent emperor of the world. As indicated in Q 10:21–22, which is itself unusual in Q, Jesus has been given authority by the Father, but without any suggestion of exaltation to heaven. Jesus continues to speak with authority through the performer(s) of the Q discourses. Whatever dichotomy may have been felt by Paul or another Jesus movement between the remembered and

---

20. Even those who recognized how different Q was in genre from the Synoptic Gospels still found Easter in the middle of Q and explained that "the 'Easter' authorization has been transferred back into the public ministry" of Jesus, as in James M. Robinson, "Jesus — from Easter to Valentinus (or to the Apostles' Creed)," *JBL* 101 (1982): 5–37.

21. M. Eugene Boring, *Sayings of the Risen Jesus: Christian Prophecy in the Synoptic Tradition* (Cambridge: Cambridge University Press, 1982); rev. ed., *The Continuing Voice of Jesus* (Louisville: Westminster/John Knox, 1991).

22. John S. Kloppenborg, "'Easter Faith' and the Sayings Gospel Q," *Semeia* 49 (1990): 84. On the following see ibid., 80–90.

recited words of Jesus as a historical figure of the past and the "word of the Lord" as a revelation in the present,[23] no such dichotomy appears in the Q discourses. But there is a third alternative: Jesus still speaks in the recitation of his speech by his spokesperson. Through the performer(s) of Q discourses Jesus continues as proclaimer of the kingdom and the renewal of Israel, with authoritative presence effective in his recited speech. The remembered speech of Jesus comes alive again in the performer's recitation.[24]

While speaking for Jesus, the Q performers were speaking before the local gatherings of communities of a movement. In no case is Q material a matter of individual transmission of sayings heard from another individual, via a better or poorer memory. Q performers not only appear to have been addressing communities of people but were apparently performing the discourses repeatedly before the same communities. Again this can be deduced from the content of the discourses. The sending out of envoys by the communities of an aggressive new movement would not have been a once-in-a-decade occurrence. Encouragement to boldly petition God for the kingdom and relief of economic pressures would have been helpful on a regularly repeated basis. Encouragement of those anxious about basic necessities of life to "seek the kingdom of God and these things will be given you" and the admonition of those delivered up to the authorities to bold confession would have been repeated regularly. The renewal of the covenant would also have been reenacted regularly. The covenantal community withdrawn into the wilderness at Qumran reenacted its covenant renewal (at least) when new members were inducted into the community (1 QS 1–2). Regular reenactment of covenant renewal would have been appropriate and helpful for the village-based communities of the Q movement in connection with the severe economic pressures on the village households and the strains thus placed on local social-economic interaction (as evident in Q 6:27–42). Even the condemnation of rulers and their representatives would have been regularly performed as one of the ways of maintaining solidarity over against those rulers and their retainers, who seemed so insensitive to the ways in which they so deleteriously affected the lives of the people. It is difficult to detect any indication of whether or not performers of the Q discourses would have moved from community to community, somewhat the way Paul or Prisca and Aquila worked as catalysts of new local communities, before leaving them to local leadership, teaching and regularly reciting traditions such as the "words of institution" of the Lord's Supper and the crucifixion-resurrection creed (1 Cor. 11:23–26; 15:3–5). On the surface of things, it seems more likely that local leaders, resident in the communities, became the performers. This surmise would be confirmed by analogy with the "assemblies" (= *synagogai* in Greek) of village communities in Galilee and elsewhere, in which those who led prayers at regular local gatherings and served

---

23. Even that may be a dichotomy in the modern mind and not in that of Paul, who cites a Jesus saying against divorce as a command from "the Lord."

24. Werner Kelber, *The Oral and Written Gospel* (Philadelphia: Fortress, 1983), 20.

as collectors of goods for the poor were indigenous to the village communities and not Pharisees or scribes from outside.

Again a comparison may help highlight the point that the performers of Q discourses were addressing communities of a movement (about social-economic relations among themselves and political-economic relations with their rulers). The sapiential teachings of Ben Sira, which belong to the instructional genre, were also speeches delivered orally, speeches then written down in his book of wisdom. Like the Q materials, the sapiential speeches of Ben Sira are arranged in discourses devoted to certain topics. Ben Sira's sapiential discourses, however, are addresses to individuals, not communities. Sirach 3:1–16 addresses a son about honoring his parents; 3:30–4:10 addresses a "son" about deeds of charity to the poor; 11:29–34 offers advice about hospitality; 13:1–7 advises against dealings with the wealthy and powerful; 29:1–13 encourages helping the poor for the com- mandment's sake — all addressed to individuals, apparently those of similar scribal station in the society, perhaps individual scribal students. By contrast with these instructional speeches addressed by the sage to individuals, apparently students, the Q performers addressed communities of people about their social interaction, about their common situation and difficulties, and about their common rulers.

As spokespersons for Jesus, the Q performers were cast in a prophetic role, serving in a prophetic office, repeatedly in discourse after discourse. Given the standard concepts of the New Testament field, this will be more readily apparent in some discourses than in others. It is most obvious perhaps where the forms of the material are readily recognizable in the field as being in the tradition of Israelite prophetic literature. Thus in the woes against the Pharisees in Q 11:39– 52 and the lament over Jerusalem in Q 13:34–35 it is readily apparent that the performer assumes the mantle of Jesus the prophet condemning oppressive rulers. Similarly, in discourses where the material was previously classified as prophetic or apocalyptic — such as the prophetic threat and announcement in Q 3:7–9, 16–17; the prophetic dialogue in which Jesus is the fulfilling prophet and John the Baptist is named explicitly "a prophet and more than a prophet" (Q 7:18– 35); the prophetic sayings in which Jesus' preaching is analogous to that of Jonah (Q 11:29–32); the declaration and warning of 12:49–59; and the sanctioning discourse in Q 17:23–27 — the prophetic role of the performer is readily apparent.

Further, in the discourses previously labeled as sapiential, even though they are not typical of or even similar to Jewish sapiential literature, Jesus' and the Q performers' role is also prophetic, as can be discerned from review of Israelite tra- dition. The original Mosaic covenant, of course, was given through Moses. And Moses, as the prophet who communicated with God and in effect led the deliv- erance and founded the covenantal people of Israel, was understood in Israelite tradition as the prototype of all later prophets. Thus Jesus and the performers who brought his speech repeatedly to presence in the Q movement were enacting the role of the new Moses in delivering the covenant renewal discourse. Elijah, the most prominent and remembered prophet from the northern tribes of Israel, had been the great renewer of Israel. In the biblical as well as popular tradition he apparently headed the renewal movement led by scores of spirit-filled *bene-nabi'im* (who had to hide from the repressive as well as oppressive Ahab and Jezebel), constructed the altar of twelve symbolic stones, and commissioned his protégé, Elisha, as his envoy and successor as prophetic leader of the renewal of Israel over against its rulers. In the mission discourse, particularly as introduced by the three brief dialogues, Jesus takes up or assumes the role of the new Elijah commissioning envoys for the ongoing work of the renewal of Israel. In connection with the renewal of Israel over against its rulers, the discourse in Q 12:2–12 can also be seen as prophetic, not simply in the threat of 12:8–9 but in the whole exhortation to fearless confession in the face of persecution and repression. And in renewing Jesus' speech, the Q performers also put on the mantle of the prophets of renewal.

The prophetic role of the Q performers in reciting the speech of Jesus, the final prophet of renewal of Israel, is broader and more active than what is imagined by previous advocates of Q as prophetic or by the critics of Q as prophetic. The debate has focused narrowly on the form and classification of individual sayings. One concern was to explain the origin and transmission of sayings attributed to Jesus.[25] The model of prophet this debate had in mind was that of the receiver and pronouncer of a revelation from the Lord. Another concern was to identify the macro-*gattung* of Q as a literary document as well as the micro-*gattungen* of individual sayings. Again the model of prophet was the receiver and deliverer of oracles, and the background explored was mainly the prophetic books of the Hebrew Bible, which consist principally of collections of oracle fragments. Yet even the most comprehensive analysis of Q as prophetic, which claimed that both in micro-*gattungen* and in macro-*gattung* it is a prophetic book, found that it represents "an atavism in terms of the history of the genre" of the prophetic period, especially that of Elijah and Elisha.[26] That, of course, is an evaluation set up and measured by oracular prophecy, the dominant type of prophecy in the biblical prophetic books. But oracular prophecy was only one among several types practiced by prophets operative in ancient Israelite society and its literary survivals. And extrabiblical evidence indicates that another type of prophecy was more prominent than oracular prophecy in the late second-temple period, particularly among the people.[27]

The standard Christian theological construction of the origins of Christianity dominant in New Testament studies understands the origin of the church as discontinuous not only with Judaism but with Jesus' ministry as well. Only after Easter and Pentecost did Jesus' disciples form the earliest church, the Jerusalem community. And Paul is the heroic founder among the Gentiles who formed the basis of emergent orthodox Christianity. Under the impact of Enlightenment reason, liberal Christian theology and New Testament studies tended to focus on

---

25. Boring, *Continuing Voice of Jesus.*

26. Migaku Sato, *Q und Prophetie: Studien zur Gattungs- und Traditionsgeschichte der Quelle Q,* WUNT 29 (Tübingen: J. C. B. Mohr [Paul Siebeck], 1988), 301, 407.

27. Richard A. Horsley, "'Like One of the Prophets of Old': Two Types of Popular Prophecy at the Time of Jesus," *CBQ* 47 (1985): 435–63.

Jesus' teachings, partly because the narratives of his actions were full of miraculous events difficult for the modern mind to appropriate. The resulting construction of Jesus primarily as a teacher or prophet who delivered sayings remembered by individual disciples tended to separate Jesus even further from any role as a founder or leader of a movement. Not surprisingly, the solitary ethical prophet of social justice such as Amos or Jeremiah and the sapiential teacher became the models of choice from the Jewish background. Moreover, Q understood as a collection of Jesus' sayings, reinforced by the discovery at midcentury of the *Gospel of Thomas*, also a collection of Jesus' sayings, fit readily into this same understanding of Jesus as individual prophet or teacher.

Israelite biblical tradition, however, features another type of prophets that is much broader in political-religious functions; these prophets not only delivered revelatory oracles of the will and action of God but also founded and led movements.[28] The great prototype, of course, is Moses, leader of the exodus and mediator of the covenant. Following in the pattern established by Moses, Israelite liberators (*sophetim*) and prophets (*nabi'im*) from Joshua through Deborah and Gideon to Samuel both pronounced the will and action of God and led revival movements and even military campaigns as the charismatic leaders of the people, often against the threat of outside rule. Elijah and Elisha belong in this same tradition and type of prophetic leaders of renewal movements, now against oppressive domestic rule. Perhaps because he was the final successful prophet who, with his successor, Elisha, led a renewal movement, Elijah became particularly prominent in the tradition as the prophet of the renewal of Israel. Thereafter Israelites were apparently unable to generate a prophet-led movement of renewal sufficiently significant that it was included in the emergent great tradition based in Jerusalem scribal and / or ruling circles. Individual oracular prophets, however, emerged to pronounce God's indictment and sentencing of the oppressive rulers and officials. Anthologies of their much-edited and much-supplemented prophetic oracles emerged prominently among the scrolls of the emergent canon of the great tradition based in Jerusalem. Yet the prominence of Moses as leader of the exodus and mediator of the covenant was so deeply embedded in the great tradition that when a movement of dissident scribes and priests broke with the Jerusalem high priesthood and established a community at Qumran, the "righteous teacher" leading the movement assumed the role of the new Moses, leading a new exodus and establishing a renewed covenantal community, as vividly portrayed in Dead Sea Scrolls such as the Community Rule.

One major reason that Q appears as an atavism in terms of the history of the genre of prophetic books and Q's Jesus and John appear to be throwbacks to an earlier era (to Sato) is that they emerged not from the great tradition based in Jerusalem, which provides most of our textual sources for prophets and

---

28. On the following, see ibid.; Richard A. Horsley, "Popular Prophetic Movements at the Time of Jesus: Their Principal Features and Social Origins," *JSNT* 26 (1986): 3–27; and Richard A. Horsley with John S. Hanson, *Bandits, Prophets, and Messiahs* (1985; reprint, Harrisburg, Pa.: Trinity Press International, 1999), chap. 4.

prophecy, but from the popular tradition cultivated among the Judean, Samarian, and Galilean people. Except for Qumran and Josephus's claims about himself as an oracular prophet, it is difficult to find evidence for any type of prophets among Judean ruling, priestly, and intellectual-scribal circles in late second-temple times. This should not be surprising considering that in Israelite tradition both oracular prophets and prophetic leaders of movements usually spoke for the people against the rulers. Among the people in mid-first century, that is, right around the time of Jesus and the origins of Q, however, emerged prophetic figures of both types, oracular prophets such as Jesus son of Hananiah (whose prophetic woes against Jerusalem are reminiscent of Jeremiah) and prophetic leaders of movements such as Theudas, the Egyptian Jewish prophet, and a Samaritan prophet, whose role and movements were clearly patterned after those of Moses and/or Joshua (Josephus, *B.J.* 2.259–63; 6.300–309; *Ant.* 20.85–87, 97–98, 168–71). Just as we have found the text of particular Q discourses referencing and resonating with Israelite tradition, especially Israelite popular tradition, in the preceding chapters, it makes sense to examine how the whole series of Q discourses may resonate with the pattern of prophetic leaders of renewal movements evident in Israelite popular tradition, as discerned both through biblical books and through accounts of popular movements.

Jesus and the Q performers of Jesus' speech unquestionably worked out of the Israelite tradition of oracular prophecy, as explained in previous studies and in the preceding chapters. The woes against the Pharisees in Q 11:39–52, the prophetic lament over the imminent desolation of Jerusalem in Q 13:34–35, and declarations of threat in several long discourses are clearly patterned after traditional Israelite prophetic forms. It has long been noted, moreover, that Jesus' lament over the imminent desolation of Jerusalem resembles the woes over the ruling city pronounced by that other peasant-prophet, Jesus son of Hananiah. However, Jesus speaks and is portrayed in Q discourses not simply as an oracular prophet but as a prophet with a far-wider-reaching program of renewal of Israel. Already in John's announcement of the one who is coming, he will not only burn the chaff but also gather the grain into his granary, will baptize not only with the fire of judgment but also with the Spirit of renewal of the people. In Q 6:20–49, Jesus, as the new Moses, enacts a renewal of the covenant. In Q 7:18–35, he is represented as performing actions that bring about the fulfillment of age-old longings for the new age of restoration and wholeness. In Q 9:57–10:16, as the new Elijah, he commissions prophetic envoys to expand the program of renewal in healing and preaching the kingdom in other village communities. In Q 11:14–26, not only does he perform exorcisms of the alien forces possessing the people, but his exorcisms are declared to be a manifestation of the kingdom of God, portrayed in symbolic terms as a new exodus ("if, by the finger of God, I cast out demons..." [cf. Exod. 8:16–19]). Jesus and the Q performers reciting his speeches not only pronounce condemnation of rulers and their representatives for their oppression of the people but also deliver encouragement and admonition to the people to work in cooperation and solidarity, trusting the renewal process that God is initiating in the kingdom and maintaining their commitment and solidarity in the movement even under threat of persecution and death (Q 12:2–12, 22–31). Once we expand our understanding of the prophetic role to include the leaders of popular movements, a type of prophecy very much alive among the people at the time of Jesus, it is possible to see that most of the Q discourses portray and/or bring to life precisely this broader kind of prophecy.

Indeed, the pattern of prophets leading renewal movements in Israel includes the way in which the protégés of the head of the movement carry on the program of renewal in both proclamation and action. As Elijah commissioned Elisha to continue his program, so Jesus commissions envoys to expand his healing and proclamation of the kingdom of God. That pattern can easily be seen to include the relationship of the Q performers to Jesus. In regular recitation of the speech of Jesus they continue Jesus' prophetic proclamation of the kingdom among the people. They have assumed the prophetic mantle as Jesus' spokespersons. In the Q discourses, in fact, the whole movement takes on a prophetic identity. Nor should this be surprising insofar as Q discourses would have been shaped by the performers who themselves had taken on the mantle of Jesus, the (final) prophet of Israel's renewal. This prophetic identity of the whole series of discourses and the movement is evident in three connections. First, Jesus and John are portrayed throughout as prophets of renewal. John is labeled explicitly as "a prophet and more than a prophet" who is preparing the way of the new exodus in 7:26–27. Earlier in that same discourse, Jesus declares himself to be the prophet who is enacting fulfillment of the people's longings previously articulated by prophets. In the introduction to the mission discourse in Q 9:57–62, Jesus is represented as analogous to Elijah. In Q 11:29–32, Jesus's preaching is analogous to that of Jonah. And in general the Q discourses consistently represent Jesus in the role of a prophet, as noted just above. Second, Q discourses display a keen interest in the long line of persecuted and executed prophets of the past. In addition to the appearance of this as a passing reference in 6:22–23 and as the grounds on which Jerusalem is to be desolated in 13:34–35, this is elaborated as the basis for punishment of Jerusalem, including its Pharisaic representatives based there, in 11:49–51. Third, the hearers of the Q discourses themselves are addressed as the successors of the prophets, belonging to the same line of prophets persecuted and killed in the past (6:22–23) and associated with the envoys commissioned in imitation of the Elijah-Elisha relationship (9:57–10:16).

We may be able better to understand that broad prophetic role of the Q performers in the Q communities precisely not by constructing a synthetic picture of a prophet but by comparing and contrasting the similarities and differences between different movements of Jesus' believers with regard to their deployment of nomenclature for leadership, on the one hand, and the functions of those leaders, on the other. Paul distinguishes "apostles," "prophets," "teachers," deeds of power, "gifts of healing," and "forms of leadership" in 1 Cor. 12:27–28. He identifies himself as an apostle, in no uncertain terms, probably all the more adamantly because he felt insecure as "one untimely born" (1 Cor. 3:5–4:21; 15:3–11). Yet he portrays his own commissioning by the Lord as a prophetic calling like that of Jeremiah (Gal. 1:15–16), and he clearly functions as a "prophet" in receiving and communicating a "word of the Lord" (1 Thess. 4:15–17), as a "teacher" in his ongoing instruction of his assemblies in the tradition he had received (1 Cor. 11:23–26; 15:1–5), and as an organizer of those assemblies, however he would label such a function ("apostle," as in 1 Cor. 3:5–15). Clearly the nomenclature is not as important as the function; the functions are not mutually exclusive; the nomenclature is not that of discrete offices; and presumably Paul or others could serve more than one such function. Were we to examine how Paul's nomenclature would apply to Jesus as portrayed in Q discourses, he would be "all of the above." That is, Q's Jesus was an "apostle" of God, a "prophet" receiving and declaring the will of God, a "teacher" of the people in the movement, and a healer and performer of deeds of power (exorcisms), as well as an organizer of a movement. And Moses and Elijah, the two principal paradigmatic prophetic leaders of movements in Israelite tradition, had also performed all of the same functions. The Q performers appear to take on most of these functions as well: certainly those of "apostles" called or delegated by Jesus, and primarily as prophets and teachers who continue Jesus' proclamation (even though they do not match the narrower role of the prophet who receives new "words of the Lord").

In the *Didache,* "prophets" and "teachers" are closely associated (13:1–2; 15:1–2), and the "prophets" not only teach (11:10; cf. John 14:26; Rev. 2:20) but are expected and allowed to lead "worship" in the communities (e.g., "to hold eucharist as they will" [10:7], not necessarily according to the "Teaching of the Twelve Apostles" in *Didache* 9–10). Similarly, "prophets and teachers" do not appear to be sharply distinguished in the account of commissioning envoys for mission in Acts 13:12.[29] So also in Q the prophet and teacher functions do not seem to be divided. Josephus's references to Elisha as the "disciple" (*mathetes*) of Elijah (*Ant.* 8.354) may simply be an assimilation of the prophetic role to a more scribal role by the well-educated priestly aristocrat-historian. The documents left by the scribal-priestly movement at Qumran refer to its leader as the "teacher," although we are struck by the prophetic character of his role as the founder-leader of the movement. The performers in the popular movement that produced Q, however, included teaching in their broader prophetic role. The prophetic performers in Q, moreover, were in effect the leaders of worship in the community insofar as they performed discourses such as those on prayer, covenant renewal, sending out envoys, and exhorting and admonishing the people.

Finally, with regard to the Q performers and their hearers, it may be pertinent to speculate a bit on a stock phrase that Matthew has only in passages where he is following or adapting Q: "prophets and righteous ones." In Matt. 10:41, it looks like Matthew is expanding upon Q 10:16, and in Matt. 23:29, again it looks like Matthew is constructing an additional line parallel to Q 11:47. In Matt. 13:17, however, Matthew could well be representing the Q text he had in common with

---

29. So also Boring, *Continuing Voice of Jesus,* 117–19.

Luke — that is, that it was previous generations of "prophets and righteous ones" who longed to see what the Q people are seeing, not "prophets and kings," as in Luke 10:23. It is tempting in connection with the investigation in the preceding paragraphs to imagine that "prophets and righteous ones" represents the performers and other members / hearers of the Q discourses and Q communities, who see themselves in continuity with the "prophets and righteous ones" of earlier generations (cf. again Q 6:22–23; 10:21–24; 11:47–51; 13:34–35). If the phrase were determined to be Matthew's own, then it is intriguing that one who perhaps identified himself more as a "scribe" uses it only in connection with key Q passages, as if he knew that "prophets and righteous ones" was a designation of the people with whom Q material was identified. It seems singularly appropriate for members of an Israelite movement of covenant renewal led by prophetic spokespersons for the great prophet of the kingdom of God as the renewal of Israel.

This study has since the outset been battling the abstract modern Western, and particularly American, individualism that biblical interpreters project onto ancient texts and the people who composed and heard them. It may be that attempting to come to grips with the oral communication environment of antiquity and the probability that Q and Mark and Paul's letters belonged in a world of performance and hearing, not printed texts and private individual reading, will be what forces us to shift to more appropriate, relational assumptions and approaches. People, now as well as then, are embedded in social-relational networks, in patterns of power relations. As sociologists recognize, in the sense that Weber used the concept "charisma," an individual "itinerant charismatic" would be an individualistic abstraction. Charisma is not an entity but a social (indeed power) relationship between leader and followers.[30] In fact, the charismatic relationship also, virtually by definition, comes out of a particular historical social situation, for example, one of social dislocation, conflict, and distress. Sociologists and anthropologists have long since recognized that those three interrelated factors must be studied relationally in order to understand social-religious leaders and movements. Recognition that the earliest texts available for study of Jesus and his movement(s) were oral-derived literature and that they functioned in an oral communication environment leads to the necessary inclusion of a fourth factor. As recent studies of oral-derived literature have indicated — and as the investigation of Q discourses confirms — leaders and followers who form a movement in struggling to deal with their particular historical situation are also working out of a particular cultural tradition and the crisis into which it has come in their historical situation. The implications are that an adequate approach to Q or any other oral-derived text must be relational and must include the four analytical factors of leaders (e.g., performers), followers (e.g., hearers), the historical situation, and the cultural tradition in which the leaders and followers are interacting as they respond to the situation.

---

30. See Peter Worsley, preface to the revised edition of The Trumpet Shall Sound (New York: Schocken, 1957).

INDEX OF REFERENCES

HEBREW BIBLE / OLD TESTAMENT

Genesis

3:15	253
13:18	119
14	118
14:13	119
18:1	119
23:19	119
25:9	119
25–36	118
27	118
49:31	119
50:13	119

Exodus

7:26	265
8:19	97
12:11	246
19	202
20	96
20:2–17	202, 207
20–24	48
21:2–6	204
21:22	204
21:35–36	204
21–23	116, 131, 202, 207, 216, 217, 265
22:1	204
22:5	204
22:6	204
22:14	204
22:16	204
22:17	204
22:25–26	96, 200, 203, 204, 220, 221
22:26–27	221
23:4–5	96, 200
23:10–11	204, 219
23:20	96, 249, 265
24	202
31:18	97, 128
32:16	128
34:1	128

Leviticus

17–26	205
19	205, 216, 217
19:2	96, 200, 222
19:9–10	204, 219
19:17–18	96, 200, 205, 222, 223
19:18	198, 222
23:22	219
25:2–7	204

25:23–24	204
25:24–28	204
25:35	200
25:35–38	204
25:39–43	204
25:48	204
26:14–22	192
26:36	192

Numbers

5:11–31	128
5:20–22, 27	128
18:30–31	96

Deuteronomy

1:6–4:43	202
4:13	128
4:25–31	109
4:44–26:19	202
5:6–21	202
5:22	128
6:5–9	129
6:9	129
6:13	95, 257
6:16	95, 257
8:2	256
8:3	95, 257
8:7–10	256
8:16	256
9:9–11	255
9:10	97, 128
9:18–19	255
10:2	128
10:20	257
12	205
14:22–29	205
15	217
15:1–11	220
15:7–11	204, 221
15:9	204
15:12–18	204
15:15	204
16	205
17	205
17:14–20	205
18:1–8	205
18:15–20	256
19	205
19:20–22	204
22	216
22:1–4	96, 116–17, 142, 200, 222
24:10–13	96, 200, 221
27–28	202, 216
28:45–68	109

Deuteronomy (continued)

29–30	202
30:1–10	109
30:15–20	203, 217
31:10	136
32	121, 137
32:5	97
32:11	121, 282
32:20	97

Joshua

8–11	48
19:13	112
24	96, 202, 203

Judges

1:16–33	48
2:16	263
3:10	263
4:4	263
5	48
10:40–43	48
11:16–23	48

1 Samuel

8–12	49
17:44, 46	239
22:1–6	142

2 Samuel

2:1–3	49
5	102
5:1–3	49
5–7	49
6	102
7:11–17	121
15–20	49
15–21	99, 102
15:30	246
15:35	142

1 Kings

1–5	49
4–5	53
8	102
9:10–11	49
11–12	99, 102
12	49
12:24	239
14:11	239
16:4	239
17:8–15	112
17–22	50
18:4	240, 289
18:17	281
18–19	111
19	108, 264, 281
19:1–18	255
19:19–21	238, 240
21:1–4	204
21:10 [LXX]	238
21:24	239
22	273

2 Kings

1–10	50
14:25	112
16:3	273
21:6	273
22–23	135–36

1 Chronicles

21:15	254

2 Chronicles

20:7	253

Ezra

8	136
9:6–15	109
9:11, 12	136

Nehemiah

1:5–11	109
4:3	238
5:1–13	206
8:2–3	136
8:4–6	136
8:8	136
8:14–15	136
9	110, 137, 203, 207
9:5–37	109
9:26	111
9:38–10:39	203
9–10	203, 218
10:32–39	53

Psalms

9	105, 263
10:18	105, 263
35	105, 263
58	105, 263
62:10	238
72:4	105, 263
76:9	105, 263
78	137, 192
78:18	192
78:21	192
78:62–63	192
79:2	239
82:1–4	105, 263
90:11–12	95
94	105, 263
96:13	105
98:9	105
103:6	105, 263
103 [LXX] 103:12	239
105	137
106	137
106 (107):3	65, 69
106:6–46	109
107:4	242
117 (118):26	97
118(117[LXX])	282
118:25–26	142
140:12	105, 263
146:7	105, 263

Proverbs

1	199
1:1–9:18	148, 197, 199, 203, 225
1:2–7	199
1:8–19	199
1:20–33	199, 293
2:1–22	197, 225
2:1–3:4	225
2:20–22	197
3:1–4	225
3:13–35	199
6:20–49	199
6:25–29	199
8	117
10:1–22:16	148
14:1–4	198
22:17	77
22:17–23:11	148
22:17–24:22	77
24:23–34	148
28:15	245
31:10–31	148

Song of Solomon

2:15	238

Isaiah

1:21	97
3:10–11	253
3:13–15	193
5:8–10	286
5:11–13	286
5:18–24	97, 113, 286
5:26–29	248
13:10	73
17:13	253
18:3–6	242
18:5–6	239
20:5–6	248
23	247
26:7–19	264
26:19	264
27:12–13	65, 242
29:5	253
29:18–21	264
30:15	248
33:11	253
34	264
34:4	73
35:5–6	96
40	273
40:3	142, 253
40:3–5	253
41:15	253
42:1	105
42:5–6	283, 284
42:6–7	96, 264
43:5–6	65, 69
43:5–7	242
45:8	193
49:6	105
51:17–18	282

61:1	96, 264
65:18–25	275

Jeremiah

1:10	192
4:4, 26 (LXX)	192
4:5–8	248
4:12	193
5:14	192
7:1–15	110
7:21–22	110
7:21–35	110
7:31	273
7:33	239
9:4	248
11:16	192
13:24	253
14:13	192
14:15–16	192
15:3	239
15:14	192
15:17	248
16:1–8	241
16:4	239
17:27	192
17:58	92
19:4–5	273
19:7	239
20:9	192
21:12	192
21:14	192
22:1–9	97, 121
22:5	121
23:29	192
25:1–14	110
25:4	110
26:7–23	281
26:20–23	108, 111
27:32 (LXX)	192
29	110
29:17–19	110
31:27–34	224
32	205
32:35	273
34	205
35	110
51:33	242

Lamentations

2:3	192
2:13–17	113
4:11	192

Ezekiel

5	192
10:2	192
10:6	192
13:4	238
15	192
21:3	192
22:23–27	244
22:27	96
24:15–24	241

Ezekiel (continued)

26	247
27	247
27:13	248
28	247
34:5	239
36:5	192
37:1–14	254, 258

Daniel

2:35	253
4:21	239
7	71, 91
7:9–14	274
7:11–12	274
7:13–14	3
7:26–27	274
7:27	3
9:4–19	109

Hosea

2:14	239
4:1	97
4:1–3	115, 288
6:11	242
7:10	248
10:12ff	253
11:5	248
11:11	65
12:2	193
12:3–7	115, 288
12:7	97
12:10	193
13:3	253
14:12	193

Joel

2:2	193
2:28–29	254, 258
2:30–31	73
2:30–32	193
3:12–13 (4:10 LXX)	242
4:4–8	247

Amos

1:9–10	247
2:8	96, 200
4:6–10	248
5:1–3	97
5:2–3	281
5:14–15	193
5:16–17	281
6:1–7	97, 286
8:9	73
8:11	193
8:12	193

Micah

2:1–5	286
3:5–7	193
3:8	193
3:9–12	282
4:11–13	242
4:12	253

6:8	97, 115, 288
6:12	193
7:1	193
7:6	65, 97, 193

Habakkuk

2:9–12	286
2:15–17	286
2:19	286

Zephaniah

2:2	253
3:3	96

Haggai

1:12	92

Zechariah

2:10	283
7:9	97, 115
8:7–8	65, 283, 284
9:2–4	247
9:9	142
10:10	65

Malachi

3(–4)	265
3:1–5	265
3:1	96, 142, 249, 253
3:22–24	265
4:4–6	265

Tobit

3:1–6	109
4:5–19	198
4:7–8	198

Wisdom of Solomon

6–10	117

Sirach

1:15	117
3:30	227
3:30–4:10	198
4:1–5	227
4:3–5	198
4:9	226
4:10	198, 226
4:11	96
7:31	53
24	96, 97, 117, 203, 226
24:7	117
24:10–11	117
24:23	117
24:33	117
28:13–26	198
29:1	96, 203, 221, 226
29:1–13	226
34:24–27	226
35:17–22	226
36:13	106
38:24–34	117
39:32–39:4	229
38:32–39:11	117
39:1	117

44–50	106, 290
48:10	106
50:1–21	53
51:23–30	293

Baruch

1–3	110
1:15–3:8	109
3:9–4:4	117
4:4	65, 283
5:5	65, 283, 284

3 Maccabees

6:3	253

4 Maccabees

6:11	253
6:17	253
18:23	253

NEW TESTAMENT

Q (following the order and numbering in the Gospel of Luke. Pages focused on particular Q discourses or sayings are in bold type.)

3:7–9	64, 193, 215, 261, 265, 284
3:7–9, 16–17	63, 65, 87, 95, 224, 242, 250, **251–54, 261–62,** 263, 304
3:8	172, 241
3:9	72, 119, 241
3:16–17	92, 193, 263, 265, 261
3:17	72, 241
3:21–22	**254**
4:1–13	105, 143, 168, 250, 251, **254–57**
4:3	2
4:9	2
6:20	16, 17, 18, 87, 196
6:20–21	82, 209, 221, 269, 270, 296
6:20–23	195, 200, 213, **217–20,** 240
6:20–26	116, 210, **211, 217–20,** 226
6:20–49	11, 23, 66, 80, 82, 85, 86, 87, 90, 91, 96, 98, 105, 147, 169, 170, **195–201,** 205, 206, **209–27,** 258, 260, 263, 285, 296, 297, 307
6:22	71, 195, 196, 239
6:22–23	81, 195, 272, 308, 310
6:23	173
6:24–26	**217–20,** 229
6:27	96, 195, 221
6:27–28	196, 198, 201
6:27–35	268, 269
6:27–36	82, 86, 91, 96, 116, 195, 198, 200, 210, **211–14, 220–27,** 267
6:27–38	86, 209
6:27–42	200, 217, 219, 269, 303
6:27–49	88
6:29	96, 195, 196, 220, 221, 222
6:30	195, 196, 220
6:31	195
6:32	196
6:32–33	198
6:32–34	220, 222
6:33	95
6:35	3, 198, 220, 226, 278
6:36	96, 196, 226
6:37	195, 196, 263
6:37–38	196, 224
6:37–42	196, 210, **214–15,** 221, **223–24**
6:38	195, 196, 223
6:38–39	224
6:39	196, 223
6:39–45	195
6:40	**214**
6:41–42	196, 223, 224
6:43–44	85, 224
6:43–45	196, 198, 210, **215,** 223, **224**
6:46	2
6:46–49	86, 197, 210, **215, 224–25,** 225, 248
6:47–49	200, 216
7:1–10	63, 300
7:2	64, 256
7:2–9	94, 259, 300
7:6	2
7:6–9	64
7:9	64, 230, 262
7:18–19	264
7:18–23	64
7:18–28	66, 92
7:18–35	63, 65, 86, 88, 92, 96, 98, 116, 258, 260, 265, **263–66,** 270, 296, 299, 300, 301, 304, 307
7:22	264
7:22–23	264
7:23	264
7:24–25	79, 86
7:24–26	81
7:24–28	64, 98, 264
7:25	240
7:25–27	296, 308
7:26	265
7:27	98, 141, 143, 249
7:28	17, 81, 87, 265
7:31	68, 298, 299
7:31–35	64, 66, 89, 117, 270
7:32	210
7:34	71, 239
7:35	3, 67, 74, 239
9:57–58	228, 229, 230, **238–40**
9:57–62	2, 66, 96, 230, 233, 234, **238–41,** 249, 262, 297

Q (continued)

9:57–10:16	*11, 23, 88, 105, 169,* **228, 230, 234–38,** *242, 259, 260, 297, 301, 307, 308*
9:58	*71, 240*
9:59–60	*228, 229, 240,* **240–41**
9:59–62	*18*
9:60	*17, 241*
9:61–62	**241**
9:62	*17, 241*
10:2	*232,* **242–43**
10:2–16	*66, 82, 86, 89, 90, 92, 96, 168, 169,* **228–34,** *242–48*
10:3	*96, 232, 242,* **243–45,** *249, 272*
10:3–4	*233*
10:3–10	*240*
10:4	*229, 231, 241,* **245–46**
10:4–11	*230, 232*
10:5–7	*233, 241, 246, 248*
10:5–8	*82*
10:5–11	**246–47**
10:7	*96*
10:8–11	*233, 246, 248, 297*
10:9	*16, 17, 87, 238, 249*
10:11	*16, 17, 87*
10:12	*96*
10:12–15	*233,* **247–48**
10:13–15	*65, 66, 96, 229, 243, 249, 300*
10:16	*81, 233, 243,* **248,** *249, 301*
10:21	*99, 118*
10:21–22	*302*
10:21–24	*66, 96, 116, 233, 243, 292, 310*
10:22	*2*
10:23–24	*72*
11:2	*87*
11:2–4	*3, 16, 17, 66, 82, 86, 88, 90, 91, 96, 147, 219, 221, 260,* **266–68,** *295, 296, 297*
11:4	*271, 272, 278*
11:9–13	*66, 82, 86, 88, 90, 147, 260,* **266–68,** *295, 296*
11:14–20	*89, 168*
11:14–26	*63, 64, 69, 88, 89, 242, 270, 299, 307*
11:19–20	*65*
11:20	*17, 65, 87*
11:23	*65*
11:24–26	*65*
11:29	*65*
11:29–32	*63, 64, 65, 68, 69, 88, 89, 97, 111, 280, 298, 299, 300, 304, 308*
11:29–32 (–36)	*270*
11:30	*71, 111, 113, 239, 299*
11:31	*67, 120, 265*
11:31–32	*3, 64, 65*
11:33	*65*
11:33–36	*65*
11:34	*65*
11:35	*121*
11:36	*65*
11:39	*114, 241, 245, 278*
11:39–41	*285, 287*
11:39–42	*275*
11:39–52	*57, 63, 64, 69, 86, 88, 90, 92, 97, 98, 112–13, 114, 118, 169, 170, 229, 247, 261, 262, 270, 275, 279, 280,* **285–91,** *292, 293, 298, 300, 301, 304*
11:42	*113, 114, 278, 285, 287, 288*
11:43	*286*
11:44	*114, 285, 287*
11:46	*99, 241, 286, 287*
11:47–48	*108, 110, 111, 287, 288, 291*
11:47–51	*89, 108, 109, 110, 289, 310*
11:49	*67*
11:49–51	*3, 64, 65, 69, 74, 89, 92, 111, 117, 173, 248, 249, 263, 280, 285, 288, 298, 299, 308*
11:50–51	*68, 298*
11:52	*287, 287*
12:2	*273, 293*
12:2–12	*66, 82, 86, 87, 88, 89, 90, 92, 97, 147, 168, 169, 248,* **271–74,** *297, 301, 305, 308*
12:4	*272, 297*
12:4–7	*18, 293*
12:5	*271*
12:8–9	*3, 70, 71, 271, 273, 274, 274, 305*
12:10	*239, 274, 274*
12:11–12	*271, 272*
12:13–14	*67*
12:22–31	*269*
12:22–31(–32)	*18, 82, 86, 87, 88, 90, 92, 97, 120, 147, 219, 221, 260,* **268–70,** *293, 296, 301, 308*
12:22–34	*66*
12:27	*265*
12:30	*95*
12:31	*16, 17, 87, 268*
12:32	*268, 269*
12:33	*67*
12:33–34	*268*
12:33–35	*269*
12:35	*91*
12:39	*65, 85*
12:39–40	*3, 81, 85, 87, 88, 97, 275*
12:39–46	*90*
12:39–59	*63, 64, 71, 80*
12:40	*65, 71, 91, 239*
12:41–46	*275*
12:42–46	*85, 87, 88*
12:49	*72, 81, 85, 241*
12:49–59	*87, 92, 97,* **189–94,** *304*
12:51–53	*65, 79, 85, 86, 90*
12:51–59	*85*
12:52	*89*
12:52–53	*81*

12:54–55	65
12:54–56	65, 81
12:56	85
12:57	263
12:57–58	65
12:57–59	65
13:18–19	17, 87
13:18–21	88, 90
13:24–30	66
13:28–29 (& 13:29–28)	17, 65, 68, 69, 86, 87, 88, 89, 92, 94, 95, 97, 107, 116, 119, 169, 173, 229, 242, 262, 263, 279, **283–84**, 298, 299, 300
13:28–30	66
13:34	67, 173, 281
13:34–35	66, 68, 74, 86, 88, 89, 92, 97, 98, 107, 108, 109, 110, 113, 169, 170, 248, 249, 261, 262, 263, 275, **279–83**, 284, 288, 304, 307, 308, 310
13:35	121
14:16–24	66, 86, 88, 92, 97, 279, **284–85**
14:24	284
14:26	18, 229, 241
14:26–27	86, 88, 279, 293
14:27	230, 273
14:34–35	86, 279
15:4–7	86
16:13	86, 87, 88, 293
16:16	17, 87, 88, 115, 248, 272
16:16–18	97, 114, 115
16:17	86, 88, 116
16:17–18	114
16:18	86, 88, 116
17:1–6	86, 88, 90, 92, 209
17:23–24	65
17:23–37	27, 63, 64, 71, 86, 88, 89, 90, 91, 97, 262, **275–76**, 304
17:24	3, 65, 70, 71, 113, 239, 276
17:26	3, 65, 70, 71, 113, 239, 276
17:29	72
17:30	3, 65, 70, 71, 113, 239, 276
17:37b	65
19:27	262
22:28–30	17, 69, 87, 88, 92, 98, 105, 107–8, 230, 243, **262–63**
22:30	262, 263, 277, 297

Matthew

3	261
3:1	253
3:7	261
4:3	253
4:15	244
5:1	200, 219
5:20–48	221
5:38–48	91

5:47	95, 244
5–7	90
6:7	244
6:34	269
7:28	78
8:19	230
8:22	230
10	90
10:5	244
10:6	244
10:20	257
10:24–25	214
10:38	230
10:41	309
11:25–27	74
11:25–30	74
12:18, 21	244
12:34	268
12:38	299
13	90
13:17	309
13:25, 28	220
13:42	273
13:50	273
15:14	214
16:1–4	299
18:17	244
19:21	35
19:28	262
20:1–16	243
21:5	142
21:43	244
23	54, 288
23:15	273
23:33	273
23:29	309
24	27
24:27	239
24:37	239
24:39	239
24–25	3, 78, 90, 91, 302
25:32	244
26:1	77
28:18	302
28:19	244

Mark

1:2–3	142
1:14–15	238
1:16–20	238
1:21, 39	249
2:1–12	218
2:25–26	142
3:22	180, 270
3:23–29	168
4	90
6:1–2	141
6:7–9	233
6:8–9	245
6:7–13	168, 233, 238
6:8–13	230, 232

Mark (continued)

6:10	233
6:11	233
6:17–29	245
7:1	180
7:1–13	57
7:6	143
7:9–10	142
8:11–12	299
8:34–38	168
9:2–8	238
9:12–13	143
10:2–9	116
10:3–5	143
10:4	142
10:6	142
10:8	142
10:19	142
10:22	142
10:28	262
10.35–45	221
11:2–8	142
11:9–10	142
11:17	143
12:1–8	282
12:10	143
12:18–27	143
13	73, 74, 91, 275
13:8	73
13:9–11	272
13:24–25	73 n 49
14:21	143
14:27	143
14:49	143

Luke

1–2	113
3	261
3:3	253
3:4–6	253
4:16–20	141
6:12	200
6:16	257
6:40	214, 223
6:45	198
7:43	263
9:57	230
9:59	230
9:61	230
10:13–15	46
10:21–22	74
10:23	310
11:39–52	57
11:49–51	74
12:11–12	272
12:32	268
13:31–33	239
14:1	54
17:22–32	74
17:23–37	275
17:28–29	275

John

14:26	309

Acts

5:36	108
6	284
7	274
12:20	247
13:12	309
26:7	106

1 Corinthians

2:8–9	79
3:5–15	309
3:5–4:21	308
9:2	44
10:5–11	137
11:23–26	303, 309
12:27–28	308
15:1–5	309
15:3–5	143, 303
15:3–11	308

2 Corinthians

10–13	44
11:13	243

Galatians

1:15–16	302, 309
2:1–10	243

Philippians

3:2	243

1 Thessalonians

4:15–17	302, 309

Revelation

2:20	309
6:12–17	73
21:10–14	106

JEWISH TEXTS

1 Enoch

1–36	77
26–27	273
37–71	77
42	96, 97
42:1–2	117
54:1–6	273
56:1–4	273
57:1	65, 283
89:13–27	244
90:24–27	273
92–105	99
94:6–9	286
94–105	57, 113, 2196
95:3	113
95:4–7	286
96:2	113
97:7–20	286
98:2–8	286
98:9–15	286

98:12	113
98:14–16	113
99:1–2	286
99:2	113
99:11–16	286
100:7–9	186
103:1–3	113
104:2, 6	113
104:10–13	113

2 Enoch
42:6–14	197

2 Baruch
70:2	242

4 Ezra
5:18	244
9:1–21	242

Jubilees
13:25–27	119
19:16–29	118
22:10–30	118
23:1–3	118
38	118

Psalms of Solomon
8:23	244
9:9–10	119
11:2	284
11:2–3	65, 283, 284
17	106–7
17:4	107
17:24	107
17:26–28	107
17:26–32	277
17:28–30	107
17:28–32	69, 263
17:30	107
17:36	107

Testament of Judah
9	118
24–25	263
25:1	107

Testament of Levi
2–5, 13–19	77

Testament of Benjamin
10:10	248

Pseudo-Aristeas
208	198

Pseudo-Philo, Biblical Antiquities
10	137

Vitae Prophetarum (Lives of the Prophets)
1:8, 9	290
1:14, 15	290
10	112
10:10	111

DEAD SEA SCROLLS

CD (Damascus Document)
1:1–6:11	207
3:13–6:11	207
4:13–21	116
6:11–7:4	207
6:20–21	209
7:2–3	209
7:4–6, 8–10	207
9:2–5	209
9:8	41
10:10	41
10:14	41
16:10	41
16:13	41

1QH (Thanksgiving Hymns) 138
4	97, 287

1QM (War Scroll) 138
1–2	97
2:2–3	106
5:1–3	106

1QS (Community Rule) 138, 167, 206–9
1–2	303
1–3	139
1:17–18	207
1:19–2:1	207
2:2–4	208
2:2–11	207
2:5–10	208
2:12–19	207, 208
2:19–22	209
3:6–9	254
3:13–14	207
3:13–4:28	206, 207
3:15–4:1	206
3–4	97, 139
4:2–6	206, 224
4:2–14	208
4:6–8	207, 224
4:9–11	206, 224
4:12–14	207, 224
4:18–24	209
5:1–6:23	207
5:4–6	209
5:6–11	209
5:25–6:1	209
6:3	139
6:14–16	209
6:20–21	209
6:24–7:26	207
6:27–39	209
8:1–4	69, 106, 263
8:10–19	207
8:12–16	253
9:12–10:5	207
9:12–11:24	207
9:19–21	253
10–11	139

1QSa (Appendix A to 1QS)
2:21–23   138

1QSb=1Q28b (Appendix B to 1QS)   138

1QT
18:14–16   106

1Q27
1:6   113

4QpsDanAa=4Q246
2:1–2   113

4Q256   139

4Q258   139, 167

4Q259   139, 167

4Q408   138

4Q503   138

4Q507–9   138

4Q525   197

4QS184–85   138

Josephus
The Jewish War (B.J.)
1.238–39   247
1.326   57
2.56   57
2.126   22246
2:229   137
2.259–63   307
2.261–63   108, 265, 281
2.562–68   58
4.106–16   58
5.55   290
6.300–301   113
6.300–309   307
Jewish Antiquities (Ant.)
4.209   136
4.210   127
7:392–94   290
8.165–75   120
8.354   309
9.206–14   111
11.66, 107   105
13.257–58   55, 56
13.296–97   100, 139
13.318–19   55, 102
13.408–9   140
14.297–98   247
14.450   57
17.271   57
18.36–38   58
18:85–87   108
18.116–19   59
19.116–19   245
20.85–87   307
20:95   290
20.97–98   108, 265, 307
20.169–71   108, 265, 281, 307

Contra Apionem
2.175   127
2.178   127
2.204   127
Vita
134–35   137

Philo Judaeus, *ad Gaium*
115   127
210   127

RABBINIC TEXTS

m. Ber. 4:3   127
m.Bik. 3:7   127
m. Sabb. 1:3   127
m. Sukk. 3:10   127
m. Sotah
1:7   223
7:8   136
m. Abot 3:17/18   225
b. Arak. 16b   223
b. Gitt. 57a   289
b. Sanh. 89b   289
Abot R. Nathan A 24   225
Midrah on Ecclesiastes
3:16 #1   289
10:4 #1   289

EARLY CHRISTIAN TEXTS

Barnabas
18–20   91
21:1   208

1 Clement
13:1–2   78
13:2   196
46:7–8   78

Ignatius, *Epistle to the Ephesians*
6:1   248

***Didache* (Did.)**
1:2   91
1:3   78, 91
1:3–5   196, 201
1–6   91
2   201
6:2   209
6:2–3   35
6:3   40
7:1   40
7:4   40
8:2   143
8:2–3   91
9:1   40
9–10   43, 309
10:1   40

Didache *(continued)*

10:7	43, 309
11:3	143
11:3–6	40, 41
11:3–12	35
11:4	248
11:4–6	43
11:7	43, 303
11:8	43
11:9	43
11:10	43
11:11	43
11:12	43
11:13	43
11–13	35, 92
12:1	41
12:1–5	41, 43
12:7–12	41
13	43
13:1–2	309
15:1–2	309
15:3–4	92, 143
15:4	41
16	91, 275
16:6	73

Polycarp, *Letter to the Philippians*

2:3	196

Acts of Paul and Thecla

5–6	197

Gospel of Thomas

1	75
2	267
3	79
5	89
6	80, 86, 89
10	85
11	79
14a	80
16	85, 86
17	79
18	79
19	75, 79
21	89
29	79
34	85
35	89
38	75
39	89

45	85
47a–b	85
49	79
50	79
51	79
52	79
54	85
68	85
69a	85
69b	85
73	89
78	79, 86
85	79
89	89
91	85
92	267
95	267
95	80, 85, 86
102	89
110	80, 86
111	79
113	79
114	78

Justin Martyr, *Dialogue with Trypho* (*Dial.*)

18:1	78
31:2	78
39:4	78
62:3	78
76:5	78
79:3	78

GREEK AND LATIN WRITERS

Aristophanes

Acharnians 383–479	133
Thesmophoriazusae 95–265	133

Dio Chrysostom

20.20	133
31.50–53	130

Diodorus Siculus

12.12–13	125

Plutarch, *Tiberias Gracchus*

9.4–5.828c	240

Quintilian, *Inst.* 5.11.19 — 133

Varro, *Rust.* 1.17.4 — 130

General Index

Abraham, 95, 97, 118, 172, 284
Achtemeier, Paul, 140, 144, 147
Adams, A., 35
agrarian society, 52
Aitken, Ellen, 214
Allison, Dale C. Jr., 69, 95, 238, 242, 283
Andersen, Oivind, 128, 129, 156, 157
anointed son of David, 106–7
anxiety, about necessities, 268–70
aphorisms. *See* individual sayings
apocalyptic(ism), 19, 63–66, 69–75
apocalyptic literature, Judean, 172, 274
apocalyptic (prophetic, judgmental) sayings,
    63–66, 76–80
"apocalyptic Son of Man," 79
apostles, 41–45, 308–9
assemblies. *See* synagogues
Audet, J.-P., 40
Aune, David E., 40, 42, 43
authority of scripture, 143–44
Avigad, Nahman, 290

Baltzer, Klaus, 201, 202, 206, 207, 209, 213
Bar-Ilan, Meir, 127
Barkay, Gabriel, 128
Basso, Keith H., 163
Bauman, Richard, 164, 166
Ben Sira, 100, 106, 120, 172, 304
Beowulf, 165, 171, 173
Bernstein, B., 178, 171, 179
Betz, Hans-Dieter, 29, 197, 232
biblical texts. *See* scripture
Boring, M. Eugene, 43, 70, 302, 305, 309
Bornkamm, G., 43, 62
Botha, Pieter J. J., 131, 132, 146, 157, 158, 159
Bultmann, Rudolf, 15, 18, 21, 22, 62, 63, 65, 70,
    73, 77, 79, 83, 84, 151, 152, 175
Burridge, Kenelm, 37

Carruthers, Mary L., 124
Catchpole, David, 244
charisma, 34–45
Charlesworth, James H., 107, 137, 232
Chinook tales (oral literature), 168, 187
Christian theological concepts, 2–4, 9, 24–27,
    46, 68, 94
christology, 2–3, 68, 70–71, 153
Clanchy, Michael T., 124, 157

codes, 171–72, 205
    elaborated/restricted, 178
    purity, 172
Collins, Adela Yarbro, 78
Collins, John J., 63, 77, 262
communication, process of, 300–301
communicative event, 182–83
communities/movement, 7–9, 147–48, 159, 166,
    168–69, 174–75, 248, 265, 267, 270, 276,
    280, 297, 303–4
community/movement, concerns of, 166,
    168–69, 260
Community Rule, 167, 206–8, 217, 224
composition/authors, 155, 158–59, 292, 294
compositional analysis, 195–96
conflict, 69, 158, 172, 220, 229, 270, 288,
    298–99, 310
context and content of sayings, 210, 220, 265,
    269
context, relational, 238
context, situation, 295
Coote, Mary P., 100
Coote, Robert B., 100
Cotter, Wendy J., 118, 270, 299
covenant, 104
    Mosaic, 201–3, 206, 208, 296
    and political-economic life, 204–6
covenant renewal, 203, 226, 259, 303, 307
    ceremony, 139, 202, 206, 209
    discourse, 216–25
covenantal blessings, 197
covenantal forms and structure, 139, 200–8,
    211, 216–17, 219
covenantal law(s)/law code, 96, 131, 202, 204,
    216, 220–21, 285
covenantal teaching, 96, 197–201, 203–6, 208,
    211, 216, 220–22, 224–25
Crossan, John Dominic, 22, 27, 29, 148
Cynic philosophers, 4, 17, 231–32

Damascus Document, 207, 224
Dead Sea scrolls, 100, 116, 137, 206, 253
debt/debtors, 204, 222–23, 226, 267, 269–70
Deuteronomistic History, 108–11
"deuteronomistic" view of history, 108–11
Deuteronomy, Book of, 202–3, 205, 257
Dewey, Joanna, 146, 157, 158, 159
dialect, 171, 178
Dibelius, Martin, 83, 84, 151, 175

Didache, 34–45, 91–92
"discipleship," 228–33
discourses, 11, 23–24, 84–93, 147–48, 166, 168, 173, 196, 233, 261, 296, 298, 300–302, 304
discourses, blocking of, 12, 211–17
Doane, A. N., 167
Doran, Robert, 118, 238
Draper, Jonathan A., 4, 12, 13, 29, 34, 35, 36, 163, 188, 231

economic interaction, 220–21, 223, 226
economic necessities, 267
economic relations, 210, 220–23
economic viability, 204–5, 219
"Egyptian" Jewish prophet, 108, 291, 307
Eichrodt, Walther, 201
Eisenstein, Elizabeth, 124
Elijah, 49, 96, 104, 108, 112, 238, 255, 259, 265, 304–6, 307, 308
Elijah, new, 307
Elijah's commissioning Elisha, 240–41, 249, 297, 308
Elisha, 49, 96, 104, 238, 259, 306
Elliott, John H., 29, 231
Epistle of Enoch, 100, 286
ethnography of speaking, 163
exalted Lord (Son of Man), Jesus as, 302

family, 59
field of discourse, 164, 182
Finnegan, Ruth, 153, 176, 183, 184
Fitzmyer, Joseph A., 113
Foley, John Miles, 7, 8, 10, 159–66, 168, 170, 171, 173, 176, 178, 179, 181–86, 210
form and function, 83, 85–90, 286–87
form criticism, 83–84, 151–52, 169, 175
Freyne, Sean, 48, 57
fulfillment, 96, 98, 264
function, 8, 83–90, 248–49, 300

Gager, John G., 173
Galilee (Galileans), 9, 46–60, 102, 112, 179–80, 219, 277, 298
Galilee, history of, 48–52
Gamble, Harry Y., 123, 127
gathering of dispersed Israelites, 95, 97, 283–84
Gee, J. P., 176
genre, 75–82
Gerhardsson, Birger, 144
Giddens, Anthony, 54
Goodman, Martin, 101, 127
Goody, Jack, 124, 148, 176
Gray, Rebecca, 172, 291
Gunkel, Hermann, 151, 175
Gutcher-Walls, Patricia, 109
Güttgemanns, Erhard, 159

Hadot, Pierre, 134
Halliday, M. A. K., 161, 164, 165, 171, 176, 177, 179, 181, 182
Hanson, John S., 69, 99, 245, 253, 306
Hanson, K. C., 101
Harnack, Adolf von, 4, 18–28, 34–36, 41, 45, 85, 231, 301
Harrington, Daniel J., 124, 137
Harris, William V., 123, 125, 126, 129, 131, 132, 133, 180, 294
Havelock, Erik, 123, 147, 154, 156, 157, 158
hearers/listening audience, 160–62, 166
Henderson, Ian, 139, 143
Hengel, Martin, 47, 127
Herington, J., 133
Hermann, P., 131
hermeneutics, 86
Herod Antipas, 52–54, 58–59, 98, 265
Herod the Great, 51, 53
Herod the Great, building program of, 290
high priesthood/high priests/high priestly aristocracy, 53, 56–58, 277, 281
Hill, David, 42
Hillers, Delbert R., 118
historical context, 27, 46–60, 159
Hoffmann, Paul, 70, 73, 229, 230, 244
Holbek, Bengt, 128
Holmberg, B., 37
Homeric epics, 165, 168, 171, 173
Horsley, Richard A., 29, 34, 35, 43, 48, 50–55, 57–59, 61, 63, 68, 69, 85, 93–96, 98–103, 105, 120, 121, 172, 180, 200, 220, 223, 229, 231, 232, 242, 245, 247, 253, 262, 263, 265, 272, 273, 275, 276, 279, 292, 294, 295, 300, 305, 306
Hymes, Dell, 163–68, 175, 176, 183, 185–89, 251, 254

immanent (inherent) meaning, 161, 166, 173
imperial records/propaganda, 131–32
individual sayings (aphorisms), 15–18, 83–84, 152, 229–33
individualism/individualistic interpretation, 4, 15–23, 26
individuals, 304
inscriptions, 129–32
instructional literature/genre, 81–82, 92, 304
instructions for envoys, 235, 242, 245–47
interpretive frame, 163–64
Iser, Wolfgang, 161, 176
Israelite covenantal tradition, 201–6, 225, 285
Israelite tradition, 5, 9, 24, 28, 55–56, 59–60, 94–122, 137, 142, 144, 171, 173–74, 198, 238, 244, 253, 259, 273, 275, 280, 282–83
    contested, 104–22, 225
    and resistance, 173–74
"itinerant radicalism," 228–32

Jacobson, Arland D., 27, 62, 72, 94, 108, 109, 117, 118, 146, 197, 229, 240, 248, 280
Jaffee, Martin S., 140
Jansen, Waldemar, 247
Jauss, Hans Robert, 161, 176
Jeremiah, 108, 110, 281–82
Jeremias, Joachim, 65, 175, 290
Jerusalem, 101–2, 120–21, 180, 278, 282, 298–99
Jerusalem rule, 50, 56–57, 103, 261, 282
Jerusalem temple-state, 53, 57, 96, 102
Jesus son of Hananiah, 113, 172, 291, 307
John the Baptist, 59, 108, 172, 238, 265, 304
Jonah, 111–12, 299, 308
Joshua, 291
judgment, 247, 273, 276
judgment (divine), suddenness of, 98, 275–76

Kaddish, 266
Käsemann, E., 42, 70, 73
Kautsky, John H., 53
Keck, Leander E., 152
Kee, H. C., 70, 107
Kelber, Werner, 6, 8, 10, 22, 68, 83, 124, 134, 138, 145–47, 149–60, 303
kingdom of God, 16–17, 19, 87, 96, 116, 238, 262, 265–70, 283–84
Kloppenborg, John S., 3, 5, 15, 47, 53, 54, 61–69, 71–75, 77, 80–85, 94, 95, 98, 114, 115, 121, 141, 145, 146, 195, 197–99, 211, 219, 223, 228–30, 232, 233, 239, 241, 243, 244, 250, 252, 273, 275, 277, 279, 292–94, 299, 300, 302
Koester, Helmut, 62, 63, 68, 73, 74, 76–81, 83, 131, 145, 153, 157, 196
Kretschmar, G., 35, 36, 41

land/ancestral inheritance, 204
Law. See Torah
law and the prophets, 115–16
"laws of the Judeans," 50, 56, 102
Lévi-Strauss, Claude, 180
liberal theology, 18–22, 25–26
Lightfoot, J. B., 41, 156
lists, 148
literacy (literate), 6–8, 123–25, 150, 155, 157
  limited, 125–27, 145
  in service of oral communication, 125, 128–31, 133–35
  social location of, 125–27, 129–30
literary production, 132–35
logoi/"words," 77–78
longings, fulfillment of, 81, 96, 264, 284, 296, 299, 301, 308
Lord, Albert, 7, 123, 158, 163, 167, 175, 176
Lührmann, Dieter, 62, 68, 70, 73, 80, 229

MacDonald, M. Y., 37
Machinist, Peter, 132
Mack, Burton L., 16, 17, 18, 26, 27, 29, 47, 66, 80, 94, 100, 123, 156, 231
Mark, Gospel of, 152–60
martyrdom, 273–74
  of Stephen, 274
Mason, Steve, 54
measured verse, 186–89, 211, 251
memory, 130–31, 140, 142, 148, 156
Mendenhall, George, 201
metonymic referencing, 160–63, 165–66, 170–74, 182, 184, 191–93, 251–52, 254–56, 258–59, 264, 273, 275
Miller, Robert J., 110, 111
mission, 229, 232
"mission" discourse, 228–29, 233–34, 249
mission to Israel, 243–44
mode of discourse, 164, 182
model of literacy, 151–52
Mosaic covenantal tradition, 55, 96, 139
Moses, 96, 255, 265, 291, 304, 306
Moses, new, 307
motives/motivation, 224–25, 227

Nagy, Gregory, 168, 176
narrative, 168
Neusner, Jacob, 114, 223, 225, 287
Niditch, Susan, 123, 128, 129, 130, 131, 135, 136, 138, 155
Niederwimmer, Klaus, 36, 41, 42, 43
Noah, 275
Nolan, Albert, 183

Oakman, Douglas, 101
O'Keeffe, Katherine O'Brien, 125
1 (Ethiopic) Enoch, 77
Ong, Walter, 124, 145, 152, 153, 154, 157, 158, 176
Opland, J., 176, 183
oral/orality, 6–8, 123–24, 144, 150–51, 153, 157
oral communication, 5–8, 12–13, 123–49, 152, 155, 157, 159–60, 163, 182, 295, 297, 300, 310
  in Judea and Galilee, 135–40
oral-derived texts/literature, 5–7, 10–12, 25, 144–46, 150, 152, 156, 159–60, 163, 165, 167, 210–11, 257, 294, 300, 310
oral formulaic theory, 158–60, 175
oral patterns, 184, 234–36, 251–52, 255, 269, 271
oral performance, dynamics of, 160–66
oral tradition, 142, 151–52, 154, 156, 159
oral transmission, 152–53, 159–60
orality vs. literacy, 152–57

Parry, Milman, 7, 123, 146, 158, 162, 163, 167, 175, 176
Patterson, Steven J., 36
Pearson, Birger, 61, 63, 238
peasants, 219
Penfield, Joyce, 256
performance, situation/context of, 168–70
performance context (arena), 163–66, 169, 274, 280
performance/recitation, 7–13, 127, 133, 138–39, 141, 144–47, 156, 159–66, 175, 184, 210, 234, 252, 255, 294, 303, 310
performative speech, 278–80, 301
performers (prophets) as spokespersons for Jesus, 301–3, 308
Perrin, Norman, 70
persecution, 270–74
Person, Raymond F. Jr., 138
Peterson, E., 35
Pharisees (and scribes/lawyers), 54, 56, 97–102, 104, 113–16, 118–19, 127, 139, 144, 158, 172, 180, 226, 228, 270, 273–74, 278–79, 285–91, 293–94, 298–99
Piper, Ronald A., 196, 198, 199, 214, 223
Plato, 154, 156–57
poetry, 133
political-economic life, 204–6
poor, the, 204, 226, 269, 284
popular figures/movements, 59, 272, 274
popular tradition, 111, 222, 278, 288. See also tradition, little
poverty, 60, 269
prayer, 266–68, 295
print culture, 6, 83, 124, 155–56, 158
prophetic forms, 112–13, 247, 279–84
prophetic lament, 279–82
prophetic mission, 241
prophetic movements, 249, 272
prophetic oracle, 283, 298, 305
prophetic performers, 300–310
prophetic role, 304–5, 308
prophetic sayings, 79–82. See also apocalyptic sayings
prophetic tradition, 220
prophets, 43–45, 49, 55, 108–12, 173, 220, 265, 280–83, 299, 304, 306, 308–9
announcement of, 251–54, 259
functions of, 308–9
killing or rejection of, 108–11, 173, 281, 288
as leaders of movements, 264–65, 306–8
legends of, 288–91
martyrdom of, 289
memorialization/monuments to, 110, 132, 288–91, 299
oracular, 307
testing of, 96, 254, 259
types of, 305–8

Q
compared with Didache, 91–92
compared with Gospel of Thomas, 61, 76, 78–82, 89–90, 147
compared with Gospel of Matthew, 90–91
as a collection of sayings, 23–27, 84
oral features of, 184, 188–89
as scribal transcript of repeated oral performance, 167
as a sequence of discourses, 23–27, 85–93, 147–48, 173, 258–59, 260–61, 263, 298, 301–2
stratigraphy of, 5, 61–67, 77, 80, 83
structure of, 86–88
Qumran community, 100, 104, 106, 116, 138, 167, 206, 253

Reed, Jonathan L., 112
regional differences, 277, 298
register, 164–66, 169–71, 173, 181–82, 193, 210, 261, 265, 280, 285, 296
religious role, 30–34
renewal (restoration) of Israel, 96, 105–8, 238, 249, 258–59, 260–70, 277–80, 283–85, 305–6
renewal movement, 295–99
rhetorical situation, 160, 220
Richardson, Peter, 51, 119, 290
Robbins, Vernon, 141
Robinson, J. A. T., 238
Robinson, James M., 2, 3, 12, 61, 62, 63, 68, 71, 73, 74, 75, 76, 77, 81, 83, 93, 145, 146, 231, 232, 239, 276, 302
Roman client-rulers, 53, 273
Roman (re-)conquest, 51, 53
rulers, 53–54, 98, 158, 173, 180, 193, 218, 240, 244–45, 261, 272–73, 277–78, 281, 298–99, 304–5
in Jerusalem, 278–85, 298
repression by, 270–74

Safrai, S., 127
Said, Edward, W., 179
Samaritan prophet, 108, 307
Sanders, E. P., 151
sapiential literature, 197–99, 225
sapiential teaching, 226, 228, 304
sapiential (wisdom) sayings, 11, 15, 17, 25, 66–67, 76, 78–80, 82, 197–200, 203
Sato, Migaku, 93, 247, 305
Schiffman, Lawrence H., 116
schools, lack of, 126–27
Schutz, J. H., 36, 37
Schweitzer, Albert, 19, 70, 73
Schwemer, Anna Maria, 112, 289
Scott, James C., 99, 100–103, 115, 180, 181, 205
scribes. See Pharisees

scripture, 98, 103, 141, 143
    recitation of, 140–44
    reference to, 140–44, 256–57
scrolls, sacred, 257
sending of envoys, 233, 235, 242, 248
Sepphoris, 58–59, 101, 112, 240
sequence of discourses, 258–59
Sherzer, Joel, 164, 165, 186
social context of meaning, 84, 153, 159, 165,
    174, 210
social interaction, 223–24
social location, 179, 225–26
social role/function, 287–88
Solomon, 97, 119–20
Son of Man. See christology
"son of man" (phrase), 71, 239, 274, 302
speeches. See discourses, Q as discourses
Speyer, Wolfgang, 135
Steck, Odil Hannes, 73, 108, 109, 280
Stegemann, Wolfgang, 29, 231
Stock, Brian, 124, 162
Street, Brian, 124
Sunden, Hjalmar, 30, 31, 32, 33
Swain, Simon, 290
synagogues (=assemblies), 52–53, 136–37,
    293–94, 303

Tannehill, Robert R., 220
Taylor, Joan, 238
Tcherikover, Victor, 294
teachers, 308–9
Tedlock, Dennis, 163, 176, 185, 186
temple, 290
tenor of discourse, 164, 182
text (word), 7, 163, 165–66
Theissen, Gerd, 29–39, 41, 43–45, 48, 80, 230,
    269, 300, 301
Theudas, 108, 291, 307
Thomas, Gospel of, 1, 15, 17, 75–80, 82, 84–86,
    147–48
Thomas, Rosalind, 125, 128, 129, 130, 131, 133,
    134, 146
Tiberias, 58–59, 98, 101, 240
tithes, 56, 115
Tödt, Heinz E., 70
Torah/Law (of Moses), 54, 97, 114–17, 135,
    197–98, 200, 203, 226, 258, 285–87
    recitation of, 135–40
    scrolls/books of, 135–39
Tov, Emanuel, 138
tradition, 8, 10, 161–63, 170–74, 310
    great, 56, 98–122, 171–72, 174, 180, 185, 278
    little, 56, 98–122, 172, 174, 180, 184
    of knowledge, 161

transcript, 167
    hidden, 181
    official, 180
transliteration, 190, 211–17, 234–36
transmission, of sayings, 238, 300, 305
Troeltsch, Ernst, 18, 19, 20, 21, 22
Tuckett, Christopher M., 35, 63, 67, 75, 76, 81,
    95, 114, 116, 211, 232, 238, 240, 244, 277,
    292
twelve tribes of Israel, 98, 106–8, 263
"two-ways" teaching, 203, 225–26

Ulrich, Eugene, 138, 155
Uro, Risto, 229, 232

Vaage, Leif, 17, 29, 81, 94, 146, 231
VanderKam, James, 138, 155
Vermes, Geza, 197
Vielhauer, Philipp, 73
villages, 52–53, 55–56, 59, 101–2, 126, 221,
    226, 233, 246, 249, 278, 280, 282, 288,
    293, 296–98, 303–4
Vööbus, A., 35

"wandering charismatics" (hypothesis), 4,
    29–45, 230, 300
Watt, Ian, 124
Webb, Robert L., 238
Weber, Max, 4, 30, 34, 35, 36, 37, 38, 39, 40,
    44, 45, 231, 301, 310
Weiss, Johannes, 19, 70
wilderness, 95, 264–65
Wintermute, O. S., 137
Wisdom, 3, 96–97, 117–18, 199, 203, 226
woes, prophetic, 97, 112–13, 285–91
Worsley, Peter, 37, 310
Wright, R. B., 107
writing
    ancillary functions of, 144
    in everyday life, 128–30
    magical, 128–29
    in service of oral communication, 125,
        128–30, 134
    in service of the state, 130–32
    uses of, 128–34
    see also literacy
written literature, 132–35

Yadin, Yigael, 290
Youtie, Herbert C., 53, 126, 294

Zeitlin, I. M., 38
Zeller, Dieter, 62, 198